EDWARD CARSON QC

EDWARD CARSON QC

by

EDWARD MARJORIBANKS

PREFACE

by

THE RT HON VISCOUNT HAILSHAM DCL LLD

COVER ILLUSTRATION

EDWARD CARSON IN THE HOUSE OF COMMONS
(VANITY FAIR LITHOGRAPH)

First published in Great Britain in 1932 by Victor Gollancz Ltd
as Volume One of *The Life of Lord Carson*

This edition published by —

THE HOUSE OF EMSLIE
3 Hatton Place
Edinburgh
EH9 1UD

www.emsliesquared.com

Hardback   ISBN 978-0-9567745-0-7
Paperback   ISBN 978-0-9567745-1-4

British Library Cataloguing-in-Publication Data
A Catalogue record for this book
is available on request from the British Library

Distributed in the United Kingdom by Central Books
99 Wallis Road London E9 5LN
Tel: 44 (0)845 458 9911 Fax: 44 (0)845 458 9912

Cover by M R Design
Set by THE HOUSE OF EMSLIE
Printed and bound by CTP Printers, Cape

Publisher's Note

This book was first published in 1932 as Volume One of *The Life of Lord Carson* by Edward Marjoribanks. The current edition, now published independently of volumes two and three by Ian Colvin, is entitled *Edward Carson QC* because it is predominantly a riveting account of the career of one of the greatest of all advocates. Edward Carson QC once said of his profession: 'It's the only thing I'm proud of.'

The author, himself an advocate and member of the House of Commons, provides an eloquent and unique insight into the genius of Carson's advocacy, and vividly recounts some of the remarkable parliamentary performances of Carson the champion of Irish Unionism.

We considered attempting to excise the politics in favour of the law, but soon discarded the idea: politics and law were so intertwined in Carson's career that any attempt to separate them would distort 'the reality of the situation', do a disservice to readers, and be disrespectful of the author. The result is a full re-publication of the aforesaid first volume, with minor editorial changes to modernise the text, but with no change of any substance (apart from the addition of a short editorial note at the end of the chapter entitled 'The Jameson Raid Case', in view of subsequent disclosures).

This edition is published as a tribute to Edward Carson QC, *primus inter pares*, and to his biographer Edward Marjoribanks, who tells the story so well.

C A Emslie
February 2011

Preface

Some two and a half years ago, Edward Marjoribanks received an invitation to write the story of Lord Carson's life. He seized the opportunity with enthusiasm; and, in spite of the preoccupations of Parliament and of the Bar, he devoted all his energies to the production of a biography which should do justice to the character and career of one of the great figures of the last half century. When he died, in April last, he had completed the composition and revision of the first half of the book, and he had accumulated a mass of material in the shape of Press cuttings, correspondence, notes of interviews, and the like, for the second half. I have had the difficult task of deciding what should be done with the portion completed by him. It so happens that the point reached is one which may well be regarded as a turning point in Lord Carson's career, his acceptance of the invitation to become the Leader of Ulster in the year 1910. What had been written, therefore, could stand as a volume complete in itself; indeed, Edward had himself become anxious to issue the book in two separate volumes, with an interval between the publication of the two. After very careful consideration, and after consultation with some of the author's friends, I have reached the conclusion that the right course is to publish the work as it stands, down to this point, and to hand over the material collected for the later years to whatever successor Lord Carson may select. The result of this decision is the present volume. I hope and believe that the reader will agree with me in regarding it as a memorial worthy of the great character which it portrays, as well as a credit to the literary talent and perceptive intuition of its author.

Hailsham
27 May 1932

Contents

1	Early Life	1
2	King's Inn and the Leinster Circuit	18
3	Gladstone's Irish Land Bill	39
4	The Croagh Orphanage Case	76
5	'Coercion Carson'	88
6	Balfour in Ireland	97
7	Crimes Act Cases	118
8	QC and MP	146
9	St Stephen's and the Temple	153
10	'A New Force in Politics'	167
11	A Fight in the House	183
12	Deadly Cross-examinations	191
13	More Forensic Triumphs	199
14	The Oscar Wilde Case	215
15	Leader of the Bar	262
16	Ben Tillett and W S Gilbert	272
17	The Jameson Raid Case	280
18	Carson v Balfour	293
19	Fighting for the Union	307
20	Law Officer of the Crown	316
21	The Trial of 'Colonel' Lynch	327
22	The Chapman Poisoning Case	338
23	The Slater Agency Case	347
24	The Alaska Boundary Case	368
25	George Wyndham and Lloyd George	387
26	Home Rule and Protection	397
27	Opposition and Private Practice Again	406
28	Redmond, Birrell and 'Limehouse'	419
29	Cadbury v Standard Newspapers	440
30	Lever and the Daily Mail	455
31	J B Joel v Robert Sievier	465
32	The Archer-Shee Case	471
	Index to main cases	505

1. Early Life

‘A very Bayard both of the Bar and of public and private life’ – so wrote a political opponent at the height of political controversy, a colleague at the Bar at the close of an historic rivalry of many years in the Courts, and a devoted personal friend in the course of a long and intimate friendship. Thus did Rufus Isaacs, Jew and Liberal, salute Edward Carson, Irishman and Conservative, when leaving the Bar to take his seat as Lord Chief Justice of England. 'If I cease to believe in Edward Carson, I cease to believe in men. I do not believe that any "honour", any money, or any other human inducement could tempt Carson to any course that he deemed unworthy or dishonourable,' said Sir John Ross to Lord Iveagh on the only occasion when the wisdom of Carson's leadership was called in question among his followers. 'I would trust my soul to Carson,' said Mr Timothy Healy, Catholic and first Governor-General of the Irish Free State. It is often said that, until death comes and the mists clear away, and posterity can stand back and see the human portrait in perspective, the lives of all historical personalities must remain mysterious and enigmatic. Soon after Disraeli's death, a famous historian wrote a biographical essay on the Conservative statesman, asking the question: 'was the man charlatan or genius?' and writers have been busied ever since with enquiry into the great Minister's personal motives. Indeed, modern critical biography has strongly developed into the science of discovering the private motives of self-interest behind the public actions and gestures of great men. It must be acknowledged that this search, fascinating in itself, has often been rewarded by success. But what shall the biographer say of the disinterested man, surely the rarest and most interesting of human creatures? Of the man who, so far from seeking great reward, stands aside that others may receive it, who shows an obstinacy not in ambition but in modesty, who again and again sacrifices his own interests, political, professional, physical, financial, to a cause in which he need never have involved himself, but to which he has given his word, who never asked the humblest of his followers to do the thing which he would not do himself? Such surely would be the disinterested man. This is a man whose public and private actions proceed alike from the same principles and directly bespeak his character. Such a man must also be the most interesting study to the historian and the psychologist. For self-interest is a dull and gross thing, once discovered; it is sensual, and shared by man in common with the beasts; but it is the man who acts without self-interest whose actions, whether wise or no, are most interesting, because they are derived from that which after all most clearly distinguishes humanity from other creatures, the voice of conscience; and in estimating them we are face to face with what is most divine in man. A cynical contemporary world will question the existence of such a person still walking among them; and, indeed, the burden of proof lies upon his biographer. But his task is at least a positive and a direct one; that of proof rather than scepticism, of narrative rather than of scrutiny.

Edward Carson's place in Irish history is already assured. A Southern Irishman, he is the founder of Northern Ireland as a political unit. Yet the foundation of Northern Ireland was not the object for which he fought: it represents a compromise after a long and grim struggle, but it was a compromise which never could have been made without the devotion, the courage, and the judgment of Edward Carson. The Northern Parliament can really be said to be his personal achievement and monument. The work which, despite an incurable modesty and diffidence, he did for England at the greatest crisis of her history is less well known and little appreciated except by those who saw Carson in action as Leader of the Opposition in the fateful year 1915-1916. On his appointment as Lord of Appeal, F S Oliver, one of the most critical political observers of our time, wrote to him: 'Our country owes you much – far more than it at present understands; but some day, I think, it will realise and fully acknowledge its debt. By that time you and I may be dead: but that is a small matter.' It is the object of the present writer to call attention to the importance of Carson's work during the greatest crisis of British history. As an advocate it would probably be agreed that Carson stood head and shoulders above any pleader of this century. But a great advocate's fame is always written in the sand, and he leaves behind him no permanent memorial; he becomes a tradition in the profession for a little while, and for a few short years stories go the rounds of the Courts and the Temple before they are attributed to some other person. Nevertheless, so remarkable and unique was Carson's advocacy that in itself it is worthy of scholarly research and presentation. His virulent invective, his uncanny skill in laying traps for unwary feet, his power of making witnesses say ridiculous things by an almost diabolical mastery of the arts of cross-examination, his superb power of seeing the one essential point in a case, his courage in abandoning everything else and in staking the whole issue perhaps on a single question; the strange weight which his great personality and expressive voice lent to everything he said would supply more than enough material for a biography, if he had never entered politics: and it must be remembered that he spent at practice of the Law the best years of his life. It was only when, at the age of fifty-seven and in failing health, he undertook the most arduous political leadership of recent times, that politics became his first interest, and only held him till, his task, as he thought, achieved, he returned to his first love, the Law, on the foundation of the Ulster Parliament.

The public knows Carson as a man who has spent most of his life in fighting in the Courts and in Parliament, who has raised an army of a hundred thousand men and sent by his advocacy many men to prison: they picture him perhaps as a grim personage, as 'Coercion' Carson, an embodiment of the unbending spirit of Ulster. How false is such an impression! Rather is he the gentlest of men: his favourite text is, 'Suffer little children to come unto me', and he is happiest when joining in the games of children. His beautiful Southern Irish voice prepares the new acquaintance for the charming smile which breaks up and belies the grimness of his Roman features. His long sensitive hands, with their almost feminine slimness and delicacy, would seem unsuitable to any man but an artist. There is something rare and exotic about his personality, something neither English nor Irish but nevertheless strikingly patrician, which must have led many observers to speculate concerning his ancestry. Behind the dogged and fearless politician, the ardent, tireless, and relentless advocate, there has always been the sensitive soul of a simple Irish gentleman, which has sought and found expression in personal friendship. Health is one of the greatest of God's gifts, but ill health from early youth brings advantages in its train: it disciplines the human spirit and economises its resources. 'Had I had F E's health, I should have been dead long ago,' Carson once said to me. Handicapped by a delicate and fickle constitution, he has found self-expression in two fields, work and friendship. Other men of more vigorous health have found resources in varied recreations, as amateurs either of taste, of sport, or of art. 'I have no resources except my friends,' Edward Carson once said to his brother. The same brother once induced him to buy a set of clubs so that he might be able to give his dear friend and patron, Arthur Balfour, a game of golf, but even for this pastime Carson had neither the strength nor inclination. For recreation he has always found it necessary to rely on the reciprocity of human sympathy given and received. 'You are a brave, loyal, and affectionate man, and deserve all the love you get,' wrote Lady Oxford in a charming and generous letter to the most formidable political opponent of her husband's premiership, and no one who knows him would question the truth of her tribute. A great life concentrated in work and love is indeed a fine subject, but it is in the former that the biographer must needs collect and present his material: there are some things too deep for his enquiry, and, in the long life-story which it is my privilege to unfold, I would beg the reader to remember that there is perforce much that must be left unsaid. Edward Henry Carson was born on 8 February 1854. He was born at the most distressful time in his country's history. O'Connell's heroic voice was only lately stilled at Westminster and in the Four Courts, but Ireland lay under the shadow of the ghastly famine which had robbed her of two million of her people. The Celt was leaving Ireland for America in increasing numbers. The stately buildings of Grattan's capital stood as monuments of past days of spacious hope over the growing slums of an impoverished city. The country was as yet too weak and stricken to embark on the bitter political controversy with the North and the sister isle, in which the little child born at 25 Harcourt Street was to play so historic a part. The Fenian movement was not yet in being.

His parentage was an interesting one. His father, whose identical name he bore, was nearly descended from one of the Italian architects and designers whose talent had been employed in architectural and decorative works by patrons in Scotland in the latter part of the eighteenth century. This eighteenth-century 'Carsoni', after working in Scotland and living in Dumfriesshire, settled in Dublin, and was perhaps responsible for some of the exquisite decoration of the Dublin houses of the bright period of culture which flourished under Grattan's Parliament. The family abbreviated their name into the common Ulster name of Carson. Lord Carson's father, an architect like his forebear, became in his time Vice-President of the Royal Institute of Irish Architects: but, despite his Italian blood, he lived and died a devout Presbyterian. In appearance he was of middle height, but fair and good-looking, and had, as his son's friends will not be surprised to hear, an 'excellent nose'. He sat on the Dublin Corporation under the unconventional, but not unreasonable, label of a 'Liberal-Conservative'. He was the youngest of three brothers: both his seniors, James and William, remained bachelors, and became clergymen of the Episcopal Church of Ireland. The latter was an interesting person, and showed a quixotry akin to that of his nephew. William Carson became a doctor, went north, and built up an excellent practice in Ulster. But he suddenly felt a call to the Church, and went down to Tipperary to minister as a priest in a poor country parish, where his medical skill became proverbial. He used to concern himself not only with the spiritual but also the physical health of his parishioners, Catholics as well as Protestants. Often outside his door there would be a long line of horsedrawn carts which had brought the sick from far and wide to be treated by this good Protestant clergyman. Lord Carson's mother belonged to an historic family of the 'middle nation', as the Anglo-Irish are sometimes called. She was Isabella Lambert, of Castle Ellen, County Galway, and a descendant of General Lambert, who, as one of Cromwell's principal major-generals, had been appointed Lord Lieutenant of Ireland, and had on one occasion broken up the Parliament at Westminster. He was described as a man of ferocious courage, and it is interesting that his blood flows in Carson's veins. Ellen Lambert's mother was a Seymour, and this family descended from an officer of King William III who had been granted considerable estates in County Galway after the glorious revolution of 1688 and the Irish Rebellion. Thus, although not an Ulsterman, Lord Carson can lineally claim to Protestant and Orange tradition by right of inheritance. Indeed, he was initiated into the Orange Order before he came of age. His mother was described as a regular 'Lambert', with the blue eyes, dark hair, and clear complexion, characteristic rather of the 'old inhabitants of the island' than of the Anglo-Irish.

Edward Carson was one of a family of six, four boys and two girls. The eldest boy, William, became a solicitor, but had too much of the Irish love of horses and hunting to make an outstanding success of his profession. Colonel Walter Carson, a year younger than Edward, became a medical officer in the Army, and, after many years of distinguished service, has retired. One of his sisters, Ellen Seymour, married an English officer of the line, Captain Thackeray, a relative of the novelist, who was stationed at Dublin, and afterwards became a Resident Magistrate in Ireland. The other, Isabella, married a solicitor, Mr St George Robinson, Crown Solicitor in Sligo, and had by him two sons, one of whom was killed in the war, and both of whom Lord Carson loved as if they had been his own sons. The family was a very united one but from early days 'Ned' stood out as the most remarkable of them all. He was his father's favourite, who from his earliest years destined him for the Bar. Although never strong in health, he was the only tall one of them all. Even as a child he began to show that strange mixture of reserve and affection with which all his close friends are familiar. There was something about him which made him seem aloof and different from other children. His childhood was spent at his parents' house in Harcourt Street, Dublin. The Carson brothers and sisters, like all other

Dublin children, had the spaciousness of Phoenix Park as a playground, and, nearer at hand to Harcourt Street, the then private, now public, gardens of Stephen's Green.

Edward Carson also enjoyed from time to time a country life: he paid many visits to his uncle, the owner of Castle Ellen, and became devoted to a beautiful cousin, Katie Lambert, who was his hostess there both as a child and a young woman. At Castle Ellen, among his mother's people, Edward Carson was brought in touch with the old traditions of Anglo-Irish Protestant culture, and became imbued with that peculiar pride in, and loyalty for, Great Britain which was the tradition of the 'Pale', and survived all the difficulties between the two islands, and never wavered till the end. The old saying of Wolf Tone was still true of Ireland at that time. She was composed of 'separate nations met and settled together, not mingled but convened: uncemented parts that do not cleave ... to ... each other'. The unfortunate history of Ireland had combined a difference of race with a distinction both of class and religion. In the South the masses of the people had become debased by the disabilities placed upon them because of their religion: even Protestant peasants of English blood tended to become Catholics, while the well-to-do Catholics tended to conform to the religion of their own class. Thus upon the Protestant minority had been conferred the privileges of a governing class of alien race, a tragic relationship not to be found elsewhere in the British Isles. Naturally this position conferred upon them an intellectual and physical superiority over the masses of the people. But equally they could never feel secure. Unlike their fellow-Protestants in the North, who were in a majority, they were surrounded by a people whom ignorance and disability had degraded; perhaps the dominant doctrine of Protestantism is that man may and must go straight to his God; to the cultured

Irish Protestant, the faith of the Irish Catholic, with his belief in the Saints and the Blessed Virgin as intermediaries, seemed that of a barbarian and an idolater. They felt that their possessions and their faith were always in danger at the hands of the people round them, and it was to England that they looked for the protection of their traditions and their faith. Unlike that of the Presbyterian North, which was Scottish and democratic, their culture was English and aristocratic. If the hand of English justice were withdrawn, they saw themselves the victims of brutal crime and violence; indeed, there was much evidence which justified their fears: and yet upon them, as upon the old inhabitants of the island, had fallen the heavy hand of English legislation in the eighteenth century. The whole situation was a hateful legacy of the past, and, although no one alive was responsible for it, the harvest of bitterness and hatred was reaped by Carson's generation more than by any other. It was, however, a real patriotism, a love and reliance on England, that Carson learnt from his mother's people, yet the meaning of a bitter taunt once thrown at him by an opponent is easily understood: 'He has no country – he has a caste.' Yet too, as is well known, there was something in the atmosphere of Ireland that often made these Anglo-Saxons more Irish than the Irish themselves; and so happy racially is the blend of English and Irish, and so brilliant and fertile of genius has this admixture of blood been proven to be again and again, that the fact that it was confined largely to the governing class must be regarded as one of the real tragedies of our history. To the illustrious list of Anglo-Irish genius, which includes such diverse names as Swift, Burke, Grattan, Wellington, and Parnell, must be added, too, that of Edward Carson. 'Although a Unionist,' said Mr Tim Healy to me of him, 'he never was un-Irish.'

Carson's father, although in good practice, was never a

rich man, and frankly told his sons that he could only provide them with a good education and then leave them to make their way in the world. Edward, his second and favourite son, he always destined for the Bar, though neither as a child nor as a youth did the son himself wish to be a barrister. The great advocate that was to be always had a leaning for the Church, and also had an early talent for draughtsmanship, which his father as an architect admired without encouraging. He would not listen to the idea of his son going into the Church. Years afterwards, after an all-night sitting on an Irish Bill, as he sat cheek by jowl with Arthur Balfour, Carson said to the latter towards eight o'clock in the morning, 'Well, now I have to go and get shaved and go to the Courts without an hour's sleep – what a bore.' Balfour, who was known to dislike lawyers, but loved Carson, observed, 'How very tiresome. But what else would you have done?' 'I should have been a parson,' replied the other, 'with plenty of time to read and lots of children.' 'I know you too well,' Balfour smiled. 'You'd have been a bishop in no time, and the trouble you'd have had with all your Irish curates would have been worse than the House of Commons and the Bar combined.'

Nor did his father countenance the idea of this precious son of his following in his footsteps. As a youth he would occasionally go down to his father's office, and work out a drawing in perspective for him. 'You're doing this better than I did when I was older than you,' said his father, 'but you're not to go on with it. You've to be a barrister.' In fact, as Carson himself has said in a homely expression, 'I was put to the Bar.'

The first step in the good education which his father was to provide for him was attending a little day-school with his two brothers, William and Walter, kept by the Rev Mr James Rice, in the same Harcourt Street where his family resided.

He there met one of his future colleagues at the Irish Bar, Blood, afterwards King's Counsel. According to the latter's recollection, Carson even as a small boy had read widely amongst the speeches of the later Georgian era. He even committed some of them to memory, and sometimes he would recite passages to his schoolfellows with considerable fervour. At the age of twelve and a half he removed to Arlington House, Portarlington, a small public school chiefly attended by the sons of Protestant professional men. Here too he was accompanied by his two brothers, William and Walter, and here he made many friendships. Not long after the brothers went to the school the Rev F H Wall LLD succeeded his father as headmaster, and Edward Carson made of him a lifelong friend. Edward's reserved but straightforward character, although he was not a brilliant scholar, immediately attracted his headmaster, and the two spent summer holidays together in Wales and Switzerland. When the shy schoolboy had attained a position of influence, he was not forgetful of his old friend. He obtained for him on his retirement, from Mr Balfour, a valuable Crown living in which Dr Wall spent the closing years of his life. He watched the remarkable career of his most distinguished pupil with eager and affectionate interest, and never failed to write to him at any step in his career.

Among his contemporaries he made lasting friendships with William Ridgeway, afterwards the celebrated Cambridge Professor of Archaeology, who obtained his well-earned knighthood in 1918 through Carson's influence, and Stirling Berry, afterwards Bishop of Killaloe; but perhaps his greatest friend was the most brilliant boy in the school, James Shannon, who was to embark on the same profession and on the same circuit with Carson; but the race is not always to the swift, nor the battle to the strong, and the gods loved him over well.

At Arlington House, Carson did not greatly distinguish himself as a scholar, although he showed a marked preference for literary and classical studies. As a student of eighteenth-century rhetoric he became an orator in the school debating-society. A weak heart prevented him from excelling in athletics as his brothers did, yet he worked steadily, and he held his own both in the classroom and in the school games: moreover, he became known and respected as a fine manly fellow, and Walter Carson remembers at least one occasion when his brother Ned resorted to his fists; his victim was one Potts, afterwards an officer of artillery, but the cause of the contest remains obscure. His schoolfellows, however, never guessed even remotely the mighty character which was developing beneath the overgrown frame of 'Rawbones' Carson – for such was the nickname of his youth. This became abbreviated into 'Bones'. He even adopted the name himself, and for a long time would sign himself, in his letters to his friends, with crude schoolboy Latinity as 'Ossa'. Despite his delicate health, there was already a strength and dignity in this overgrown schoolboy, which was recognised and appealed to by his schoolmates. The younger boys came to look upon this rather aloof and moody sixth-form boy as their champion when they were bullied or badly treated, and several of these, as their letters bear witness, have not yet forgotten his kindness. On one occasion, after a cricket match, a dispute arose about some small matter, which eventually led to words. One of the opposition team, a man almost, was particularly objectionable to a smaller boy, and Carson challenged him to fight. Soon they were both hard at it, and the stronger boy was beaten down by the extraordinary fierceness of Carson, which astonished even his friends. The child is the father to the man, and it is this spirit of combativeness, whenever his sense of justice or his sense of chivalry were roused, which has run through and connected every period, private or public, legal or political, of Carson's career. Only one incident could have given his schoolfellows a hint of that ruthlessness of enquiry and analysis which was to bring him fame and fortune and carry him to a foremost place in national affairs. On one occasion a complaint had been made by some of the boys of the mysterious disappearance of some of their belongings; an investigation into the matter was made by a junta of the head class, of which Carson was a member; he assumed the role of inquisitor and judge, as he did so often in later days to His Majesty's Ministers. Although a half-hearted admission of guilt was made by the wretched boy under suspicion, there still remained some missing money to be accounted for. All the boy's possessions had been ransacked in vain. Carson noticed that the culprit kept looking at his feet. 'Take off your boots,' said Carson in his best Green Street and Old Bailey manner; the missing coins were at once found. The writer cannot help thinking that the story must have been recounted to the Vice-President of the Royal Institute of Irish Architects, and that it hardened him in his determination to make his son a barrister, and to keep him from the Church.

At all events, the father was faithful to his promise; he sent his son to the University which had trained the minds of so many of the most illustrious of his countrymen. There is little that is mediaeval about Trinity College, Dublin; it breathes into its students the spacious atmosphere of the eighteenth century, when the Irish capital was becoming one of the most elegant and graceful cities in Europe. Further, the students had this advantage over their brothers of Oxford and Cambridge: the two great English Universities overshadow the provincial towns which so largely depend upon them. Professors are professors in Oxford and Cambridge, and dons are dons; in Trinity they are courtiers and men of the world, in constant touch with the many currents of life of a capital city. Typical of them was Professor Mahaffey, who had just become a Fellow when Carson entered as an undergraduate. Perhaps this is the cause of the rare distinction which Trinity College throws around its alumni. In Carson's time the undergraduates were mainly Protestants, although a few Catholics took advantage of the best education in Ireland, and the University was beginning to become a meeting-place for the middle nation and the old inhabitants of the island. At the midsummer entrance examination of 1871 he earned a 'high place' in classics, and in Michaelmas 1871 a junior exhibition. He is said to have missed a scholarship only by a mark and a half. At the littlego examination he was placed in the first class. He secured several second class honours in classics, but graduated with an ordinary pass degree. He thus achieved a creditable University career, but could not yet be said to have shown any signs of brilliance. There was no one who predicted for him anything like the future which lay before him. John Ross and James Campbell, who were to swim after him and around him like planets round a sun, both had faultless academic careers, as also had William Ridgeway, his schoolmate at Arlington House. Yet perhaps the foremost all-round man of his time was Seymour Bushe, whose quick, versatile, brilliant mind was to give him a long start over Carson at the Bar, but whose life was set all awry by a sincere but disastrous romance; to say that Seymour Bushe was the foremost of his generation is a great deal, for Carson's class included the name of a man of acknowledged genius, Oscar Wilde, the son of the well-known oculist, Sir William Wilde, and his poetess wife. Sir Dunbar Barton says of Seymour Bushe, 'In him and in Arthur Balfour the culture of Greece and Rome seemed to come alive again in everything they did or said.' Contrary to widely current story, Carson and Wilde were contemporaries, but never friends. Carson's fastidious and Spartan nature was repelled, and not amused, by the perfumes and extravagant raiment that had already begun to hang about Wilde. But they knew and spoke to each other, these two diverse Irishmen, for whom so dramatic a scene and so tragic a relationship were prepared by Fate. For they were both reading classics in the same year, the one a brilliant, soaring scholar, the other a plodding, pedestrian student, or so it appeared. Indeed, it would be difficult to imagine human creatures more different than these two fellow-students, the ascetic, retiring, manly, slowly developing young rhetorician and the aesthetic, flamboyant, effeminate, and precocious poet.

Carson's health had not improved as he grew into manhood, and he took small interest in athletic sports; he belonged to the Trinity Rowing Club, rowed now and then, and also played a game called 'hurley' which was the precursor of modern hockey. It was rather in the College Historical Society, the old Debating Society of the University, that he began to show his real promise. He was an assiduous speaker at the debates, and on several occasions the society showed him favour. He obtained 'the marked thanks' of the society for oratory; he obtained the second medal for 'Composition', which he presented to his sweetheart and cousin, Katie Lambert. The subject of this essay was not legal or political, but aesthetic; it was entitled 'Early Excursions into the Realms of Art'. He was elected to be librarian in 1876, but he was defeated as a candidate for the coveted chief office of the auditorship in the 'General Election', 1877-1878. Charles O'Connor, afterwards Irish Lord Chancellor, was elected as a 'Home Ruler' with twenty-eight votes: Carson was second with twenty-one votes as a 'Protestant Liberal'; and A W Samuels, afterwards Irish Law Officer and Carson's colleague as member for Trinity College, was last with twenty votes as a 'Protestant Episcopalian Conservative'.

On another occasion he might have been elected auditor, but he stood aside and supported his friend John Ross in a struggle with Arthur Samuels. In this early self-denial, which we will see repeated again and again, in a coveted ambition we have a real glimpse of the full-grown man.

In those days Carson was a Radical, as was remembered by Oscar Wilde many years afterwards, but even then a dogged defender of the Union. This perilous subject, as likely to promote disorder, was only allowed to be introduced in an indirect way in motions in such terms as 'That Pitt's Irish Policy was worthy of a wise and upright statesman', and 'That Mr Lecky's views on Federalism deserve our approval'. Nor was his Radicalism free from those prejudices which must in the end evolve the true Tory. Whereas he spoke in favour of the abolition of capital punishment, and raised his voice in favour of the disestablishment of the Church and in approval of the French Revolution and women's suffrage, he defended the dramatic tastes of the times, the legislative powers of the Hereditary Chamber, the system of land tenure in Ireland, and denounced the memory of Cromwell. In all his speeches was observed a certain maturity, and, as a contemporary writes, 'a horror at all injustice and wrong and a transparent love of uprightness and fair play'.

As librarian it was his duty to keep and sign the minutes of the society, and on 20 December 1876 this modest youth was pleased to sign himself, somewhat prematurely, 'E H Carson QC, Attorney-General'. Altogether, at the end of his Trinity career, Carson was beginning to find himself, and, although his University career was only an ordinary one, he had won from all his contemporaries who knew him a deep respect, not so much for his intellect, but for his character.

Nor did this character show itself always along the paths of conventional rectitude. Ned Carson was far from being the model undergraduate. He nearly lost his degree by an outburst of high spirits during a state visit to Dublin by the Duke of Marlborough as Lord Lieutenant. He seated himself on a high railing in the precincts of the college, and threw squibs at the crowd below. 'Come down,' shouted the Rev Dr J H Jellet, Vice-Provost of Trinity, in a great rage, 'or you'll be rusticated.' 'I've only a dozen more,' answered Carson, and did not descend until he had run out of ammunition. He was summoned before a disciplinary board of dons for this defiance of authority, but they could do nothing with him. Dr Palmer, Carson's own classical tutor, to whom he was devoted, was a member of the Court, and feared that his pupil might indeed be rusticated.

'You really ought to say you're sorry, Mr Carson,' he said.

'D'you really think I ought to tell that lie?' was Ned Carson's retort.

The authorities could not bring themselves to rusticate him. What could these cultured Irish gentlemen do with so obstinate and honourable a rebel, except dismiss him with a severe caution, and burst into laughter as soon as his back was turned?

Over in England, in an older University, another undergraduate, young Asquith of Balliol, was carrying all before him in the academic world. He too one day was to be challenged, and to see his policy frustrated by the same iron, unrepentant determination in the defiance of authority, after nearly forty years of hard experience of life and law and politics had steeled and matured, but never changed or broken, the spirit of this redoubtable undergraduate.

2. King's Inn and the Leinster Circuit

In the year following that in which Edward Carson had described himself as QC and Attorney-General he was 'called' as a humble member of the outer Bar by Lord Chancellor John Thomas Ball. For nearly ten years he was to win his way slowly along the not very lucrative, but nevertheless friendly and companionable, road to fortune provided by the Bar of Ireland. According to the rule of the day, he had perforce spent a little time in the wider legal atmosphere of the Temple. Every aspirant to the Irish Bar had in those days to keep four terms in one of the English Inns of Court by 'eating dinners'. This, in Carson's own words, was 'one of the badges of servitude on the Irish nation'; further, before being admitted to his English Inn, he, like all other Irish students, had to obtain the signature of two English barristers as guarantors to vouch for his personal honour, 'lest he might steal the silver spoons'. One of his guarantors was a young Irishman and a family connection, named Charles Bell, whom Carson was to lead on many occasions in the distant future. In this manner young Irish law students acquired something of the tradition of the Temple and in return enriched the libraries and the halls of the old Inns by their Irish charm and conversation. But, as Carson ate his dinners and bowed to his messmates before taking wine with them in the beautiful and historic Middle Temple Hall, he had no thought that he would ever live to be treasurer of this great English Inn, and to be reputed the greatest of all the advocates at the English Bar. The 'Very Bayard' of the Bar took his dinners in the hall of the Knights Templar with no ambition for the great position that was to be his; his ambitions were modest and were exclusively Irish. His life was to be spent at the Four Courts in Green Street and on the Leinster Circuit; it was different perhaps with men like James Shannon, John Ross, Seymour Bushe, and James Campbell. They were brilliant scholars, and might perhaps aspire to any high position even outside Ireland.

His decision to go to the Bar was not favoured by his mother's family; although one of her brothers was a solicitor, among these people of the Ascendancy lingered a tradition, which was dying hard, that it was disgraceful for a gentleman to earn his living save in the Services. Yet perhaps, after all, it was little concern of theirs what this impecunious nephew did: he must earn his living, and it was of course out of the question, in any event, for their daughter to think of marrying her penniless cousin. He had given her his medal for composition, and it was a symbol of his first deep affection; and anyone who knows his sincere and affectionate nature can guess that this was no small thing. But Edward Carson had too proud and sensitive a character to press a suit which was unwelcome to her parents and which would offer so precarious a future for his dear cousin; he therefore put behind him all possibilities of a happy consummation of his boyhood's romance; and so Katherine Lambert was not allowed by Fate to share his great future. For him, or so it seemed, lay a humbler path so looked down upon by the Lamberts, with perhaps at the end of the road the dignity of a County Court Judgeship.

Nevertheless, the Irish Bar was one of the best clubs to which a young Irish gentleman might belong: in those days it was very much a continuation of Trinity College life, and, with a few exceptions, a close preserve of its Protestant alumni; for most of its members were then Protestants and Unionists. It was a smaller and homelier corporation than the English Bar, and, although its prizes were less and its fees were lower, it made up in good-fellowship what it lacked in guineas. Barristers had no separate chambers at or near the

Four Courts, one of the most beautiful and noble buildings in the Empire, unhappily and wantonly destroyed by Rory O'Connor in 1922. This building was so called because opening off the circular main hall were the Chancery, the Queen's Bench, the Common Pleas, and the Exchequer Courts. The criminal trials for Dublin were held in the old Court House in Green Street, some half-mile away. In the main building was the famous 'Bar Library', the place 'where barristers most did congregate'. The main room was rectangular, with narrow galleries round the sides, under which were the bookshelves, a small octagonal room at each corner, and another room, the 'Long Room', running at right angles and opening off one side. The entrance used was through one of the small rooms, which became an anteroom in which solicitors and their clerks could speak to counsel. The barristers sat on forms at long desks, or at 'the Round Table', a large table in the centre of the main room and opposite the chief fireplace (where twelve men sat), or at small round tables or separate desks in the corner rooms, or occupied any other available space. The accommodation was quite insufficient for the number requiring it, and the Bar were packed like children in a poor school of the bad old days, but with far more discomfort than would now be tolerated in such a place. But it will easily be seen that at such close quarters the members of the Bar were a much closer association than their brethren in London, that jealousy and backbiting were so uncomfortable as to become really impossible, and that friendship and good-fellowship were not only general but necessary in such conditions.

Every barrister then lived in the city, and came to Court regularly every morning. Having robed and bewigged himself, whether expecting to be in Court or not, he went to the library and began his work or prepared to go to Court.

As in the House of Commons, though not strictly entitled under the regulations to any special seat, each man could acquire by custom his own. In Ireland, owing to the limited amount of legal business, there was not the same possibility of specialising as in England, and a junior barrister had to be prepared to take a case or advise proceedings in any of the Courts. This general knowledge, perforce acquired, was very useful to Carson when he came to the English Bar, and on many occasions he surprised the English Judges and his own colleagues, such as A H Bremner, with his acquaintance with the most abstruse legal doctrines which are as a closed book to the ordinary English Common lawyer. Nevertheless, the library had its rough divisions. For instance, the 'Long Room' was the abode chiefly of Chancery men and conveyancers. So far as not engaged in Court, everyone spent the day in the library, and the pampered English practitioner, with his private chambers and his senior and junior clerk, may well wonder how these Irishmen managed to transact their business.

At the entrance to the main room stood a 'crier' – this formidable official was in Carson's time an ex-trooper named Bramley, with a clear, powerful voice. Solicitors or their clerks – barristers had none – requiring to see a barrister, or to summon him to Court, came to the library door and mentioned the name of their counsel. Bramley then shouted the name – his voice would have reached far beyond the uttermost corner of the library – and the barrister immediately stopped his drafting or reading and went to the door. Bramley's voice retained its power from early morning till the shadows fell, and, in justice be it recorded, the ex-trooper's throat needed very little lubrication. He kept by him a printed sheet with the names of the barristers, and a man leaving the library would say where he was going – such as 'Rolls', 'Common Pleas', or 'Exchequer'. Bramley then entered a note of this address after the man's name, and if, when subsequently wanted, he did not respond when his name was called, Bramley would tell the enquirer where to look for him. The shouting of the names and the tramping of the men between their seats and the door made a great noise. In addition to this, the 'library boys' (some of these attendants were very old men) were obliged to go trotting or tottering about at their quickest speed in their search for the books called for by the members of the Bar. Further, there was much talk and laughter – quite unrestrained – chiefly at the fire and the Round Table, the centre of legal gossip and scandal of the Kingdom of Ireland. To the newcomer, like Carson in 1877, the place seemed more like pandemonium than a place to work. He wondered how he would, if a solicitor ever paid a call on him, even hear his name called above the hubbub, let alone do any study in such a place. Soon, however, like everybody else, he became used to it, and grew able to shut his ears to every sound but Bramley's stentorian 'E H Carson', a cry at first rarely heard, but one which grew almost monotonous in its frequency as the years passed. Moreover, Carson learned in the library that a general noise, no matter how loud, is not so distressing to the worker as two persons in close proximity holding a whispered conversation.

When Carson was called, the barristers' black brief bags were brought from their houses every morning to the library by the poor old 'bagwomen', a wretched-looking class who carried the heavy bags of briefs, and sometimes books as well, on their backs, or wheeled them in makeshift perambulators. Wretched-looking as they were, these old ladies had a sturdy and impeccable honesty, for the briefs were never tampered with or stolen or lost; and the only delay which I have been able to gather from the memory of the Irish Bar was occasioned when some bags spent a night in a public-house on their way from the Court, an occurrence which caused serious and general inconvenience. One of the 'bagwomen' was a great character, and was called 'Snuffy Maggie', but, like many other excellent institutions of the past, the bagwomen had their day, and were, soon after Carson's call, replaced by a more modern method of transport. This was composed of two horse-drawn vans, which collected the briefs from the barristers' homes in the morning and delivered them at night, and was known – by comparison with the bagwomen, I suppose – as the 'Legal Express'.

The library system had very great advantages; gentlemen of the Bar from the 'six quarters of Ireland' – there were in 1877 six circuits – were thrown together, and, as the Catholics and Nationalists began to come to the Bar, the library became a fine centre of friendship and comradeship between men who were politically and religiously opposed. Indeed, the Bar library was the best social club in Dublin. Moreover, it was a great advantage for a young man to be thrown amongst men older and more experienced than himself; and a junior could always ask for assistance from a senior, and such help was freely given. Counsel engaged together in a case could discuss their business together, and the most useful consultations were those informal ones held in the library. More formal consultations were held in counsel's house in the evening, or in a consultation room at the Courts immediately before or after the Courts rose. The 'formal' consultations, however, frequently degenerated into informality, being held at home among Irishmen, and libations in claret and champagne were freely poured out to the legal Muse, who is never thus honoured by her English devotees in their dignified professional chambers.

In the library as a young man of twenty-three, Carson first made the acquaintance of his later chief, Edward Gibson, then Disraeli's Irish Attorney-General, and afterwards Lord Ashbourne, three times Irish Lord Chancellor and a Cabinet Minister, a noble and broad-minded Irish gentleman and man of the world. Gerald FitzGibbon was then his Solicitor-General, a very versatile and eloquent man; there, too, on the other hand, he saw the great Isaac Butt QC, the father of the Home Rule movement, a generous and gentle Irishman, then about to give place in the Nationalist movement to the strange and dark genius of Parnell. He also became acquainted with Peter O'Brien, who was to share with him a close and dangerous association a decade later. There, too, among his contemporaries he found his great friend James Shannon, already making a name for himself, and was soon joined by Seymour Bushe and John Ross. The Judicature Act, which reformed and simplified the legal system of Ireland, only came into force a year after Carson's call, so that he worked for a year under the ancient regime. There was still a Chief Justice of the King's Bench, George Chichester May, who was then becoming old and deaf; a Chief Justice of the Common Pleas, Michael Morris, afterwards Lord Killanin, a strong Unionist and a great power in Ireland, but a man for whom Carson, in his independence of character, was to entertain without concealment a strong antipathy; finally, Christopher Palles presided over the 'Barons' of the Exchequer: his appointment had been wrung unwillingly from Mr Gladstone in 1875, but until the troubled days of 1918 he was to adorn the Irish Bench and serve the Irish people by his superb intelligence, his deep knowledge of the law, his independence of character. He was a great lawyer and a fearless judge. His knowledge of law was deep and universal, and his judgments are quoted with reverence wherever the Common Law runs. Carson became devoted to him from the earliest days for his wisdom and kindliness. The Exchequer, in those days, was a marked contrast to the Common Pleas: it was far more technical. The plaintiff could, under the old system, select his Court for a Common Law action, and Lord Killanin well stated the rule which used to guide the Junior Bar when advising proceedings: 'If you have law on your side, but no merits, bring your action in the Exchequer; if you have merits, but little or no law, go to the Common Pleas; but if you have neither law nor merits, try the Queen's Bench, because there is no knowing what they may not do there'. With the operation of the Judicature Act the practice on the Common Law side became uniform, and Carson was not teased by these problems after his first year.

Like all young barristers, Carson went as 'pupil' for a year to an experienced junior for a fee of fifty guineas. The master chosen for him was George Price, an equity practitioner whose conveyances were works of art, but who was tongue-tied in Court. However, the Chancery Judges were very patient with him. He was a strange master to launch Edward Carson, that artist in rhetoric, enquiry, and irony, upon his legal career. However, draughtsmanship can be taught, but advocacy such as Carson's can only come from innate capacity and long practice, so that perhaps after all his father chose for him the right master. There was never any real danger that Carson's genius would be wasted in equity draughtsmanship. With George Price, Carson learnt the invaluable art of 'pleading'. The first stage of every civil suit is the formal abstract of the contentions of each side, drawn up and signed by the junior barrister. The general rule is that argument and evidence at the trial cannot be allowed to go beyond the issues so defined in the pleadings. Although the rules are much laxer as to 'pleading' than they were in Carson's day, many cases have been won or lost on the pleadings. Amendments at the last minute can be very expensive, and many a junior has had to hang his head in shame for a mistake or omission in his

'Statement of Claim' or 'Defence'.

Carson had to make his way, and he had little influence to help him. His first brief was a difficult and very technical one which arose out of the absence from Ireland of one of the parties to a lawsuit, who had therefore to be served with notice of the proceedings by 'substituted service'. Carson had to argue the validity of such service, and the Judge complimented him enthusiastically on the way in which he acquitted himself: in this technical case there was little scope for the great advocate that was to be to show his powers of rhetoric or enquiry.

A clergyman named the Rev M Bradshaw always claimed to have given him one of his first briefs. Mr Bradshaw sought to prohibit a certain vicar of St Bartholomew's Church, Dublin, from placing a cross on the altar or Communion table. Carson won the case, and the vicar was ordered to remove the cross, but, being of an ingenious turn of mind, he suspended the cross from a long wire attached to the roof, so that it hung about half an inch above, and clear of, the altar. Thus does the Irish mind escape from the decisions of the law!

The first big case in which he was briefed was obtained by his father's influence: indeed, the father had the experience of being examined in chief by his tall son; the case concerned a building contract in which Mr Carson senior had been engaged as architect. Young Carson was for the defendant, who resisted the claim by the builder. He had prudently pleaded, entirely on his own initiative, that it was a term in the contract that the architect's certificate should be a condition precedent to payment, although he had never been allowed to see the contract by the plaintiff's solicitors. The plaintiffs in the end were forced to produce the contract in Court by Chief Baron Palles, and the clause which Carson had pleaded was found to be included in it. Thus, after a long fight, Carson won his case, and had the satisfaction of knowing that his client had won by his sagacious pleading. It must also have been a satisfaction to the father, who had 'put him to the Bar', to see him win the case which his influence had brought. Moreover, this building case, with all its details, gave young Carson a real opportunity to try his hand at cross-examination. The fee and the refreshers also were satisfactory. 'I lived on that case for a long time,' Lord Carson has confessed. His father was only to live a few more years, and died in 1881, at the age of fifty-nine; but, even so, he lived to see his favourite son on the way to making a good living, and to be proud of him for that reason, although there was as yet no clear promise of a great career.

For Carson's was a reputation which grew slowly on Irish soil. Irish solicitors loved a man who could talk; they were worse than their English brethren on 'solicitors' points': having raised points without number, good, bad, and indifferent, in their briefs, they liked to have the satisfaction of seeing their counsel argue them. But Carson would not oblige them; he had an uncanny power of seeing the real point, the winning point, in a case, and had further the courage to rely upon that point to the exclusion of all others. For this reason, until his judgment was vindicated again and again by long success, his advocacy was unpopular with Irish solicitors, who preferred a counsel like Seymour Bushe, who could and would take up with ease, eloquence, and charm any line of argument supplied to him by his professional client.

Almost his first appearance in the Criminal Court at Green Street was to defend a number of Trinity College students, personal friends of his own, for an assault which arose out of the Metropolitan Regatta. They had put money on the winning crew with a bookmaker, who welshed; he was captured by his clients, who relieved him of what money he had, and were about to throw him into the sea when the police rescued him. He was vindictive, and brought a prosecution against the Trinity men, who forthwith instructed Ned Carson for the defence.

'How did you know they were going to drown you?' asked Carson.

'Is it how did I know? Begorra, I knew right enough. Didn't they howld me by the leg over the say wall!'

'Which leg?' asked Carson, with a terrible droop of an eyelid. 'Was it your *black* leg?'

Under this and a few similar sallies, the prosecutor, who was known for his glib and witty tongue, collapsed. He admitted afterwards that Mr Carson was one too many for him. 'Ah, bedad,' said he, 'ye may say what ye like, but that Carson's a champion: he'd puzzle and fluster the very Divil himself.'

It was quite a frequent occurrence in Dublin for a prosecution to arise as a result of a man 'falling' into the Liffey, and it was counsel's duty to probe into the circumstances which preceded such an accident. Carson used to make the party explain in precise detail how the misadventure arose. In a case of this kind, when he was for the prosecution, he asked the defendant, 'Just tell me your account of how this man got into the river.' The defendant had learnt his story by heart: indeed, he afterwards told Carson with a grin, 'We had a great rehearsal last night, all about your cross-examination.' At all events, the result was a masterpiece of testimony. 'It was this way,' he said. 'We had a slight quarrel, whereon he turned his backside to me, and he pulled up the tail of his coat, and said, "Can you tell me the time of day?" and thereupon I felt myself insulted, and I took him gently in my arms, and, applying no more force than was necessary, threw him into the river, which is the assault complained of.' The poor man was much bewildered when his eloquent defence was interpreted as an admission of guilt! A few months after his call, his mother's brother, Mr Lambert the solicitor, went down Green Street, and came into Court just in time to hear his forceful nephew saying, 'Gentlemen of the jury, I'm sure your throats are not large enough to swallow that.' He went away much impressed with Ned's forensic abilities, feeling confident that such eloquence would be sure to make its way.

It was on the Leinster Circuit, and in the County Courts on that circuit, that Carson learnt the ways of the Irish people, and how to open their hearts by cross-examination: he chose the Leinster Circuit because it was there that his great friend James Shannon had begun to practise, one of the most brilliant and lovable young men of his time at Trinity. Carson loved him, and James Shannon, being, quite apart from his talents, the son of a solicitor, immediately sprang into a good practice. In those early days his achievements and his ambitions easily surpassed those of Carson. He was full of vitality, and was not handicapped by the bad health which pursued Carson from his teens and which compelled him to give up athletic sports while at Trinity. Nevertheless, he died a few years after his call, from a malignant attack of diphtheria, and Carson, at great personal risk to his own health, went to see him as he lay dying; indeed, Shannon almost died in his friend's arms. His last never-forgotten and strangely moving words to Carson were, 'Give up the world, Ned, and meet me in heaven.' James Shannon's poor young wife, who had vainly besought Carson not to go in and see him, followed her brilliant young husband to the grave a few days later, a victim to the same disease. The death of his best friend was a milestone in Carson's experience; life was, perhaps, never quite so gay after James Shannon was gone, and who shall say that this last dramatic salute and exhortation to his friend were not a permanent influence in the latter's long and singularly unselfish life? To the biographer of that life, as he is faced with this incident,

Fate presents herself in her most inscrutable form. Of these two young men, affectionate friends and competitors in the self-same field, for the one, the more ambitious, robust, and successful, was decreed an untimely death and a name unknown save to his intimate contemporaries; for the other, diffident in mind and delicate in body, length of days, world-wide fame and the leadership of a nation.

As in the Four Courts, so on circuit, the members of the Bar were very much a band of brothers. There was a strong *esprit de corps* and rivalry between the different circuits. Carson's circuit numbered only forty members, and was known by the members of the Home Circuit as the 'Forty Thieves', because, by an ingenious method of altering the order of the towns visited on Assize, they acquired much of the surplus work which had previously been remitted from Dublin to the Home Circuit. There were six circuits in 1877, the Home, the Leinster, the Munster, the Connaught, the North-East, and the North-West. Every Circuit had its 'Father', its 'Town Steward', its 'Junior' and its 'Treasurer'. In the earlier days there had been a 'Waggoner' in charge of the Bar 'waggon', which carted the barristers' briefs and luggage along the rough roads of the Irish countryside. After the day's work was done and the dinner was eaten, the brethren of the Bar mess used to amuse themselves by calling to the attention of the Father that one of his 'sons' had committed an offence against the Bar rules, such as 'addressing a meeting in a ladies' boarding school', or issuing an election address, or taking a special fee on another circuit, and by pleading that the delinquent be forthwith tried. Counsel was appointed on each side, and the prisoner, if found guilty, was fined in a dozen of claret. All this bred good-fellowship among the members, but this did not prevent personal attacks of the most violent kind being made in Court the next day by one 'son' against another, which were taken as a matter of course at the Irish Bar, although they would be fiercely resented in England. When Carson was Crown Counsel, T L O'Shaunessy, afterwards a Judge, would say of his opponent to the jury, in defending a prisoner: 'This Castle hack, coming down here in the intolerant pride of ascendancy.' But Carson, recognising the convention, would pay no attention to such observations, and, indeed, the 'Castle hack', when he became a power in the land over the St George's Channel, was to exercise a strong influence for O'Shaunessy's preferment. Carson himself, the most courteous of men, never adopted these methods, unless wantonly provoked, and found the polite manners of the English Courts both surprising and pleasant. However, these rude methods were really only symptomatic of a real and sturdy independence at the Irish Bar. Impartial observers have often criticised the English Bar for undue subservience, in outward manners at any rate, to the Bench. This was very different in Ireland; according to Sir Thomas Molony, the last Lord Chief Justice of Ireland, who bravely kept up all the pomp and circumstance of the Judges of Assize through the dangerous times of the Rebellion, a Judge in Ireland would be rather surprised if his suggestion was accepted by counsel; Judges were not infrequently made to apologise to counsel in open Court, and even Palles, great lawyer that he was, was not too proud to do this on at least one occasion. Carson at any rate was determined not to be set upon in Court. Mr Justice Lawson, although a just man, had a very rude tongue, and Carson, as a young man, was afraid of him. However, after he had been abused a number of times by Lawson, he was determined to have it out with him. Carson was once appearing for a solicitor, whose professional status was at stake, before three Judges, sitting 'in bank'. After hearing Carson for a while, Lawson blurted out roughly, 'Mr Carson, you've got no case.' Carson, unperturbed, continued for another twenty minutes, only to be interrupted again by Lawson's 'Mr Carson, I say you've got no case.' Carson then turned politely to Lawson with that grim dignity of his which was powerful even in so young a man. 'My lord,' he said, 'I heard you say that twenty minutes ago, and knew it would be useless to argue the merits of my case with your lordship. Since then I have not addressed one word to your lordship; I've been addressing the other Judges, and may I be allowed to go on without your lordship's interruptions?' Such perseverance and independence were rewarded by a majority judgment for Edward Carson's client. Mr Justice Lawson had been taught a lesson by Carson, as many Judges were thereafter, but he bore no ill-will. Afterwards, when Lawson was about to go on the Leinster Circuit, he met Carson in the Courts. 'Did you know I was coming the Leinster, Ned Carson?' he said, 'and will you promise not to be setting upon me in every town?' He received one of those smiles which transfigure Carson's face from grimness to real beauty. 'My lord, I will,' he answered, 'if you'll promise me that if you'll be strong, you'll be merciful.' Later Mr Justice Lawson was able to do Carson a good turn. Carson was engaged with John Gibson QC, a brother to Lord Ashbourne, afterwards Irish Attorney-General, in a difficult case of slander of title, a class of case which, as every lawyer knows, requires the most careful preliminary 'pleading'. John Gibson, a man who suffered from an overdose of undigested case law, thoughtlessly and cruelly said at the consultation, in the presence of the client, 'On the pleadings (which had of course been drafted by Carson) it is impossible to win this case.' This observation, true or not, was calculated to do great professional damage to the young junior. Carson replied boldly to the Queen's Counsel, also in the presence of the client, 'I do not know what you are talking about, John Gibson.' They then went into Court, before Mr Justice Lawson, everybody engaged in the case in bad humour with the others. Gibson testily opened the case, feeling convinced that his junior's pleadings had prevented him from putting the right line before the jury, and then left Carson to deal with the witnesses and finish the case as best he could by himself. After Gibson's departure the case began to mend, and it became obvious that Carson was going to win. At this stage there was a rustle of a silk gown, and Gibson came fussily back into Court, thinking the case had been lost. 'Did you remember to give notice of appeal?' he said. Carson had the satisfaction of replying, 'The Judge is with us: we are going to win.' Even then Gibson did not spare Carson. He jumped up, and said, 'My lord, I ask leave to amend the pleadings.' Lawson replied in his most terrible manner, 'No amendment is necessary; I never saw more accurate pleadings in my life.' Not for nothing had Carson served an apprenticeship with an equity draughtsman. Neither did John Gibson, with true Irish generosity, bear his junior any ill-will on account of this discomfiture, but in the end chose Carson, on whose judgment he had been taught to rely, to be his Crown Counsel, an appointment which led directly to his fame and fortune.

Among the places which His Majesty's Justices of Assize visited on the Leinster Circuit were Tipperary, Wicklow, Wexford, Carlow, and Kildare. Before Carson obtained a footing at Assizes, he had first to win his way in the County Courts of the same circuit. Justice in the old Irish County Courts had the merits of extraordinary cheapness. A suit could be brought for a sum of £5 at a cost of about 12s 6d, and up to £10 a fully-blown 'counsellor' could be had for half a guinea; and the Irish litigant would expect full value for his money from his 'counsellor', and usually got it. But a County Court practice was not without its difficulties; one was the preternatural antiquity of the Bench. For the old County

Court Judges were of a rare style, and usually of a great old age: whenever a man obtained an official position in Ireland, he endeavoured to hold on to it till grim death literally parted him from his salary. For instance, Judge Wall, who was stone deaf, presided over the County Court of Tipperary. One day Carson, who had been engaged elsewhere, met the Judge on the platform of Tipperary station.

'Well, Judge,' he said, 'had you an interesting case in Court today?'

'Eh?' he said, and Carson had to shout the question out again.

'Oh, yes,' he replied, 'a very interesting case. I am not certain what it was about. I think it was a choral society complaining about an instrument. I suppose it was a harmonium.' The next morning Carson discovered that this alleged musical action really concerned the price and quality of a Singer's sewing machine.

Carson's powerful voice was admirably suited to impress tribunals of this nature, and he began to be busy in the County Courts, especially before old Judge Waters at Waterford. His clients, too, were a wonderful class of men. On one occasion, when Carson was pleading a case, he could not help noticing a rustic-looking fellow biting his mouth and looking first at him and then at the Judge. In the luncheon interval, Carson went over to the hotel opposite the Court. As he returned to Court, the same rustic-looking fellow tugged at his sleeve.

'Might you be Counsellor Carson?' asked the countryman.

'Yes.'

'Have you a bit of a case for Michael Corrigan?'

'No.'

'Look here, counsellor, I'm Mick.'

Young Carson, knowing that a barrister can only be approached through a solicitor, said, 'You had better speak to

Mr Patrick Burke, the solicitor.'

'Paddy is my man,' rejoined the countryman, and then, with a most confidential air, as if he was frightened that anyone might hear him, he whispered, 'Come over here, counsellor, and I've got something very private to say to ye.' He then pulled his hat well over his face, so that no one could recognise him, and summoned up all his courage to say, 'If ye win that bit of a case for me, I'll give ye five shillings for yerself.' Carson, properly instructed by Mr Patrick Burke, won the case for the client, but he never saw the five shillings!

At other times outside the County Courts he would be accosted by similar homely individuals, with the same confidential, 'Will ye speak to me, counsellor?' Then would follow, 'On Thursday last I was served with the Grace of God. I have it in my pocket.'

'Well,' Carson would say, 'show it to me, and I'll tell you what to do with it.'

The frightened man or woman would then produce to Carson a crumpled subpoena *duces tecum*, ordering them to bring some document to Court. 'It's a compulsory,' they would complain.

These County Courts were a great school for cross-examination; the simple Irish folk would come to Court with some extraordinary story all rehearsed and learnt by heart: they were determined to win their cases, and yet were in terror of the priests and of hell-fire if they should commit perjury. They did not care for the spirit of truth, so long as they could make some literal claim to veracity. Some of their devices were ludicrous and pathetic in their ingenuous ingenuity. A number of witnesses were called to prove the validity of a signature to a will: the allegation was that the woman was dead when the will was signed. All the witnesses who had been at the bedside swore one after the other that 'at any rate she had life in her'. And, indeed, so it was: for they had put a live fly in the woman's mouth. These were a very difficult class of witnesses to deal with, and, of course, the figures of illiteracy at that time in Ireland were tragically high.

Nor did Carson always have to deal with such witnesses on the opposite side: he had many of his own. They would come and plead pathetically for advice: 'What am I to say?' Carson always dealt with them in one way. 'You must tell the truth,' he would say. But frequently their simple yet cunning and tortuous minds had no sense of truth, and his simple advice often fell upon uncomprehending ears.

One of his earliest lessons in cross-examination was gained in an action brought by a 'fancy class' girl to recover certain presents from a man who refused to implement his promise of marriage. This was one of his earliest cases, and Carson was very green. In cross-examination of the man, since he could think of no better question to ask, and was quite at a loss, he simply said, 'Why don't you give the lady back her presents?'

The witness began to bite his hat, as Irish peasants would when they were puzzled or embarrassed. Then he looked Carson straight in the face. 'I think, yer honour,' he said, 'that's a very leading question.' The man was quite unable to answer the simple question, which was the very root of the case. This set Carson thinking that it is always necessary in cross-examination to ask a 'very leading question' which lies at the very root of the action. This experience laid the foundation of the famous Carson method of cross-examination, which consisted in asking very few, very embarrassing questions, and then leaving the witness alone. This was a very new method in Ireland, and it perplexed the people, but this wonderful gift of his was only really appreciated when he came to England. 'He was so very relevant,' says Lord Darling, 'so unlike all the other Irishmen we had seen: he simply would not talk balderdash.' In its finest form this method appeared in a divorce case many years later in London. Carson was appearing for the wife, who would have left the Court ruined and penniless had the jury found against her. She had a self-righteous, narrow-minded husband, whose neglect had perhaps led her into indiscretions. Carson liked the little woman, and all his human sympathies were aroused on her behalf: he was determined to win her case for her. He rose to cross-examine the husband, who was standing in the witness-box, with a huge pile of correspondence in front of him which he had been manipulating in order to prove himself in the right. Carson assumed his most terrible air. 'When did you leave off loving your wife?' he asked slowly. The question was one of rare insight, but so surprised the husband that he could say nothing in reply, and began again to search for some letter or other in the pile of correspondence. 'Ah,' said Carson, in dramatic disgust, 'you won't find that in any document; now tell me, will you, when did you leave off loving your wife?' From that moment the jury saw the true situation as between the pedantic, unsympathetic husband and the affectionate, foolish little wife, and found in the end for the latter.

Another quality which Carson learnt from his Irish witnesses was a refusal to be put off from his real question by any skilful evasion, at which the Irish were adepts. He was once cross-examining a theatrical expert on the value of his experience in the music-hall business.

'How long have you been in the music-hall business, Mr Cox?'

'Theatres and music-halls, twenty-one years.'

'Mr Cox, how long have you been in the *music-hall* business?'

After a short pause the answer was, 'Seven months.'

How many advocates, who had not the advantage of a training in the Waterford County Court, would have been put off by that skilful evasion, 'Theatres and music-halls, twenty-one years'?

To this early period belongs a famous story, which has wrongly been attributed to other advocates, including Lord Reading; but it nevertheless belongs to Carson and the Irish County Court of the past. There was a witness in the box whose good character was relevant to the weight of his testimony.

'Arre ye a teetotaller?' asks Carson of the bottle-nosed man in the box. A titter is heard in Court.

'No, I'm not,' says the bottle-nosed man, feeling himself insulted by the question, as Carson knew he would.

'Arre ye a modtherate dhrinker?'

No answer from the bottle-nosed one, who begins to scent danger.

'Should I be roight if I called ye a heavy dhrinker?'

'That's my business,' replies the bottle-nosed one, drawing himself up proudly, thinking he has scored off clever Counsellor Carson. Then comes the knockout.

'Have ye any *other* business?' comes in a slow, gentle voice from Counsellor Carson.

But it must not be thought that Carson always got the best of his witty fellow-countrymen when he was pitted against them in his wig and gown. He was once cross-examining a farmer as to the purchase of some cattle at a fair, and he asked, 'Have you got a receipt for the money?' Paddy turned scornfully from Carson to the Judge and said, 'Yer honour, I wonder if that man was ever in a fair, and did he ever sell cattle?'

3. Gladstone's Irish Land Bill

In 1881 Mr Gladstone brought in his Irish Land Bill, which, apart from its many political repercussions, brought the Bar an enormous amount of work, both in the County Courts and before the Commission set up in Dublin. A typically Irish misadventure marred the opening of this Court. Mr Parnell and the Land League, which was organised against landlords to secure reduced rents, much as trades unionists are now organised against employers to maintain fair wages, had already made their influence felt in the British Parliament, and Mr Gladstone knew their power. It was, therefore, particularly unfortunate that in November 1881, after the three Commissioners had entered the Court with great pomp, when the registrar was directed to open the Court officially, he should declare in a loud voice, 'The Court of the Land League is now open.'

At all events, tenants were now enabled to go to the County Court and ask the Judge to assess their holdings at 'fair rents'. This was a much-needed reform; there was a fundamental difference between the Irish and English land systems which the English public, with their natural respect for the 'sanctity of contract', had long failed to appreciate. The Irish tenant had no fixity of tenure, and, if he attempted to improve his land, his rents as a rule would rise as a result of his expenditure. Rents were in many instances far too high for the return given by the land, and, the landlords insisting on arrears, the tenants were always liable to eviction for non-payment of rent. In spite of the ambiguous attitude of Mr Parnell as to the patronage of the Land Act by the Irish people, there was a rush to the County Courts in order to take advantage of Mr Gladstone's measure, and it is said that the result was a crop of half a million lawsuits. If the Act was in the end of great advantage to the people of the land, it was of immediate advantage to the Irish Bar. Tim Healy, in his memoirs, says it is impossible to exaggerate the interest taken in land cases at this epoch: to landlords, every defeat seemed a Waterloo; to tenants, every victory an Austerlitz. Edward Carson's abilities were already known to the people of the Leinster Circuit; the discomfiture of the bottle-nosed one had spread far and wide, and it is fair to say that the tenants discovered his talents before the landlords were compelled to take notice of them. Many was the 'fair rent' which 'Counsellor Carson' secured for the poor people of the Leinster Circuit in those days. In one of these cases the landlord had gone to the expense of calling three 'valuators' (the Irish term for 'valuer') to inform the County Court Judge of the high value of a certain field rented by Carson's client. Carson asked that the other two valuators should be out of Court while one of them was giving the Court the advantage of his expert testimony. The first valuator came in, and, after being carefully examined in detail as to the field, gave its fair annual rent as £10 15s 2d. The second valuator gave precisely the same assessment. Carson let them alone, but when the third valuator came and repeated exactly the same figure, he considered that his turn had come to intervene.

Carson: 'Ye said ye went over the field carefully, by yourself?'
Witness: 'Yes.'
Carson: 'What sort of a field did ye find it?'
Witness: 'It had a wall all round it: I noticed everything about it.'
Carson: 'Did ye notice any coincidences about the field?'
Witness: 'Yes, indeed. I didn't rightly recall it at first, but now ye come to remind me, there was a little heap of them lying up in a corner of the field by themselves.'

So successful was Carson as an advocate for the tenants, and so fiercely did he throw himself into his cases, that a deputation once called upon him to beg him to be the 'No Rent' and 'Nationalist' member for Waterford. They could scarcely believe their ears when he told the deputation that he was a Unionist with his living to make and no thought of politics.

In the County Courts, Edward Carson was beginning to build himself up a practice for the Assizes. In Ireland they had a system by which the litigant could for a very small expense bring his case before the Judge of Assize by what was known as 'Civil Bill Appeals'. For any sum under £50 there was an appeal from the County Court Judge to the Judge of Assize on fact or law; and any litigant could get, for a case concerning any sum under £50, the best man on the circuit – for example, Carson in his most prosperous days – for three guineas, and, for a case involving a sum under £25, for two guineas. Thus His Majesty's 'Red' Judges of Assize came into contact with the common people, their joys and sorrows, their quarrels and grievances, and brought their knowledge back to the capital of the kingdom. When Carson was beginning to get on he showed great kindness to younger men, and did not neglect to give them friendly advice. Thomas Molony, who was known, because of a certain praying gesture of his hands when pleading, as the 'Mother Superior' (although his high courage during the troubles as Ireland's last Lord Chief Justice belies any suggestion of feminine weakness), recalls how, when he was losing the ground he had won by talking for too long, he felt a strong pull on his gown from the ruthless but friendly Carson, who was not engaged in the case. 'He became extremely brilliant, and always extremely tenacious: he was, even as a youth, full of mature wisdom in managing juries; he was always a good fighter and a clean fighter,' says Chief Justice Molony of him.

Another of Carson's brethren on the Leinster Circuit was a

certain Wexford landowner's son named John Redmond. He was a 'right good man to make a speech', but he lost himself in his oratory. In Ireland, oratory is taken for granted, and what is needed is knowledge of the people and their tricks, a lore in which Carson was steeped; Redmond was incapable of an insinuating cross-examination. However, Redmond by his natural eloquence did quite well for himself on circuit, and defended prisoners with some distinction. Carson, who was to find himself as the antagonist of Redmond in matters which were to challenge the attention of the world, was once in those early days his opponent in a murder trial. Carson prosecuted, and Redmond was for the defence. Two boys had gone into a poor old woman's shop in a country district, who earned a scanty livelihood by selling bits of tobacco: she was found dead soon afterwards, and some tobacco and a few coppers were found to have been stolen. Some tobacco and some coppers were subsequently found in a loft where the prisoners were proved to have slept. Amongst the coppers was a halfpenny with a hole in it, and a witness was called who proved that he had, shortly before the old woman's death, bought from her tuppence worth of tobacco, and that he had paid for it with a halfpenny with a hole in it. Redmond defended the case with great skill, according to his opponent. Carson had a facility for writing light verse which has never deserted him, and, when Redmond had finished his eloquent address for the prisoners, he was handed the following verses in Carson's hand, summarising the arguments on each side.

> *'If a halfpenny is evidence, I think on the whole*
> *I find in your case a terrible hole.*
> *If tobacco is evidence, so Redmond spoke,*
> *I think that your case must all end in smoke.'*

Despite Redmond's eloquence, the prisoners, both of whom were very young, were convicted. One was hanged and the other reprieved.

It might seem slightly shocking to the lay mind for young counsel to write flippant rhymes when they are mutually engaged on a trial for a man's life, but it must be remembered that by the time of this case Carson had become professionally hardened to the lawless state of Ireland, and to crimes of violence and their penalties. In his very first murder case, Carson had defended two soldiers on the Leinster Circuit for murder: they were convicted and sentenced to death; after the grim ritual of the black cap and the sentence of death, the jury sent a note to the Judge. Carson at once rose in his place, determined to take advantage of the situation.

'If that is a recommendation to mercy, my lord ...' he began.

The Judge: 'No, Mr Carson, it is nothing of the sort.'

The jury then took the idea which Carson's words had suggested to them. They put their heads together, and in a minute the foreman jumped up and said, 'But we would like to recommend them to mercy.' Carson was deeply overwhelmed by the solemnity of the occasion and by the fact that his clients had been condemned to death. In his concern for them he went to visit them in prison soon afterwards with a view to a petition for reprieve: he was almost in tears, but what was his ironic surprise when he found his late clients playing leap-frog with the other prisoners in the prison yard, but an hour or so after they had been condemned to die.

In many of his early prosecutions Carson was faced by what was known as a 'Tipperary alibi'. This was a defence which sought to establish, not only the absence from the fatal scene of the prisoner, but also of the principal Crown witnesses who came to give first-hand evidence. Some of the

'Tipperary alibis' were very carefully concocted, and very difficult to break down, but Carson's penetrating mind was the one specially fitted for this work. Another well-known Irish defence was the 'Westmeath alibi', by which the criminals and their confederates would prepare in advance a story of the prisoner's absence from the fatal scene, and his presence with witnesses at the fatal time at another place. They would afterwards describe in the smallest detail what they did on the night of the murder, at a place far distant; they would actually have visited that distant place on a previous date for the purposes of the alibi. After four or five years on the Leinster Circuit, Carson was beginning to make a name for himself; but work was not nearly so plentiful on that circuit as it was on the Munster, and Carson applied to join the Munster Circuit. He was, however, blackballed, not because of any objection to his personal character or personality, but simply because the Munster barristers were afraid of his formidable competition. Indeed, his 'blackballing' was regarded in Dublin as a very great compliment to the young advocate.

In reading the above pages, and considering their anecdotes in ordered sequence, the reader may perhaps think that Carson's progress was easy and predestined by his ability. Such a view would be wrong. Although both in Dublin and on circuit he frequently held briefs, his progress was slow, and the remuneration which he received was small. A letter from a Mr Frederick Fenton, who briefed him in those early days, congratulating Carson on his appointment as a Lord of Appeal, came to him like an echo of the past in 1921. 'In the 'eighties I often handed to your lordship briefs marked half a guinea. Very often, I fear, the fee did not accompany the brief. I also have delivered similar briefs at your then house in Dublin ... I have been present at consultations of counsel when the late Dr Houston QC, and the late Mr

David Lynch QC, were your leaders. I have heard from you great speeches to juries on briefs marked two guineas, and the late Mr Tooney once remarked to me, "He is killing at the money". I have many anecdotes about your lordship of those days stored in my memory, and your lordship can quite understand the satisfaction I feel when I contemplate the great position in English and Irish history your lordship's name will ever occupy.'

Nevertheless, the first two years at the Bar were hardly able to keep him in pocket-money, and it was at this unpropitious moment that he had chosen to marry. He had been boating, one summer evening – a favourite relaxation in those days – at a seaside resort near Dublin; as he came ashore, the beauty of a slim, fair-haired girl first challenged, then captivated his attention. He immediately enquired of a friend as to who she was; her name was Miss Sarah Annette Foster Kirwan, the adopted daughter of Mr Persse Kirwan, formerly of Tristan Lodge, County Galway. Edward Carson was at once introduced to her at his own request by his friend, and for him it was love at first sight. He had about fifty guineas saved in the bank, and she was without fortune. But Carson would listen to no counsel of delay from his family, who were naturally opposed to such an improvident marriage; and in a very short time the almost briefless barrister was a married man, and had already thrown gages to fortune. For a short time after they married, Mr and Mrs Edward Carson lived in the house of old Mr Kirwan. Then, under the old gentleman's roof, began a hard and dogged struggle for a foothold in life. A year after their marriage in 1880, their eldest son, William Henry Lambert, was born, and, although Carson's practice scarcely justified the step, they moved into a small house of his own in Herbert Place. But he was determined to succeed, and, when there were no briefs, he used to sit up into the small hours studying law. Idleness was hateful to him; his ambition was not presumptuous, but there was something in his nature which found failure in anything undertaken repellent: in truth, it was not his way to fail, and gradually the briefs began to come in. Expeditions into the country, and to the Dublin Theatre, used to follow a successful week on circuit or at the Four Courts: for Carson has never been a man to hoard his money, and even now, after being probably the most expensive counsel to brief in the history of the Bar, he is not a rich man. If money had ever been one of the serious considerations of his life, he would certainly have amassed one of the largest fortunes of his times made at the Bar, or elsewhere. Nor, even in those early days of first success, when there actually began to be a little more money in the bank than was needed for current expenses, was his generosity confined to members of his own family. Ireland was always a poor country, and in 1880 a cruel famine was imminent, and Ireland was faced with a harvest only less bad than that of the terrible year of 1849, which had changed the face of Ireland. A fund of £181 000 was collected from all over the world for the relief of the distressed Irish people. Carson performed many acts of generosity to colleagues and other people who were not so well equipped for success as he was. This was told me by Mr Tim Healy a very short time before he died. 'Yet,' he added, 'I never heard a word of self-praise from Carson for the numerous works of charity and generosity which he did.' Tim Healy was not called to the Bar till 1884, but he had already made his personality, a strange, bitter-sweet, human alloy of childlike gentleness and cynical ferocity, strongly felt in the House of Commons. From the first, Healy and Carson were personal friends, although one was an inheritor of the Protestant Ascendancy and a Unionist in the old tradition of the Dublin Bar, and the other a passionate Nationalist, the trusted lieutenant of Parnell, who belonged to that different class of Irishmen, sprung from the peasantry and small farmers, then beginning to take their share in the professions and in other branches of Irish life. Many and bitter were the fights they had in Court, but the Irish gentleman in each of them called out for the other's affection. Once, in a country inn, after a hard-fought case, they had a bottle of claret together, and enjoyed each other's company to the full. After the meal was over, Carson smiled, and, turning his deep blue eyes on his colleague, said, 'You know really, Tim, you're quite a decent fellow when you're in good company: will you tell me why you're such an awful blackguard over there in Westminster?' To which Tim, rolling up those curious light brown eyes of his, replied, 'Really, Ned, will ye tell me this: do ye think honestly that any other role would suit me?' When Carson welcomed Healy to the Irish Bar, just as when Healy welcomed Carson some years later at Westminster, each of them realised that in the other he had an opponent worthy of his steel. They were constant opponents, and Healy noticed with what great seriousness Carson took his work; after a case he would be bathed in perspiration, and, moreover, he had no confidence in his health. In a *habeas corpus* case, where there had been a 'mixed marriage' and the two religions each claimed the 'body' of a child for its education, Tim Healy won on technical grounds, but, to his great delight and admiration, Carson made a wonderful speech 'on the merits', as a result of which Healy's client was deprived of costs. As they went out of Court, Tim said, 'That was a wonderful speech you made, Ned. You must have had a grand breakfast to have done it. What did ye have?'

'A bottle of medicine,' replied Carson gloomily.

For, although his parents were displeased at his early

marriage, it was probably a most fortunate event in his life. Soon afterwards, he was struck down, after one of the long journeys in the winter which his profession enjoined, with an attack of typhoid, which all but proved fatal. His wife nursed him devotedly through this illness, and in his opinion saved his life. Indeed, through all those difficult years of making his way, she was a wonderful helpmate to him; and in later times, when Carson, rather to her bewilderment, became a great man, and her own health failed badly, her husband never forgot her devotion and service to him in the early days, and she was repaid in the end by the wonderful patience and consideration which he in turn showed her, when continued illness had made her unable to give him the same assistance and comradeship which had helped and encouraged him in Dublin long before.

A successful lawyer's rise to fame is, at some stage or another, usually facilitated, after the early struggles, by a *cause célèbre*. Lawyers themselves, as a rule, look upon litigation as the very last resort of a prudent man; but, fortunately for them, there are people who are minded differently, and look upon litigation, not only as a means to the defence of their rights and as a remedy for their wrongs, but as a means of living, and as a joy in itself. It is fortunate for the lawyers that there are such people. It was thus that Fortune presented herself to Carson, in the eccentric form of Miss Anthony, the celebrated 'lady litigant' of the Dublin Courts. Her introduction to the joys of litigation was literally 'accidental'. She came from Waterford, and was ejected by a railway porter from a train compartment for travelling without a ticket. Fortunately for her, and for Carson, who was subsequently briefed for her, she received injuries in the course of ejection. However, so suspicious was she of the law, that when the case was about to come on at the Dungarvan Assizes, she had not yet briefed her 'counsellor'.

Carson was still lying in bed at his Inn, when a wild-eyed and middle aged lady rushed into his bedroom and tried to 'retain' him on the spot. After he had referred her to a solicitor, he undertook her case. Her advocate recovered heavy damages before the jury; an indignant railway company appealed, and Carson was the leading and ultimately successful figure in a long story of protracted litigation, in which the whole law of negligence was discussed. But Carson, in winning fame for himself in this way, gave his client an unfortunate taste for litigation which was at length to bring her to ruin: his great skill in conducting her case, both on facts and law, taught her so much that henceforward she dispensed with the services of an advocate; and she was remarkably successful, although Carson himself defended several cases against her. On one of those occasions she violently assailed the personal character both of her late champion and of his mother. 'And your mother was no better than she should be,' she flung at him. 'My poor saintly mother!' said Carson to his solicitor. She paid a tradesman, for bacon supplied, with a jewel; she then issued a writ against the tradesman for illegally taking pledges, and so recovered her property; next she sued a priest for the implied slander of passing her over when she presented herself for Holy Communion, and received a sum in settlement of her action from the priest, who feared for his reputation; she also sued a rate collector for excess in his collection: she lost her action this time, and soon after she persuaded a Christian Brotherhood to take her sheep into their field to save them from the execution; she then proceeded to borrow money from these unsuspecting brethren on her sheep and, to avoid repayment, and remembering her success with the gem, she sued them for the return of the animals, and so frightened them from going into Court. Having defeated outright a large railway corporation, the Irish priesthood, and rendered the victory of the local authority nugatory, and, indeed, turned it to her own advantage, she turned her attention to the legal profession itself: for next in the order of her victims came a solicitor, who, receiving from her a writ for slander and never having heard of Miss Anthony, threw it into the waste-paper basket, and had £1 000 given against him in default of appearance. She had become the terror of the whole professional and trading community. She was now a privileged, almost a sacrosanct person: she was accorded free travel, and no tradesman dared to sue her for her unpaid bills. Eventually, however, the assistance of the Irish Lord Chancellor, who had jurisdiction over lunatics, dangerous and otherwise, was invoked, and she became an inmate of the Cork County Asylum. There she hanged herself, but so frightened were the editors of newspapers that she might still sue them for libel that her death was never reported. Carson had no lot nor part in his old client's certification, although he had acquired a practice before the Lord Chancellor's Commissioner in lunacy. After he had been successful in proving one of his fellow-countrymen insane, a man who had been listening entranced to his argument came up and congratulated him gravely upon his performance. 'I'm the alleged lunatic,' said the stranger, 'and I've never heard a fairer statement.'

Carson's practice, however, was not only concerned with the pathos and bathos of the Irish character, its mischief and its quarrels. These experiences were only light flashes in the darkening horizon of Irish life, which was reflected from many aspects in Carson's practice as it grew in importance. The murder of Mr Gladstone's nephew, Lord Frederick Cavendish, in Phoenix Park, on the very day in 1882 when he landed in Ireland, the circumstances of which are described in the next chapter, and the long enquiry and trial which succeeded, disclosed the existence of the formation of armed secret societies whose object was the murder of officials and landlords. It was not generally known how widely these societies were spreading and to what extent the conspirators were armed, but two murder trials, in which Carson was briefed for the defence, illustrate respectively the alarming conditions prevailing both in the city of Dublin and over the countryside.

The first was known as the Dorset Street tragedy. On 28 March 1882, a respectable young artisan named Joseph MacMahon, employed in the printing trade, left his mother's house at about nine o'clock in the morning, accompanied by two close friends of the came class, John Brennan and Thomas Martin. His mother had watched him anxiously during breakfast; he could not eat, and said that he was too ill to go to work: she thought that he had something on his mind. At midday the three young men walked together into a public-house kept by a Mrs Dunlop in Dorset Street, and asked for a private room. They were shown into a little place which was separated from the bar by a partition which did not quite reach to the ceiling. There was a crowd of people in the bar at the time, so that little attention was paid to the low conversation which was being held in the little room. Five minutes later, there rang out the loud report of a revolver shot, and smoke was seen curling over the partition. One of the three young men, John Brennan, rushed out of the little room, forced his way through the astonished crowd, and took to his heels. As he opened the door in the partition, the dead body of Joseph MacMahon, who had entered the shop so shortly before, full of the vigour of life and health, fell out on to the floor of the saloon bar. A crowd then gave immediate pursuit to John Brennan, and one of the number, after a short hue and cry of 'Stop the murderer', pulled him off a jaunting-car onto which he had jumped, and his arrest swiftly followed. The third young man, Thomas Martin, remained with the dead body. Two revolvers were found lying on the floor of the little room, one fully loaded, the other lacking the one cartridge which had been fired. The latter was pointing towards MacMahon. Five other revolver bullets were found under a seat in the room. In MacMahon's house there was found a small armoury: more revolver cartridges, 143 rounds of rifle ammunition, rifles, bayonets, and some articles for cleaning firearms.

The case was tried in April before Chief Baron Palles and a jury of the 'wild flowers of Tullahogue'. James Murphy QC and William O'Brien QC appeared for the prosecution, and Carson defended the prisoners single-handed. The event had taken place when everybody in Dublin was talking about the Phoenix Park murders and the knife and the bullet were feared by all respectable citizens, and the case caused considerable alarm. 'What brought these three men here with these deadly weapons?' asked Murphy. 'There is at present an alarming state of affairs prevailing in this city. We cannot tell to what secret obligations these young men are bound, or what they may have been planning to do that day.' Popular feeling ran high in Dublin against the murder gangs, and at this moment, if at any, a conviction was likely. Carson's defence was that the whole affair was an accident: he called the carman to prove that Brennan had told him to drive back to Mrs Dunlop's public-house to help a dying man, and also called witnesses to prove the hitherto exemplary characters of the accused. This made the case all the more strange and alarming. What were these three respectable young men meeting together for? For what were they turning their homes into arsenals? Carson made a powerful speech, calling upon the jury to dismiss all these matters from their minds: no man should be convicted on a capital charge on account of the state of the city. 'You must put out of your minds any speculation as to what may have been the object of these young men going into the snuggery. You have here a charge of murder without evidence of any motive whatsoever. Have you ever in the course of your experience heard of a murder perpetrated thus? In the midst of a crowded shop, in broad daylight, with two policemen in the street outside? Is it likely, I ask you, that if a murder was *intended*, the murderer would use a weapon which must bring upon him immediate detection? I do not ask for mercy,' concluded Carson; 'I demand justice.' At 4.25 the Lord Chief Baron summed up for an hour against the prisoners. 'Why these fully loaded revolvers?' he said. 'Why did Brennan have the revolver in his hands? Why were both fully loaded? You can only judge men's motives by their acts.' The jury retired, and had not agreed on their verdict at eleven o'clock that night. Finally William O'Brien QC asked for the jury to be discharged. 'I do not believe,' he said, 'that the jury have tried to consider this case at all: this is another example of the failure of this tribunal.' The prisoners were tried at the next Commission at Green Street in August before Mr Justice Lawson, and they remained in gaol during the interval. In the course of the case the Crown saw that it was hopeless to go forward for a verdict on the capital charge, and accepted from Carson a plea of guilty on the lesser count of 'manslaughter', and the two men were sentenced to terms of imprisonment. Carson said, 'I could not resist the finding that the accidental going off of the pistol was the cause of MacMahon's death. But negligence is a relative term. Accidents with revolvers are of almost daily occurrence. No motive has been shown, and up to the last minute the three men had been bound together by the closest ties of friendship.'

Mr Justice Lawson, however, could not take Carson's view

of this as a mere unfortunate accident. 'I can only say,' he observed gravely, 'that this case reveals the deplorable state of the society in which we live. It is most disquieting that three decent men of the artisan class should be found in the possession of these formidable weapons, especially when there is a proclamation against the use of them. Yet there they were, sitting together, planning something or other, in a public-house in the middle of the day. It is more disquieting that a verdict, even of manslaughter, could not be had from the former jury.'

Carson's success on the capital charge had not reassured the public, or those entrusted with the administration of the law; yet in this case at least there was a hue and cry raised, and the man who had killed his friend was pursued and caught by members of the public. In later days assassinations of defenceless people took place in broad daylight and in a busy street, and the assassins were allowed to escape in full view of the crowd. Later Carson received the most ironical message of gratitude from Mrs Brennan, the mother of the prisoner. The Phoenix Park murders soon followed the Dorset Street tragedy. Carson might well have been thanked for his conduct of the case, but Mrs Brennan came to thank him for advising her son to plead guilty so that he was in prison at the time of the Phoenix Park murders. Otherwise, said his mother, he would have been compelled by his oath to have taken an active part in the conspiracy.

In the following year Carson appeared for the defence in a far more celebrated and tragic murder trial, which was reported all over the English-speaking world.

On 2 April 1882, Mrs Henry Smythe, of 33 FitzWilliam Place, Dublin, took her two girls, who had been introduced to Dublin society, on an Easter visit to the beautiful country mansion, Barbavilla House, County Westmeath, the seat of their uncle, Barlow Smythe, Justice of Peace and senior Deputy-Lieutenant of the County. Other districts might be dangerous enough and some landlords might be in danger, but it surely seemed that Mr Smythe and his guests would be safe enough in his lovely Georgian home. Until just the other day he had not evicted a tenant for fifty years: the most amicable relations existed between him and his tenantry. He had recently sent a circular to all of them, generously offering to each and all of them the free registration of reduced rents before the new Land Commission, with all legal costs to be charged to the estate. This circular letter had begun with the words 'My friends'. It was true that he had recently evicted a farmer named Riggs, who had rented a large farm, and had refused to pay rent for years. He had offered land to Riggs at a nominal rent, and even to pay him an annuity to protect him and his family. But Riggs refused to accept these offers, and it was understood that he had some organisation behind him. He had been a Fenian in old days. However, it could hardly be probable that the other tenants would take strong measures against their generous landlord for the sake of one obstinate and foolish old man, who was clearly in the wrong. At all events, Mr Barlow Smythe, who loved Ireland and had spent his whole life at Barbavilla, working among and on behalf of his tenantry, had the greatest confidence in his people. He had in his time received many threats. But they had come to nothing; and he was an old man now, quite confident and fearless.

There was a happy house-party at Barbavilla; there were two young officers asked by the young ladies, and a kinswoman of the family, Lady Harriett Monk, who was also a personal friend to the Queen. The day after Mrs Henry Smythe's arrival it was Palm Sunday, and the family set out for the Anglican church close by at Collinstown. It was a lovely spring morning, and the young ladies walked to church by a short cut through the woods. Their uncle chaperoned them on their walk to church, while his sister-in-law and Lady Harriett followed in the closed brougham. It was a short and pleasant drive to the church of not much more than a mile. The young ladies and gentlemen came out after matins, and left the elder members of the party to partake in the celebration of Holy Communion. As they walked home, one of the girls heard a low whistle in the trees and noticed a sound of rustling in the leaves of a thicket as they passed, but little attention was paid to this, and the four young people continued their walk home, chatting and laughing as they went.

Later, Mr Barlow Smythe, his sister-in-law, and Lady Harriett Monk, when the Communion Service was over, got into the carriage shortly before two o'clock. Mrs Smythe chose the seat with her back to the horses on the right-hand side. This would have been the seat normally occupied by a gentleman, but her brother-in-law was an old man, and she left the back seats for him and Lady Harriett. The horses trotted along the road and turned into the drive, a smiling green landscape lay on either side of the road, and all the world seemed at peace. A winding avenue about a third of a mile led up to Barbavilla House. The house did not break upon view until the visitor had reached almost the end of the drive, being hidden by trees with which it was surrounded. The avenue was planted at intervals with trees, sometimes at a distance from each other, sometimes in clumps. The carriage had come within 150 yards of the house, which was not yet in view, when two explosions were heard, so loud that Mr Barlow Smythe did not recognise them as gunfire. He first thought that there had arisen some tremendous hailstorm. The coachman stooped down and asked if anyone was hurt. 'No,' said Mr Smythe. The horses then became frightened; the coachman saw a man on the left, partially concealed by the branch of a tree, but standing on a slight eminence. He was stooping; another loud report was heard, and the circular glass front of the brougham was smashed to pieces; the windows were splashed all over with what appeared to be mud. Mrs Smythe fell forward, as if frightened, as the shots were fired; 'Good God, we are under fire,' said her brother-in-law, as the horses galloped towards the mansion.

It was only when they reached the house that Mrs Smythe was discovered to be dead: her brains had been blown out by the gunshot at close range, and she was horribly mutilated. Her wounds were frightful, and what Mr Smythe had thought was mud was really the blood and brains of the poor lady. Meanwhile the assailants had completely disappeared. The news spread quickly, and soon a crowd of sympathetic people were assembled at Barbavilla House. The police and the resident magistrate arrived from Mullingar. They found no sign or trace of the assassins, except the path of the bullets through the leaves of the thicket, and a bottle which was lying hard by, containing a little whiskey.

The news of this terrible murder was soon all over the world, and, because the victim was a woman, excited more horror than that of Lord Frederick Cavendish, which occurred on 6 May. The *Freeman's Journal*, the organ of Nationalist opinion, mournfully said in its leading article, 'Time was when the presence of a woman would have stayed the assassin's hand, but the bloody events of this year reveal men merciless and regardless'. *The Times* described it as the most dreadful and desperate murder which had yet been added to the foul list of agrarian crimes.

The inquest was held, and, although many people all over the countryside must have known a great deal about the murder, not one person would come forward to identify the murderers. The verdict of the jury was that 'Mrs Maria

Smythe had been brutally murdered by some person or persons unknown'. In the bitterness of his spirit, Barlow Smythe wrote on Good Friday a terrible circular letter to his tenants, which contrasted tragically with the one that had gone before. 'I do not', he wrote, 'go through the former farce of calling you friends. Few of you are so. Most of you by your silence assent to the deed of blood, and many of you only regret that one who has passed his life and spent his income among you was not the victim. Some of you knew what was intended and are as guilty in God's sight as the murderers. I must, however, address you, and wish you to know that those among you who are liable to rents are in future to pay to a non-resident agent, who can make no future allowances nor do anything on the property not strictly required by law. You may regret the murder, because of the fatal mistake (which you, of course, hope to rectify), as prejudicial to your Land League, but not as against God's command, "Thou shalt do no murder". May He lead some of you to repentance, and give you forgiveness, whose death is now being commemorated by all who call themselves Christians in this unhallowed land. – W B Smythe, Barbavilla House, Good Friday, 1882.'

It was obvious that Barlow Smythe was right, and that he himself was the intended victim; indeed, for many years in West Meath the tragedy was remembered as 'the accident', in the sense that the wrong person had been murdered.

Barlow Smythe wrote another bitter letter to Mr Gladstone, to whose recent policy of conciliation he attributed the tragedy: 'Sir, –Your practical adhesion to the principle that force is no remedy in the case of Irish savagery, has culminated here in making it easy for the assassin guerrilla of the Land League to murder my sister-in-law not long after noonday returning from church with me. I lay the guilt of the deed of blood at your door in the face of the whole country, supported as you are in that part of your policy by the "no-rent" Members of Parliament, their Press and some Irish bishops. I have to add that the terrorism existing under the protection of your police is so tremendous that I know there are few of those who abhor the crime who would venture to denounce the assassins had they seen them and that, were they to do so, their lives would be forfeited, while the prisoners would almost as surely escape after the farce of a trial by jury. – W B Smythe, Senior DL, County Westmeath.'

Mr Gladstone, himself overwhelmed by the murder of his nephew Lord Frederick Cavendish, whom he had sent to the forefront to initiate his policy of conciliation, replied 'expressing his deep and heartfelt sympathy on the occasion of this terrible outrage', and the Queen also sent a message of condolence.

Meanwhile the police had been pursuing their enquiries in vain. The evicted tenant, Richard Riggs, and his family were arrested, but it was obvious that they at least were innocent; then a month passed and no new light was thrown on the tragedy; finally, in the *Gazette* of 27 May the huge reward of £2 000 was offered for information leading to the conviction of the murderers, and a free pardon for any accomplices who would come forward.

Even this exceptional offer of reward, an odious method relied on by the Crown in the last resort and often successful in the case of much smaller sums, failed to break the silence which hung over Westmeath. People whispered together in corners about the 'accident', and few young men left the neighbourhood, but no information reached the police upon which even an enquiry under the Crimes Act could be based. The conspiracy of murder was succeeded by a far wider, and very ominous, conspiracy of silence.

At last, over a year after the death of Mrs Smythe, an

informer came forward: he was a peasant named Patrick M'Keon, who lived near Barbavilla House. His information, and that of his son, who bore the same name, justified a number of arrests, and an enquiry before Captain Boileau, the resident magistrate, under Mr Gladstone's recently enacted Crimes Act, began on 20 June 1883. Nine prisoners, apparently of the well-to-do farmer class, came up before the magistrate as suspects.

Patrick M'Keon and his son told an amazing story. They said that they had attended a dance at 'the Widow Fagan's' on 24 March 1882. Thither Michael Fagan and Daniel Curley, already by June 1883 executed for the murder of Lord Frederick Cavendish and Mr Burke, had come with a mysterious personage known as E Mack. It was frequently the case that these murder societies in Ireland held their meetings when the people were come together for a wake or a dance: if there was no dead body at hand, a dance would be arranged for, and the swearing in would take place, and perhaps innocent but inquisitive persons would be drawn into the net. According to M'Keon, Curley stated that it was proposed to revive the Fenians; it was now obvious, he said, that the independence of Ireland could not be won in the open field; it could rather be obtained by secret methods, in the pursuance of which one man would be worth ten. The object of the new society, which was to be called the 'Assassination Society', was the 'removal of tyrants'. He gave a list of tyrants, including the names of William Barlow Smythe, his brother, and the Earl of Longford. M'Keon forbade his son to take the oath, and stood aside with him and a few others while the rest, a goodly company, formed a circle, and swore an oath, as a book was passed round. During the proceedings a flute-player played dance tunes. Then a smaller number were taken aside by Fagan and Curley. When M'Keon was giving the names of the persons present at the meeting, and identifying the prisoners, the men in the dock laughed with loud contempt. The same incident occurred when the 'Invincibles' had appeared in Dublin during the preliminary investigations into the Phoenix Park murders.

M'Keon the younger connected the society formed at the Widow Fagan's with the actual murder. He had been a blacksmith at the time of the murder, working for a man, named John Walshe, and lived in his house, which was close to Barbavilla. A young man named Robert Elliott, another journeyman blacksmith, also worked and lived at Walshe's house. Elliott was possessed, to M'Keon's knowledge, of a cut-down gun, and on the day of the murder this was seen projecting over his waistcoat. Young M'Keon saw him, with four of the prisoners in the dock, on the morning of the murder, and about one o'clock they went together 'towards the black bog in the direction of Barbavilla'; he then lost sight of them. While he was eating dinner a little later, he heard six shots fired, and soon the news came that a lady had been shot dead. After dinner, M'Keon saw a man furtively emerging out of a corner of a place called 'The White Fields' to the back of Walshe's forge. It was Robert Elliott, and he was carrying his dreadful cut-down shotgun. He told M'Keon he was dry, and searched for a bottle in his pocket. 'I must have left it in Barbavilla Wood,' he said, 'where I was lying for some time at the foot of a tree. I was firing at a black crow, but the right one is down.' M'Keon said that he had heard a lady was shot, and the police were everywhere. 'I thought it was the master,' said Elliott. The next morning M'Keon saw Elliott breaking up the firearm: he put some fragments in the fire, and hid the rest in an old wall. At the close of his evidence, the witness identified the prisoners: they did not laugh now. 'I can call witnesses to prove that I was at Castlepollard all this time,' said Elliott. If M'Keon was to be believed, the conspiracy had been unmasked. But who could believe informers, themselves implicated in the conspiracy? Then the police remembered the whiskey bottle they had found in the wood: M'Keon's casual mention of Elliott's discovery of the loss of his bottle was some corroboration; perhaps there might be more. Head Constable Lynch made a search in John Walshe's wall, and found the lock of a gun, its trigger, and a trigger guard.

The long enquiry proceeded from week to week, and from month to month; at each hearing the friends of the prisoners gathered round the Court for a sight of them, and wild lamentations were heard. At first so brazen and confident, the prisoners began to show careworn expressions, especially Elliott and a man whom Carson was to defend named Magrath, who was a man of some wealth and position, and a Poor Law Guardian. At one of the hearings, Rose Reilly, a young woman, gave evidence with extreme reluctance. Pat Hanlon, one of the prisoners, was living in her mother's house, which was situated about a mile from the place of the murder. He slept there the night before the murder. He earned his living by making brooms. 'At about dinner-time he went away to gather sticks,' she said. 'He might have been an hour away. It was after church time, about two o'clock, when he came back.'

As a result of this evidence further arrests were made, and at the next hearing there were seventeen prisoners, and it was necessary to guard the Courthouse with a strong detachment of military and police; the road from the gaol to the Court was thronged by the people; newspaper correspondents from all over the world were present; and now the story of the Phoenix Park enquiry repeated itself. One of the prisoners, Pat Hanlon, implicated by Rose Reilly's evidence, disappeared from the dock, and appeared in the witness-box. His story was that he had gone out to collect branches in the wood, when he saw four of the prisoners go into the wood at Barbavilla, and then, after six shots were fired, come running out of the wood, scattering in different directions. After Hanlon came forward, all the seventeen prisoners were committed for trial at the Commission Court in Green Street at the next Assizes, fifteen months after the murder.

On 11 December 1883, the evidence against four men who had been identified as those who had stolen down to Barbavilla Wood on the day of the murder was put before the grand jury, who were asked to find a 'true bill' against them all for the murder of Mrs Smythe; but, as a result, they only found such a 'true bill' against Robert Elliott, while against the others they only found a true bill 'of conspiring to murder William Barlow Smythe'. The Crown elected to proceed against all four prisoners, including Elliott, on the latter charge.

At the trial before the Lord Chief Justice in Green Street, the Crown was represented by the McDermot QC and Peter O'Brien QC, afterwards Attorney-Generals respectively to Mr Gladstone and Lord Salisbury, and Constantine Molley QC. The McDermot was also the Prince of Koolavin and a great hereditary Irish chieftain, and is one of the few examples of an aristocrat who has made a success as a lawyer. Peter O'Brien was surnamed 'The Packer', and much is recorded of him in a later chapter. The prisoners were represented by Dr Boyd QC and Mr Edward Carson. There were numerous challenges of jurymen before the trial began.

The Crown witnesses, whose evidence has already been summarised, came forward, but the defence was able to discredit them past recognition. Pat M'Keon was not a good character: he had been in trouble for small offences as a lad; he had married a wife, and, in order to avoid supporting her, he had joined the Army, swearing a false declaration that he was not married. It was to avoid punishment for this perjury that he had probably come forward to give evidence in the Barbavilla case. He said that his lie about his marriage was perfectly honest and excusable, 'as he did not kiss the book'.

'Can you tell as many lies as you like if you don't kiss the book?' asked Dr Boyd. 'Yes, sir, you can,' was the answer. He also admitted that if he had taken the oath at the Widow Fagan's he would have been quite willing to assassinate people, and that he was not in the least shocked by the objects of the society.

The informer Hanlon, however, was not called by the Crown at all, and this fact was noted by Carson.

Dr Boyd opened the defence; he poured scorn on the pitiful evidence of the prosecution, collected so sedulously after months of enquiry. Was this the best that the Crown could do even now? His defence was a complete and cast-iron 'Tipperary alibi'. He could prove not only the absence of Robert Elliott in Castlepollard on the tragic Sunday, but he could also prove that young Pat M'Keon was not in the places he said he was on that day, or on the night of 24 March. There had been no meeting and no dance held at the Widow Fagan's on that night, and as for Pat M'Keon, he could prove that gentleman to have been in Castlepollard at that date and time, under the influence of drink.

Carson called a number of these witnesses: about a dozen were called altogether to establish the 'alibis': seven went to show there was no meeting at the Widow Fagan's and three to establish an alibi at Castlepollard for Elliott; the other two were called to prove that Pat M'Keon was elsewhere. The evidence of these witnesses at the first trial is not very fully reported, but a cross-examination of two witnesses in one of the later trials serves as an example of the way in which an alibi carefully prepared in advance could be shaken. A man and his wife named Kennedy swore that they had seen Elliott wearing a new hat in Castlepollard on the Sunday of the murder: they had met him at midday, and he had dined in their house from 1.30 to 2.30. Under cross-examination, Kennedy was forced to admit that he was not sure on which Sunday it was that this had happened. John Carter, a barber at Castlepollard, swore that he had cut Elliott's hair at the time of the murder. But he had told the police beforehand that he had not cut Elliott's hair. He was cross-examined by the McDermot.

'Was that a lie?' – 'Yes.'

'Intentional?' – 'No.'

'Did you also tell the police that you did not drink with him at all?' – 'I did.'

'Was that a lie?' – 'It was.'

'Did you tell that lie on purpose?' asked the McDermot.

'Well, I knew it was against the law to drink on Sunday,' was the amazing answer of the law-abiding barber.

'Do you ever tell the truth to the police?' pursued the McDermot. 'No, I do not,' replied the barber emphatically, amid the loud laughter of the Court.

It was established in cross-examination that a number of the witnesses, who told precisely the same story about Elliott's presence in Castlepollard at the time of the murder, had stayed together at the same house on the night before the trial, no doubt holding a grand dress rehearsal against Peter's cross-examination. It seemed also as if they had carefully planned the 'alibi' by a personal visit of Elliott to Castlepollard before the crime was committed.

Yet it was amazing that so many respectable witnesses could be called to commit perjury, and tell a tale which fitted so logically together. This network of concocted and prepared evidence, as it unfolded itself, made the advocates for the prosecution more anxious than ever for a conviction. If these men were to go free, no landlord's life would be safe in any part of Ireland. This sense of responsibility made Peter O'Brien forget that an outward attitude of judicial indifference is one of the most powerful weapons in the armoury of a prosecutor. On several occasions during the evidence he had had heated passages with Dr Boyd QC; finally, in an audible whisper, he called his adversary a 'damned coward', and precipitated an amazing scene, even for Ireland, between two eminent counsel.

'He has just called me across the table a "damned coward",' shouted Dr Boyd to Lord Morris.

'I declare,' said his lordship, 'that is most improper language, Mr O'Brien.'

'It was simply between ourselves,' said O'Brien, with an aggrieved air.

'It was not between ourselves,' said Dr Boyd.

'Yes, my lord,' added Mr Carson, joining in the fray, 'and he challenged Dr Boyd outside to contradict it.'

'Dr Boyd,' said Peter O'Brien, 'from the beginning to end of this case has been insolent in his manner towards me.'

'But no gentleman,' chided the Lord Chief Justice, 'should have used such language as is now imputed to you.'

'I am sorry,' said Peter, 'because it was said in Court, but from beginning to end Dr Boyd has been most insulting to us at this side of the table. My character is in the hands of the Bar.'

'Oh, indeed,' interjected Dr Boyd; 'the less said about your character the better. I respectfully ask your lordship to make the counsel who made use of such an improper expression retract it.'

'You have been guilty, Mr O'Brien,' sternly observed Lord Morris, 'of very scandalous and improper language. You should not only withdraw, but apologise for having used it.'

But Peter was obdurate. 'I simply withdraw the observation,' he said. 'The observation was simply addressed to Dr Boyd personally, and not within the hearing of the Court or public.'

Both counsel then resumed their seats, and the hearing proceeded; however, the attention of the jury had been lifted away from the tragedy of Barbavilla and the lying witnesses, who thought that no lie was wrong unless the book was kissed and who boasted of never telling the truth to the police, on to the personalities of the opposing advocates.

John Walshe, the blacksmith where M'Keon and Elliott had worked together, said that the latter had left his house early on the Sunday morning to go to Castlepollard to have his hair cut. He had returned in the evening, having had his hair cut and wearing a new hat. Every minute of Elliott's day on the fatal Sunday had now been accounted for. Moreover, added Walshe casually, M'Keon and Elliott had been on very bad terms. In the course of the cross-examination of this witness, Peter O'Brien was again in trouble. The witness admitted that after dinner, later than two o'clock, one of his men went out, got up a tree, and shouted loudly, 'Coo-coo.'

'Ah,' said Peter, 'I see, the signal.'

'That is a most improper observation,' objected Dr Boyd.

'It is,' said the Chief Justice.

But O'Brien saw that this might be an essential part of the story which was disclosing itself piece by piece, like a Chinese puzzle. 'Was the "coo-coo" cry to announce that the police were coming?' he asked. 'I know nothing about it,' said the witness, 'except that the boy told me he was up the tree shouting "coo-coo": I heard the cry myself. I first heard of the murder when the police passed my door.'

After all the evidence had been called for the defence, the prisoners being not then competent to give evidence for themselves, the Court adjourned. When leading counsel fall out, a young man comes into his own. Dr Boyd probably thought that, after the rather disgraceful scene with O'Brien, it would be wiser in his clients' interests to allow his junior to make the final speech. So Carson, only twenty-nine years old, had the tremendous good fortune of playing the culminating part in what was probably the most famous trial all over Great Britain and America at that time, and matching himself against two of the acknowledged leaders of the Bar. It was a great opportunity.

He based his appeal not so much on the evidence of the defence – indeed, he avoided it – but on the unreliable nature of the evidence for the prosecution. He suggested that the whole story was similar to the account which had appeared in the newspapers in the Phoenix Park case, and that the M'Keons' evidence was a pitiful imitation of it. Once more he argued that the 'state of the country' was no argument for a specific conviction. 'There is much,' he began gravely, 'that is agreed between us and the Crown. There were many things in the opening statement of the McDermot with which we heartily concur; at least in the extreme horror of the crime committed on Sunday, 2 April 1882; another matter of agreement is that for a long time, through the length and breadth of our land, has existed an impunity for crime which threatens to uproot society and overthrow law and order. I would be as glad as any man to see the true culprits brought to justice.' All this the McDermot had said, and Carson conceded it. 'But,' he asked impressively, 'at what time in the history of this country has it ever been more requisite that jurors should be careful only to act on the clearest and strictest proof? No matter what abhorrence you feel for the crime, you must act on the evidence alone. You must not speculate, or attempt to find by speculation, a case against the prisoners at the Bar. God forbid that that day shall ever come when our laws will be changed, and jurors allowed to act on speculation. I see nothing to justify the assertion that law and order is reasserting itself. Were these two creatures, the M'Keons, these two confederates, coming forward to assert law and order? Their whole evidence is a solemn mimicry of the Phoenix Park cases. Why were the names E Mack and Daniel Curley introduced? To what use was the term "to remove tyrants", the phrase of James Carey, the approver in those cases, used?' Carson then used with consummate skill for a young man the fact that the informer Hanlon had not been put into the witness box. 'I accuse the Crown of having shamefully withheld evidence which would have conclusively shown that the M'Keons were fabricators, liars, and villains. What were they? They were, upon their own showing, approvers of the deepest dye, steeped, according to their own words, with the blood that had been shed throughout the country. You cannot believe them, according to the law, without corroboration. Where is it? Where is Hanlon the informer, the man who, to save his life, gave evidence with regard to Mrs Smythe's assassination, the man who has made a deposition in the present case; the man who was alleged by the M'Keons to have been present at the meeting of the 24th, and who, it was alleged, went down to the demesne gate on the occasion of the murder? Where is this Crown informer Hanlon? Why is he not here to corroborate the story of the M'Keons? He has saved his life. The Crown has *purchased* his evidence, and still he is not produced; and yet, unless I am very surprised, he is in the precincts of this Court. The Crown now suggest to me that *we* may read Hanlon's deposition given before the resident magistrate. Gentlemen, the Crown may not read it themselves without producing the witness. But the Crown dare not produce him, because Hanlon would have given the lie to the M'Keons. This, gentlemen, is not the way to get at justice. This *thirst* by the Crown to secure a conviction is not the way to secure an *honest* conviction.'

After having dealt in detail with the evidence, in concluding he implored the jury 'not to allow yourselves to be led away by any desire of righting society, which has been talked of by my learned friend. I hope it will right itself by fair means, but juries are not to be asked to convict innocent men in order that this desired state of affairs may come sooner.'

It is interesting to record that later, when Carson became the principal Crown prosecutor in Ireland, he never used the argument of 'the state of Ireland' to secure his convictions: he always adhered with deadly effect to the evidence of the crime in each specific case, without reference to the wider field of crime and politics all over Ireland.

This speech of Carson's was much talked about in the King's Inn and in the newspapers the next day. It was an outstanding performance for a young man in his twenties, who had stepped into the breach at the last moment. His words had obviously had an effect upon the jury. For his speech had been one of studied moderation: it was he, and not the prosecution, who had called on the jury to decide according to the evidence, and the evidence alone. Peter O'Brien himself was much impressed by his young opponent's speech, and remembered it in his favour, when Mr Balfour asked him to retain him as Attorney-General's chief prosecuting Counsel some years later.

O'Brien again fell back on prejudice. Why, Michael Fagan, the Phoenix Park murderer, the lieutenant of Curley, had resided at the Widow Fagan's house. Was it not likely that an evil conspiracy would be cradled at such a place? Of course. As for Hanlon not being called, or prosecuted, this was the reason. If he were put in the dock, according to the law he could not give evidence for the prisoners; if the Crown put him in the witness-box, they would be forced to waive a prosecution against him. 'It is true,' he said, 'that he is in the precincts of this Court, and I challenge Mr Carson to call him.'

Just as the Lord Chief Justice was about to sum up, a juror named Hely asked his lordship to adjourn, as he was physically worn out, and could not pay sufficient attention to his lordship's address. Another juryman protested that one of his colleagues was 'half mad', and quite unsuitable for his juror's duty. Lord Morris said that the case must go on with the present jury, but adjourned until the next morning. This adjournment was fatal. The next day only eleven jurymen appeared, and evidence was given that the twelfth had fallen down in a fit when getting out of bed. Dr Boyd, who considered that Carson's speech had achieved a great effect on behalf of the prisoners, applied that the case should go on with eleven jurors, but the Chief Justice said that there was no precedent for this in a criminal case, and adjourned the case for the arrival of the absent juryman. Medical evidence was, however, given that the man's mental state made him quite unfit for his duty as a juryman, and all the proceedings of the long three days' trial were rendered null and void, and the prisoners were committed to the next Assize. Of all the speeches that were delivered for the defence in the four long trials which succeeded, Carson's reads as much the most impressive and incisive. Meanwhile the Crown were able to strengthen the case by further evidence, and it was as well for justice, perhaps, that Carson's speech was not allowed to go to the jury for decision.

The second trial of these prisoners before Lord Morris was heard on 11 February 1884; Carson did not appear for any of the prisoners on this occasion. After several days, the case ended in a disagreement, the *Freeman's Journal* alleging that eleven out of the twelve men were in favour of convicting all the prisoners.

The third trial was heard before the Lord Chief Baron in

April, and two more prisoners were put in the dock. On this occasion the Crown had fresh evidence brought from the gaols by two gaolbirds, Joseph Mahon and Peter Kevin. The first said that Elliott had come to him for a night's lodging when he was employed as a watchman in Navan. Elliott told him then that he was a blacksmith, and had been compelled to leave a nice job in Westmeath because of Mrs Smythe's murder: 'he had had a finger in the pie, and was pushed into it.' This witness was now serving a sentence for sending a threatening notice to a landlord: he was thoroughly discredited in cross-examination, and shown to be thoroughly disreputable. The second gaolbird said that one of the prisoners, Fitzpatrick, had confessed to him in prison.

On the last day of this trial, a Wednesday, once more only eleven jurymen were ready in the jury-box. One of the panel said Joseph FitzGerald, who had received a threatening notice, was found to be absent. It was then disclosed that by a curious circumstance all the jurymen serving in this case had been sent notices which should only have been sent to jurymen required to be present for subsequent trials, summoning them for 'Thursday'. Mr FitzGerald had fallen into the trap. He was sent for, but, when he arrived, asked to be excused on account of the threatening letter. The Chief Baron told him he must go on with his duty. After a long retirement this jury found the prisoners guilty. One of their number, a man named Swords, said, 'We are as innocent as a child unborn.' The Chief Baron sentenced them each to ten years' penal servitude.

It was thought that the conviction of these men would have a very good effect in the country: as Peter O'Brien said, 'Justice, slow and sometimes baffled, but ever sure, has triumphed in the end.' But the Crown were not yet satisfied. On 9 June six more of the Barbavilla prisoners were put on their trial for conspiracy to murder Mr Barlow Smythe, this time before Mr Justice Lawson at Green Street. O'Brien, now a serjeant-at-law, led the McDermot and Constantine Molloy for the Crown. Dr Webb QC and Edward Carson represented a prisoner named John Magrath, an old farmer of some wealth and position, who was a Poor Law Guardian, had been an inmate of an asylum, and had paid rent even in 1881, the year of the 'No Rent' manifesto. The rest were represented by other counsel. The only distinguishing feature of this trial from the previous ones was that another prisoner, Cole, had four days before the trial turned approver and entered the witness-box to give evidence against his colleagues. He told substantially the same story as M'Keon, but added a last link to the chain of evidence. He said that a meeting of the conspirators was held at nine o'clock on the night before the murder; that Arthur Swords, who had been already convicted, told off others, including himself and Hanlon and others of the prisoners, to place themselves next day at intervals along the avenue, instructed, when Smythe returned from church, to fire. 'I could not help joining the society,' said Cole, 'because if I did not do so I should suffer.' Poor Rose Reilly, giving evidence for the third time, being asked if she had sworn certain statements, said, 'I will swear no more. I am tired swearing.' Dr Webb's appeal on behalf of John Magrath was very different from Carson's restrained and logical argument, and typically Irish. 'May eternal justice, of which all earthly justice is the mere outward form, shadow your consultations with its manifestation, and induce you to come to the conclusion which I consider you ought to come to, namely that there is no evidence to convict these men.'

The jury went away at four o'clock, and hours afterwards they found themselves totally unable to agree. The Judge discharged them, and announced that special jurors would be summoned on heavy fines on the following Tuesday to try the prisoners at that same Assize. When Tuesday came, Peter the Packer was determined to leave as little to chance as possible, and used all his keenness of wit and vision to detect sympathisers with the Land League, and make them 'stand by'. At last a jury to his satisfaction had been empanelled. It was said to have been one of Peter's best efforts. An amusing incident occurred between the witness Rose Reilly, who, now giving evidence for the fourth time, positively refused to say a word in answer to Peter: she was too ill, she said.

'Come, now,' said Peter, in his most ingratiating manner, 'had ye not a beefsteak for your breakfast? Come, now, Rose, answer the question.'

'Not a word,' persisted Rose Reilly.

She then proceeded to leave the table, and when half-way down she again refused to answer O'Brien. Finally she created much amusement by sitting down on the steps, and covering her head with her cloak.

'Tell her,' said the Judge sternly, 'I will have to send her to gaol if she does not answer.'

'I don't care where you send me,' said the witness, sobbing. 'I will go anywhere sooner than talk to that man.'

'The serjeant is not a ladies' man,' observed one of the counsel drily.

'He is too great a bully for that,' Rose answered. Finally the obstinate lady was allowed to retire, and the Crown had to do without her. In the end the jury, after considering the case for two hours, found all the prisoners guilty, but recommended them to mercy, especially the prisoner John Magrath. At this stage a woman in the gallery began to cry, 'Oh, John! Oh, John!' The Judge gave all the prisoners seven years' penal servitude except John Magrath, who was sentenced to one year's imprisonment. The prisoners then saluted their friends in the gallery, where weeping and lamentation were set up. 'We will come out as innocent as we went in. We have been found guilty by a packed jury,' said one of the prisoners. Thus, two years and two months after the tragedy of Barbavilla, the conspirators, many of whom had no doubt entered the conspiracy against their will, paid the penalty of the best years of their lives, but not their lives themselves, for this terrible murder.

4. The Croagh Orphanage Case

The foundation of Carson's career had been laid entirely in Southern Ireland. Save that he had been initiated as an Orangeman at the age of nineteen, he knew very little of that other Ireland which lies north of the Boyne: his knowledge of human nature had been acquired among the whimsical people of the South, and his own steadfast nature was there trained to deal with all the phases of their talkative and mercurial temperament. The mind and manners of the North, where the dour spirit of Scotland seems to have been hardened and intensified far beyond its native asperity, and of which he was to become the uncrowned king, was little known to him. But when the Ulster spirit did become known to Carson, he was drawn to it immediately; he found the Ulstermen to be men after his own heart. 'When I first knew them,' Lord Carson has said to me, 'I found the Ulster Scots a most extraordinary lot: they are the most blunt, ill-mannered, outspoken fellows. One of them would listen to instructions with a stolid patience and apparent agreement for a quarter of an hour, and then suddenly say at the end, "I will not".'

He too was a man after their own Ulster hearts, had they but known it. They were wholly unlike even the Protestants of the South, to whom Carson belonged. In the South the Protestants were aristocrats and Conservatives, with Saxon and Norman traditions dividing them from the common people. Here the common people were democrats and Liberals, acknowledging no social superior as master; independent as few men are in private life; they had furnished leaders of the American Revolution, and a long succession of American Presidents, and, far from being Conservatives, they were by nature Radicals, and no fear of 'Captain Moonlight', if ever he dared to show his face in Ulster, would have deterred a

Northern juryman from finding the proper verdict.

His first visit as counsel for the defence for a special fee to the North-East Circuit at Belfast is of peculiar biographical interest, because the case not only made a great reputation for Carson in the North, long before it was ever dreamed that he would, after William III, be the greatest Ulster hero, but because he was faced for the first time in a case of importance with a jury of Ulster Scots. Your North-East Ulsterman, although he has certain deep, imperishable sentiments, is not easily accessible to sentimental considerations, as any Southern counsellor soon found who tried to bring him to the melting mood with the view of getting a verdict out of him along that line. Such a course only amuses the North-East Ulsterman: for at his best he is one of the most efficient jurymen in the world, especially in dealing with guilt; he is acute, honest, and absolutely fearless. The emotional side of a case he very properly leaves to the Judge.

The celebrated 'Croagh Orphanage' case was tried for two days before Chief Baron Palles, and Carson was briefed, with a 'special fee' required by the rules of the Bar when a man takes a brief outside his own circuit, since the venue was Belfast, and on the North-East Circuit. The case was tried here on a change of venue on the motion of the prosecution, as a result of a disagreement by the jury in a previous trial on a similar indictment at Kildare. The case was truly a *cause célèbre*, and was talked about all over Ireland, and even in England; and a great crowd came to watch the proceedings in the Assize Court of Belfast.

An Episcopalian clergyman, the Rev Mr Cotton, had, it seemed, in his latter days surrendered the official cure of souls, and taken to philanthropic work: he had founded an orphanage in Croagh, in the County of Kildare. The place was run by voluntary subscriptions, and it appeared that Mr Cotton had, in search thereof, ranged over the three kingdoms. Cotton's happy hunting-ground was the bourgeoisie of the great English towns. There, in Liverpool or Birmingham, notebook in hand, he would drop in on some prosperous merchant and blandly remind him of the generous subscription that he had given on a previous occasion, a subscription which had its share in bringing gladness and light to the hearts of the dear little Protestant innocents at the Croagh Orphanage. Then he would produce a leaflet containing a hymn regularly sung by the children, expressing their deep debt of gratitude to those generous benefactors who had provided them with daily bread, and spiritual guidance in the person of the Rev Mr Cotton. What generous-hearted, middle-class, church-going or chapel-going Englishman, well-to-do and with his cheque-book handy, could withstand such an appeal to his Protestant pocket? Unfortunately, however, for Carson, it came out in evidence that no account of pecuniary help so rendered ever saw the light: no balance sheet ever showed the way the money went, when it had once passed into the pious hands of the Rev Mr Cotton.

Now the offence charged was that the children of the orphanage were neglected, maltreated, and starved. So shocking were the allegations of the indictment that, if they were true, Dotheboys Hall would have appeared a home of luxury and easy comfort compared with Cotton's orphanage, and it would have seemed that any child taken into that ogre's den might be fairly reckoned to have forfeited one-half of its chances of ever seeing manhood. How many children really perished in that fearful place will never be known. There were no visitors, no committee, nobody from without that had any authority within the dismal precincts of the orphanage. At length it attracted the attention of the ever-vigilant RIC, and was raided by some of their officers. Some of the children, typical cases of starvation and neglect, were taken to Dublin and examined by doctors, who confirmed the suspicions of the police; the result was the prosecution of the Rev Mr Cotton.

There followed the abortive trial at Kildare, in which Carson's advocacy secured a disagreement, and then the second trial at Belfast. Carson's task was a difficult and an ungrateful one, but two things told in favour of his client. First, the said reverend client's saint-like appearance and demeanour. Here was a venerable clergyman, approaching the Psalmist's limit of human life, garbed in becoming clerical, and yet not offensively sacerdotal, cloth: his neck-cloth was of the old voluminous, innocent sort, tied in front in a rather awkward bow. No wonder the soft-hearted Kildare jury had disagreed. How should a shepherd in his quest for money on behalf of the stray, orphaned lambs occupy himself with the tying of a neck-cloth? His bearing was that of a primitive Christian in the presence of a Propraetor. Nor did he have the disadvantage of faculties unimpaired. He suffered not only from the ordinary infirmities of old age and from the malice of his enemies, but he was pathetically deaf, so deaf that he was compelled to wear, attached to each ear, a little metal plate in the form of concave shell, that apparently served the purpose of an ear-trumpet. When, in the course of the trial, a strong point was made against him, of course he never heard; but one of his friends, a sort of interpreter of calumny, speaking into his ear, explained or quoted; then followed an extra-clerical look of the resigned and forgiving Christian martyr on his pained but benign countenance. In a word, he seemed just the person to be a father to the fatherless, and to desire nothing more in this world than to receive in his loving old arms those whom the mysterious providence of heaven had deprived of their natural protectors. A veritable Dr Primrose this, a Vicar of Wakefield, yet he found himself treated as if he had acted like the Jenkins of the same story.

Another unexpected turn in favour of Carson's client was the evidence of a woman who had been a sort of matron at the orphanage. Carson did not do much with her in direct examination, because they had, both of them, by the rules of evidence to be relevant; but when the prosecuting counsel's indiscreet questions led her into irrelevancies, she was magnificent. The prosecutor found himself baffled at every turn by her answers, and, indeed, saw his questions turned into arguments for the defence. Yet the witness was quiet, obliging, and to all appearances disarmingly candid. At last he gave it up, but, before sitting down, he kept for a parting shot the suggestion that her evidence was biased. 'Of course, you are engaged as assistant matron at this precious orphanage?' he sneered. 'Oh, no,' replied the lady, with the utmost sweetness. 'Mr Cotton dispensed with my services some time ago.'

The Ulster jury was not, however, to be confounded like the men of Kildare. Carson found himself addressing a different and peculiarly unresponsive audience: their faces were not eloquent with emotion like those of the Southern Irish. The aspect of the jury told him nothing of what they intended to do. The stolid Ulster jury could not know that this tall Southerner who had been addressing them would live to be their beloved leader, who would never 'ask them to do what he would not do himself'; nor could he know that he was addressing an audience of what were to be 'his own people'. Nor would that Ulster jury, had it been gifted with such vision into the future, have been deflected from their duty by political considerations of that kind: at all events they retired, and, after a considerable consultation, they found Cotton guilty on all the counts.

After the verdict was announced, an incident occurred which was long recounted and discussed on the North-Eastern

Circuit. As the Chief Baron was about to speak, Mr Carson asked to be heard. 'My lord,' he said, 'with great reluctance, but under a deep sense of the duty I owe my client, I submit that in trying this case as it stands on the indictment, your lordship has been all along acting *ultra vires*: your lordship has, in fact, no jurisdiction.'

A great sensation was produced in Court. Had Carson foiled the canny Ulster jurymen after all, and, by keeping a point of law till the end, rendered the verdict null and void? At all events, how could he dare to challenge the very jurisdiction of the great Lord Chief Baron, after he had patiently tried the case for two days! He went on to argue that the indictment drawn for the Belfast jury was not identical with that drawn for the Kildare jury: and how could you have a change of venue except on an identical indictment? As a matter of fact, the Kildare indictment, in passing through the Attorney-General's office in Dublin, had received the addition of one or two new cases of cruelty or neglect, which, added to the Carlow indictment, might at Belfast have contributed to the conviction: but, argued Carson, these additions, tacked on to the Kildare indictment and then presented to the Belfast jury, rendered nugatory the entire proceedings at Belfast.

Carson, indeed, had slyly kept this point of law until the end; a formal objection at the beginning could only have harmed his case; a jury never likes a case which shelters behind technicalities; he knew how to lay low, and now he produced his trump card. It is easy to imagine the feelings of the Crown solicitors when this surprise was sprung upon them. They were furious at Carson's audacity, and it was generally expected that Palles would sweep aside this conjuror's device to defeat justice by a strong rebuke to the counsel who had questioned his jurisdiction. But Palles was a man who always decided according to the law. 'Upon my word,' said the Lord Chief Baron, 'Mr Carson, I believe you're right.' He then went on to compliment Carson on his courage and his learning, and said he would reserve sentence, subject to the decision of the Court of Crown Cases Reserved, on the validity of the verdict. He was about to do so when Mr Carson, whose keen advocacy was never baulked by compliments, again stood up, and made an appeal in mitigation of sentence the like of which many lawyers of old standing who were in Court declared that they had never heard. Thanks to the busy hand of an eye-witness, I am able to reproduce the actual words, but not, perhaps, the effect of that speech. Pleas in mitigation, especially when the prisoner has pleaded 'not guilty', are among the hardest tasks of the criminal advocate. He is not addressing a jury, but a seasoned lawyer, who has judged human nature in its wickedness and weakness from his judicial seat for years, and who, in this case, had seen the facts thrashed out from beginning to end; in truth, an advocate needs the tongue of an angel to make an impression under such circumstances. With consummate skill Carson dwelt upon every fact that could tell in favour of his client, while, without seeming to do so, he kept in the background, or glossed over, every fact that would prejudice the accused in the eyes of the man who was to pass sentence upon him: and through it all he never forgot that he was addressing, not a jury, but a Judge. If quoted fully, it may serve as a model for any young counsel faced with a similar duty.

'I beseech,' he said, 'your lordship to consider the position of this old man. At the time of disestablishment he, even then advanced in life, sacrificed his own interests in order to promote the interests of the religious body to which he belonged. In all the long period of his ministry, there never was a whisper that he was selfish, or avaricious, or careless of the suffering of others. Is it according to our experience of human nature that vicious qualities should suddenly display themselves in a man within the verge of old age? He started the orphanage. Who, entering upon such a course, could reasonably look forward to ease or opulence, and, in heaven's name, who could think that any personal ends could be served by systematic neglect of the orphans? My client, in engaging in such a work, was very ill-advised – especially as he proceeded on the absurd principle (respectable enough in itself, but impossible to be carried out) that, as far as possible, no orphan that applied for admission should be turned away from the door of the orphanage. In short, it is abundantly clear that my client is not a man of business, and that he is weak, unpractical, prone to trust where he ought to suspect, and, for so old a man, singularly, absurdly sanguine. Not the man, I admit, to manage an orphanage the support of which depended absolutely on his own exertions, but not of necessity a criminal. There is in the evidence absolutely nothing to show that he was long-headed or hard-hearted. Look how his idea of receiving, if possible, all those who applied – look how it worked out. The number of the applicants was very soon so great that even he had to draw the line ... There simply was no more room. But worse: happy would it have been for him if the orphanage had been only full – full to overflowing – of reasonably healthy children. But, in carrying out his absurd, if charitable, notion, he received many children that were hopelessly diseased – the offspring of dissolute, debilitated, and diseased parents. Those beings, wretchedly nourished, even scrofulous, these proved the ruin of the place: for the orphanage funds were not sufficient to provide them with proper food, never to speak of medical attendance; and many were deposited at the orphanage – often by selfish relatives who wanted to be rid of them – when they ought in fact to have been sent to a hospital. Meantime, to obtain funds, this old man was compelled to be as constantly on the road as if he had been a commercial traveller. The orphanage saw very little of him: and, while he toiled to collect funds, the working of the place devolved very much on others. As a matter of fact, the receiving of children, and the treatment of them, passed out of his hands into the hands of those who, not being responsible, were doubtless often reckless in expenditure: in short, he was like many a business man who, do what he will, is powerless to keep down his outlay, while his income is stationary or shows a decided shrinkage. What, under the circumstances, did my client do? Just what many a business man does: he went on, hoping for a better day. At this juncture the police interfered, and the present proceedings were instituted. Legally, of course, my client is guilty: *qui facit per alium facit per se.* But the prerogative of mercy lies with your lordship. Pray reflect on the enforced, yet fruitless, hopeless conditions of this old man, who in an evil hour for himself and others undertook duties which very soon he found that he could neither discharge nor escape from. He went from town to town, virtually a beggar, and all the money he obtained he threw into the apparently bottomless pit of the orphanage, only to hear, as he often did, that the expenses incurred in connection with the treatment of scrofulous children alone swallowed up the greater part of this or that considerable remittance. My client was very foolish, hoping always for some turn in the luck: but I find it hard to consider him as a mere vulgar criminal. I trust implicitly in your lordship's sense of fair play, your feelings of human sympathy, and perhaps I might venture to add of equity, when you come to pass sentence on this broken old man.'

Thus Ulster listened to the first great speech in Belfast of Edward Carson: for a great speech it was, delivered, not in the breathless manner of many Irish advocates, but with deliberation – in the slow, Southern, melodious, and wonderfully expressive voice that Ulster was afterwards to know and love so well. F E Smith's speech in mitigation of Goudie's sentence in the *Liverpool Bank* fraud case has often been held up for admiration as a model for such things, but for the present writer it lacks both the humanity and the comprehensiveness of this effort. Also F E Smith had not the disadvantages of Carson: his client had pleaded guilty. He had not already urged every relevant consideration in a hard-fought case: he was putting forward Goudie's case for the first time. At all events, this speech of Carson's, although it was only a clever and powerful restatement of all that he already knew, made a visible effect on the Chief Baron, who postponed sentence till the next Assize. Also hard-bitten and experienced lawyers who listened in Court confessed that Carson's speech made them at least for the moment look on the venerable figure in the dock in quite a different light, and some of the audience were moved to tears. Yet it was not merely the form of the speech which carried such memorable weight, but the force which the rare and mature dignity of the young advocate added to the words. It also illustrates the restraint and pertinacity of Edward Carson as a man and as an advocate. Many would have made their formal objection at the beginning, and prejudiced at the outset, instead of assisting, their client's case: the art of the advocate is not only to prepare the best weapons to be used in the fight, but to know at what time to use them. Many, too, would have left the Judge to pass what sentence seemed best to him, or would have had nothing more to say. Carson left the Court immediately after his speech, having to catch the Limited Mail train to Dublin, and could not wait to receive the congratulations of the hospitable North-East Bar mess, but he had established for himself a legal reputation in Ulster.

It remains only to record the decision of the Court of Crown Cases Reserved. That Court affirmed the competence of the Chief Baron to try the case on the indictment presented at Belfast. There was, however, among their lordships sitting on this Bench, one notable and distinguished dissentient, the Lord Chief Baron Palles himself, the greatest lawyer of them all, who declared for his own 'incompetence'; and, with the greatest respect to the majority, there were not lacking men learned in the law who considered that Palles and Carson were right. At the next Assizes, however, sentence was at long last passed on Cotton; he was given two years' imprisonment, a light punishment for those more severe days, having regard to the nature of the offences proved against him and their disastrous consequences to human life. Moreover, after all that Carson, doing his duty as his advocate, said on his behalf, it is melancholy to record that, when he came out of gaol, he was again prosecuted on a similar charge, and again convicted. Be that as it may, it was the defence of this miserable old man which first showed Ulster the persistence, the ability, the eloquence, and the devoted sense of duty, even in a losing cause, of the man who was one day to become their own great national advocate and champion.

It is interesting also to record that at this time Carson found the Ulster way of speaking the Queen's Irish very difficult to understand. In the course of the Assize he was bidden to dinner by the Judges. He hired a cab, which climbed slowly up the hill towards the Judges' lodgings. Carson begged the cabman to go faster, as he was late for dinner. 'Can't get up th' Hell,' explained the Jehu. Carson thought the man said, 'Can't you get to Hell,' made no further protests, but reflected on the unmannerly behaviour of Ulstermen to the strangers within their gate. It was strange that where there was to be such complete understanding between a man and a whole people, their association should begin with a misunderstanding arising out of contrasting accents.

5. 'Coercion Carson'

By the year 1886, Carson had acquired a leading position among his contemporaries at the Irish Bar. Had it not been for his delicate health, which his critical attack of pneumonia had permanently impaired, he could have looked forward to a successful career terminating with an honourable appointment to the High Court Bench in Dublin; his health alone stood in the way of such an ambition; the hard work was telling upon him, and he still looked forward only to some more humble appointment on the County Court Bench or as a resident magistrate. Few successful barristers of that or any other day owed less to favour than Edward Carson, whose reputation as a powerful advocate and a skilful and relentless cross-examiner had become well established. Hitherto his status had been solely professional; his life had been limited by his duty as an advocate; he was in no sense a public figure, nor was he identified in the public eye by adherence to any cause. He was still a Liberal and a Unionist, an admirer of Gladstone; but he had appeared on no political platform: his active interest in politics had ceased ten years back, when his career at the Historical Society had terminated. Yet he had increased, out of all knowledge, in power and intellect. Dr Purser of Trinity College informed me that it was not generally thought that Carson would make a striking success in life: the donnish mind must necessarily judge a man by academic talent. Carson's mind had developed slowly, yet with each year at the Bar his colleagues saw it growing more formidable. When he went to the Bar it was as if a plant had been set to grow in a soil which exactly suited it. His increasing competence and ability had not escaped the notice of the Bench and the leaders of the Bar, and, in 1886, John Gibson, recently appointed Irish Attorney-General by the new Conservative administration, nominated him to be his Crown counsel, or, in the language of the Bar, Attorney-General's 'devil'. This was not only a position of much responsibility and honour for a young man of thirty-two years, but, as will be shown, a post of the greatest personal danger. Carson did not hesitate to accept it. Apart from this, it speaks much both for the ability of Mr Carson and for the generosity of the Attorney-General that he should select for promotion a young man who had openly flouted him, and whose judgment had once proved superior to his own.

To realise the significance of Carson's appointment, and what acceptance of the position meant, it is absolutely necessary to make a digression into the history of Irish politics during the first six years of the 'eighties. Hereafter Carson was to be no longer a private citizen, but a public character, feared, loathed, execrated, yet admired alike by friend and foe. He entered political life by as dangerous a door as ever has been opened for a politician; his daily life for the next three years was, at least, as hazardous as any soldier's on active service in modern warfare. Moreover, the eyes of England, and indeed of the world, were upon him: with his new duties the name of 'Coercion Carson' leapt into notoriety and fame. In March 1887, Lord Salisbury said, 'All the politics of the moment are summarised in the word Ireland'; and Labouchere had written to Randolph Churchill, 'There are only two policies for Ireland: "Coercion" or a domestic legislature; all else is intrigue.' The fate of the two great political parties in England, which Labouchere described as 'two gangs greedy for office', and the government of the proud British Empire, with all its unprecedented commercial prosperity, depended on the poor, distressed little island across St George's Channel, where 'Coercion Carson', a young man of thirty-two, had a momentous task assigned to him.

Rarely, if ever, has a lawyer been asked to play so decisively the part of a man of action in the execution of his duty as an advocate. How had all this come about – and why was a shy barrister of delicate health, gifted with a mind like a sword and a nerve like steel, asked to perform such a role?

It is indeed a melancholy and tangled history, this oft-told tale, and neither English political party can emerge with credit from the shifting sands of intrigue which resulted first from Parnell's relentless extra-Parliamentary pressure on the majority Liberal Government and then from his direct Parliamentary bargaining with each party in turn, after he had acquired in 1885 the balance of power. The web was at once cut by the unequivocal decision in favour of the Union by the Conservative Government in December 1885, after an indecisive General Election. One party at least had shown its hand, and Mr Gladstone was to follow almost at once with an equally clear declaration for separation.

Mr Gladstone's land legislation in the 'seventies had not cured the state of Ireland; a succession of bad crops had made the rents irrecoverable; notices to quit created havoc everywhere; and special methods under the Peace Preservation Act had to be used to keep the country free from the worse kind of lawlessness: legitimate grievances against the system of land tenure and the land hunger of the peasants had become intermingled with, and were exploited by, the political movement which claimed Home Rule as a solution for all the ills of Ireland; and a third factor, the criminal element, which always seeks its own loathsome profit where the law is difficult to uphold, was their potent, if unwelcome, ally. Nevertheless, in 1880 Home Rule was not yet a practical proposition, and when Beaconsfield decided on a dissolution he wrote to his Irish Viceroy that 'all men of light and leading will resist the destructive doctrine of the severance of the constitutional tie which unites Ireland to Great Britain in that bond which has favoured the power and prosperity of both'. Meanwhile, neither a bare mention of Home Rule nor even a promise to amend the Land Laws was found in Gladstone's Midlothian address.

But Lord Beaconsfield's sun had set forever: the new Parliament comprised 349 Liberals, 243 Conservatives, and 60 Home Rulers: the Liberals had thus a comfortable majority over all parties. Mr W E Forster, a man of light and leading, was sent to Ireland as Chief Secretary with Lord Cowper as his Viceroy. He went reluctantly, 'in the spirit of a soldier who is sent to the front by his chief', but full of humane intentions for the 'union of hearts' between the two islands. Mr Gladstone did not renew the Peace Preservation Act, devised for the protection of life and property in Ireland by exceptional criminal procedure. Perhaps it would have been wiser to introduce reform under the cover of such an Act, for the very next day Mr Parnell showed how he would use the clemency of the Government: America, he said, had sent him back with a message that she would give Ireland nothing for charity, but 'millions to break the land system'; a man had offered him £5 for bread, and £20 for lead; he spoke proudly and defiantly, like the formidable man he was, at a time when the world had subscribed nearly £250 000 in charity to save Ireland from famine. Further, it was known that the Government was to introduce some sort of an Irish Land Bill, and, to encourage the Liberal Government in liberality, to the electors of Ennis he introduced for the first time the terrible spectre of 'Captain Boycott', which was to stalk over Ireland with 'Captain Moonlight' for many a year. 'Now, what are you going to do to a tenant who bids for a farm from which his neighbour has been evicted?' he said; there were loud cries of 'Kill him!' – 'Shoot him!' Parnell coldly proceeded: 'Now, I think I heard somebody say "Shoot him". But I wish to point out a very much better way – a more Christian and charitable way – which will give the lost sinner an opportunity of repenting. When a man takes a farm from which another man has been evicted, you must show him in the streets of the town, you must show him on the roadside where you meet him, you must show him at the shop counter, you must show him at the fair, and in the market-place, and even in the house of worship, by leaving him severely alone, by putting him in a moral Coventry, by isolating him from his kind, as if he were a leper of old. You must show him your detestation of the crime he has committed; and you may depend upon it that there will be no man so full of avarice, so lost to shame, as to dare the public opinion of all right-thinking men, and to transgress your unwritten code of laws.'

The system was at once put into operation: 'Courts' sat to administer the terrible 'unwritten code' and to decree the boycott; whether desired or no, criminal allies were not wanting to the Land League; they began their work in earnest, and assassinations became frequent. Among the victims was a nobleman named Lord Mountmorris. Finally, Mr Forster was driven to insist on a policy of repression. Criminal proceedings were commenced against Parnell and other Irish leaders, which ended in a disagreement of the jury and a great increase in his prestige and bitterness. In January 1881 the new Coercion Act, giving special powers of arrest, enquiry, and a summary criminal procedure, was introduced by Mr Forster with a heavy and, indeed, almost a breaking heart. 'If I could have foreseen it, I would never have entered Parliament,' he said. It was carried on 2 March, in the face of the most persistent, scientific, and violent Irish obstruction: the closure was invented as a device to deal with this new kind of opposition; however, in April of the same year a Land Bill, highly beneficial to the Irish peasant, became law. The Act founded the Land Commission, and embodied the principles of fair rent, fixity of tenure, and free disposal of landed property for the tenants. It gave no more than was just; yet the boon had been granted, not as a free gift, but as the reward of lawless and cruel agitation. Parnell knew this, and so did the Irish people; nor did the Land League give the Act their wholehearted approval; its effect was doubtful, and Parnell advised the Irish tenants in general not to avail themselves of the machinery of the Act by applying to the Courts for 'fair rents' until certain test cases had been decided, and decided favourably. This disgusted and infuriated Mr Gladstone, who began to think that Parnell was politically impossible and was determined to ruin any attempt, however generous, by English statesmen to help Ireland. He made the ominous statement 'that the resources of civilisation were not exhausted'; and the Government, which had failed to convict Parnell before a jury, decided to arrest him under the new Coercion Act. On 12 October he was safely lodged in Kilmainham gaol.

A hundred years had passed since Grattan had won independence for his Parliament, and its centenary was indeed an unhappy one for the Niobe of Nations. Terror and bloodshed under the new Crimes Act were increasing rather than declining, although many of the Parliamentary leaders were in gaol. Parnell had been right: on the eve of his arrest he had prophesied in a vivid phrase that, were he imprisoned, 'Captain Moonlight' would take his place; his strong and ruthless hand being removed, the last vestiges of restraint were withdrawn from the agitation. Many years later another Liberal Government was to remember the imprisonment of Parnell, when considering what to do with an even more powerful leader. Henceforward the needy tenants were not only minded not to pay any portion of their rents, but were also determined by every means of intimidation in their power to prevent their richer neighbours from doing so; the assassin's knife and pistol aided them; witnesses and juries were alike terrorised, and refused to do their duty. In desperation the Government released Parnell from prison, and promised a bill to relieve tenants from arrears of rent: once more Parnell had shown his power, and his influence had availed, it seemed, to curb the campaign of lawlessness. The policy of coercion was now abandoned, and Cowper and Forster had to make way for a new Executive, untainted with that tradition of government. Gladstone sent Lord Spencer as Viceroy, and his own nephew by marriage, Lord Frederick Cavendish, an almost untried politician, as Chief Secretary; conciliation was in the air; perfect weather coincided with the new political atmosphere, and cheered the impressionable Irish people. Lord Frederick was welcomed like a prince on that beautiful summer's day, and it seemed that a new era of the 'Union of Hearts' was about to begin. But history is ruthless; and the laws of cause and effect do not cease to operate by the sudden and imperious request of one man, who has set a complex train of events in motion. Powerful as Mr Parnell was, his policy had made possible a nationwide alliance between crime and politics: 'Captain Moonlight' had already stridden out into the light of day, and could not be so easily banished or arbitrarily controlled as the sixty talkers in the House of Commons. Towards evening on the day of his arrival, Lord Frederick Cavendish was walking in Phoenix Park with Mr Thomas Burke, the Permanent Under-Secretary of State. The sun was still shining brightly, but they were both murdered brutally under its light by a gang of a secret society, known as the Invincibles, whose purpose was murder and one of whose organisers was a member of the Dublin Town Council.

Ireland's day of hope was blotted out in a night of despair.

Parnell at once issued a manifesto appealing for the detection and punishment of the murderers, and the jury at the inquest expressed the 'hope that the Almighty Disposer of events will enable the constituted authorities to discover the assassins, so that they may be brought to speedy justice'. Ireland hung her head in shame and knew that her cause had been irreparably injured for many years to come. From England there came a stern demand for measures of precaution, and even for vengeance, although, when the gang were at length discovered, tried, and hanged, largely through the devotion, sagacity, and courage of John Adye Currie, the Dublin magistrate, poor Lady Frederick Cavendish sent an ivory cross to the murderer of her husband as a token of forgiveness. Such, however, was not the mood of the English people or her Government. On 9 May, Sir William Harcourt introduced a far stronger Coercion Act than the last, which in effect suspended trial by jury. 'Every juryman,' he said, 'looks with dread upon the levelled pistol at his heart, the dagger at his back, and the bullet of the rifle in his home at night.' Even Parnell could not offer anything but a dejected and half-hearted opposition to this measure. Mr Gladstone sought to attach responsibility to him: he said that the Irish Party had not instigated these murders, but they could have prevented them. Yet the Irish Judges passed a resolution against the Crimes Act, and one, Baron FitzGerald, resigned rather than be a party to its administration. The Act remained in operation for three years, but nevertheless, in the words of Judge Currie, 'murder and outrage stalked through the land at noonday and were as the pestilence that flieth by night'.

In October 1882 the National League was formed, which made Home Rule, and not the land question, its principal concern, and, in 1884, Gladstone's new Franchise Act was passed, an event pregnant with importance for the Irish Party.

The Act increased the Irish representation considerably, and trebled the Irish voters. Heretofore the higher property qualifications had prevented the Nationalists from overwhelming the polls in Ireland. The Orangemen in the North foresaw the certain consequences of the change, and began a violent agitation. They saw that the new franchise would give the Nationalists the balance of power, and that this might mean Home Rule. Meanwhile under the Union they had prospered exceedingly, and developed the country out of all recognition: their ancestors had been the strength of Grattan's Parliament, but Catholic emancipation and the democratic franchise had intervened, and they knew that in an All Ireland Parliament they would be under the heel of the South. 'Captain Boycott' and 'Captain Moonlight' would then hold sway in Ulster, and this must never be; no surrender. So apprehensive did Ulster become that Sir Stafford Northcote, leader of the Conservatives in the House, found it necessary to tell Belfast not to 'fire off your guns in the gaiety of your hearts'; and Colonel King-Harman MP told the Orangemen 'to keep the cartridge in the rifle'. Nevertheless, Ulstermen, far and wide, began to arm: but their methods were very different from those of the South; as Tim Healy records, 'the Orange rioter never moves without orders: unlike the Nationalist mobster, he is a disciplined unit'. How true this judgment is will be shown abundantly by the history of Carson's leadership as contrasted with that of Parnell. Already the whirlwind was being sown between North and South.

6. Balfour in Ireland

In August 1885 the Crimes Act was to expire, and, when it became known that Gladstone proposed to renew certain of its provisions, the Irish Party began to veer towards the Conservatives, who, in turn, knowing that the strength of the Irish Party would be much increased as a result of the lowered franchise, did not reject their advances. Meanwhile the Liberal Cabinet had failed to agree on a scheme for an 'Irish Central Board' which it was proposed should be set up over a reformed system of local government in Ireland, although the scheme had the approval of Parnell. The Irish joined with the Tories to beat the Liberals on the Budget proposals in June 1885. Lord Salisbury formed a minority Government to carry on business until the General Election in November: it will be observed that he did not renew the Crimes Act and proposed a Land Purchase Act which was acceptable to Parnell. He appointed a Viceroy, Lord Carnarvon, who had definitely expressed himself in a letter to him as being in favour of Home Rule; he had himself used language at least consistent with Home Rule; and it was known that the Conservatives had been negotiating with Parnell. Nevertheless, in November the General Election was fought without the electorate being enlightened by either party as to their policy on Home Rule, although the Irish question was the dominant issue in British politics. The election was disappointing to the Conservatives, and indecisive. The Liberals lost twenty seats, and the Conservatives and Irish together outnumbered them by only four. Ireland, however, had spoken with no uncertain voice for Home Rule; even in Ulster there was a majority; and this was not lost on Mr Gladstone. However, the Conservative Cabinet after the election decided unequivocally against Home Rule.

Some say that the party had regained its soul: at all events they reverted to Disraeli's affirmation of the Union, a policy which undoubtedly coincided with the Queen's views, and which was to give them supremacy in politics, except for one interval, for close on twenty years: yet, to any critical student of the period, the grave and ugly suspicion must present itself that the Conservatives had far from decided against Home Rule between June and November 1885, and were quite prepared to bargain with Parnell in return for Parliamentary support which would have ensured them a safe Parliamentary majority. But the result of the elections negatived such a possibility, and the Conservatives shook the dust of Home Rule off their feet. A challenging affirmation of the Union was a feature of the Queen's Speech of January 1886, and of course the Government was soon heavily defeated. Mr Gladstone formed a Government, and, although he persuaded Joseph Chamberlain, already a convinced Unionist, to join his Ministry, the results of the election on the new franchise in Ireland had already decided him to espouse Home Rule as his last crusade. Meanwhile, Randolph Churchill, well aware of the divided counsels of the Liberal Party, saw that a new alignment of parties on the Unionist and Home Rule division would with good fortune secure a decisive majority for the Unionists, and that the Conservatives would be the preponderant partner in the new alliance. Moreover, he was convinced that there was a winning card in the pack. 'I decided some time ago', he wrote bluntly to his friend Lord Justice FitzGibbon on 16 February 1886, 'that if the GOM went for Home Rule, the Orange card would be the only one to play. Please God it may turn out the ace of trumps and not the two'. He was as good as his word: on 22 February he had crossed the Channel and landed at Larne. 'He was welcomed like a king,' wrote his illustrious son. Indeed, the Unionists of Ulster realised that at long last the mighty Conservative Party had espoused their cause, and that they were no longer alone; the night of doubt and sorrow was ended; they had not been abandoned to Parnell and the Moonlighters after all. Yet, loving discipline and leadership as they did, they had no outstanding leader of their own; so they took Lord Randolph to their hearts, acclaiming him as their champion, and marched past him seventy thousand strong. His vivid and adventurous spirit was stirred and uplifted, faced as he was by a national emotion aroused by himself, such as he had never seen. His words were as clear and explicit as Parnell's to the Southerners, but far more eloquent and inspiring. For he was promoting no hateful, stealthy, unchristian boycott of friends and neighbours, but open, organised, 'loyal' rebellion in defence of the Union, the Queen, and the Protestant faith.

'Now may be the time,' he said, 'to show whether all those ceremonies and forms which are practised in Orange Lodges are really living symbols or only idle and meaningless ceremonies. ... The loyalists in Ulster should wait and watch – organise and prepare. Diligence and vigilance ought to be your watchword, so that the blow, if it does come, may not come upon you as a thief in the night and may not find you unready and taken by surprise.' Then he promised help from England to loyal Ulster. 'I do not hesitate to tell you most truly that ... there will not be wanting to you those of position and influence in England who would be willing to cast in their lot with you, and who, whatever the result, will share your fortunes and your fate.' Finally, to a great multitude already profoundly moved, he quoted the stirring and magnificently appropriate words:

> *'The combat deepens; on, ye brave,*
> *Who rush to glory or the grave.*
> *Wave, Ulster – all thy banners wave,*
> *And charge with all thy chivalry.'*

So with these words he departed, as swiftly as he had come, and never to return, but leaving an indelible memory behind him; and no one knew that there was in Dublin a plodding Southern Irish barrister, working hard on his briefs, at the Four Courts, upon whose shoulders his mantle would fall. In a few days, in a letter to a Liberal Unionist, the new hero of Belfast had written: 'Ulster will fight and Ulster will be right'; and the Ulster movement was born – a new movement, indeed, but militant with the sentiment of old ideals, cherished religious convictions, and a proud history, boldly challenging the older Nationalist cause with their indirect methods of boycott and intrigue.

Meanwhile, Mr Gladstone – with the loss of his powerful lieutenant, Chamberlain, his party seriously split – pressed on with his 'Better Government of Ireland Bill'. On 8 April he moved the first reading, which was formally carried. The Bill was bound up with a Land Bill, and proposed an Irish Parliament and an Irish Executive for domestic affairs, reserving to the Crown, *inter alia*, imperial matters of defence, foreign policy, trade, and post office; also the Irish members, the cause of so much intrigue and obstruction, were to be removed from Westminster. Yet in May 1886, after Mr Gladstone had used every legitimate party device behind the scenes, and all his wonderful gifts of rhetorical persuasion from the Treasury Bench, to bring back the seceding Unionist Liberals, the Bill was defeated on second reading by 341 votes to 311, amid scenes of unprecedented public excitement and with the issue open till the last. But his words, though they failed of their effect, were memorable, and carry to the present-day reader something of the weight of prophecy: 'If it be a just and reasonable demand, we cannot hasten too soon to meet it, and we will not wait until the day of disaster, the day of difficulty, and, I will add, the day of dishonour, to yield, as we have so often yielded to necessity, that which we were unwilling to yield to justice.'

A General Election followed in July: in Ulster the excitement, intensified by Lord Randolph's visit, broke out into riot and bloodshed; for in 1886 there was no hand strong enough to control them. Scores were killed on both sides; many, to hide their dead, buried them in back yards. Policemen were murdered by Orangemen in Belfast, and the RIC who fired back at the Orangemen were known as 'Morley's Murderers'. For Morley had been Chief Secretary for a few months. Nevertheless, the result of the elections was decisive. Lord Randolph's card had won. The United Kingdom declared by a majority of 118 for the Conservatives and Liberal Unionists against Gladstone and Parnell. The Union was saved, and the new Salisbury Government, reinforced by the powerful alliance of Joseph Chamberlain and his followers, seemed secure for years.

And now the Conservatives, pledged again and again against any form of Home Rule, had to set about governing Ireland: it was no light task. Passions had been inflamed; the fears of Ulster, though they had not been realised, were not yet allayed, and savage riots continued: the hopes of the South had been raised almost to certainty, and then dashed to the ground. The Government pledged itself to maintain the law, whether against the Orangemen of Belfast or the Moonlighters of the South: Sir Michael Hicks-Beach, who had led the Conservatives in Opposition, was sent to Dublin as a strong Chief Secretary; Salisbury made John Gibson his

Irish Attorney-General, and he in turn appointed Edward Carson as his Crown counsel or chief of staff, in his dangerous and important task of restoring order under the law in Ireland.

The experience of the Conservative Government of 1886 was almost that of the Liberal Government of 1880. The Nationalist Party, realising that any question of Home Rule was indefinitely postponed, fell back upon the old agrarian grievances. The Land Act of 1881, as interpreted by the Courts, denied to leaseholders and other classes of tenants the right to apply to the Courts for 'fair rents' to be fixed, and the bad season of 1886 pressed hardly on yet others whose rents had already been fixed. An Irish Land Bill for their relief, proposed by an Irish member, was rejected in the Commons, and soon afterwards was initiated the celebrated 'Plan of Campaign', which it became Carson's duty to suppress: the Plan was signed by Tim Harrington MP and although it was repudiated by Parnell, who was ill, it had originated in a suggestion of his own four years before. The Plan was shortly this: where eviction was threatened, a 'fair rent' was to be offered by the tenant; if it was refused by the landlord, the sum offered was to be deposited with a local committee, which would, if the landlord persisted, be used to fight him on behalf of the tenant. Chief Baron Palles decided against the legality of the Plan, although acknowledging that it had emanated from 'a master mind', and ultimately the Vatican itself condemned it. The chief promoters of the Plan, including many MPs, were prosecuted for conspiracy. This trial, in which the Chief Secretary was subpoenaed as a witness, ended, as had Parnell's trial, in a disagreement of the jury; and the Government, as had Mr Gladstone's, resorted once more to coercion. But Sir Michael Hicks-Beach resigned, after a charge to the grand jury by Chief Baron Palles which almost openly charged him with neglect of duty, and gave way to the most notable of all Irish Chief Secretaries.

'Twenty years of resolute government' was Salisbury's grim prescription after the defeat of the Home Rule Bill: an old and tried leader like Hicks-Beach had not availed; maybe, after all, this was a task for youth, and Salisbury, like Gladstone before him, decided to send a nephew to Ireland – the grave of reputations – and with very different results. This nephew of his had already acquired a Parliamentary reputation; it had taken him two years to bother to make a maiden speech, and then it was an effort which baffled the Parliamentary reporters. Later he had joined Lord Randolph's Fourth Party: his delicate appearance, which won him the name of the 'Tiger Lily', his air of abstraction, his preoccupation with an inconclusive philosophy, all concealed the nerve of iron which was to win him a grimmer title. Lord Salisbury must have known his nephew well before giving him the post, but few others did; the appointment was criticised and even derided, as had been that of Lord Frederick Cavendish. In March 1887 he expounded with steely urbanity, on its second reading, the strongest 'Coercion Act' which had ever been introduced into Parliament, on the same day on which *The Times* first published the famous letters, purporting to be signed by Parnell, but really forged by the miserable Pigott, and sold for thousands of pounds, implicating the Irish leader in the Invincible conspiracy: it was carried by a large majority, and the 'Tiger Lily' went over to Dublin to become 'Bloody Balfour'.

Shortly, the provisions of this drastic Act were as follows: the Lord Lieutenant could, by 'proclaiming' a district, bring it under the 'Crimes Act'; in such a district a criminal trial could be removed to another part of the country, at the instance of the Crown, and could be placed before a 'special' jury – that is, a jury with a property qualification, instead of a 'common' jury – and extensive powers of 'challenging' the jury were implicit in this provision. He could also in such a district proclaim any association 'dangerous' and forthwith suppress it; in addition, such offences as intimidation or conspiracy, directed to interfere with the law of landlord and tenant and peaceable occupation of land, the taking part in riots or unlawful assemblies, or obstruction offered to an officer of the law could be tried without a jury before two resident magistrates; in addition, any person could be summoned to give evidence, although such evidence might incriminate him, before a resident magistrate, where a crime had passed undetected.

Balfour lost no time in making the acquaintance of his Irish Executive, and the men upon whom he was to rely: he impressed them all. With Lord Frederick's terrible fate to warn him, he at once began to drive about alone in a jaunting-car, and the Irish noted his courage and began to admire him. Much as they were to hate him, they never fired at him once during all his time as Chief Secretary. 'I never knew a man with more iron courage,' said Lord Atkinson to me, who was soon to become his Irish Solicitor-General; 'I never saw him show the slightest symptom of fear.'

One day he asked Lord Ashbourne to give a dinner for him to meet the members of the Bar. A large number of the 'gentlemen of the long robe' were asked to the dinner, and Balfour went round all the guests with a smile for each: when he passed a young man, tall and spare, with a grim determined countenance and deep blue eyes, something made him stop. Edward Carson, aged thirty-two, was presented to the Chief Secretary, his senior by only a few years. 'So you're Edward Carson,' he said, 'I am glad to meet you: there's a great deal I should like to say to you.' There was an immediate and spontaneous attraction between them: they were much of a height, and, although it would be hard to imagine a greater contrast in physiognomy between the young man of Celtic and Italian descent and the finest flower of Lowland Scotland, their figures were so similar in their slimness and elegance that Carson was afterwards addressed by Baron Dowse as 'Balfour Junior', for he had always been most carefully well-dressed. Edward Carson's smile, and the blue eyes that met his own, straight and true, charmed Arthur Balfour. This attraction to a lawyer was rare, for one of Balfour's few indiscretions was the frequent and open admission that he disliked lawyers: this antipathy was specially aroused by his Irish Lord Chancellor, Lord Ashbourne. Once, when they sat together considering the drafting of a Bill, Balfour suggested the alteration of one word in Ashbourne's draft. 'I like that word,' said the Lord Chancellor, 'I wouldn't alter it.' 'Ah,' rejoined Balfour quietly, 'then perhaps you could put it into another Act.' Carson, who was always intensely proud of his profession, regarded Balfour's dislike of lawyers with amusement and as something of a pose. 'You know, you're not a bit like a lawyer, Carson,' Balfour once said to his friend. 'That's not a compliment,' was Carson's curt reply. Yet Balfour himself was far from innocent of legal lore and subtleties; his fine intelligence had mastered the complicated land legislation pertaining to Ireland as comprehensively as had the mind of any professional lawyer; and, when Balfour would rail at the legal mind and its arid power of abstraction and preoccupation with detail, Carson would reply, 'You know, A J B, you're the very best lawyer I ever came across.' If Carson attracted Balfour, the new Chief Secretary was a revelation to Carson – 'I was only a provincial country lawyer, and, until I saw Arthur Balfour, I had never guessed that such an animal could exist.' And, indeed, the young statesman, in the early prime of life, with his handsome and refined appearance and maturity of mind, could hardly be matched in the three kingdoms as a figure of combined grace, culture, wisdom, and strength of character. That a public man could interest himself in the abstractions of philosophy without in any way losing his grasp of practical life or administrative duties amazed the provincial lawyer, who had left whatever he had touched of these matters behind in the lecture-rooms of Trinity College, Dublin; that a man could show manners perfectly suited to every occasion, and the next moment, if necessity arose, could become cold and indeed ruthless, seemed highly paradoxical; that one who appeared to enjoy the softer graces of life with such elegant detachment could drive about alone, both his hands occupied with the reins, where he knew assassins were lurking with their knives and pistols, revealed indeed an 'animal' in whose real existence it was difficult to believe. It was a great lesson, not only for Carson, but for Ireland, to have such a man set over her even when his prescribed duty was to enforce 'twenty years of resolute government'. For once, England had sent of her very best, her finest flower, to Ireland: the strength of his hand was soon apparent, and what began as a grim and efficient association between the two men for the restoration of law and order in Ireland ripened and widened into a lifelong respect and friendship for each other. For over two years 'Bloody Balfour' was to assert his authority by proclamation over the south and west of Ireland, and 'Coercion Carson', by his rapidly developing legal skill and his contemptuous disregard for danger, was to see that nothing dangerous escaped from the meshes of the law, and from day to day they both of them carried their lives in their hands.

Early in 1887, John Gibson became a Judge, and Peter O'Brien, serjeant-at-law, well known throughout Ireland as 'Peter the Packer', afterwards Lord Chief Justice of Ireland, took his place. The appointment of Crown counsel was personal to the Attorney-General, and normally Carson would have been succeeded by another man; but Balfour already considered Carson indispensable, and prevailed on O'Brien to retain him as Crown counsel. O'Brien was a character, and was always known as 'Peter' throughout the length and breadth of Ireland, a sign of the popularity which he never lost. Once, years later, when he was Lord Chief Justice, a humble village postmistress, whom he had known years before, sent him a cry of distress: 'Mr Peter, I am in trouble with the Postmaster-General. You promised to help me if I needed it; I need it now.' He crossed the Channel, and interceded with his old master, Mr Balfour, then Prime Minister, successfully on her behalf; that was the kind of man he was. He had a most dramatic and friendly way of cross-examining. 'Just tell me this, Bridget,' he once said to a witness. The ample Irish mother in the witness-box drew herself up and observed haughtily, 'Mrs Luby, if you please, to *you*, Peter.' Despite his broad humanity, he used the Crimes Act with striking effect. 'If it had not been for him', writes Sir John Ross, 'the whole country would soon have gone into chaos'. It is not surprising that Peter and Carson soon became very intimate. Peter had been a plucky, fighting advocate, but he was not of the legal or intellectual calibre of his 'devil'. He saw Carson was a man among men, and used to encourage and hearten him when Carson's sometimes melancholy nature became despondent. O'Brien came to rely very much on Carson's judgment. Once at the end of a long consultation before a very difficult case with many eminent counsel engaged, Carson diffidently stated his view of the course to be taken, which was quite a simple one. 'I always said this fellow had the last half-mile in him,' said Peter, and accepted Carson's view. The onerous task was no strain on the latter's courage, but it was upon his health; once he sent in his resignation to Peter and applied for a vacant County Court Judgeship. Peter refused it him and bade him reflect. 'Here you are, Ned Carson, thirty-four years old: if I do what you ask, in ten years you'll be a County Court Judge; in twenty years you'll be a County Court Judge; maybe in fifty years you'll be a County Court Judge; and the Almighty meant you for bigger things than that.' And so the wise and kindly Attorney-General, knowing his great gifts, saved Carson from obscurity. It is almost certain that, if O'Brien had been unkind enough to grant Carson's request, the history of Ireland, and indeed England, might have been a very different chapter. The very danger of their association brought the two men together: on one occasion O'Brien, as he often did, saw Carson off at the Dublin station when the latter was leaving the city to conduct an important prosecution. Carson noticed that a man, who had been following the two of them through the Dublin streets, took his seat in a compartment in the same coach. Soon after the train started he observed the man creeping stealthily along the corridor of the train. Carson calmly drew his revolver and pointed it at the man. The latter crept away down the corridor of the train, and was able to evade all attempts at identification and search by the guard and the railway officials. There can be little doubt that he was an intended assassin.

Peter O'Brien gained for himself the title 'Peter the Packer' by his extensive exercise of the Crown right, under an Irish Juries Act, of directing jurors summoned for criminal cases, when called, to stand aside, and so excluding from the jury-box those who, it was believed, would not under any circumstances convict a prisoner, save in cases of cattle or sheep stealing or similar offences against small Irish farmers and peasants to whom such convictions were important. This was really the only means at the time of securing a *real* trial; most criminal trials in country venues were only forms and farces. If exclusion according to law, of those who were known or reasonably believed to be sure to bring in a verdict of acquittal, no matter what the evidence, be jury packing, O'Brien deserved his title. Peter's practice was quite within the law, and the right was a necessary protection against the effect of a Juries Act, carried by Lord O'Hagan in 1871, which placed the safety of the public in the hands of the 'Wild Flowers of Tullahogue'. About that time an enterprising manufacturer of perfume had brought out a scent which he called 'The Wild Flowers of Tullahogue'. When O'Hagan carried his Act, which lowered the qualification for jurymen, and admitted to the jury-box a class of peasants largely illiterate and quite unfitted for the discharge of judicial duties, his new juries were immediately called 'The Wild Flowers of Tullahogue'. It was said that once when the new jurymen were first ordered by the Clerk of Assize 'to take their usual places' as gentlemen of the jury, they all scrambled into the dock. One of the most important tasks of Crown counsel in the days of the Crimes Act was to detect land-leaguers among those summoned to go into the jury-box: the Crown had a right to challenge six jurymen in a case of misdemeanour, and twenty in a case of felony, and any more if the Crown counsel could 'show cause': all sorts of devices were used by sympathisers of the prisoners to get into the jury-box, or to create prejudice against the Crown; some of the jurors summoned would ask Carson whether they could 'stand by', and, if he granted their request, would complain that they had been made to stand by, simply because they were Catholics. Of course, the prisoner had his challenges as well; when counsel was for the defence, it was the golden rule 'to challenge any man with a clean collar'. The empanelling of a jury was therefore often a matter of hours, and even days. This laborious preliminary, which is also a feature of modern American trials, is entirely absent from the English Courts. Carson is said to have once asked an English lawyer at what stage a trial in England began. 'Oh, when the jury is sworn,' was the answer. 'That's curious,' was the Irishman's comment, 'with us it's all finished when that business is over.'

Carson's appointment as Crown counsel, the part played by him in the prosecutions under the Crimes Act, his friendship with Balfour, and his subsequent promotion by the latter's influence, have been the subject of critical and hostile comment by his fellow-countrymen both at the time and long afterwards, and perhaps the place to deal with the matter is here. In the famous Home Rule debate in March 1914, after Carson had accused Mr Winston Churchill of being a 'turncoat' and as being 'a politician on the make', Mr Joe Devlin retorted by saying that Carson was no better. 'When a young lawyer,' he said, 'in a moment of youthful and generous enthusiasm follows the banner of a great cause for the sake of all that is good in it, and becomes an ardent Home Ruler, and then, when the forces of honour and justice are beaten, joins the forces of a powerful enemy – that is what I pronounce a "man on the make".' After Carson had, for once very excited, pronounced his statement as an 'infamous lie', Mr Devlin referred to the fact that Carson had been a member of the National Liberal Club. The latter fact was undoubtedly true, but the inference drawn from it that Carson was ever a Home Ruler or ever changed his coat upon that question was erroneous, and ignores the whole complicated political history of the year 1885, when neither party declared itself on Home Rule, which it has been attempted to outline at the beginning of this chapter; indeed, during the year 1885, and up to the Queen's Speech in 1886, it would have been quite possible to be a Home Ruler and remain an orthodox

Conservative. Now, it appears that Carson was elected to the National Liberal Club in June 1886, the month in which Mr Gladstone moved the second reading of the Home Rule Bill. This would not have committed him to Home Rule, for Joseph Chamberlain and his seventy followers considered themselves at that time and for many years to come as being quite as good Liberals as Mr Gladstone: it was Mr Gladstone whom they regarded as the 'turncoat', who seemed to them to have gone back on many previous utterances; nor was there any undue heresy hunt in the National Liberal Club, since Mr Gladstone's one object was to win the Liberal Unionists back to the fold. After the following General Election it might have been said with greater accuracy that Home Rule was an essential element in the Liberal faith. But there was neither in 1886, nor later, any declaration in favour of Home Rule required to be signed by new members by the committee of the National Liberal Club, which Mr Devlin claimed in his speech was the fact. The only declaration required was 'I am a Liberal'; indeed, as Mr Alexander Millar wrote to *The Times*, soon after Mr Devlin's speech, he had himself, having become a convinced supporter of the Union and the Ulster cause, written to the committee of the National Liberal Club, offering to resign on that ground, but had received a reply that such a course was entirely unnecessary. Mr Devlin's statement, therefore, based no doubt on a rather gross misconception, that Carson became a Home Ruler by joining the National Liberal Club, and became a Unionist only on being given a lucrative appointment, must remain absolutely unjustified. In fact Carson was proposed for the club by Cecil Roche, the most determined opponent of Home Rule in southern Ireland. Moreover, in 1886, almost as soon as it was formed at Birmingham, immediately after the debate on the first Home Rule Bill, Carson joined Joseph Chamberlain's

Liberal Unionist Association; but he was still a Liberal, and it was not until the next century that the Liberal Unionists really lost their separate identity; in 1914, indeed, they had become almost merged with the Conservatives, and many, who were ignorant of their political history, were startled to hear that Carson had ever been a Liberal at any time; but he had never concealed the fact, and, indeed, had prided himself upon it. We can go back even farther and find that Carson, in the Dublin Historical Society, although a professed Liberal, even an ardent Radical, was a strong supporter of the Union. Years later, he again insisted on his Liberalism to his own disadvantage, if also on his Unionism, when, by Balfour's influence, he was first a prospective Parliamentary candidate for Trinity College; the electors almost demanded a professing Tory, and even Balfour could not persuade Carson to stand as such; he would stand only as a Liberal Unionist, and was faced with a powerful Tory opponent in consequence. This Unionism had been born and bred in him, as a Lambert and as an Irishman of the Pale. 'From the time that I said my humble prayer at my mother's knee,' he said in one of his 1914 speeches, 'proud as I am of being an Irishman, I was taught to think that I ought to look upon England as the great prototype of a justice-loving, religion-loving, and in every respect a trusted nation, which in colonisation brought all its great qualities to bear on securing the happiness of the people.' Mr Tim Healy first mentioned the Devlin incident to the present writer, and laughed at the idea of Carson being a turncoat on the question of the Union; indeed, he was surprised that Carson had taken the taunt so seriously. The trouble about Carson, he said, was that the idea of the Union had been instilled into him at an early age; and with Carson any idea, once adopted, will get into the marrow of his bones and go to the grave with him. His own criticism of Carson was of a very different order. 'If Carson had been of the stuff of which turncoats are made, he would never have had his great power over the North, and the history of Ireland might have been much happier. But Carson is a man who would never change. It is absurd to talk of Carson as a turncoat. No one that knew him took it seriously. He was a man whose word you could rely on. When he said "Yes", it was "Yes"; if it was "No" with him, it meant "No". He said "No" all his life to a United Ireland, more's the pity. But I would trust my soul to Carson.'

Nevertheless, hard things were said of him at the time, and he had to listen to bitter taunts both in the Courts, even from colleagues, and from the Press. One published article stated that 'The Crimes Act fed him, clothed him, took him to the Gaiety Theatre on Saturday night, and equipped him with a jaunting-car on Sunday afternoon'. A crooked journalist once brought him a very abusive article, with a hint that it might be worth his while to buy the article so that it should not see the light of day. 'Go to it,' said Carson, with cold disdain. 'That's the sort of filth that'll be the manure upon which my reputation will flourish.'

It is, however, true that his association and friendship with Arthur Balfour did alter his life and turn his talents into a political channel, along which they would otherwise probably never have flowed. This wonderful superior being who had descended upon Ireland became almost an object of worship for the young lawyer; although Arthur Balfour never put himself above his new Irish friends, any more than he did with anyone else, nor presumed to lecture them on the course they ought to pursue, his broad outlook began to influence and widen that of Carson; he would listen to Carson's suggestions as gravely and respectfully as if the Irish barrister were the Marquess of Salisbury, and gradually, without any assumption of patronage, he made him understand that there were ambitions which Carson might entertain, both for the good of himself and his country, beyond the Irish County Court Bench, no doubt in its way a very admirable institution. Little by little the views of the 'provincial Irish lawyer' began to develop and take wing; he began to see that across St George's Channel there was a field at Westminster, and perhaps another in the Temple, where the talents which he must have known were quickening within him and, leaving John Ross, James Campbell, Seymour Bushe, and all the other Trinity stars far behind, would find even greater scope than in the execution of the Crimes Act.

Yet the task of counsel engaged for the Crown under the Act was exacting enough; not only was the work extremely dangerous, and of great State importance, but it called for no ordinary ability. It would be worse than useless for Dublin Castle to 'proclaim' a district unless convictions could be obtained in proper cases: it was the one aim of the Nationalist leaders to render such 'proclamations' a mockery by defeating the Crown in the Courts. Crown counsel could not afford to fear death; his eyes and his mind had always to be on the alert, and, in addition, it was essential for him to be a fine lawyer. The ordinary practitioner, with a keen mind for cross-examination and a gift for the gab, who can do well without learning in the criminal Courts, was not good enough here: the difficult duty of challenging when the juries were empanelled has already been mentioned, and Counsel were beset by many kinds of minor conspiracy at the very outset. Sometimes a number of prisoners would be in the dock together; these people would rarely give their names, and as soon as a police officer had identified one by name, and his eyes were turned away, another man would take his place wearing his coat and muffler. The depositions were frequently stolen. After it was all over for him, Carson was once asked whether he had at times been afraid for his life. 'No,' replied Carson, 'but I was in constant dread that my depositions would be stolen.' Also there was an appeal, by way of re-hearing under the Act, to the County Court Judge; and from him an appeal by *certiorari* to quash the conviction in the Exchequer division; or the prisoner's counsel would invoke the procedure of *habeas corpus*. Every kind of technicality would be relied upon, and Chief Baron Palles, who always acted on the strictest interpretation of the law, would quash the conviction if only a slight mistake had been made by counsel or magistrates in the Court below. The reports of the cases on appeal reveal the nicest and most difficult points of criminal law and procedure; for instance, in one of the many cases in which Carson prosecuted the redoubtable Mr William O'Brien MP, the depositions were stolen in the middle of the hearing; it was essential under the law that there should be full depositions recorded for the purposes of appeal; the magistrates innocently began the case again from the beginning, taking down, of course, full depositions of the renewed proceedings. But the Chief Baron held the conviction invalid, because the loss of the first depositions had never been strictly proved or deposed to before the fresh start was made. On a later occasion, owing to scenes of the wildest disorder, the Bench cleared the Court: Mr O'Brien then contended that a criminal trial should be *coram publico*, and left the Court with his advisers; his exit was made *vi et armis*; one policeman was knocked down who tried to prevent his departure; sentence was pronounced in his absence. On appeal, his counsel, Mr Tim Healy, contended with great solemnity and learning that the conviction should be quashed because sentence had been pronounced in the absence of the prisoner; and his learning very nearly succeeded. Again, a conviction was quashed because, although there was ample other evidence to secure a conviction, a policeman, called mainly to prove a formality, refused to produce a confidential report after he had mentioned it. Yet it was extraordinary how the wary feet of Counsellor Carson evaded all the pitfalls which were set for him. Sir John Ross describes him as a 'tower of strength' in all these matters: no matter what surprise was sprung, he sat in Court 'calm and unmoved'. One incident has almost a Nelson touch. The Chief Secretary used a difficult secret code with Carson, and in an important prosecution communications in this code would often pass between them. At the moment when a trial was about to commence, Carson received a telegram in this secret Castle code, ordering him to abandon the trial and offer no evidence against the prisoner. Carson just glanced at it and said to the Crown solicitor immediately, 'It's not genuine: it's a forgery.' He continued the case on his own responsibility, and the interruption was hardly noticed. His only grounds for pronouncing the document a forgery was his certainty that Balfour would never thus have 'let him down'. But he was right: the telegram, although a perfect example of the art of a copyist, had never passed through the post office; it was, however, never discovered who had sent it, or how the secret of the code had been discovered. All this may sound interesting and adventurous, but it was a stern duty on which he was engaged. Underlying the long and technical judgments, expressed in wonderful English, of the Chief Baron, one can clearly observe the sad and lawless state of the Irish countryside and the cruelty and miseries which resulted from the agitation. One reads of proscribed peasants who had, maybe unwittingly, occupied land for their cattle forbidden by the National League, and who were consequently refused the necessities of life, even a crust of bread, by the terrified tradespeople. 'We keep no bread, only for customers; we'll not have you for a customer,' they told him. 'I was boycotted,' said one of the unfortunates. 'I could get no provisions of any kind, or anything else, through the town, not as much as a halfpenny candle, and no one would speak to me. I was popular, and would be popular now, only the people are afraid of one another.'

Breaking through his polished English and legal phrases, the reader can detect the grief and anger of the Lord Chief Baron, who was a Catholic, that the priests themselves, the proper guardians of the poor simple folk, were inciting them to such conduct. '*Quis custodiet ipsos custodes?*' 'Now we have the anointed priest of God, who from his pulpit on Sundays will inculcate upon his parishioners the paramount duty of justice and charity to all men, irrespective of the mode in which men may have treated them. Then you have the reverend gentleman telling the people that they ought by combined action to boycott this man. All this he tells them – he standing there as a priest of God, and of the Church to which I assume they belonged, and even referring to the possibility of the unfortunate man "dying without the last Sacraments, being cut off in his sins without being granted one moment to make his peace with God".' We read of a bailiff being roasted alive; of poor beasts maimed and with their tails cut, lest their owner, not liked by the National League, might be able to sell them; of young girls stripped and ill-used, and left to go home naked: this was the field in which 'Coercion Carson' laboured during these years.

7. Crimes Act Cases

It fell to Carson's lot to be counsel in the first prosecution under the Crimes Act – before two resident magistrates; the prisoners were that very eloquent politician, Mr William O'Brien MP, and a Mr Mandeville. The country round Mitchelstown had become a 'proclaimed' district; the National League had been suppressed as illegal, so Mr William O'Brien MP thought he would show Mr Balfour the futility of such policy by addressing two mass meetings inciting the tenants to be faithful to the Plan of Campaign. Perhaps owing to the terrorisation of the people, he hoped that it would be impossible to obtain evidence as to the meeting or the speeches.

The circumstances of the trial were in many ways extraordinary, and became famous. There was tremendous public excitement when the Court sat at Mitchelstown on 9 September 1887; all the shopkeepers closed their houses, and from all the surrounding districts contingents poured in to take part in a monster demonstration of the National League which was fixed to take place in the market square as a protest against Coercion, in which several English members of Parliament had arranged to be present, including Mr Henry Labouchere, and a party of Society ladies. Among other notable politicians present were Mr Brunner MP, Mr Dillon MP, Mr Condon MP, Mr Gill MP and Captain O'Shea MP. From early morning large crowds of people, led by bands, had poured into the town, which was gaily decorated with flags, evergreens, and streamers bearing various mottoes. When the Court sat, the crowds were flanked by men on horseback, who tried to prevent the police from entering the Court. But the young Crown counsel had no such difficulty: his features went, probably for the last time in Ireland, unrecognised, and he was able to make his way into Court without difficulty: indeed, Mr Dillon asked him politely if he was the resident magistrate. He had driven over in a car from Fermoy, as it had been impossible to book a room for the Crown counsel at Mitchelstown. When the carman saw the excited crowds in the latter town he whispered to Carson, 'This is a dangerous business, your honour. Do you mind if I throw up my cap and say, "Three cheers for William O'Brien"?' 'Not in the least,' said the young Crown counsel, and the man did so.

At half-past twelve a tall, lean figure, which was to become so well known to the south of Ireland, rose in Court, and said: 'May I ask you, will you constitute the Court under the Crimes Act?' One of the magistrates, Mr Eaton, agreed, but, when Carson looked round, there was no sign of the prisoners who were on bail. Carson then applied for warrants for the prisoners' arrest. 'What about a warrant for an MP when the House is sitting?' asked Mr Eaton nervously.

'It makes no matter,' replied Carson, and told them why. The warrants were granted, and the Court adjourned. After the adjournment, a fearful riot began: the crowd hurled themselves on the police, pelting them with stones, and injuring several severely; the latter formed solid square, and tried to keep their assailants back without firing, but the crowd, numbering 1 500, armed with sticks and missiles, compelled the police to fall back. The crowd then broke every window in the police barracks, and clearly meant to sack them. Under the greatest provocation the police, as they retired, fired a volley: one man was shot dead and another fell mortally wounded. A scene of the wildest confusion followed, and the distinguished English visitors, such as Labouchere, began to appreciate the predicament to which their love of Irish freedom had brought them. Labouchere, for one, took refuge in a shop which opened its doors to him, and hid under the counter, it is said, until the crowd, shocked by the bloodshed, fell back before the charge of an overwhelming force of police. This melancholy occurrence became known as the Mitchelstown Massacre, and Mr Gladstone's memorable phrase, 'Remember Mitchelstown', rang through Great Britain as a dreadful and practical argument against Coercion and for Home Rule. A decade before he had roused the whole country on behalf of the Armenian Christians, whose fate could not be laid at our door. Dizzy, to his disaster, had dismissed their misfortunes as 'coffee house' babble; but Gladstone had brought him down. Now, Mitchelstown was nearer at home, and the direct result of the first executive act of Conservative Coercion. Under these grievous auspices the first prosecution under the Crimes Act began. This is not the occasion to assess the ultimate responsibility for the bloodshed at Mitchelstown, but the English sympathisers, whose presence greatly impressed the Irish crowd, must bear their share of the blame for the trial of strength of the mob against the armed forces of the Crown.

Carson has always taken the gravest view, not so much of the riot itself, as of the Liberal politicians who encouraged it and condoned it afterwards. In his view it set the most serious and disastrous precedent, which has led to the disintegration of the British Empire. 'I had no objections,' he said to me, 'to a constitutional agitation for Home Rule, but so long as British authority was there, the wicked thing was to encourage murder and outrage, which the Liberal Party undoubtedly did. I thought that this was the end of the Liberal Party then and I think so now. Only in 1906 did they get a majority without the Irish vote. There really has not been a Liberal Party since then. But unfortunately they have brought down far more than themselves.'

Meanwhile, Counsellor Carson, already in a moment execrated and well known – his face and build were not made for obscurity – had been watching the storm from the Court window, absolutely unmoved; shillalahs and stones were in the air; curses and cries of vengeance were raised against him and the Government he represented; he was urged by the police again and again to hurry away: they could not be responsible for his safety. Would he not leave, they begged him, by a side door? He refused to do so. 'The King's highway was made for all,' he told them, 'and by that will I go, or not at all.' It was useless to dissuade him. The Court door opened, and an eye-witness, who had been present at some of the worst riots in Ireland, described what he saw as almost miraculous. The villain of the hour, for whom the crowd has been waiting, the hated 'Castle hack', who has procured the arrest of Ireland's latest hero, William O'Brien, steps out alone and unarmed save for a blackthorn stick in his hand, and for a moment or two surveys the scene before him. He sees the howling, infuriated mob, thirsting for vengeance, breaking like a rough sea on the steps of the Courthouse; the windows on all sides filled with shrieking women; the wild brandishing of sticks, the showers of stones, the mad struggles with the police. He is recognised, and there is a great shout: 'To hell with Carson'. For a minute it looks as if there will be a rush on him, but he meets them with a look of scornful amusement; then he strolls slowly down the steps of the Court with that very slow gait of his, walking with toes slightly turned in. There is a sudden and extraordinary change in the demeanour of the multitude: perhaps it is something in the strange insolence and courage of his action, always attractive to Irishmen, that awes them; perhaps there is something which sobers them in the physical aspect of the man: the tall, elegant figure with its spare dignity; the narrow pale face and the deep-set eyes; the wide mouth, twisted by a wry smile, half defiant, half cynical; at any rate, the loud cries are succeeded by a low, long-drawn murmur, ugly enough in itself but very different from the previous tumult; the hands are dropped, and even the murmur begins to die away into silence, as a passage mysteriously opens in the crowd; then again the crowd psychology manifests a change in their attitude. Respect and admiration give way to incredulity and curiosity. Can they have been well informed after all? Could a man have dared to have walked alone through them all, if he had really obtained a warrant against their hero? Perhaps the rumour which had caused the riot was wrong. 'Is it true that ye got a warrant for the arrest of O'Brien?' he was asked again and again, and a sea of faces looked eagerly for an answer. Here again was a test of courage, but Carson did not flinch. 'I did,' he answered, and still he makes his way unharmed through the midst of his enemies to an hotel, while Labby, maybe, is still hiding ignominiously beneath the counter. Even then, having left his papers there, he considered that it was still his duty to return: he foresaw the dangers of misrepresentation. Mr Balfour must be informed of the true facts: so back he returns to the scene of the disturbance. The crowds are now dispersing; but there are several pools of blood in the square, and the ground is covered with stones. He finds one party of forty-five police in the square: every one of them bears signs of rough treatment; many of them are suffering from severe wounds; then he passes on to inspect the detachment of the barracks: these have fared no better. One of their number, Constable Leahy, who had given evidence against O'Brien, had been singled out for special attack by the mob: he was to be a cripple all his life. Carson never forgot the sight of him, and four years later, when Mr Gladstone referred to him as being recovered, and as having received ample compensation for the injuries, which were inevitable after such ill-advised orders to the police, he wrote to *The Times*: 'So far from being recovered, as Mr Gladstone alleges, he has ever been, and will always be, a helpless, paralysed cripple. Of all the horrible phases of Parnellism, I beg to assert that the effort of the Ex-Premier to excuse the attempted murder of Constable Leahy, and the murder of Inspector Martin, is the most revolting.'

This was indeed a baptism of fire for a mere lawyer with a new appointment: nothing now need really surprise him; and, indeed, the memory of his mastery of the crowd at Mitchelstown might well have equipped him for all the dangers and contingencies of his long and adventurous career. After having faced that angry mob alone and unarmed, what mattered the bitter taunts of advocates and journalists in the Courts and in the Press, the indignation of flushed, elderly politicians in the House of Commons, the cold disdain of the noblemen of England in the House of Lords? He had faced a mob at Mitchelstown that wished to tear him limb from limb; he had shrugged his shoulders, and passed through them. Such an experience cannot but give strength, and perhaps also arrogance, to the man who has endured it: certainly it tempered and hardened the cold courage which was requisite for a man called upon to play the part assigned to him in the life-and-death struggle against the forces opposed to the Government for the next few years. The impassive, cynical face which he turned to the hostile crowds on this and many other occasions won for him a sinister and almost mythical reputation, among the common folk, as a sort of demon who bore a charmed life.

A fortnight later the two prisoners had been arrested and lodged in Cork Gaol: then the trial began in real earnest. Public interest grew; every day the *Freeman* published a bulletin giving the result of an interview with O'Brien, and the details of his daily life in prison. O'Brien's journey from Cork Gaol to Mitchelstown might have been envied by a Caesar: huge cheering crowds at every railway station;

cordons of police; bouquets of flowers from pretty women; finally, on the last stage of the journey from Fermoy Station to Mitchelstown, the precautions were such as might be adopted by a convoy entering an enemy's country: scouts galloped before the party, and a number of infantry went through the fields beating the hedges; at intervals halts were made to allow the scouts to come back with their reports; round the prisoner's carriage trotted a glittering guard of Hussars. As the cavalcade passed by, people came out from every cottage, waving green boughs and cheering. Finally Mitchelstown was reached. The prisoner, now escorted by Dragoons and police with rifles, was met with tumultuous cheering from the large crowd that had gathered in the fatal square, where was stationed a troop of Hussars with drawn sabres, a company of Royal Scots Fusiliers with fixed bayonets, two large bodies of police – one body with rifles, the other with batons; meanwhile another troop of Hussars was busy moving through the streets to keep them clear. Before O'Brien reached the door from which Carson had made his dramatic departure, two more bouquets had been presented to him by ladies, and he was joined by many distinguished sympathisers, headed by John Dillon. In such supercharged atmosphere the trial began. When Carson came in, O'Brien asked Harrington who was the tall young man. 'That's Carson,' said the latter. 'He looks very young,' said O'Brien.

After the tense atmosphere of drama which had prevailed at the previous hearing, and up till O'Brien's entry into Court, the proceedings were, by contrast, begun with strange formality. Mr Tim Harrington MP, who was in his turn to be prosecuted, appeared for the defence, and argued that his client could not be tried for two speeches on one information; but the Court was inclined to rule against him, and Carson proceeded to deal with both speeches in his opening. Tim

Harrington was continually rising to protest. 'This is an effort to prejudice the case of my client,' he said. 'That is the usual blatter,' replied Carson, and proceeded unperturbed. 'I denounce this,' shouted Harrington, after an interval, 'as an outrage on the liberty of my friend.' 'I will submit to any ruling the Bench makes, but his remarks about outrage on liberty I treat with contempt,' rejoined Carson. 'I would advise you not to indulge in language of that kind, as I am a capital hand at it myself,' persisted Harrington. 'That is only the emanation of an excited mind, and I don't heed it,' said Carson. The only evidence really needed for a conviction was that of the police, who had taken a note of O'Brien's oratory. Harrington raised every kind of objection to the form of the note, and the formality, which the Irish mind is never able to sustain for very long, rapidly degenerated into farce and personalities.

'Oh, go on,' said Carson, in an aside; 'this is proper humbug!'

But Harrington had overheard. 'It is not a proper humbug. You are a humbug to use such language.'

Carson: 'Don't address me, please.'

Harrington: 'I have not the slightest ambition to have a lifelong acquaintance with you.'

Carson (*with a grim smile*): 'It looks as if you did.'

The witness then interposed in the argument of counsel by saying that he had left the meeting 'when it began to stir'.

Harrington: 'That's an Irish answer, any way.'

Carson: 'It is none the worse for that.'

Harrington: 'I'm very glad you're so good an Irishman.'

Carson: 'As good as you.'

In the course of another Crown witness's evidence, Harrington observed to Carson, 'You are low, mean, and contemptible, venal and corrupt. You think by this display you will get some position from the Tory Government, for whom you are doing this job.'

At this sally there was loud applause from the public in Court, and a general uproar; after Harrington had refused, quite naturally, to guarantee the future good behaviour of the Court, the Court was cleared of the public.

In the course of the evidence of Inspector O'Sullivan, it appeared that another report of O'Brien's speech was in the possession of the police; although it was in almost precisely the same terms as the previous report, it was found marked 'Not to be used'. The existence of this second document had been made known to Harrington by a 'traitor' in Dublin Castle. This gave Mr Harrington a legitimate excuse for a loud demonstration.

'I say,' he said, 'that this document was deliberately suppressed by the Crown. I am saying that it is the prosecution who are doing it. I say it was deliberately suppressed for the purpose of making it more easy to imprison my friend.'

Carson: 'That is a pure fabrication.'

Harrington: 'That is a lie, sir.'

On the Bench threatening to remove Mr Harrington, the latter announced that he would remove himself, and take no more part in this solemn farce. He thereupon flung down his brief and left the Court with his solicitor, and the Court adjourned. This dramatic exit had been arranged between O'Brien and Harrington. Carson heard them arranging it. Harrington was to seize some pretext for leaving the Court so that O'Brien could make the speech.

The officials of the Court and counsel were well protected at the adjournment by military and the police; however, another Nationalist member of Parliament, little Dr Tanner, who seemed, as often, to be under the influence of violent emotion, and who had kept on saying during the hearing, 'That fellow Carson is a real scoundrel', got access to Carson and shook his fist in his face. 'You are a mean, ruffianly coward,' he said, 'and I'll take care that before you leave Mitchelstown your head and both your legs will be smashed.'

At the sitting of the Court, Carson saw Tanner sitting just below him in Court, very neat and dapper; he referred to the fact that a Nationalist MP, under the guise of a gentleman, was in Court, who had violently threatened him, at which Dr Tanner was observed shamefacedly to slink out of Court.

O'Brien, deprived of Mr Tim Harrington's valuable legal assistance, now conducted his own defence, which was an eloquent, but quite irrelevant, defence of the Nationalist cause. The magistrates could do nothing to stop him, and he concluded with the statement that no public-spirited magistrate ought to condemn him for hasty words uttered when his blood was boiling, and that the question the Court ought really to decide was whether or no a great wrong was not being done to the tenants whom he had addressed. 'I will be very proud,' he said, 'to suffer something for a people proved worthy of suffering. I appeal to the great jury of English public opinion, confident that they will reverse the decree now passed upon me.'

It is fair to record that the speech reads amazingly well today in the old print of the *Freeman's Journal*, and its effect on the crowded Court, packed again on the second day with his friends and sympathisers, must have been great. But, as he knew himself, his eloquence was of no avail for the immediate issue, and he and his fellow-prisoner were sentenced to three months' imprisonment. Bail was, however, allowed, and a number of ingenious expedients were applied by way of appeal to prevent the sentence being effective; and although in the end the appeal was unsuccessful, much water of the Liffey flowed past Dublin before O'Brien saw the prison cells, and refused, during his imprisonment, as a protest, to wear his 'breeches'. Indeed, as he admitted in a speech immediately afterwards, the sole reason for his appeal was to gain time, and to delay his imprisonment, so that he could help to carry on the Plan of Campaign, and stir up trouble for the Government.

They were to meet on many occasions, and Carson was almost invariably the man chosen to prosecute William O'Brien, always a dangerous duty to the advocate. Their relationship became almost a matter of routine, and O'Brien once said, 'This young man thinks he has a passion for prosecuting me.' On appeal from this case, before Mr Hamilton, the Recorder of Cork, the menacing attitude of the crowd became even more critical than at Mitchelstown: there at least the threats and riot had been outside the four walls of the Court, but now an effort was made to break up the session of the Court; the crowd rushed forward to rescue O'Brien and the young prosecutor stood at his desk with his papers in front of him and a revolver in his hand for five minutes, keeping the people at bay, until order had been restored by the police.

So many were their encounters, as advocate and prisoner, that it is impossible to record them all, but one or two are worthy of mention. Early in the spring of 1888 Coercion had made an appreciable effect, and the forces of order were gaining ground; but Mr Balfour made the premature statement in the House of Commons that the Land League was a thing of the past. This observation was well calculated to touch O'Brien's vanity, and he was soon in a ferment of agitation once again. 'Balfour has said,' he exclaimed, 'that the League is a thing of the past. We will fasten him to that phrase, and it will be his epitaph as a statesman. He is either the most audacious liar that ever swore the lid off the pot, or the most arrant donkey that ever floundered up to his neck in an Irish bog, and some 10 000 people will contradict him next Sunday ... It is not the Mitchelstown branch of the Land League, but the Mitchelstown rent office, that is really suppressed.'

He was once more prosecuted for attending a meeting of an illegal society in a proclaimed district. The usual precautions were taken, preliminaries gone through, which were always associated with a trial of Mr O'Brien. A regiment of Hussars was in attendance, and all the rest of it. Carson was for the prosecution and Tim Healy for the defence. The defence was an amusing refinement of logic and Hibernian in the extreme. The meeting had not been a meeting of the National League as such, but it had merely been a peaceful demonstration of citizens of the County of Galway convened together to protest against Balfour's false statement that the National League was dead in that district, when it was really very much alive: it was a public meeting called together to give Balfour the lie, to expose the ministerial statement, and to promote the good relations of the two countries, which could not exist by falsehood, by the bold declaration of the truth. This was the defence of Tim Healy, most skilful of Parliamentary obstructionists, and it was very diverting, although *The Times* testily described the subtlety of his argument as being 'so impenetrable that only the defendant's counsel can understand it'; again the *Thunderer* said, 'The defence would be ridiculous, if the proceedings were not so utterly dull.' After proving the speech by reports, Carson had to put in evidence the 'proclamation' of the district and of the illegality of the National League in order to establish the competency of the Court under the Crimes Act. Tim Healy solemnly objected. 'This is not evidence against Mr O'Brien,' he said. 'The Lord Lieutenant's opinion of the legality of the meeting cannot affect Mr O'Brien. His opinion may be very good about Punchestown or horseracing.'

The Lord Lieutenant was the Marquess of Londonderry, a

notable sportsman with whom Carson was already on intimate terms of friendship. 'I think,' retorted Carson scornfully, 'that that is the most scandalous observation to make about His Excellency, the representative of Her Majesty in this country.'

Surely the Muse of History must have laughed up her sleeve: the irony of this is deep; for Carson, who was upholding the dignity of His Excellency, was one day to defy the authority of his successor, not by words, but by 100 000 armed men; and the insolent young legal critic of the Marquess of Londonderry was one day to step into his shoes as the 'Representative of His Majesty' in Ireland as first Governor-General of the Irish Free State.

In opening the defence, Mr Healy announced that he would call every single man, woman, and child, who had attended the meeting, several thousands strong if necessary, to prove that the meeting was not officially that of the National League; and at once he began to play this game of solemn farce, which he, with his training of Parliamentary obstruction under Parnell, was well qualified to do: his purpose was mere obstruction and to keep Mr O'Brien, who was on bail, out of prison as long as possible. Carson cross-examined a few witnesses until he saw that Healy intended to be as good as his word. 'Go on producing your witnesses,' he said wearily. The magistrate tried to rule the procession of witnesses out as irrelevant repetition, but in vain: for thick and fast they came, in seemingly inexhaustible supply. The case might thus have dragged on for weeks if, on the third or fourth day, the depositions and all the official documents in the case had not been stolen while in the custody of the Court. The whole case had to begin wearily afresh; Carson asked that the loss of the depositions should be strictly proved, but the magistrates said that was unnecessary. Tim Healy was delighted at this, because he knew that there would be a bull point in the appeal before the Chief Baron, as indeed it proved. O'Brien called no witness for the defence, as he had a political engagement at Mitchelstown and wished to be released on bail pending the appeal.

Eventually the Chief Baron quashed the conviction on the ground that the loss of the depositions had not been strictly proved, and sent the case back to the magistrates to be tried a third time. A year later Carson and Healy again faced each other in another William O'Brien case at Tralee. This time Healy was not so calm: he refused to give in his cross-examination a certain police chief the title of 'Colonel', which was his due, and called him simply by his surname. He did this again and again, and at last succeeded in infuriating the resident magistrate, who said that the officer was entitled to his military rank. 'Whatever he may be,' retorted Healy with asperity, 'I think he is a sneak.' The magistrate then ordered Healy out of Court. He refused to go, and a scene of wild confusion followed, in which a solicitor rushed to the help of Healy, and the people, according to *The Times* report, 'in a most disgraceful way began to hoot the magistrates'. Carson was most distressed, and 'for the honour of the Bar' had tried to make peace between the Bench and his learned friend. He immediately proposed an adjournment to enable O'Brien to obtain other legal assistance. O'Brien, seeing a good ground for appeal slipping from under his feet, shouted indignantly, 'Unquestionably, no. If it were to purchase heaven for me, I would not.'

'In calmer moments, Mr O'Brien,' said Carson courteously, 'take a different course.'

Next day the police and military were reinforced, and drawn up outside the Court. O'Brien appeared without counsel. He said: 'I only want my speeches read to the public, if I am to get six months.' He told the clerk to read them distinctly, and the usual sentence followed, and O'Brien was released on bail, pending an appeal.

It was Carson's duty to prosecute during those years the greater number of the political leaders of Ireland, and his skill in obtaining convictions against even such skilled advocates as Tim Healy became proverbial; it was fatal to be prosecuted by Carson. Perhaps the most picturesque occasion of all was the prosecution of the Lord Mayor of Dublin himself, the Right Honourable T D Sullivan, in 1887 for publishing a notice of a meeting of the National League in his newspaper, the *Nation*. The city council decided by special resolution to attend their Lord Mayor's trial in state from the Mansion House to the Police Court. So his lordship proceeded in court dress, wearing his mayoral robes, attended by the sword and mace carried by the city marshal, the town clerk, and the members of the Corporation following in a carriage procession. On entering the Court, his worship walked to the table in front of the dock, and the sword-bearer gravely followed him. The police inspectors stopped this, and the City Fathers, with their minions, were forced to return to the gallery for the rest of the case. When the Mayor was acquitted by the magistrate on a point of law, the homeward progress of the Lord Mayor was even more triumphant than that of his outward journey, and the cheers of the crowd were so insistent at the Mansion House that they were rewarded by a mayoral speech from the balcony. Alas, when Carson took the case to the Exchequer Division, the Chief Baron pronounced that the magistrate was wrong in law, and the poor Lord Mayor had to go to prison after all.

The last case in which Carson and O'Brien met was the prosecution of five men at the Cork Assizes for taking part in the Tipperary riots in 1890. O'Brien appeared in this case as a witness, to prove that the crowd which had come to Tipperary to see him prosecuted there once again was a perfectly peaceful gathering, and had been scandalously manhandled by the police under their commandant, Colonel Caddell. Nor was O'Brien the most distinguished witness in the case. The Right Hon John Morley, ex-Chief Secretary for Ireland, who had accompanied O'Brien to the trial, also gave evidence for the defence. Tipperary had recently been the scene of terrible rioting: it had, a few months previous to O'Brien's trial, almost been laid waste, and property damaged to the value of £50 000. The prosecution of O'Brien, therefore, which had led so many times, as we have seen, to serious rioting, at Tipperary, was of special moment to the police, and careful preparations and dispositions of troops were made. Once more the presence of English members of Parliament probably conduced to the public disorder, which, as usual, occurred; as Carson said in his opening, 'When these English gentlemen are brought over to witness some of the terrible ways of the RIC, something of this sort is always got up in some way or other; and when they go back they make political capital out of it.' It fell to Carson, now an Irish QC, to cross-examine John Morley. His conduct of the Crimes Act prosecutions had been fully reported in *The Times*; accounts of his intrepid courage and caustic words had already been read with interest by those interested in Ireland; but it was his cross-examination of Morley that really made him famous to the English public as a whole. Now Carson, although he had not prosecuted O'Brien in the case in question, was really the greatest expert in the world on the results on public behaviour of the prosecution of William O'Brien. Morley had made an unfortunate speech at Manchester, saying that two English village policemen could have dealt with the whole affair. There were many amusing passages between the two clever men during Morley's interrogation; it was good-humoured throughout, and, according to Carson, the occasion 'made his friendship with Morley'. He made great play with the 'two village constables', and asked him, if he had been Chief Secretary – he had been compelled when in that position to suppress very grievous riots in Belfast, as everyone knew – if he would have used two village constables. Morley had to say, 'No. I should have allowed the crowd to go on till it reached the point of disorder which called for police intervention.'

'At what particular point would you intervene?' – 'When there was a breach of the public peace.'

'Unless a policeman were wounded, you would not say there was very serious disorder?' – 'Oh, I would not say that.'

Finally, Morley had to admit, when pressed, to political prejudice. 'I cannot drop my politics,' he said, 'at Tipperary railway station.'

The trial lasted several days, and, when Mr Justice Munroe was summing up to the jury, an extraordinary event occurred. A heavy piece of wood fell on Carson's head. The Judge, knowing of the many dangers and vicissitudes through which the young QC had passed, and of his charmed life, looked up anxiously to see if he was hurt, and what was the cause. Had they got him at last?

'I think, my lord, it was accidental,' said Carson.

His lordship went on with his charge, but very soon there was a cry of 'Fire'. The Court was crowded, and there was a smell of smoke, but the Judge said it was only a chimney smoking, and continued. There followed, however, an ominous crackle, and it was soon seen that the woodwork of the Court was ablaze. The Court was adjourned, but there was no panic, and the Judge, sitting calmly on the bench like Casabianca, was the last to leave. Whether it was arson or accident will never be known; but at all events the crowd was delighted and amused at the disaster: as someone said, when Carson and O'Brien met the sparks were sure to fly. When the flames reached the figure of Justice on the cornice and the Union Jack flying on the mast came crashing down and was burnt, the delight of the crowd knew no bounds. This was a portent indeed. The whole Courthouse was destroyed, and the county records, some of great value and antiquity, were burnt.

The next day the Court met again elsewhere. Two of the prisoners were acquitted, and the jury disagreed about three of them. Eleven jurymen were for a conviction, and one, an ardent member of the National League, held out. 'We had not challenged him,' said Carson, 'he looked so eminently respectable.' With one member of the League on the jury it was of course almost impossible to secure a conviction in such a case.

The prosecution, in the face of hostile and menacing crowds, of national heroes so intrepid that they never feared the discomforts of Kilmainham Gaol, was not the only duty that fell to Crown counsel in those days: sometimes they had to prosecute humbler folk who committed crimes far graver in the eyes of the law and of humanity, but who, according to strongly held opinions, were influenced or motivated, directly or indirectly, by those unselfish and idealistic patriots in the cause of freedom, or the organisations set up under their auspices. Major Traill, one of the resident magistrates, divided those who committed these outrages into three classes: the fanatics, the hired assassins, and others upon whom duty under the rules of their own organisation, which they might have light-heartedly joined without knowing its true and secret purpose, fell by lot or detail to carry out some terrible act, their own death being the penalty for disobedience. These Irish cases stand, therefore, on quite a different basis from normal crime, and in the case of the unwilling assassin, upon whom the fatal lot has fallen to act, special considerations of pity arise, which do not belong to ordinary criminals. On the other hand, the hired assassin is an even more loathsome creature than the most cruel or cold-blooded poisoner who seeks his own gain. The case of the Queen against Hayes and Moriarty, in which Carson was engaged with Peter O'Brien for the Crown, serves as an example among many of the latter class. On 31 January 1887, John Carroll, the parish clerk in Lixnaw, eight miles from Tralee, was woken up at about six o'clock in the morning by a girl's cry, 'Get up, for God's sake; my father's dying.' He hastened out into the road, and found there a young girl, daughter of a neighbour, Norah Fitzmaurice, trying to tend her father, who was lying in a pool of blood by the roadside, bleeding and mortally hurt by several wounds inflicted from gunshots. It was a fine winter's night, and the moon was shining down with uncanny brightness. He helped to carry the poor old man – he was sixty-six – into a neighbour's house, and to make him comfortable. The village priest, the Rev John Sheehan, was summoned, and arrived in time to give James Fitzmaurice the last rites of the Roman Church. It was not till the light that the police arrived; Norah Fitzmaurice told them a pitiful and broken story. Her father was a 'boycotted' man, and he had been granted police protection; that night he had had to take some pigs to market at Lixnaw for the fair on the following day; he had driven away with them from his farm at about 5.30 am in his cart, his pigs railed off on the cart behind. At first Constables Hunt and Ryan of the RIC followed behind at a distance, until Fitzmaurice told them that the moon was bright, and he would not need them; father and daughter then proceeded onwards by themselves until they reached a dark stretch of the road with a wall on one side and thick foliage on the other; there they encountered a man whose appearance aroused the young woman's suspicions; he was not disguised, like the man in the Barbavilla case, but he looked keenly at the old man and his daughter, as if he were seeking to recognise someone; then, as the cart passed a bend in the road near a bridge from which a long straight strip of road led into the village of Lixnaw, the old man dismounted to ease his horse, and walked behind the cart still carrying his whip. The girl saw that the stranger was following them, and had been joined by another man; she saw that they were both low, thickset fellows; she saw them begin to run, as if to catch up the cart. Knowing that her father was 'boycotted', and fearing foul play, she begged her father to climb back into the cart; but he was a friendly old man, and, weary of the boycott by his neighbours, he turned round to begin a friendly chat. The girl heard angry words almost at once; she saw her father raising his whip, then beaten down and overpowered by the two young men, who each fired at him at point-blank range with some sort of firearm; her horse was startled, it tried to bolt before she could get down to look to her father; the old man dragged himself towards her, calling out loudly that he was dead; meanwhile the assailants had disappeared.

The deed had been a bold one, committed so close to the village and within a few yards of inhabited houses; when the police questioned the poor girl as to whether she had recognised either of the two men, she said it was a mystery, but the police were sure from her behaviour that she really knew more about the matter. Inside the house lay the body of her father, covered by a white sheet, near the fire: she took a last look at his face and saw that his brow was contracted as if he had been in pain before death, and through the sheet she saw the blood soaking from his wounds; then, her fear overcome by emotion, she began to whisper to the police: she told them that the two men were short and thickset and that one was like

Mike Carroll, the son of the clerk, who was sitting in the chair in the kitchen; she gave the heights of the men, but not their names. Afterwards it was understood that she had identified two men. At all events, two young men, Daniel Hayes and Daniel Moriarty, the former a stranger to the district, the latter a lodger in a house close to the scene of the murder, had been arrested and were committed for trial. The trial took place before Mr Justice O'Brien at the Wicklow Assizes on 28 March; Peter the Packer and Edward Carson were counsel for the prosecution, and Mr Martin Burke defended the prisoners. The facts of the night of 31 January were recounted and proved by Norah Fitzmaurice, who showed herself a most unwilling and ambiguous witness on the first day of the trial: her identification of the two witnesses was not convincing, and she seemed restrained by some overmastering fear. The Crown had valuable information connecting the prisoner with the Land League, but this was reserved by the wary Carson for cross-examination. After the adjournment she had an interview with O'Brien and Carson, telling them that one of the murderers was certainly Hayes. On the next day Sergeant Harris of the RIC told how he had come to arrest Moriarty: he watched Norah Fitzmaurice walking along the village street and pass Moriarty. He saw the girl speak to him and then look earnestly after him.

On the third day of the trial Mr Burke opened the defence: he said he could frame a complete alibi. He would call witnesses to prove that the prisoners were sleeping peacefully miles away at the time the murder was committed; he said that the girl had told quite a different story in Court to that which she had told the police. The police, he said, had obviously influenced her mind by suggestion. Of course, witnesses were called who framed a careful 'Westmeath alibi'; and so circumstantial was their account that their evidence was difficult to shake; but

Carson took it as common form, as being carefully prepared in advance, always possible in a conspiracy. It was otherwise with the more independent evidence. John Carroll, the parish clerk, was called to contradict the evidence of Norah Fitzmaurice: according to his account, he had asked her, 'Why do you pick on Danny Moriarty?' She had replied, 'I don't think he is the man at all.' Peter O'Brien then rose to cross-examine: the witness perforce admitted that the girl had named Hayes to him as the murderer, and that he had described this as a lie. But there were further questions. Had the witness subscribed to the fund for the defence? No, but he had been invited so to do by the solicitor for the defence and Thomas Dowling, local secretary of the National League. Was he a member of the National League? Thereupon O'Brien put to the witness a resolution of the League concerning the murdered man, and the history of the old man's misfortunes emerged. On Sunday, 12 June, a resolution had been moved and seconded that 'as James Fitzmaurice of Ahabeg still persists in allowing his cattle to graze on the farm from which his brother Edmund was recently evicted, we hereby call on the public to treat him as a land-grabber of the most infamous kind'. Afterwards another resolution was passed referring to Fitzmaurice as a miserable man, who had 'been so base and unnatural as to grab his brother's land'.

This murder had indeed arisen, like so many other crimes, as a result of an embittered dispute between brothers concerning some land at Ahabeg: it appeared that up to two months before the murder James and Edmund were joint tenants of certain land belonging to Mr S M Russey of Tralee: there was, however, a great difference between the brothers: while James was industrious and thrifty, Edmund was otherwise. Edmund fell into arrears with his share of the rent, and so both tenants were evicted; ultimately James redeemed the arrears of rent and took over the whole property, and, though he offered to give his brother a third of the land and to stock it for him, his brother regarded his action as an outrage on fraternal decency. He won the sympathy and interest of the Land League, who summoned James before them; the latter refused to come, and the hostile resolution was passed. From this moment his fate was sealed. Public opinion had been roused to a high pitch by the idea of a man 'stealing his brother's land'; the poor old man was held up almost as a fratricide, and the most stringent boycott was put into operation; he was afforded police protection, with which he unfortunately dispensed on the night of his death; all his movements were being carefully watched.

The witness upon whose evidence Carson and O'Brien had really burnt the midnight oil was the priest, the Rev Father Sheehan, who had performed the last duties for the dying man; the defence unwisely called him as their most important witness. Norah, it appeared, had told this priest on the morning after the murder that she did not know the murderer. 'Oh, no, father,' she had said. 'But one of them was a stout low fellow, and the other was for all the world like that boy.' She had then pointed at the son of the last witness, John Carroll: this was a considerable score for the defence as the boy was in Court and wholly unlike either of the prisoners.

Not in vain had Carson studied the Irish mind: had the priest given the girl any advice? Oh, yes, he had told her to be cautious as to what she said. When was that? That was after she had identified the two prisoners: he had told her she should not swear anything that she had not known for certain. He might have admonished her to be cautious again after her father's burial; and had he so advised her, being her pastor, and knowing that she would pay heed? Yes, that was so. He had said to her, 'Do you suppose that anyone would be so foolish as to walk before a number of policemen, past the house where the murdered man lay, if he had committed the crime?' What did she reply? She said 'that he might well have done so'. Then the priest had again cautioned her: 'was she convicting him simply because of a grey coat and a brown hat, which the prisoner had, which were like what she had seen on the murderer? '

The poor girl's reluctance to identify the two prisoners was now more than explained, and the case looked black indeed for the prisoners. They returned to their cells, and Moriarty, no doubt remembering that the informer in the Phoenix Park case had turned King's evidence and saved his neck, thought to do likewise by turning 'approver' in the same way. This was a constant feature of these trials. Carson was asleep, and was dragged out of bed by the Crown solicitor to deal with the new situation. He had to consider Moriarty's detailed confession to the crime, which was written and signed by his own hand. But he was sure that the jury would convict, and did not see why this foul creature should escape his punishment in this way. O'Brien was not at first disposed to agree, but he was persuaded. Moriarty, however, persisted, and, seeking to win golden opinions, gave the police a statement implicating Hayes and five other men; when he knew that the Crown was obdurate, he attempted to commit suicide by breaking his cell window and trying to cut his throat with the glass. The gaoler, awakened by the sound of smashing glass, prevented him; he appeared in the dock next day with sticking-plaster concealing the wound in his throat.

Mr Justice O'Brien charged the jury for five hours strongly against the prisoners' interests. 'The murder,' he said, 'is plainly the result of a conspiracy. I will not stop to enquire into the causes at work.' The fact of the prisoners being strangers to each other did not weaken the case against them: it was often so, he said, in conspiracies, when men were selected to do such dreadful work. After a retirement of half an hour, the jury returned with a verdict of guilty against both prisoners, and Carson's judgment was proved right. Neither man, by the rules of evidence then prevalent, could give evidence on his own behalf; but when sentence was pronounced Hayes said, 'I defy the rope: I am innocent.' Moriarty too called out that he was innocent, when his written confession of guilt, which had not been used by the Crown, was lying on the desk in front of Carson. Moriarty at first confessed, but recanted immediately before his execution. 'I made a false statement,' he wrote, 'in Wicklow Prison about 10 pm on the night when I was found guilty, when I accused men that I did not know, whether they were or not. I am going before my God tomorrow, and I am after telling the truth, and the reason I made that statement was to try and save my own neck.' But Hayes protested his innocence throughout the proceedings; his last written words were, 'I would die a thousand deaths before I would go to God with a lie on my lips. I declare to God that you, Gerry Fitzmaurice, I never did see to my knowledge. I did not shoot you on that morning; I do not know who shot you; Moriarty I did not know in my life before. I was not with you that morning; I forgive all who swore my life away; may God forgive me as I forgive them. – Daniel Hayes'

When the Black Flag was hoisted to show that the men had been hanged, a loud wailing was set up by the dead men's relatives; but the sequel was interesting. Mr Thomas Dowling, the local secretary of the Land League, who had signed the resolutions against Fitzmaurice, organised a cruel boycott of Norah Fitzmaurice: when she went into Mass for the first time after the trial he made the whole congregation go out; she was protected in church by forty armed policemen. Dowling was prosecuted for this under the Crimes Act, and sentenced to six months' imprisonment. His counsel defended his action as 'an error in taste'. But so persistent was the boycott that a relief fund was raised on her behalf in England; later she married an officer of the RIC, and it is to be hoped that she found happiness after her troubles, although to be married to a member of that gallant corps meant a life of constant anxiety.

The circumstances of the case made a profound impression on public opinion, and it was at this time that the Vatican made its famous edict in condemnation of the Plan of Campaign, which induced one witty Ulsterman to say to a Catholic, 'Say, Paddy, have ye heard the news? The Pope's turned Protestant.'

So, for three long years, 'Coercion Carson' went about Ireland doing his difficult and dangerous duty against the agitator, the moonlighter and the Fenian, and the Parliamentary Nationalist, in the face of the most turbulent opposition and daily threats to his life. The political leaders hated him no less than the rest, with the exception of his friends and colleagues Tim Healy and John Redmond: for these two, although the latter was prosecuted by him successfully at least once, always found him 'the same friendly fellow' even in the embarrassing duty of prosecuting them and their friends. Carson met Redmond in counsel's robing-room in an Assize Court at the time of the famous 'split' in the Nationalist Party as the result of Parnell's citation as co-respondent in Captain O'Shea's divorce case, when the Irish leader, deserted by half his party, was wearing out his health by his invincible and arrogant spirit in a desperate and losing campaign. 'Are you too going to desert your leader in his hour of need, John Redmond?' asked Carson. 'No,' replied Redmond; 'would I be leaving him because of the love of his life?' 'I'm glad to hear it,' said Carson, and it was this answer that made Carson Redmond's friend till his dying day. The other Nationalist leaders, however, regarded Carson's advocacy with a certain humorous fatalism. As one of them wrote many years afterwards, 'If, being a Nationalist, you made a speech to which Dublin Castle took exception, and were prosecuted by Edward Carson, you might just as well make arrangements for six months' imprisonment in Kilmainham Gaol before you went into Court.' But many of the humbler agitators regarded him as a sort of dreadful ogre, whose name was used to frighten children. Against his own express wishes, he was shadowed by police night and day, and sometimes, when he drove about, armed police would beat the hedges and explore the woods on each side of the road. Had it not been for these precautions, he could hardly have escaped assassination. His name was respected and feared, but it was also bitterly hated; he came to be known as a man without compassion and without fear. Threatening letters came almost every day with unfailing regularity; postcards with skull and crossbones; model coffins were sent to him; and humble people who dared to speak to him were subjected to cruel boycott. There were curses and threats as he drove by, and he was once stoned in the streets, for which some of his assailants were sent to prison for six months. 'It was a very nasty feeling,' said Carson, 'to feel the stones flying through the air so near one.' It was small wonder that his wife, when she saw him go off to his work any morning, did not know whether she would see him next alive or dead.

All this left the young Crown prosecutor cold: the threats and attempts at intimidation only hardened the nerve and will of 'Coercion Carson'. The scene at Mitchelstown had taught him to despise danger; and, though his exceptional charm was always able to win, not merely admiration and devotion from his associates and subordinates, but sincere affection from allies and opponents alike, he cared neither for popularity nor unpopularity. He had his duty to perform, and, moreover, he fully understood the implications of that duty: a strong conviction of the necessity of his work reinforced his sense of professional zeal. No man saw more of the secret machinations of the forces of disorder, and his deepest sympathies were aroused by the sufferings of the unfortunate, and often helpless, victims of the widespread conspiracy which was producing outrage and conspiracy all over the south and west of Ireland. No man was more convinced than he that Ireland needed twenty years' resolute government by the strong hand of England; the grim facts disclosed by every prosecution under the Crimes Act were being stored up in his mind as a new and concrete argument for the Union. It sometimes happens that a man is considered intransigent and unreasonable by others whose wisdom, compared to the knowledge of that man, is but ignorance. What English 'Unionist' who voted for the Irish Treaty in 1922 really guessed, or, if he had ever known, remembered what a mass and depth of experience and knowledge lay behind that bitter, accusing, and memorable speech of the newly appointed law lord?

8. QC and MP

In 1889 Peter the Packer achieved his life's ambition, and became Lord Chief Justice of Ireland. He advised Carson to apply for a 'silk gown', and to become one of the 'Queen's Counsel in Ireland learned in the law'. After three such strenuous years as a junior, Carson was not unwilling to take the risk always involved in 'taking silk', whether in Dublin or London. Henceforward he would not be concerned in any of the often lucrative preliminaries of a lawsuit, such as pleading and so on; his duty was now to 'lead' in Court. He could all the more easily leave his Crown appointment because, under Balfour's stern rule, things had definitely begun to improve in Ireland. Crime was conspicuously on the decline. *The Times* review of the year in Ireland was able to state that 'the pledge of success given at the beginning of the year has been fully redeemed. ... The dark forebodings which for a long time were heard on every side have given place to expressions of hope and confidence.' There had been a bumper harvest, and money was being spent far more freely in the pursuit of business, charity, and pleasure. Ireland was no longer the Niobe of Nations. There is no greater pleasure than in being shown the good consequences of hard work; and to Carson at any rate, as to others concerned in the Irish Executive, it looked at the end of 1889 as if their courage and diligence had been of much practical value to the island. Both Balfour and Carson were alive and unhurt, and it seemed as if the black chapter which had begun with the murder of Lord Frederick Cavendish was closed.

Carson was only thirty-five years old and a QC, the youngest in Ireland; henceforward he was chiefly to be engaged on civil work, till his career took him away to England. He now had a nice house in Merrion Square, and a little country house at

Sorrento, in County Dublin, which overlooked the bay. So blue is the face of the sea there in summer that it was easy for him to imagine himself by a flight of Irish fancy as in the Mediterranean. It was hardly possible at the Irish Bar to earn more than £3 000 a year; but living was cheap in Ireland, and Carson was becoming a very prosperous man. Although chiefly engaged at *nisi prius*, he was sometimes briefed in the more important prosecutions for the Crown. Among such cases was the celebrated trial of Father McFadden and his fellow-prisoners for the murder of Inspector Martin, known as the Gweedore Case. Father McFadden was one of the priests who was most actively engaged in promoting the Plan of Campaign among his people. His chapel, which was built in a hollow, was connected with his house by an elevated causeway. Inspector Martin was sent to arrest him, with a few policemen, a quite inadequate force having regard to the feeling at the time. After the priest had celebrated Mass, the inspector met the priest on the causeway, and notified him that he must arrest him under the Crimes Act. The priest asked for the warrant, and this was in the hands of the sergeant, who was at some distance. The priest then struggled with the inspector, and a large crowd of people saw this happen on the causeway from below, as if it had been a stage. They rushed up to save the reverend father, and Inspector Martin drew his sword and slowly retreated before the crowd with the priest; as he retreated, someone struck him on the head with a heavy stake from behind, rendering him unconscious. The crowd then rushed and showered blows upon him, which killed him. After a trial of many days, one prisoner was convicted of manslaughter, and others, including McFadden, under the advice of Tim Healy, who was defending, pleaded guilty to a minor count. The case, which excited tremendous interest in England, was chiefly conducted by the Attorney-General, who led Carson and a number of other counsel, for the Crown. Two curious facts, well calculated to impress the superstitious mind, emerged in this trial. A night or two before his death, Inspector Martin dined at the Gweedore Hotel, the thirteenth to twelve other messmates. On the night before the murder, one of the policemen who had been observing and guarding McFadden's house at night in the moonlight came running in with terror to tell his comrades that he had seen the body of a policeman lying dead at the priest's door. The others at once came up to see and to bring succour to the dead officer, if there was one, but they found not a soul there, alive or dead.

If Carson never forgot Mitchelstown, neither did Mr Gladstone, and his speeches against Coercion had made, with the wonderful eloquence and inspiration of his last crusade, a deep impression on the sentimental English people. *The Times*, a great strength of the Unionist cause, had blundered badly in purchasing the clumsy and vulgar Piggott forgeries and attributing them to Parnell. The Government had also blundered badly by practically associating themselves with *The Times*, and using the forgeries as an argument for the Irish policy, and, further, in appointing an unconstitutional tribunal, called the Special Commission, consisting of three Judges sitting without a jury but armed with powers of enquiry into the affairs of Irish politicians, which recalled the days of the Star Chamber to the liberal conscience of the people. Although a mass of information was acquired unfavourable to the Nationalist cause, the only matter remembered by the public was that the miserable forger Piggott had confessed to forging the letters purporting to be in Parnell's handwriting, and implicating him in the Invincible conspiracy, and that the Government had, in effect, put an innocent man on his trial by unconstitutional means on the strength of a forgery which any competent expert in handwriting would at once have condemned. Later, when Parnell's personal tragedy broke up the Irish Party, and there was no unity among the Irishmen themselves, the Gladstonian appeal to English public opinion soon recovered from this temporary setback and gathered increasing force as the time approached for a General Election. The country began to ask itself: has all this coercion of a people, and persecution of its leaders, done much good? May not the Grand Old Man have been right after all?

Balfour had retired from the Chief Secretary's lodge before the General Election, and had returned in triumph from Ireland, heretofore the grave of political reputations, with greatly increased prestige, to lead the House of Commons. Long before he reached this high position, he had made up his mind to bring Carson to Westminster if he could; but the lawyer was hard to persuade; he had his career mapped out for the Bar, and for the Bar alone; besides, he was not a Conservative, but a Liberal Unionist; the Liberal Unionists had sat aloof during the whole of the Salisbury administration, and it was doubtful if Chamberlain, the Radical and one-time Republican, would ever advise them to join a Conservative administration. Balfour, as leader of the House, was still preoccupied with Irish policy, and he was missing Carson's counsel.

On the eve of the General Election, Balfour decided to make Carson his Irish Solicitor-General if he could procure for him a seat. This was a high honour for so young a man. There was to be a vacancy by the retirement of Serjeant Madden QC in the representation of Trinity College, Dublin, which was a two-member constituency, and Balfour thought that the prospects of a seat at his old College would attract Carson, and eventually he persuaded him to stand if he were offered a seat. Meanwhile, however, there was difficulty among the dons of Trinity

College. Dublin University was historically a Conservative stronghold, and had invariably returned two true-blue Tories. But Carson, with his Radical past well known to the Historical Society, could only stand as a Liberal, and a very keen contest on party lines ensued, the solitary contest which he had to face in twenty-six years as member for Trinity College. The other candidates were David Plunkett QC, afterwards Lord Rathmore, whose election was a foregone conclusion, and Colonel J C Lowry. Feeling ran high among the dons. The Vice-Provost, Joseph Carson, commonly known as 'bloody old Joe', said that the University had never been 'tainted with Liberalism', and wrote a letter to the newspapers expressing the hope that no one would be induced to vote for Edward Carson in the false belief of any relationship between the candidate and Joseph Carson. Edward Carson replied that he was glad the Vice-Provost had taken this course, as otherwise in his own interests he would have had to make clear to the public that he was no kinsman to Joseph Carson. The contest was almost one between the Bench of Bishops and the Queen's Bench. Among the voters, all the bishops were on Lowry's committee, while all the Queen's Counsel, except one who was the Colonel's brother-in-law, supported Carson. The ballot-box had not yet been introduced into the academic atmosphere, and voting was by show of hands. It can well be imagined that these Parliamentary elections were made the most of by members of the University. Carson liked it, as all through his life he enjoyed 'a good rag'. The candidates had to appear in academic dress on the hustings and to show cause by speeches why they should be elected, but the undergraduates made such a deafening tumult that it was impossible to be heard. The result of the poll was, however, an easy victory for 'Coercion Carson', already rather a hero for personal if not for political reasons at his old University. The poor Colonel, while Carson had been draped in the full glory of the dress of a Master of Arts, had been forced to appear in an undergraduate's gown, since he had won no degree. The result of the poll was: Right Hon D R Plunkett QC: 2 188; E H Carson QC: 1 609; Colonel J C Lowry: 897. He was the first Liberal ever to be elected to the British Parliament by Dublin University since the union. Immediately after the election Carson went out to Vice-Regal Lodge to attend a reception after the wedding of the Lord Lieutenant's daughter as the newly elected member for the University. He met there Archbishop Alexander, the Primate of Ireland, who had taken a strong and leading part against Carson in the election; but his gentle and charming wife, the writer of many hymns, came up to him at Vice-Regal Lodge and said, 'But I was on your side all the time, Mr Carson.'

The new member heaved a sigh of relief: he was glad to be member for Trinity College, but regarded the whole incident as irrelevant to his career and as a foible of Arthur Balfour. 'Well, thank God that's all over,' he said to a friend. 'I'll be staying in Parliament for two or three years, then I'll go on the Bench at the Four Courts and lead a quiet life.'

In a week or two he was crossing St George's Channel on his way to Westminster, with his friend John Ross, recently elected for Londonderry, where, before he went on the highest Judicial Bench of Great Britain, many stormy and adventurous years awaited him. The quiet life for which he longed, and to which four years of daily peril had perhaps entitled him, was postponed for just on thirty years. Fortune was beckoning her modest and reluctant favourite onwards to a great career. As he stood by John Ross's side, his eyes were not cast hopefully towards London, but affectionately back to the city where he had been born and educated, and where he had worked indefatigably for fifteen years.

9. St Stephen's and The Temple

The general election of 1892 reversed the decision which the country had clearly given on the Union in 1886, although the Nationalists and the Parnellites lost three seats in Ireland to the Unionists. The Conservatives lost 48 seats, the Liberal Unionists dropped from 78 to 47, and together the Home Rule Liberals and Nationalists had a majority of 40. The decisive voice of Lord Randolph Churchill, who had resigned the leadership of the Commons on a small matter of economy, was already faltering, and the hand of a fatal malady was already heavy upon him. Moreover, Mr Gladstone, despite Home Rule, which had threatened to ruin the Liberal Party and terminate his leadership, was once more leader of the greatest party in the State. This was at least a great *tour de force* of courage and vitality at his age. Lord Salisbury, however, determined to face Parliament with a Queen's speech, although it was obvious the Government must go out on the debate on the Address. The office of Solicitor-General for Ireland, which had fallen to Carson on Balfour's recommendation, was clearly to be held by him on very transitory tenure. A few days' debate on the Address, and then he would be an Irish QC whose livelihood was in Dublin, but who would constantly have to be in attendance at Westminster to vote and to give advice to Arthur Balfour in the vital Home Rule debates which were sure to follow.

Perhaps he might be able to pick up some practice in England: he hardly thought so; it would be better to remain in Dublin, so far as he could, where his name had already been made. He did not appreciate that, from the very full reports which *The Times* had given to his Crimes Act cases, his name was already widely known in England.

Shortly before 4 August 1892, the day when Parliament

was to meet, Mr Charles Darling QC MP was sitting in a club in Pall Mall, and was introduced to Edward Carson QC (Ireland) MP, the new Irish Solicitor-General. Darling had followed closely Carson's exploits in the Irish Courts, and his satirical mind had been much amused by the trenchant humour which was often found in the reports of Carson's arguments.

'I suppose you've come over to practise here, and take the bread out of our mouths?' said the English QC.

'No,' said the Irish QC, who knew absolutely nothing of the mode of life of the English Bar, 'but I dare say I'll have a desk in the library.'

Darling was at first puzzled, but, on learning from Carson the manner of practice in Dublin, explained to him that every English barrister must join with two or three colleagues in a set of chambers, sharing the rent and the services of a clerk with the others, the latter fixing and taking a percentage on the fees and keeping the books. Carson looked very discouraged. 'It'll be no use my taking chambers here,' he said. 'I'll be no one, and nobody'll know me.'

Darling took his hand eagerly. 'Look here, Carson,' he said, 'you mustn't think we haven't heard a lot about you over here. Arthur Balfour thinks the world of you. You let me paint your name outside my chambers, and you'll have five times my practice in a year.'

Carson smiled. 'I know I won't,' he said, 'but I'll bet you a shilling.'

Darling had been greatly captivated by that smile of Carson's; and, with the half-assent that was implied in Carson's bet, he went off to the Temple and gave orders that the name E H Carson, without the initials 'QC', because Carson was rated as a junior at the English Bar, was to be painted over the door of his chambers in No 3 Dr Johnson's

Buildings under that of his own. If Darling had not taken this into his own hands, Carson might never have come to the English Bar, so diffident was he concerning the chances of success for an Irishman at the English Bar. He was the first Irish QC to dare the change. Irish advocates had, of course, appeared on special occasions, and in the House of Lords, and on the whole they had not made a good impression. The violent personalities of the Four Courts were not understood; the Irishmen were considered to be bullies in cross-examination, and their oratory, even on points of law, was thought irrelevant and diffuse. In Carson the Englishmen recognised qualities very different from those of the familiar Irish advocate. The soul of courtesy in Court, both to counsel and witnesses, he led both on by his very politeness to their destruction; his speeches were an epitome of brevity; he made one sentence do the work of two. He was, indeed, about to be transplanted by Fortune – impelled into the House of Commons by Balfour's advice and patronage, and into the Temple by Darling's interest and kindness – from his native soil into another which was far more adapted to both his taste and his talent. Alike in the Temple and in Parliament, he won immediate popularity from his new English friends, as many a winning Irishman had before him; but, unlike most of the others, he accepted and welcomed without reserve the affection and homage which was at once offered to him by the Saxons, and, moreover, reciprocated eagerly these cordial sentiments. He was already a member of the Middle Temple; and, although his name had previously been painted under Darling's, he was now formally called to the English Bar.

When Carson went to take his seat in the House of Commons on 8 August 1892, and waited in the historic chamber to sign his name and take the oath as junior member of Dublin University, the familiarity of many faces about him added an irony to the impressive ceremony, which must necessarily impress every new member, however distinguished or rebellious, of the Imperial Parliament. Sitting over against him was William O'Brien; there, too, were Tim Harrington, Tim Healy, little Dr Tanner, and John Redmond, sitting apart as leader of the better Parnellite faction, and many others who had been prosecuted by him and sent to prison by his advocacy. They looked with curiosity and amusement at 'Coercion Carson' in his new role, a little uneasily, perhaps, but yet surely anticipating the repayment of old scores on equal terms on the floor of the most democratic Parliament in the world.

The Conservative Government went to the debate on a short formal Queen's Speech without constructive proposals, knowing that it was to die. Carson was not to take part in the debate, but he had the experience of answering from the front bench two questions on Irish administration, and joined the roll of those few and privileged persons who appear for the first time in Parliament on the Government Front Bench. The 'Address in answer to Her Majesty's most gracious Speech' was moved in a polished speech by a colleague of Trinity days and the Four Courts, Mr Dunbar Barton. It was a debate on Home Rule from first to last, and Carson saw and heard most of the great political figures for the first time. Mr Asquith moved the Liberal amendment, expressing want of confidence, with classic dignity and grace: the Government was dead; their cause was ruined; the people had spoken. '*Roma locuta est. Causa finita est,*' said the faultless scholar of Balliol. But Carson's new friend, also a scholar, was able to turn this quotation, by a witty inversion, against him. Yes, indeed, it was Rome, the Church of Rome, that had spoken, and had decreed the result of every southern Irish election.

'The Archbishops and Bishops of Ireland have spoken,' said Mr Darling, 'the priests have acted, and the case is finished.' Then came a most interesting diversion into the main stream of discussion on the Union between England and Ireland. The new Liberal member for Finsbury, Mr D Naoriji, the first Indian ever to be elected to the British Parliament, rose and contributed a maiden speech. He spoke with deep and glowing gratitude of England's work for India, which had breathed 'new life into a land which had been decaying for centuries'. His conclusion, which expressed the hope that the connection between England and India, that comprised five-sixths of the British Empire, might long continue with benefit for the two countries, and, indeed, his whole oration seemed to be a rare argument by analogy from this exotic Gladstonian, not against but for the Union, and was a strange contrast to the bitter reproaches of the Irishmen in the same debate against British rule. Mr Gladstone himself intervened later, solemnly assuring the House that Ireland was now his sole link with public life, his primary and absorbing interest. How noble he looked, how full of vitality. Carson saw him come into the House, gather himself like a guardsman at the Bar, and stalk to his place behind the box with the step of a youth. He walked like a soldier, this noble old man of eighty-three, and spoke like an angel. He was intent on his last crusade in the evening of his days, and Carson was there, in his prime, to frustrate him; but he listened spellbound to the rival of Beaconsfield, the lieutenant of Palmerston, the pupil of Peel, who had sat in the unreformed Parliament for a pocket borough, and, although now the great leader of popular opinion, with all Britain for a constituency, recalled the dignity and culture of an earlier age.

Balfour, Sir William Harcourt, Goschen, Joseph Chamberlain, John Redmond and Justin McCarthy all spoke, but it was not until late in the debate that Ulster, the rock round which the whole controversy was to break and upon which three Home Rule Bills were wrecked, was considered or even mentioned. Then, from a group above the gangway, there rose the tall, gaunt figure of Colonel Saunderson, the member for North Armagh; among these men sat John Ross, recently elected for Derry, the man who had left Carson behind at Trinity and was even now before him in the Parliamentary field with a stirring maiden speech on the Address; here, round Colonel Saunderson, high up on the seats above the gangway, sat a score or so of determined-looking men. Their grim, set faces distinguished them from the rest of the Conservative Party; there never was such a group of smileless politicians; you would get more fun from Tim Healy in five minutes than you could wring from them in five years; but they knew how to follow a lead, and how to greet their man with a chorus of steady cheers. These were the men of Ulster: this was 'the other Ireland'. As Colonel Saunderson rose, the voice of the North rang out, harsh, clear and unmistakable. He referred bitterly to the desertion and fall of Parnell: there was a time when southern Ireland had a leader, but now the real leader of the Irish Party was, the first man in the next Government would be, Dr Walsh, the Roman Archbishop of Dublin. 'I do not know to what extent he will deem it right to interfere in foreign affairs.' His conclusion was menacing. 'No man who comes over to Belfast will laugh at the Ulster loyalists. When all is said, whether the Lords reject the Bill or not, we reject it; and, though you may occupy the House of Commons for years to come with academic debates upon the value of this Home Rule Bill, when all is said, even if you pass this Bill, I say in the name of my people that I reject it.' 'Who are you?' scornfully interjected a southern voice. 'No man has a better right to say that than I,' the Colonel answered. 'I say, in their name, we will reject it, and that if you ever try to erect it in Ireland, we will crumble it into dust.'

Though William Redmond, who followed, described this peroration as a boast so absurd that anyone who had acquaintance with the province of Ulster could safely ignore it, Saunderson's rough words, challenging in the name of an organised minority the very basis of Parliamentary authority, hung ominously over the remainder of the discussion, and, indeed, over the whole range of this great debate; the scholarship of Asquith, the dexterity of Balfour, the stately grandeur of Gladstone himself, seemed to Carson but empty words in comparison with the blunt threats of this soldier man who clearly spoke for a nation which, if insignificant in size, was ready to organise to its full strength and obey him.

The Government was beaten; Gladstone formed his Home Rule administration, and Parliament was adjourned until the following January. Carson was now free to return to the Four Courts; and before he left the Irish Bar forever there was to be one notable stand by him made in the name of the Irish Bar against a distinguished member of the English judiciary imported into Ireland by Mr John Morley, the new Liberal Chief Secretary. One of the principal difficulties in Ireland was the position of the tenants who had been evicted, especially when the landlords had been strong enough to accept new tenancies from other tenants. These latter were regarded as traitors and outcasts by organised southern opinion, and there were, in consequence, few enough of them; there were not many above a thousand of these cases in all. Still, the new tenants themselves aggravated the problem. Boycotted as they were, living only by police protection, what was to become of them if the old tenants were restored? To solve this question, Morley set up the 'Evicted Tenants Commission', placing at its head Mr Justice Mathew, a man of Irish birth but whose distinguished career at the English Bar and Bench – he was really the creator of the Commercial Court – made his appointment seem wise and far-sighted.

The landlords concerned in this case were among the most unpopular of their class, and the most unpopular of all, whose name was almost a by-word, was the Marquess of Clanricarde, for whom Carson was briefed: he disliked the brief, but he knew that Clanricarde's harshness had been much exaggerated. The Plan of Campaign had exacerbated a naturally eccentric nature: his advocate was determined that justice should be done on his behalf.

Now Mr Justice Mathew, although he had his enemies, had in England built up a great reputation for impartiality and strength. The moment, however, his feet touched his native soil, he seemed to become a prejudiced person. The Court sat in a private house at 28 Merrion Square for the purposes of enquiry. Mr Justice Mathew was the President of the Commission, and took control from the start. He opened the proceedings with a lengthy statement very like a political speech, in which he argued that the policy of every Government had been for the ultimate restoration of the old tenants, and it was only too clear in which direction his own mind had decisively tended. He looked round for Lord Clanricarde, and, not seeing him, said that his presence had been expressly required. In fact, Lord Clanricarde had not been expressly invited to attend; he had not refused to do so, and fully meant to be present and examined by Carson.

'The fullest opportunity will be given him,' said the English Judge, 'to show why, as regards evicted tenants, he has declined to follow the example generally set by the landlords of his own country. If he refuses to attend …'

Carson then rose. 'I appear for him, and I don't know why these observations should be made.'

The President: 'You shall be heard presently.'

Carson: 'I am only stating that I appear here for him, and I don't know why these observations should be made.'

The President: 'I am very glad to see you, but we want Lord Clanricarde personally. We do not contemplate that the enquiry will take a course which will render the presence of counsel necessary. ... It is a great advantage for counsel to sit quiet.'

Now the Commission was about to enquire into a very complicated set of facts, and grievances were to be formulated and set against each other; right was not all on one side, and it was the duty of justice to enquire impartially and weigh the evidence. It was a case of landlord and tenant on a large scale. To make this possible it was essential that the landlords should have some notice of the allegations which it was sought to bring home against them. Carson then applied that the tenants should furnish some particulars of the charges which they were bringing against the landlords, and for an adjournment to consider them. There were witnesses in Court, well known Nationalist agitators, who were prepared to give evidence for the tenants.

Carson QC intervened before the first of these witnesses was called. 'I ask you whether we are to be prohibited from cross-examination, from going into the origin of these evictions.'

The President: 'I cannot say. I will see that justice is done.'

Mr John Roche MP, a Nationalist, was called first, and made a rambling statement on the iniquities of the landlords, little of which was first-hand evidence, and most of it hearsay.

Carson then repeated his request to cross-examine. 'May I do so after lunch?' he said.

'Yes, if you are ready,' said the President.

After lunch, however, the President had changed his mind.

Although it was very short notice to cross-examine on such a statement as had been given, there was no greater authority on this particular subject-matter in Ireland than the late Crown prosecutor. He stood ready to cross-examine. 'Am I now at liberty to cross-examine?'

'No, certainly not,' snapped Mathew.

Mr Carson: 'You told me before lunch that I should have a right to cross-examine.'

The President then told him that he might prepare questions, and, if these were considered relevant, they be put by one of the Commissioners to the witness. Carson flushed with anger: was his advocacy to be hamstrung in this way? Was the edge of his questions to be taken off by this device?

'I would ask to be heard on my right to cross-examine,' he said.

The President: 'No, no, I decline to hear you.'

Mr Carson: 'I must press this matter. I will ask for a vote to be taken by the Commissioners to see if every Commissioner takes your view. Seeing that a charge was made at the outset that Lord Clanricarde stood in a different position from any other landlord in Ireland, am I now, when the turn has come to sift the evidence before it goes to the public, to be told that I am not to be heard, and that I am not at liberty to cross-examine?'

The President: 'I will not hear you further, and I order you to withdraw.'

Mr Carson: 'I insist upon my right until every Commissioner orders me to withdraw. I will stand up here and now for justice to be done to Lord Clanricarde as well as to anyone else.'

The President (*quickly*): 'The Commissioners have consulted, and we have come to the unanimous conclusion that we will not hear you. When you have taken off your wig and gown, you will see that it is most convenient and best. You are here at present as an *amicus curiae*, and in no other capacity.'

Carson, who had never sat down, his brogue slower usual, said, 'My lord, if I am not at liberty to cross-examine, I say the whole thing is a farce and a sham. I willingly withdraw from it. I will not prostitute my position by remaining longer an advocate before an English Judge.'

'I am not sitting as a Judge,' interposed the President hotly.

'Any fool could see that,' said Carson in a low voice, but loud enough for everyone in Court to hear.

The President: 'Your observations are disgraceful.'

Then Carson heard a familiar voice behind him: it was that of Mr William O'Brien MP, who had come in unperceived. 'You are not in a Coercion Court now,' he said.

Then Mr Kenny QC, also briefed in the case, said, 'I entirely concur with the observations made by Mr Carson,' to which the President retorted, 'I say that is equally impertinent and disgraceful.' Carson then threw down his papers on the desk and walked slowly out of Court, followed by every member of the Irish Bar present.

The first leading article in *The Times* next day was devoted to a commentary on these unconventional proceedings. 'A farce and a sham', said *The Times*. 'Such was the description of the proceedings of the Evicted Tenants Commission given yesterday by Mr Carson QC … and we think our readers will agree that, in the peculiar circumstances of the case, these words, strong as they were, were not too strong. The extraordinary allocution of Mr Justice Mathew was an appropriate intervention to what followed. He refused to be bound by any of the rules of judicial procedure. The evidence of a witness, not himself a tenant, was purely hearsay, and not to allow this person, a Plan of Campaign organiser, to be subjected even to cross-examination, after a promise had been given that this would be permitted, is a method of enquiry for which no precedents exist since James II. We do not believe that Sir James Mathew's harsh and irritable observations on the conduct of the distinguished counsel who appeared in the case for the landlords in claiming their right to cross-examine will command the sympathy of the English Bar. He was too busy preparing a speech that might have been delivered by Mr Dillon or Mr Redmond on an Evicted Tenants Bill. ... He allows the Campaign organiser to bring forward damaging charges without any effective check upon them.'

Nevertheless, Carson had his critics, and wrote to state his position in *The Times*. 'If I erred, it was only because I am accustomed to practise in Courts where parties are heard before they are condemned, and where Judges never complain if they are in a respectful manner corrected as to a misapprehension on a matter of fact.'

As a result of Carson's sensational withdrawal from the enquiry with his brother barristers, the Commission lost all authority in the public eye, and shortly afterwards Mr Justice Mathew's two most distinguished colleagues on the Commission resigned, one to take up a Government appointment, the other for some other reason. Undoubtedly Carson was right in the course he took; the Commission was proceeding on grossly prejudiced lines. Such, at any rate, was Carson's sensational *adieu* to the Bar of Ireland, perhaps a fitting culmination to his distinguished and adventurous career in Dublin, bearing witness to the independence of that Bar where he had practised for nearly sixteen years; such was the challenging prelude, at the expense of a great English Judge, to the greatest legal career in England of his time.

Years afterwards, Sir Edward Marshall Hall suffered severely from continual encounters with the same powerful Judge, in which, to his great surprise, he never came off best; and he went to Carson for advice and sympathy. He got the first, but not the second. 'The difference between you and me, Marshall,' said Carson, 'is that when I have a row with a Judge, I'm always right. When you have a row with a Judge, you're always wrong!'

In order to appreciate the boldness of Carson's action, it is right to remember that he had already decided to practise at the English Bar, and that he was fully aware of the position of esteem held by Mathew in the Temple; he might well have been making for himself a powerful enemy; but in the end the two Irishmen showed magnanimity: after Carson had argued a case splendidly before Mathew, the latter sent for Carson to his private room and complimented him. The two shook hands and became real friends.

Tim Healy chuckled to himself when he read the report of Carson employing the wrecking tactics which he had so often used to such advantage himself, while William O'Brien remained behind in Court to take part in a 'farce and a sham'. The tables were already being turned, and time would come to show the wheel turned full circle. But Healy was not surprised, because he knew that Carson would show the same sturdy independence whether against an English Judge of Nationalist leanings, or even a powerful Unionist. In 1889, Michael Morris, whom Peter the Packer succeeded as Lord Chief Justice of Ireland, was promoted to the position of Lord of Appeal in Ordinary, the highest purely legal appointment which can be given. He was a very able man, and had been a leading Unionist, and was still a great power. The whole of the Bar went off to the Queen's Bench to join in the official congratulations; Healy, who hated Morris, found himself alone in the library with Carson. 'Well, Ned,' said Healy, 'what would you be doing here? Why don't you go off and congratulate your man, like the rest of them?' 'The brute,' said Carson; 'I wouldn't congratulate him.'

'Such,' said Healy, in recalling this incident to the author, 'was his independence of character.'

10. 'A New Force in Politics'

Carson returned to London early in the New Year for the meeting of Parliament which was to be inaugurated by a Liberal 'Queen's Speech', in which the vital words were to appear: 'A Bill will be submitted to you, on the earliest available occasion, to amend the provision for the Government of Ireland'. Before the introduction of the Home Rule Bill, the new 'Queen's Speech' had to be discussed, in which the subject of Ireland was again the principal theme. John Morley had repealed the provisions of the Crimes Act, which allowed secret enquiries, changes of venue, and special juries, and claimed that Ireland was made more peaceable thereby; he had also released the Gweedore prisoners.

Carson was now to become Balfour's special confidant and adviser on Irish affairs, which at this time meant the whole of politics, and the close relationship which had begun in Dublin was now to be resumed. Before Parliament assembled he received a letter dated 14 January, from an hotel in the Pyrenees, in Balfour's hand: 'My dear Carson, – I think undoubtedly something should be said about the Gweedore prisoners and I shall be most grateful if you will come to my house (to 4 Carlton Gardens) to give me any points likely to prove useful. Randolph's *obiter dictum* we need not trouble ourselves about. As you know, the Parliamentary practice is for the leader of the Opposition to follow the mover and seconder of the Address, and to make a sort of general survey of the situation; it is not supposed to be the right thing to do to couch the opening attack in very controversial language: this is left to the later stages of the debate. Perhaps you could manage to see me on Saturday or Monday, or at latest Tuesday morning. A little conversation on the Irish situation will be most valuable to me. Yours, Arthur James Balfour'.

The interview took place, and Carson thoroughly primed the leader of the Opposition with information on Ireland. After the interview it was decided that Carson should be principal 'controversial' speaker in reply to Morley in the debate on the Address upon the general state of Ireland, and particularly having regard to the Evicted Tenants Commission, the release of the prisoners in the Gweedore case, and the repeal of the Crimes Act provisions. On all of these subjects Carson was well qualified to reply: he had been counsel in the Gweedore case, and before the Commission, and no one knew more about the Crimes Act or the criminal state of Ireland. Balfour referred to Mr Justice Mathew as having enjoyed 'the unwonted luxury of delivering the verdict before he had heard the evidence', and Saunderson had caused a terrible scene by referring to Father McFadden as a 'murderous ruffian'. After appeals from Gladstone and Balfour, he consented, with a fiery look at the Nationalists, to substitute for the words 'murderous ruffian' the term 'excited politician'. A great deal of heat had thus been engendered into the debate, and Carson sat nervously by Balfour waiting to be called on to make the concluding speech. In those days the House rose at midnight, and Carson needed at least three-quarters of an hour for his speech. At length John Morley rose at 10.15: he was continually interrupted, and it was an hour and a quarter before he sat down. His main argument was a detailed examination of the state of Ireland with regard to rents and crime. His figures showed that rents were being paid better, and there was a decrease in crime. Carson had thus only half an hour to reply. Mr Darling tried to do Carson another friendly turn by moving the adjournment of the debate, but made matters worse, since a division on this question, insisted upon by the Irish members, followed, which occupied ten minutes, and there was now only a quarter of an hour left. However, the debate was automatically to adjourn at midnight until the next day, and the speaker at that moment in possession of the House had a right to resume his speech on the morrow. So Carson foiled the Nationalists' manoeuvre to embarrass him by taking an unprecedented course for a maiden speaker: he decided to make his maiden speech in two parts. In another way also he made a precedent: he was the first and last speaker within recent memory to make his maiden speech from the Front Opposition Bench on the left of the Speaker's chair. His position as ex-Solicitor-General for Ireland during a few weeks entitled him to a seat on this Bench, and to the great advantage of the use of the famous table and despatch-box when speaking. The ordinary member speaking from the back benches, rising tier on tier, has no such support, and nowhere to lay his notes save on the seat from which he has risen. Maiden speeches have occasionally been heard from the Government Front Bench on the Speaker's right, from members entering the House for the first time as members of the Government, but the writer can find no precedent for a maiden speech from the Front Opposition Bench save in the case of Edward Carson.

The House was in a stormy and angry mood. Carson's enemies had already made for him a certain reputation. Proclaimed by Nationalist members and newspapers as the most terrible and ruthless Crown prosecutor ever known, all parties at St Stephen's were curious to see what manner of man he was. His intervention was awaited with mixed feelings; but there could surely be no doubt as to the manner of his reception from one quarter of the packed House; there they sat, the Nationalist members, in a solid phalanx of seventy, ready to barrack the man who had sent so many of them to prison; in their imagination and experience he figured as something like an ogre – a fanciful picture, relieved by the

Irishman's admiration for a born fighter. Now, at long last, had come the chance to bait and humiliate their oppressor. It is an almost invariable convention to show the utmost consideration to a maiden speaker, and in the long history of the House the rule has rarely been broken; but this surely was an exceptional case: to the Nationalists he was no maiden speaker; they had often heard him. The Irish had shouted down Disraeli's maiden speech because of a grievance that O'Connell had against him; so why not 'Coercion Carson', who had sent the half of them to gaol? Everybody expected a scene. The Conservatives and Liberals alike were anxious to see how this formidable-looking person would acquit himself in an atmosphere of hostility which could be felt. He advanced towards the box, a tall, gaunt, sombre figure, faultlessly dressed, with an easy, almost languid stride. All eyes were upon him, and from the seats below the gangway there rose from the Irishmen a murmur, which presently swelled to a chorus of hooting. Mr Balfour, sitting on the Bench beside him, was seen to smile; he was confident that Carson could take care of himself.

Now, a maiden speech, even in ordinary circumstances, is as terrifying an experience as any ordeal in the world, and his outward calm concealed a turmoil of nervousness within; the savage crowd at Mitchelstown had been nothing to this. Yet it was not the Nationalist clamour that awed him; indeed, it gave him confidence, and made him feel at home; rather he was awed by the same circumstances which assail every new member rising for the first time, however distinguished already in another walk of life – the fear of 'as critical an audience as exists in the world'. When the hooting had died down, he began very quietly, and sustained this tone throughout: those who had expected fireworks were at once disappointed. It was only natural, he said, that one who had taken some part in the administration of the law in Ireland should reply to the Chief Secretary. His opening observations on Thursday night, although purely introductory and making no attempt at eloquence, somehow gained the attention of the House: the interruptions died down, and the House settled itself down to listen as it only does when it is interested. The signs of their interest are unmistakable: the chamber ceases to be a moving scene, but one in repose. Members cease to fidget or move about. There was something in the clear, simple sentences of the expressive Dublin voice which showed that the man was master of his subject, and the House always likes that. They had expected a fire-eater; and they found a sinuous snake-charmer. By the time Big Ben began to strike midnight, and the House adjourned, although he had hardly touched the main subject-matter of his speech, he had gained the ear of the House, and the battle was half won.

Nearly forty years afterwards the present writer went to Lord Carson for advice on the subject of his own maiden speech. 'Shall I try to be eloquent?' he asked. 'Yes,' answered Lord Carson, 'if you can; but, you see, I never *could* be eloquent.' In truth, he had qualities which the House of Commons likes far more than eloquence, and it recognised them in him at once. The House is invisibly paved with the lost Parliamentary reputations of eminent lawyers: they rarely make a success in the House; but this one was clearly a first-rate 'House of Commons' man.

Yet Carson, who had a strong vein of pessimism in him, did not realise his success. A friend went to see him the next day, and found him in bed, a bundle of nerves, convinced that he had made a great failure, and that he had better hurry through the remainder of his speech as best he could. Carson was often overcome by such attacks of nerves before his great Parliamentary and legal performances, but, on the scene of action, they never impaired the excellence of the performance itself. On the following day he stood at the box again, and, with the same gentle manner, was far more provocative. He swept aside John Morley's figures, as an eye-witness said, like so many cobwebs with one sweeping sentence. It was strange that rents were being paid better in a year of great and distressing agricultural depression; that showed that the payment of rent was dependent, not on the prosperity of the tenants, but on something else. He was not impressed by the slight diminution of crime: 'the course of crime depends on the course the political agitators find it convenient to take at a particular time; rents are paid, not because of the state of the tenants, but because the member for East Mayo gives the orders.'

Then he passed to the Evicted Tenants Commission; and here was a remarkable quality of this maiden speech: it literally continued, before the tribunal of the House of Commons, the proceedings which had been so abruptly terminated by his withdrawal from the Commission. He would, he said, say nothing about 'the urbanity of the Judge', but in its conception, in its proceedings, up to the day it left Dublin, the whole thing had been a monstrous pretence. 'But sir, I will venture to characterise that opening statement of the President, not only as scandalous, but as incompetent. What was the foundation for the change that was made in segregating the case of Lord Clanricarde, for whom I appeared?' Here there were loud jeers and groans, to which Carson responded. 'Yes, sir. I am not one of those counsel who selects his clients when they are on their trial. I am always quite ready to appear, to see that justice is done to any man.' He then passed on to his claim to the right to cross-examine. John Morley had already found it necessary to address a large meeting on this subject: 'As to precedents,' he said, 'I state without fear of contradiction that the procedure followed by Mr Justice

Mathew was in accordance with every precedent to be found.' Carson had then looked up the precedents: he found that out of the fifteen Irish commissions which were precedents, cross-examination had been allowed in eight cases, and in the remaining seven it was not clear that cross-examination had been applied for. Having laid Morley out on this, he brushed this score aside: no, he was not proceeding on precedent at all; he was proceeding on the inherent justice of the case; and then, by a tour de force of Parliamentary skill, he succeeded in cross-examining on the floor of the House the very man, John Roche MP, whom he had not been allowed to cross-examine before the Commission.

'The first witness examined,' he said, 'certainly rather astonished me. I had had some experience of that witness in the trial of *Blount v Byrne*. I had heard matters of the gravest responsibility proved against him in relation to the Clanricarde estate. I saw him challenged to go upon the table in that case and stand the test of cross-examination, and I saw him refuse, and in relation to these peculiar circumstances, and in relation to this identical estate, there was at least some ground for sifting the honesty of his testimony.' It appeared that a land agent of the Marquess was called 'Balaclava', because he had taken part in the historic charge. After a speech by John Roche MP, in which he had said, 'The authorities have their "Balaclava" on that day, but the people will have their "Fontenoy" another day,' the unfortunate land agent had been riddled with bullets. Further, before the Commission John Roche had said that, if Lord Clanricarde had accepted a general reduction of fifteen per cent in the rents, there would have been no trouble. In fact, John Roche had spoken at a meeting and himself signed a resolution binding the tenants not to accept a less than fifty per cent reduction of rents from the Marquess. Carson was describing how Mr Roche had been present at a riot which sought to prevent the sheriff from evicting certain tenants, when Mr Roche himself came hurrying into the House. He rose at once, and said he defied Carson to prove that he had been present for the purpose ejecting the sheriff. 'I was present at the eviction, and I was proud to be present.'

Carson raised his eyebrows and smiled. 'Exactly; I am not *accusing* the honourable member of resisting the eviction, but, having regard to the fact that he was there, and proud of it, I suggest that at least I was entitled to put one question in cross-examination.' The House laughed. Then Carson referred to another speech of Mr Roche in which he told the tenantry that they ought to throttle a certain landlord, Mr Lewis, 'until the glass eye fell out of his head.'

Mr Roche was up again on his feet, protesting. 'Mr Speaker, I did not tell the tenantry to throttle him; but I told them by adopting the Plan of Campaign they would adopt a means and method by which they would throttle him … I was led away, and I did make use of the expression that by adhering loyally to their pledges they would throttle him, and I hoped they would not loose their grasp till the glass eye fell out of his head.'

'Well, really,' rejoined Carson, amid loud and prolonged laughter, 'I will leave it to the House whether that was a matter upon which one might have been allowed to put a question to the witness.' The House was delighted: it had rarely seen Irish members given such a strong dose of their own medicine. Was it not George III who said that if you want to baste an Irishman properly, you could easily get another Irishman to turn the spit?

Mr Roche sat silent and crestfallen, and did not submit himself to further cross-examination.

Carson had lost all nervousness now: at the beginning of

his speech he had turned round to Balfour again and again, as if for reassurance, but now, absolutely confident in himself, he passed on to the release of the Gweedore prisoners, and accused Morley of exercising the prerogative of mercy in bad faith. He quoted from Morley's speeches which denounced the prosecutors and sentences, before he entered on his office or knew anything about the matter. 'I should like the House to note the judicial mind of the right honourable gentleman, who had prejudged the matter three years previously.' He then said a few words in defence of the Ulster leader, Colonel Saunderson, who had made the violent scene of disorder by rating Father McFadden as a 'murderous ruffian'. He quoted from a speech of McFadden immediately before the tragedy: 'Will they dare arrest me in Gweedore among my people?' he had said. 'It will take the whole British Army to do it; there will be some blood spilt before they take me out of it … I do not agree that the landlords are the only murderers; the police I regard as murderers, and they will have vengeance to fall on them in this world or the next.' Carson referred to a Liberal member who had boasted of intimate friendship with McFadden. 'I make no criticism,' said Carson, with a shrug of his shoulders; 'after all, the honourable gentleman is quite entitled to make his own friends: it is purely a matter of taste.'

After making the most successful maiden speech heard for many years, a blend of legal enquiry and political exposition, so near at times to the method of an advocate in the Courts, which usually the House will not tolerate, yet never lapsing from unexceptionable Parliamentary form, and a perfect House of Commons manner, so provocative and yet so restrained, so powerful, so modest, Carson concluded with a few quiet, warning phrases about the state of Ireland, and the necessity for social reform preceding political reform in that country. Finally, he thanked the House for listening to him, and expressed 'the deep obligation to the House for the manner in which it has received me.'

He was accorded a Parliamentary ovation such as few have enjoyed. At the end of his speech, which had been given frequent applause, the House cheered for several minutes, and a crowd of members rushed to congratulate him. By one speech he did what few have ever done: in the hour and a half during which he had spoken, he had gained an established Parliamentary reputation; and, although his speech lasted well into the sacred dinner-hour, when the House is usually almost empty, there was a fuller House when he sat down than when he rose. Mr Gladstone, who had listened to him intently throughout, said that that was the best maiden speech he remembered. All through his speech he had sustained the interest, not merely of the delighted back benchers, but also of the masters of debate. The lobby correspondent of the *Sheffield Telegraph* thus described the effect of his speech: 'He spoke not only with the fluency of a practised orator, but with all the consummate ease of a Parliamentary hand. Behind him were Mr Balfour smoothing his handsome head of hair in the delight of listening; Mr Goschen in an angelic rapture; Sir Edward Clarke looking as if the art of oratory was not dead; and other of the Tory leaders beaming and delighted. Ever and anon a solid roar of Unionist cheers punctuated the brilliant speech. Of the Ministers, Mr Asquith alone seemed to enjoy the speech. It evidently struck sympathetic chords. More than once he nodded his head approvingly. On all sides the opinion is ungrudgingly conceded that a rich acquisition has been made to the debating power of the House, and that the Unionists have added to their Front Bench an orator of the first rank.'

As Joseph Chamberlain drove away in his carriage with his

son Austen, he said, 'A new force has arisen in politics'; and as soon as he was home he penned this note:

'40 Prince's Gardens, SW
Friday night

Dear Mr Carson, – You must allow me to congratulate you warmly on your splendid speech. It was the best debating speech I have heard for a long while in the House of Commons, and for a maiden speech I think it was unprecedented.

Yours very truly
J Chamberlain.'

The next day *The Times* gave a leading article to his speech, and almost all newspapers, even the Liberal ones, commented on it with high praise: he had indeed cheered the whole Conservative and Unionist Parties; they had been dejected by the results of the elections, which had swept away their great majority. Gladstone confidently claimed a mandate for Home Rule, and some Conservatives were beginning to doubt. Throughout the debate this note of discouragement had been present. Now this newcomer had not only presented a convincing justification for the late Government's policy, but had clearly stated the dangers of Mr Gladstone's alternative. His personality at once attracted great attention in the Press: even the *Tailor's Gazette* noticed his beautiful frock coat. His distinctive appearance, the sweet smile on the brooding, melancholy countenance, his languid movements, were all marked down. It was said that another Irishman as remarkable and masterful as Parnell had come upon the Parliamentary scene immediately after the latter had quitted it tragically for ever. It had been said of Parnell that he always looked as if he had been fitted with someone else's eyes: the same was said of Carson, and T P O'Connor described this as 'the look of a lost soul'.

Thus did Carson, almost on the eve of his thirty-ninth birthday, achieve a Parliamentary reputation in one night. The House was not surprised at anything he did now, but he maintained his reputation by frequent and effective interventions: he was irrepressible at question time, when the Nationalists again and again tried to barrack him. 'I will not be mobbed,' he said on one occasion, looking angrily round at them. On this occasion, however, he received a strong rebuke from Mr Speaker Peel, then almost on the point of retirement. However, it was his speech on Mr Morley's Evicted Tenants Bill which set the seal upon his Parliamentary reputation. In its way it was as fine as his maiden effort. Morley proposed to take powers to restore tenants who had been evicted as long as fifteen years previously for non-payment of rent, whether the property was in the occupation of the landlord or of new tenants. The numbers of these tenants were not large, but they had been ringleaders of the Plan of Campaign, and had refused to pay rent, in the main, for political reasons. The Irish Party were insistent for their restoration, and a Bill had been promised immediately after the election by the Liberals. But two years had now passed before the question was raised. Carson, in replying to the Solicitor-General, Sir Frank Lockwood, had a splendid opportunity: the subject was his own. Two principles to which he remained faithful all his life were at stake: no property can be dealt with by the State without compensation, and no concession should be made by Government to lawless agitation. If either of these principles are transgressed, the State must suffer in authority and respect. 'It simply means this,' he said, 'that unless you pass a Bill, no matter how bad, no matter how unfair, if there is only sufficient disturbance of the peace in Ireland, you are bound to submit.

So mob law is the foundation of a Liberal Government: they rather submit to that than incur the necessity of preserving peace in Ireland. ... When I am told that a tenant who went out fifteen years ago for non-payment is to be restored, I can only think that the most profitable means of occupation for a tenant in Ireland is to be out of possession for fifteen years ... You are putting a premium on illegality. The purpose of the Bill is to restore, not tenants who could not pay, but those who could, but would not, for political reasons ... I would rather have the Government say outright, "Let the arbitrators put back these Plan of Campaign tenants and those only", and do it in the light of day ... It is equivalent to telling people that if they will only commit a sufficient number of outrages they will bring the question they desire to raise within the sphere of practical politics.' This was always to be Carson's argument. From the first he maintained that the policy of surrender to agitation could only lead to the disruption of the Empire, first in Ireland, and then elsewhere. The Conservative Party loudly cheered the bitter logic of his words. They were not always to cheer him for the same logic in the near and distant future. Meanwhile his triumph was complete. Even for a lawyer the Irish Land Laws were an intricate maze. The Bill was badly drafted. Did the Bill cover urban as well as agricultural sites? Morley could not answer. Again and again Carson turned round scornfully to the Unionists, with the scornful words, 'He doesn't know.' Morley hid his helplessness and his face in a book of reference. Carson accused Morley of sacrificing the rights of the landlords and the tenants 'to pay a political debt'. Carson was followed by a great English lawyer, Mr J B Haldane, who warmly congratulated him from the Liberal benches. He gracefully referred to Carson's immediate success at the English Bar. 'The honourable and learned member,' he said, 'has made a brilliant speech worthy of his great reputation.' The Liberal Press was hardly less grudging in its praise. 'He has done nothing,' said the *Daily News*, 'in the House to justify either his own sublime regard for himself or the mysterious confidence of his leader, but it must be admitted that his speech on the Evicted Tenants Bill was a very able performance. It is by far the best thing he has done in Parliament. Mr Balfour was in raptures over it, while half a dozen young bloods hastened to pat him demonstratively on the back for the drubbing he gave to the Government, and particularly the Irish Chief Secretary.'

Mr John Morley, despite the fact that he liked Carson as a personal friend, grew irritated by these constant attacks, which were very often on technical points of Irish law. 'Oh, that's another lawyer's point,' he said wearily one day. Westminster is a long way from Tipperary, but Carson, having the memory of the Tipperary Riots and the burnt Courthouse well in mind, retorted, 'This is the third time you've reminded me that I am a lawyer. It's the only thing I'm proud of, and I think it is a far more honourable profession than that of an agitator.'

While T P O'Connor still called him the 'dreadful Carson', a good number of his fellow-countrymen on the Irish benches began to be proud of him as an Irishman, as they were also of Colonel Saunderson; the latter had become a great admirer of Carson's knowledge and debating skill, and called him 'Sleuthhound'. He had little learning, this Ulster soldier, but he had a gift of turning what should have been a technical discussion into a heated debate on the one question for which he cared. 'Was that all right?' he asked Carson after concluding a speech on the Evicted Tenants Bill.

'You'd have better referred to the Bill,' said Carson.

'Good God, d'you ever think I'd read the beastly thing?' said Saunderson.

Saunderson did not respond in any way to the admiration

of the Irish Party: he called them the 'murdherers'. He would survey the benches on an 'Irish' night gloomily. 'There is plenty of the murdherers here tonight,' he would say with the light of battle smouldering in his eye. He it was, also, who said, 'Mr Speaker, sir, I have eighty reasons against Home Rule: there they sit' – and pointed to the Nationalist members.

Carson dealt with the ablest of them with more finesse, and they learned to be careful of his deadly blade. Swift McNeill was a Nationalist, who had been a Conservative. He was an able man, but extraordinarily ugly. He was called 'Pongo', after a celebrated ape in the Zoological Gardens. When Carson wished to goad 'Pongo' into making a speech, he used to say to Balfour, 'I'll throw him a nut to crack,' and 'Pongo' almost always 'cracked' it and wasted good Government time, to the fury of his Whips. Once he said to Carson, referring to the fact that all the ecclesiastics had supported Lowry in the Trinity election, 'Will the honourable and learned member deny that every bishop in the Anglican Church tried to keep him out of Parliament?' 'Trinity College,' retorted Carson, 'is the one place in Ireland where priests cannot dictate as to who is to get in.' Carson, although he never hated the Nationalists personally, did not court them, nor did he try to make personal friends with them, charming and agreeable as many of them were. The political difference between them was too deep, and meant too much. Nevertheless, some of them could not restrain themselves from paying a tribute to him. He was walking slowly into the lobby when he saw little Dr Tanner, who was in a merry state, pirouetting round him in a most curious way, as if he wished to say something, and dared not. At last he said, 'Mr Carson, I want to tell you I have the greatest admiration for you. Tell you what, you ought to be elected leader of the Irish race at home and abroad.'

But Dr Tanner did not have the same affection for other

Unionists. There was a certain Catholic Unionist named De Lisle: nothing annoyed the Nationalists more than a Catholic Unionist. As De Lisle was leaving the House, Dr Tanner flung himself in his way, and said, 'De Lisle, you're a bloody fool.' De Lisle, who was a big man, took him by the neck and flung him away. 'Go away, Dr Tanner,' he said, 'you're drunk.' Tanner was not short of a repartee. 'Yes,' he said, 'that's true, but, don't you see, I'll be sober tomorrow, but you'll still be a bloody fool.'

William O'Brien, whom he had prosecuted and sent to gaol, also came up to Carson, when he was beginning to succeed at the English Bar. 'I see you were in a big fat case, sir,' he said. 'Nothing like getting hold of that Saxon money.' They could not forget that he was an Irishman.

During the discussion of the Evicted Tenants Bill, Carson and Dunbar Barton were walking together arm in arm through one of the corridors of the House, discussing the innumerable wrecking amendments which they had drafted together over a weekend at Eastbourne. 'Carson and Barton,' said a Nationalist member, 'you may be the biggest blackguards on earth; I don't say you're not; but, begorra, I'd rather go to hell with you than to heaven with T W Russell.' (Russell was an English member who took up the Irish question with intense interest. He was originally a strong Unionist, but later became a Liberal and a Home Ruler.) Mr Asquith, passing by, happened to hear this observation, and was highly amused. When he met Carson later in the day, he pointed at him in imitation of the Irishman, saluting him with the words, 'I don't say you're not.'

11. A Fight in the House

Meanwhile London Society, under the leadership of the beautiful Lady Londonderry, who had been Vice-Reine in Dublin and had known him there, adopted Carson as its latest lion, and delighted in his stories and his brogue. 'He simply must not lose it; it's adorable,' said one lady of the gay 'nineties to another; and he never did. Everybody wanted to meet Mr Carson in the social and political world: he was said to be something quite new and charming. Lord and Lady Londonderry did everything they could to give him a welcome in London. 'A great friendship developed between us,' said Lord Carson to me. 'Anything like Lord Londonderry's kindness to me in those days I've never known. When I came over here, if he had been my own brother he could not have been kinder.' At Lady Randolph Churchill's house he met her elder son. The first meeting of Carson with the last-named throws an amusing and prophetic light on the Winston Churchill of later days. 'I see,' said this youth of twenty, measuring himself against the tall Irishman twice his age, 'you've been remarkably busy this session; the worst of it is that you are likely to continue to be so, as the ship of State will be in very stormy waters so long as the Government steers its present course.'

Sometimes, too, he exchanged a friendly word with distinguished political opponents. Sir William Harcourt took him aside one evening at a political party. 'You're a young man, full of enthusiasm for your cause, are you not?' 'Yes,' said Carson. 'And you put absolute trust in your leaders and your party, I can see that.' 'Yes,' said Carson. 'Well, sir,' observed Harcourt, 'sooner or later there is going to be a terrible disillusionment for you. The Conservative Party, mark my word, never yet took up a cause without betraying it in the

end; and I don't think you'll betray it with them.' At the time
Carson did not treat the taunt of the bitter old Radical against
his opponents very seriously. But after he had concluded his
speech in the Lords on the Treaty with Ireland in 1922, he
suddenly remembered Harcourt's prophecy twenty-eight
years before, and cursed himself for not using it.

During the stormy and exacting session, which lasted
through the year 1892 almost without a recess, Carson had
many opportunities to develop his Parliamentary talents. On
13 February 1893, Mr Gladstone begged leave to introduce
his second Home Rule Bill. Its great distinction from the
previous measure was the retention of Irish members at
Westminster in full force for 'Imperial' questions, contrary
to Gladstone's express declaration in 1886. It began with a
vague preamble asserting the supremacy of the Imperial
Parliament: 'whereas it is expedient, without impairing or
restricting the supreme authority of Parliament'. Certain
paramount powers were reserved to the Imperial Parliament:
peace or war, foreign affairs, customs and coinage; above all,
the whole land question, from which the entire Irish agitation
had originated and gathered its strength, was reserved to the
Imperial Parliament for three years. Those who cast vain
regrets backwards to Gladstone's second Home Rule Bill, and
curse the men who brought it down, would do well to ponder
these reservations. This was no permanent settlement, as was
claimed. Apart from the transcending difficulty of Ulster,
where the most dreadful riots would have broken out on
any attempt to force an All Ireland Parliament upon them,
there were in these reservations causes for endless disputes
and bitterness: with the Irish at Westminster still holding the
balance, and free to vote on any question of no confidence in
the Government, there is much to be said for the view that
this Home Rule Bill, so far from being a solution, would have

proved an aggravation of the Irish problem. How much of the reserved ground the Irish Parliament would have gained, and by what means and what would have been its attitude and bearing during a European War, it is not any longer useful to discuss; but at the very least it must be admitted that the opposition to this particular Home Rule Bill was well grounded, and that there was much to be said against it even by those who were convinced that the Union of hearts could only be brought about by Parliamentary separation. The Home Rule Bill settled nothing on a permanent basis, left all the old controversies open; its very preamble, declaring the supremacy of the British Parliament, was an offence to the Irish, and would have created entirely new differences and difficulties for future statesmen.

At all events, there was a great deal to be said, and the junior member for Dublin University was constantly saying it. The Bill, which was introduced by Mr Gladstone on 13 February, did not pass its third reading in the Commons until 1 September, the House enjoying no summer recess. The Opposition were determined to make the task as difficult as possible, if not impossible, for the Government. A cloture motion, drastically curtailing discussion, and setting a time-table for the Bill, was carried. Even then, before the Bill went through, 459 speeches were delivered for the Bill and 938 against it: the former took 57¼ hours, and the latter 152¾ hours of Parliamentary time. The Government only had a possible majority of forty, and the Irish party was split between the orthodox and Parnell factions: the latter were not to be relied on, and Redmond described the Bill as an 'ugly toad, bearing a precious jewel on its forehead'. But Mr Gladstone was assisted by the most able and despotic Government Chief Whip of his time, Mr Edward Marjoribanks. His Highland retainers knew all the Liberal members by sight, and were posted like sentries at every possible place of egress from the House. They had orders to send back any Liberal to the Chief's office who tried to escape 'unpaired'; by this means and by ruthless party discipline, he gave the Prime Minister a safe majority throughout the hundreds of divisions that took place during these stormy and drawn-out proceedings.

Carson was one of the most persistent members of the Opposition: by September he was practically leading it. He spoke countless times at every stage of the Bill, except the formal third reading, moving amendments, new clauses adjournments, using analogies from the Constitution of the United States, urging abstruse points of law, cross-examining, speaking for hours on the insertion or omission of an adverb or an adjective, and occasionally shouting with excitement or indignation. He crossed swords with all the great Liberal leaders of the Parliament, Gladstone, Sir Charles Russell, Harcourt, and Haldane. Armed with his knowledge of Ireland as he was, no new member had ever had a better opportunity to learn the procedure of the House than had Carson as he sat week after week, month after month, by Balfour's side during the discussion of the Bill.

Feeling ran very high throughout these debates, and finally exploded in one of the most extraordinary scenes that can ever have taken place in the House of Commons. The whole weary committee stage, in which a Bill is discussed and amended in detail, line by line, and clause by clause, was about to be concluded, and the long debate was to close automatically at 10 pm. Joe Chamberlain was describing the blind obedience of the Liberal Party to Mr Gladstone. 'Never since the time of Herod has there been such slavish adulation,' he said. The House was angry and excited at the end of these long discussions, and ready to take up a Biblical allusion. 'Judas, Judas,' shouted T P O'Connor at the man by whose action

Home Rule had been made impossible eight years before. Almost simultaneously, ten o'clock struck, and the chairman put the question for the last division on the committee stage. But Mr Vicary Gibbs, a Tory member, 'seated and covered', according to custom which binds all members who wish to address the chair after a division has been called and before the result has been declared, asked for 'the words to be taken down' as a point of order. The chairman, in the uproar, 'had not heard' the words, and many of the Unionists refused to pass from the chamber into the division lobby until action was taken; among these was Carson, who lounged on the Opposition Front Bench, provocatively shouting, 'Gag, gag,' in chorus with others, the customary Parliamentary protest of any Opposition submitted to the tyranny of 'the cloture'. Members of all parties delayed in the chamber to see what was afoot, and such was the crowd that it soon became impossible for anyone to leave the chamber to record his vote. A Liberal member, Sir J W Logan, who had been standing on the floor of the House, suddenly crossed over, with flushed face, and took a seat beside Carson on the Front Opposition Bench. It was thought by the Unionists that the menacing Liberal was about to assault Carson: whether this really was his intention, or whether he merely intended to take a seat until the crowd dispersed and he could go out and vote, will never be known, for Mr Hayes Fisher, who was sitting immediately behind Carson, heretofore and hereafter one of the quietest members of the House, seized Logan under the chin and pulled his head back over the Front Opposition Bench. Logan then struck out at Carson, and the Nationalists, with a yell, uprose in a *levée en masse* to defend their ally, but they made straight for Colonel Saunderson. This made the last-named completely happy, and with right and left he dealt havoc among the 'murdherers'; a little man – some said it was

Dr Tanner – got up on a bench and dealt him a blow from above on his bald head, but the Colonel sent him spinning from the bench with a careless wave of his arm. When the fight was at its fiercest, Marjoribanks, the Chief Whip, as strong and tall as Saunderson, was busily occupied in violently parting the combatants with his powerful arms, a task much to his taste. He was on his feet, engaged on this errand of peace, and an immaculate silk hat was still perched on his head. Now, although a member, as one among the sovereign assembly, may wear his hat in the House when sitting, it is against the rules of the House to wear one when standing up. Seeing him, the serjeant-at-arms, ignoring the general *mêlée*, advanced and tapped him gently on the arm. 'I'm sorry, Mr Marjoribanks,' he said, 'but you mustn't stand in the House with your hat on.' Sacred indeed are the traditions of the Mother of Parliaments! The fight had now become general, and there were contests in almost every quarter of the House. A cloud of dust, which did little credit to the charwoman employed in the House, began to rise around the Speaker's chair. The public in the galleries began to hiss loudly, and, although he had fared badly, Tim Healy, who always, even when most preoccupied, had an eye for the supernatural, observed a strange omen. The padded arm of a corner seat on the second bench below the gangway was seen, loosened from its fittings by the turmoil, to raise itself to an upright position. Quite suddenly the uproar ended. Members, lately locked in each other's arms, separated, and began to look shamefacedly at each other. Mr Peel, the greatest Speaker of the nineteenth century, had been sent for, and was standing in front of his chair: his strong personality had quelled a hundred storms, but he had never seen anything like this. Already honourable gentlemen felt the disdainful authority of the great Speaker.

'Will some member tell me what has occurred?' said the

Olympian one, to a House restored to absolute silence.

The Grand Old Man himself rose and tried to explain, as embarrassed and grieved as the head boy of a class who has failed to keep order in the absence of the teacher. Yet even now the incident was not over: the change of atmosphere, as often in the House of Commons, was complete and instantaneous; for there the sublime is so often followed by the ridiculous, the laughter so near to tears, and violence to reconciliation; melodrama so suddenly melts into comedy and farce. A very old Tory member – every House of Commons knows him – commonly known as 'the Buzzer', rose and pointed an accusing finger at the Prime Minister. 'All your fault,' he chanted dolefully, 'all your fault.' It was in vain that his colleagues pulled him down by the coat-tails: up he rose again, and repeated, like the raven, his monotonous refrain. For once the great orator was discomfited: nobody was listening; everyone was laughing. There, perhaps, the incident would best have ended, but T P O'Connor, the picture of remorse, rose with the air of a penitent at the confessional, and brought the mind of the House back to the discreditable origin of the scene, which he rightly traced to himself. But all inquests must have an end; the Clerk of the House began to drone out a number of clauses, which were accepted without question put. Then he used the full force of his penetrating voice. 'Order, order,' he shouted. 'Plumbers' Registration Bill – the Marquess of Carmarthen.' The spirit of the House never changes: even today such an intervention would be greeted by a mighty roar of laughter. Then the son and heir of the Duke of Leeds rose formally to move a further stage of that important measure, which dealt with the necessity of the registration of the members of that august profession for the protection of the British public, while the legislators brushed the dust off their clothes so as to return in decency to their families. Thus did talk of plumbing succeed to fisticuffs, and words to deeds: so still are the English people governed under an enlightened democracy.

12. Deadly Cross-examinations

That week had been a very eventful one for Edward Carson. Not only had he sat up night after night in the House of Commons, but, two days before the memorable scene just described, he had made his name at the English Bar in no less spectacular and decisive a way than he had during the previous February in the House of Commons by his maiden speech.

His first brief in London, strangely enough, had been in Chancery: an English solicitor sent a 'green card' in to him from the outer Lobby, and, when Carson came out, asked him if he would be willing to undertake a case in Chancery. Well, yes, he knew that Mr Carson was not experienced in the English Courts, but there was a special reason. Carson found that the litigation had arisen concerning the interpretation of a deed which had been drafted by himself as a pupil of Price the Equity draftsman in Dublin, eighteen years before. He undertook the case and defended his client's interpretation of his own draft successfully in the High Court of Justice, Chancery Division, before Mr Justice Chitty. After this he began to receive a number of briefs, but as he had only been 'called' the day before yesterday, he was junior to almost every young counsel whom he was asked to lead. One day a very confident young man named Edward Marshall Hall was sent a brief marked 'With you Mr Carson'; he had never heard of Mr Carson, and when he was told tactfully by his solicitor that, though Mr Carson was an Irishman, and in matter of call to the English Bar his junior, he, Marshall Hall, was requested to leave the Court, so that Carson might conduct the cross-examination without breaking the etiquette of the Bar, his indignation knew no bounds. But he obeyed in the end, and, if he had stayed to listen, he might even have learnt something from a method of advocacy so different from his own. He had not forgotten the incident nearly thirty years later, as can be seen from the generous letter written when Carson's retirement to the House of Lords left him as perhaps the best-known advocate at the Bar.

'Ever since the day – alas, so many years ago – when I received a brief marked "With you Mr Carson", and asked "who the dickens you were", you are the only advocate I have feared as an opponent. ... I have had to fight (and generally on the worst side) all the men who have made reputations in the Courts during the past twenty years. There was one time, and one time only, when I had the chance to lead you, in those days of long ago, but, then as now, I recognised that you were the leader, and that no accident of professional etiquette could alter the reality of that position.'

Success only waited for him in the Temple for a few weeks, but during that short period the bitter February weather added to the Irishman's gloom. Here he was in London with nothing to do: life was expensive; he now had a family of four children, two sons, William Henry Lambert, born in 1880, Walter Seymour, and two daughters, Aileen Seymour and Gladys Isabel; his savings would soon be exhausted; and why should any English solicitor come near him? One cold and wet February day, as he was crossing the Strand on his way from Dr Johnson's Buildings towards the House of Commons, a fine carriage, drawn by two horses, narrowly missed him and splashed him with mud. A tall, stout, elaborately dressed person, with velvet collar and cuffs to his overcoat, and infusing the foggy air with a strong scent of perfume, jumped out of the carriage and held out his hand. A huge white flower decorating his buttonhole matched a smaller one in that of his coachman. 'Hullo, Ned Carson, how are you?' he said. There was something familiar in his voice. Could this prosperous, middle-aged, effeminate-looking individual be the once exquisite Oscar Wilde? Oscar was friendliness itself. 'Fancy you being a Tory,' he said, 'and Arthur Balfour's right-hand man. You're coming along, Ned. Come and dine with me one day in Tite Street.' The young aesthete, who had befogged his rooms at Trinity with incense and decorated them with blue china, had developed according to type; but the prize scholar of Trinity and Oxford was becoming extremely famous, despite the studied contempt of the official critics, who had not changed their mind about him. His witty comedy, *The Importance of being Earnest*, was running in London at that time; his name was well known all over America; it was the hey-day of the *Yellow Book*, of Gilbert and Sullivan, and the cult of the beautiful; and Oscar was a sort of high priest of a sensual philosophy of wit. How different they were, these two tall Irishmen, the fat, scented, high-spirited aesthete, and the lean, ascetic-looking lawyer; yet they were bred in the same air, and had worked together in the same class. For a moment these two contrasting and widely diverging lives touched in the wet London thoroughfare on that cold February morning. They had not met since Trinity days, twenty years before; would they ever meet again? Just as likely not, for Carson knew that Wilde would never remember his casual invitation: his 'wonderful life' was at its height; he was preoccupied in a hundred ways; he could not be bothered with lawyers, even old schoolfellows. It was plain that he did not really wish to see Carson again, nor did Carson like the look of him any more than he had in the old days. Yet, had Oscar remembered that invitation, and somehow persuaded Carson to come into his house as his guest, his fate might perhaps have been so very different. For Carson's rule of conduct forbade him to accept a brief against a friend, or one who had treated him as a friend.

Mr J R Remer MP tells a story about Carson which illustrates this. Carson was retained on behalf of the *Daily Mail* for the defence in a libel action, brought by Mr Remer, for a very large fee. After he was briefed he made friends with Remer in the House of Commons, and his new friend reminded the great lawyer that they were shortly to face each other as witness and counsel. 'Oh, you're the plaintiff in that case! Well, you may be sure that I shall ring up the *Daily Mail's* solicitors tomorrow morning and tell them that they must be expecting me to have a bad cold on the day that case comes on, which'll prevent me from attending to it.' So the lucrative brief was returned.

His reputation as a deadly cross-examiner flew quickly round the Temple. It was said that there was a new Irishman in the Temple, who had not yet learned to charge English fees, who could mesmerise witnesses into a betrayal of their whole case. Some briefs arrived in chambers, the only respectable part of which was their pink tape, and the clerk duly laid them on Carson's table. Among them there was an action or two against several politicians which seemed to Carson to be thinly veiled blackmail. To his clerk's dismay, Carson took the papers and hurled them on to the landing outside, and left them for the 'instructing solicitor' to collect. 'If there is one thing I loathe and detest above all else,' he said, 'it is the raking up of a public man's private affairs against him. We're all sinners.'

There was more than one set of papers which suffered this ignominious fate, and a highly coloured story of the eccentric Irish counsel who threw his briefs into the passage began to go the round of the Inns of Court. Yet so well was his work done that a considerable number of briefs was coming into his chambers. Solicitors began to brief him quite often as a 'senior counsel', and the junior with a longer English call would tactfully leave the Court while Carson, technically his junior, made the speech or took the witness.

He only once appeared before the great Chief Justice Coleridge, then in his very last days on the Bench and soon to be succeeded by Sir Charles Russell. Carson appeared before him in a case stated by magistrates on the meaning of a section in an Act of Parliament. Carson found the magistrates' construction very absurd; so did the Lord Chief Justice.

'How could the magistrates get that out of the section?' asked Coleridge.

'I assume the learned magistrates did not find it necessary to read the section,' replied Carson.

Carson began to appear often at the Old Bailey before Mr Justice Hawkins, the greatest criminal Judge of his time, and was able to apply much that he had learnt in his early days at Green Street. Even in civil cases the same lore was sometimes useful. He was once engaged before Hawkins in an action between two Jewish purveyors of jewellery. One had succeeded in selling to the other a beautiful-looking 'pigeon-blood ruby' for £1 000, a small price for so big a gem. But the second Jew, for whom Carson appeared, was unable to dispose of it, as a customer had discovered it to be a fine piece of French paste. The second Jew sued the first Jew for having deliberately defrauded him; the first Jew's defence was that the second Jew had purchased the piece 'with his eyes open'. Both men were probably right, according to Carson's intimate view. But his first duty was to his client, the second Jew. In his cross-examination he told the usher to hand the first Jew the ruby; the witness would not take it, perhaps lest it might be evidence of assent to the sale. 'Take it, sir,' said Carson, 'it won't bite you or cut you, I think.'

'What is it you've got in your hand?' asked Carson.

Witness: 'It's now proved to be a bit of French paste.'

Carson: 'Which you sold for £1 000?'

The fellow began to cry. 'Yeth,' he said, with appropriate Hebrew gestures, 'but I thell it ath a ruby without a guarantee.'

Carson, with a sympathetic smile: 'Don't be upset; it was very prudent of you. No one is going to hurt you. Perhaps you can help me. Come, man, tell me, where are they made?'

Witness (*brightening up*): 'In Birmingham.'

Hawkins, fine lawyer that he was, used to get very bored with the Courts. He was a racing man, and his heart was away at Newmarket or Sandown during the progress of another case in which Carson was appearing at the Old Bailey; in the course of the case he handed down a note to the advocate – 'Patience Stakes: Hawkins first, Job nowhere.'

Nevertheless, the old Judge was not nearly so bored with Carson as he was with other advocates. It was his habit never to eat lunch, and he used to invite Carson into his room during the luncheon interval and make him tell Irish stories, so Carson often had to go hungry too. The Judge asked Carson earnestly on one of these occasions why he did not apply to become an English QC, and pressed him to do so. Carson took his advice, and, with only a few months practice at the English Bar, applied to the Liberal Lord Chancellor for his silk gown. The Chancellor replied that there was no precedent for the giving of a silk gown to a barrister of a few weeks' call, even when he was an Irish QC, and that the requisite period of qualification was at least nine years. Carson was not *persona grata* to the Liberal politicians, and his attack on Mr Justice Mathew had been resented by some English Judges. The gift of a silk gown lies entirely in the Chancellor's discretion, and it seemed that nothing could be done. He was in a peculiar position: although an Irish QC and an ex-Solicitor-General, he had to appear like any white-wigged novice, wearing a stuff gown in every Court except the Privy Council and the House of Lords, where, as Courts of the Empire, he was entitled to wear the dress of a QC. Carson's pride was wounded: it would have been better never to have made the application. The refusal was attributed to political reasons by Carson, who considered it an affront, not only to him personally, but to the Irish Bar. The Lord Chancellor's action was resented by many others, although he could shelter behind the fact that there was no precedent for an Irish QC coming to the English Bar and attaining such a position at it that he could apply for silk within a few weeks. Carson, however, had the cold comfort of reading the frigid comment in the newspapers that the new QCs for 1894 were 'little-known men'. He determined that he would never renew his application for silk to Lord Herschell. If the Chancellor was right he would have to remain a stuffgownsman and sit in the back row for another nine years, as Lord Brougham had done: owing to his defending Queen Caroline, all the Chancellors of George IV had refused him silk, and it was only when William IV succeeded his brother that he was made a KC, at least ten years too late. Meanwhile he had been a leading counsel in all but name, like O'Connell, who refused to be called a counsel of the British Sovereign and in the end was given a special patent as 'senior counsel', and his lack of the official dignity became simply a reproach to the Government. Carson was so clearly about to become one of the leaders of the English Bar that the idea of his remaining a junior for nine years more would have brought the etiquette of legal promotion into contempt. The matter began to be ventilated in the Press. 'This [the refusal of the silk gown] is not due to Queen Victoria', said the *Evening News*, 'but Lord Chancellor Herschell, the Keeper of the Queen's Conscience, has refused to allow him to wear his silk gown in the ordinary Courts of law. Those who know of T P O'Connor's horror of the "dreadful Carson" will readily gather he is not a *persona grata* with the present Government. That one who wears silk in the higher tribunals should be compelled to don the garb of a barrister of one year's standing in inferior Courts may appear quite consistent to Lord Herschell, but to the ordinary intelligence it is a piece of flagrant injustice.' Hawkins, who had prompted the application, wrote to Herschell, after his refusal, saying that it was a scandal that Carson was not made a QC.

The refusal of the Liberal Lord Chancellor to promote him, however, was but a straw in his way: he was certain of success.

13. More Forensic Triumphs

There was one advantage in briefing Carson which English solicitors did not fail quickly to observe and to appreciate: he hardly ever did more than one case at a time. He never used a 'devil' to represent him while he was engaged in another Court: if two cases clashed, he returned one of them. He is the only great counsel whose sense of honour to his clients imposed this iron rule strictly on himself, without which he would have at least doubled his business. As a young man he had observed the contemptuous glances and smiles on the faces of the jury when some distinguished advocate came in and tried to pick up the case in the middle without hearing any of the evidence, which might easily have changed the whole course of the case. He maintained this rule until the end, and this was why, maybe, clients were willing to raise their fees to such a high figure if only they could induce him to go into Court for them; for, once he could be brought to this stage, he never went away. During his last years at the Bar, when he was engaged in a long *cause célèbre* with nearly all the other leaders of the Bar bustling in and out of the Court around him, he overheard one member of the jury say to another, one morning before the hearing was resumed, 'That old Carson sticks to his case better than any of them.' In those early days, Carson led the most exacting life physically: he would, if he was fortunate, leave the House of Commons a little after midnight. He would rise day after day before it was light at about 4.15 am, and work on his briefs by candlelight until it was time for him to go to the Temple.

Although briefs had been flowing into Dr Johnson's Buildings very satisfactorily, his name was not widely known to the legal people, except as a promising political figure, until his first English *cause célèbre*. He had a friend on the *Evening*

News who had already taken his part in the matter of the silk gown. Now, in July 1893, the *Evening News* had a libel action of the first importance to defend against one of the first Labour members of Parliament. It was vital to them that they should secure the best possible cross-examiner, since the success of the defence would entirely depend on the admissions of the plaintiff. Carson's friend assured the Board that there was no man more experienced in browbeating members of Parliament in the Courts than 'Coercion Carson'; the management took a chance and briefed this newcomer.

The facts of the case were these: Mr Havelock Wilson, MP for Middlesbrough, an important and trusted trade union leader, was general secretary of the National Amalgamated Seamen's and Firemen's Union. The year previously he had almost succeeded in promoting a national strike. His financial administration had been violently attacked by the *Evening News*, which also published even more hostile criticism contained in letters from members of the union and others. The union's financial statements for the year 1892 were condemned as 'indicative of a greater financial effrontery than we have yet seen'. The *Evening News* spoke of 'the prodigality with which the pence of the sailors are spent by the general secretary and executive of the union'. 'The accounts', it continued, 'are so jumbled together that it is difficult to arrive at the gross cost of administering the affairs of the union. We have this scandalous state of things: of £29 000 made up of the pence of seamen, nearly £2 000 is spent on law, and over £10 000 finds its way into the pockets of general secretaries, clerks, branch officials, delegates, and the like. ... If J H Wilson MP thinks the incompetency which he has displayed in the management and affairs of the Sailors Union is to be tolerated forever he is very short-sighted.' It was also suggested that Mr Wilson had deliberately called a strike in order to burke enquiry into the financial position of the union, and most damaging of all was the allegation that the seamen were paying their pence into a hopelessly insolvent concern.

It would be difficult to imagine a libel more dangerous to a trade union leader: it only barely stopped short of accusing Wilson of dishonesty. As in all libel cases, tactics were of the first importance: the newspaper was in a fighting mood and had wished to 'justify' – that is, to prove – strictly all the facts alleged in the article. Carson preferred not to take this *onus* upon his shoulders, but, rather, to plead an alternative defence: 'fair comment on a matter of public interest', a defence less stringent, but often open to much odium. The defendant is exposed to: 'My learned friend does not attempt to justify his gross allegations', and all the rest of it.

The trial was to take place at the Guildford Assizes before Mr Justice Grantham. For the plaintiff were Mr Bernard Coleridge QC, Mr Corrie Grant, and a young junior named Rufus Isaacs, whom Carson now met for the first time, and who was to be his forensic rival for so many years. Carson led Mr H C Richards, a well-known circuiteer on the South Eastern Circuit. Mr Richards was many years Carson's senior, and solemnly retired at the beginning of the defendants' case so that Carson could begin without breach of legal etiquette. The trial was being watched, not only by trade unionists and employers' organisations, but also by the politicians all over England. There was more at stake than the issue between the parties. The year before, Mr Wilson had tried to paralyse the whole of the shipping of the country by advocating up and down the country a national strike of all seamen and firemen, and also of all associated workers. Carson was engaged on more than a lawsuit, and, although he could ill be spared from the Home Rule debates in the House, he took away from

Westminster more than 'his pair'. For not only had Mr Wilson necessarily to be at Guildford, but nearly all the Labour MPs were present in Court to support their colleague. Mr Keir Hardie MP, William Allen MP, Major Rasch MP, were there with Tom Mann and many other pioneers of the movement.

Mr Coleridge told the jury that his client was claiming £7 000 damages from this evening newspaper for the very grossest libel, which the defendants did not even attempt to justify in a manly way; the newspaper had personally charged the plaintiff with bribery and other corrupt practices. 'The paper must now prove its charge or pay damages.' This was clever tactics, because there would be a great probability of success if Carson could be induced to go beyond his plea of 'fair comment' and beyond the words of the article, and impute to Mr Wilson attempts to gain corrupt profit or advantage for himself out of the union. How vainly was the net spread in the sight of the bird: Carson was 'too old a hand'. He had taken immense trouble over this case; he had studied Wilson's election accounts for years back; he had studied the Trades Union Acts until he knew far more about trade union law than any official; he knew the rules of this particular union backwards. He had searched old newspaper files for reports of speeches by Wilson and his friends. Mr Havelock Wilson MP little knew what he was in for when he stepped confidently into the witness box, and saw the Court filled with his friends and colleagues.

Yes, he himself had founded the union in 1887. The sailors paid only sixpence a week: he had a salary of only £250 a year, but he had very little to do with the funds of the union; he was concerned with policy; local secretaries collected the money and, after deducting branch expenses, sent the rest to headquarters. All the questions were asked quietly, and Mr Wilson was engagingly candid. Then came the first sign of a red light. Had there been any defalcations by the local secretaries? Possibly; there might have been defalcations to the tune of £2 000 since the union had been formed. He had spent £201 on his Deptford, and £506 on his Bristol, Parliamentary candidature.

Carson pulled a paper out of a pile of documents.

'You say in your declaration, in your *sworn* declaration, that at Bristol the expenses of your election had been £400 odd?' Wilson nodded his head.

Carson selected another paper.

'Yet in this balance sheet there is £500 odd donated by the union for the expenses at that very contest?' – 'Yes, I cannot explain that.'

The slow voice continued, 'You also say that no club or association paid anything for you. You say *that* in your sworn declaration. How do you explain that?' – 'I did not think there was anything illegal in that at the time.'

The advocate then passed to the detail of the accounts, and showed that the union could not meet its liabilities; then he asked his 'leading question'.

'Is it not true, then, sir, that the balance sheet is a document of "financial effrontery"?' – 'No, I have seen other trade union statements of account which are not half so clear as this.' The answer was *naiveté* itself, but not as good as what followed.

'Can you suggest,' persisted Carson, 'why £19 000 should be spent on management, and only £5 000 in benefits, £2 000 of which went in law costs?'

'No,' replied Havelock Wilson, 'the man who spent the money knew all about how it was spent.' Whereon a great shout of laughter went up in Court.

'Is there a word of detail as to these "legal expenses"?' – 'No.'

Carson then dealt with the most serious aspect of the case,

from a political and industrial standpoint.

'What about this expression: "the executive are calling a strike to burke enquiry into the finances"? Was there a strike?' – 'Yes.'

'Did you say at that meeting that if there were not a strike you would be ruined?' – 'No, I do not think so.'

'Did you say you were liable to £600 on bills?' – 'I do not know. I said I had received money from various friends, which I had paid away on behalf of the union, and that I was liable for these.'

For nearly two whole days Carson patiently cross-examined the trade union leader; hardly a question miscarried; only when he had completely discredited the witness on one aspect of enquiry did he pass to another. This was not a case to which there could be any short cut; he was dealing with a well-known public man at the head of a nationwide organisation.

Next day he produced the book of rules of the union: the date of the annual meeting had been changed. Carson proved to the Judge from the rules and from the Trades Union Acts that there was no power to alter the rule dealing with the annual meeting. Yet it had been done. 'We did not act upon the rule,' Wilson admitted lamely.

Havelock Wilson, in endeavouring to promote a strike among the union and allied workers, had paid strike money to other unions, though there were strict restrictions of such payments, even to members of the union itself, under the rules.

'Is there any rule authorising you to give strike pay to members of another union, the stevedores?' (Which Wilson had done.) – 'No.'

'While you can only give strike pay to members of your own union, yet you give it to others?' – 'Yes.'

'Are you in the habit of giving large sums to other unions?' – 'Yes.'

'Did the executive committee authorise you to spend £110?' – 'No.'

'Did you do it on your own authority?' – 'Yes.'

'Did you in your sworn return for 1891, to the Registrar of Trade Unions, make any return that you had given your money away to another union, as you are required to do?'

'No, I gave the money paid, with some money paid to my own union.'

'What is the use of laying down a rule which governs the giving of money to members of your union, and handing the union's money to strangers?' – 'I do not know.'

'Did you not give the Glasgow dock labourers £400?' – 'Yes.'

'Did you not give the Sausage-skin Manufacturers Union £50?' – 'Yes.' Loud laughter at this.

'What have the sausage-skin dressers to do with seamen?' Carson looked about, bewildered, among his papers, as if mystified for an explanation, while the Court rippled with laughter. Then his brow cleared, as if a load had been lifted off his mind. 'Ah,' he said, 'was not this union in Deptford, where you were a candidate?' A damaging suggestion this, but all Wilson could say was his usual, 'I cannot say.'

There was worse still to come from the point of view of trade union opinion. The *Evening News* had alleged that part of the moneys of the union had been paid to the masters of seamen's lodging-house keepers in the ports, who in one way or another acquire great influence over seamen.

'I come down to one of the alleged libels. Some of the money of the union went to organise the boarding masters. Did not you practically make them agents of the union?' – 'Yes, you may put that construction on it.'

'Have you denounced the boarding masters as "thieves and crimps"?' – 'I had called crimps crimps.' (The expression 'crimp' means an agent of a ship who procures a seaman, by getting him drunk or by other unfair means, to take service on a ship against his will.)

'What *do* you mean?' – 'I called some of them crimps.'

'Whenever the shipowners made use of the boarding masters, they were always thieves and crimps?' – 'Not always, sometimes.'

'In 1892, did you form the Boarding Masters Association?' – 'It was necessary to make use of them to get the subscriptions from the men.'

The member for Middlesbrough was showing visible distress, mopping his brow from time to time, and looking round for his friends to prompt him, for which he had to be rebuked. But the *coup de grace* was yet to come. There had recently been a Parliamentary Labour Commission to enquire into conditions of the workers. In the pile of accounts produced by Wilson, Carson languidly fastened on one item by chance.

'What is this item of £44 given as payment to witnesses at the Labour Commission? Do not the Government pay witnesses?' – 'Yes.'

'Why do you pay yours as well?' No answer this time, not even 'I do not know'. The question is repeated. – 'These men told me they had been employed by the Shipping Board to ruin the union and me, and I asked them to go before the Commission to say so. Thirty pounds were given them against a possible boycott by the shipowners, and to enable them to start in business.'

'Why was one of these witnesses here today?' This last question was too much for Havelock Wilson, who incontinently broke down and burst into tears in the box; he was unable to continue under cross-examination, and was led out of Court in a pitiful condition by his friends, sobbing like a woman and the tears streaming down his cheeks. This had happened to Carson twice since he had practised in England. Really, witnesses in England were very thin-skinned. Yet, in the whole of the two days' questioning, there cannot be found one instance of bullying the witness. To have made a Jewish dealer and a hardened trade union leader cry in the witness-box in the space of three months was no mean achievement. Either times must have changed in the mercantile or working communities, or advocates were giants in those days.

On the third day of the trial, Wilson had to be recalled for more of this slow torture. Carson only went into one more question, the £2 000 which was the sum attributable to 'legal expenses' out of a total of £5 000 paid in benefits. It transpired that, of the £2 000, £600 had been paid to launch an unsuccessful criminal prosecution against a member of the union for calling Wilson 'a thief, a villain and a rascal' – further, the prosecution had been dismissed.

Carson's triumph was already complete. His cross-examination stands as an almost perfected example of the art in a complicated case; he took all the gravest sentences of the alleged libels, and as a culmination of each part of his enquiry he had either made Wilson admit the truth or the probability of every one of the libels, or hang his head and say 'I do not know'.

Carson scorned to prolong the case, and took a most exceptional course: he called no witnesses for the defence, and made a short speech. This was a rare case, he said. There was really no need to waste the jury's time with witnesses for the defence. The plaintiff had proved the defendants' case. There was no allegation of personal corruption against Wilson, but of hopeless incompetence. In a fund in which so many thousands of poor sailors were concerned, it was the duty of the Press to bring to the public notice the vast sum that was being paid in management. The weekly pence of these poor fellows had purchased them nothing but an elaborate and costly system of management with the plaintiff at its head. Every rule of the union bearing on finance had been admittedly broken.

The jury, after a short discussion, returned, giving a verdict for the defendants, except on one isolated sentence, for which they awarded the plaintiff the generous sum of one farthing.

The ideal dream of every advocate had been fulfilled: the plaintiff had been forced, out of his own mouth, again and again to admit the justice of the defendant's case. *The Times* gave a leading article to the case, and, after paying a tribute to 'Mr Carson's most thorough and searching cross-examination', said that 'rarely has there been such a fiasco in a law court'. Very seldom has the result of a civil libel case, concerned mainly with figures, aroused such widespread public interest. Every newspaper of any importance throughout England gave an article to it, and Carson's performance was commented on by most of them; and rarely, if ever, has any counsel received such widespread praise and notice for a single performance. Indeed, he woke up the next day to find himself more famous in the law courts than his maiden speech had made him in the House. This success, however, pleased him more. 'The law was always my first love,' he said; and, indeed, the success was a most notable one. This was no ordinary lawsuit. The *Evening News* had taken its courage in both hands to expose what was undoubtedly a public scandal, and its courage had been vindicated; but the case was even more important, and by no means harmful in the end, to the trade union movement. Carson's cross-examination had graphically revealed the state of affairs which existed at a time when a vast sum was raised by the pence of working men, and administered by working-class orators with no experience or knowledge of finance and no sense of obligation to be bound by their own rules. The result of the case was to shake the confidence of the men in their 'bosses', and was a strong inducement to trade unions all over the country to set their house in order. The Seamen's and Firemen's Union was split in twain as a result of the action, and Mr Havelock Wilson never recovered his commanding position in the Labour movement. At the next election his handsome majority at Middlesbrough was turned into a decisive defeat. But he had not yet learnt wisdom: the very next day after Carson's victory he persisted in continuing another action against the *Shipping Gazette* for reprinting the identical *Evening News* articles, from which his name and certain strong passages had been omitted. Apparently he considered that his defeat had been caused by Carson's devastating methods, and Carson was not briefed for the *Shipping Gazette*. Now he wished to vindicate himself. Of course he lost, and the funds of his union had been squandered on another expensive and fruitless action. Even now the trade union love of the law was not exhausted. Tom Mann made a violent harangue attributing the defeat of his colleague to the unfair advocacy of Carson, and hinted at an appeal to other Courts and other Judges where justice would be done. But, meanwhile, one of the seamen wrote to Carson expressing their thanks for what he had done. 'When the union had not a shilling in its coffers, Wilson had the audacity to try and get us all out on strike and starve, as a last desperate effort to prevent the union going to the dogs'.

An old advocate of great experience and vast bulk, Pat Murphy QC, who was engaged in a later case, had listened all through Carson's cross-examination, and observed to a colleague after the Court rose, 'This man is a better advocate than Charles Russell, and he is a better advocate than Edward Clarke.' They were the unquestioned leaders of the Bar at the time. All these compliments he accepted with his exemplary modesty, but the one compliment which pleased him most was a telegram sent from the library of the Four Courts, signed by a representative committee of the Irish Bar, congratulating their old colleague on his brilliant performance. They were growing very proud of him in Ireland.

The silk gown could no longer in decency be denied: Lord Chancellor Herschell was really forced by circumstances to create a precedent. Indeed, Carson was sounded diplomatically as to whether he would graciously accept the honour from his hands. He had made up his mind not to apply again on his own initiative, but he had no desire to be intransigent at his own expense. And so he went down alone to receive his patent from the Lord Chancellor. This the writer thinks almost unprecedented. Every year a number of junior counsel are given their promotion 'to the front row', in the spring, and as a rule no more are made until the next year. They all go down together to receive their patents from the Lord Chancellor in the House of Lords. Then they go the round of all the Courts and are called 'within the Bar' by the presiding Judge: they are dressed in their full dress with full-bottomed wigs, silk gowns, knee-breeches, and buckled shoes. The business of the Courts is suspended when the usher informs the Judge of the arrival of the new King's Counsel. They pass through the length of the 'front row', the Judge says, 'Mr So-and-So, do you move?' Mr So-and-So KC then bows low to the Bench, turns round and bows to the 'outer Bar' to right and left, is bowed to in turn by the juniors, and passes out; and so through all the weary round of the Courts. Carson performed these ancient rites in solitary grandeur. When he went down to the House of Lords, the Lord Chancellor handed him his patent, and the two bewigged men bowed to each other: not a word was spoken by either of them, nor did the Chancellor even offer Carson his hand. Then he made his dignified progress round the Courts by himself. By the time, however, that he reached the Chancery Courts, Mr Justice Kekewich had finished his list, and had adjourned his Court, so here at least Carson was saved a little ceremony.

It so happened that on the very next day, the first on which Mr Edward Carson QC MP appeared as a leading counsel in the English Courts, he was briefed to appear in a Chancery action before Mr Justice Kekewich. Now, his lordship was a most learned lawyer, and a great stickler for form and precedent; he was not, however, a great Judge. It was of him that a learned counsel said in the Court of Appeal, 'My lords, this is an appeal from the judgment of Mr Justice Kekewich, but that is not my only ground of appeal.' When Mr Carson rose to open his case from the Queen's Counsel's row, this learned Judge began to fume and fret. 'Mr Carson, I can't hear you.' Carson courteously raised his voice a little louder, only to be met by the same observation from the Bench. The comedy repeated itself until Carson was shouting, and receiving the same reply. At length the new QC said, 'My lord, I give it up. I can think, for some reason not known to me, your Lordship does not wish to hear me. It has never been my experience in the past that my voice is not audible to the Bench.' The Judge then fussily observed, 'Mr Carson, you don't take my point. You have not been called within the Bar of my Court. I don't propose to send you home to put on your knee-breeches, as perhaps I should.'

'I should hope not,' said Carson in his deep brogue.

'What's that? What's that you say?' said the Judge. 'I warn you, I shall tolerate no impertinence.'

'I thought your lordship could not hear me,' observed Carson, and the case proceeded.

The prophecies of the newspapers were now speedily fulfilled, and in full measure. The quiet jog-trot chambers in

Dr Johnson's Buildings suddenly changed their character, as chambers in the Temple often do when suddenly the word goes round Ely Place, Lincoln's Inn and Mincing Lane that a new comet has risen in the legal firmament or that an old star has moved its headquarters.

He now was meeting, and receiving the congratulations and patronage of, most of the great English legal luminaries. One night after a dinner, Lord James of Hereford, a versatile man just short of genius in many spheres, came up to Carson and gave him a lecture of half an hour on his future. 'It might pay you to stay over here, as I hear you have a faculty for cross-examination. It might *pay* you to stay. You might be made a Judge in time.'

'This was at a time,' said Carson, 'when I was really getting on.' Indeed, it was at the time when Carson was being widely talked of as the successor to Sir Charles Russell, a greater advocate than Lord James ever was.

Carson had now been called to the Bar of England for a year, and the time had come to settle accounts. Charles Darling came into Carson's room one day and said, 'I've been going through my fees and I find you owe me a bet.' Carson, who had a horror of gambling, looked up, surprised. 'I told you,' said Darling, 'that if you allowed me to paint your name over my door, you'd have five times my practice within a year.' With all respect to the learned Judge, his judgment was right: Carson, according to the strict terms of the bet, *was* owing him a shilling. In a few days, Carson brought Darling a beautiful Irish blackthorn stick, with a silver band, which had cost exactly a shilling, around it, and bearing the inscription 'CD from EC, 1894', still a treasured possession of the famous Judge. 'It has been carried,' said Carson, 'by Cecil Roche, the fearless resident magistrate, and it has done good service on the heads of my fellow-countrymen. It has a "sword grip" and it won't turn in your hand, as it grew between two stones.'

By November 1892 Carson had achieved the hallmark of fame in those days. *Vanity Fair* accorded him the patronage of a column of biography by 'Jehu Junior', and a cartoon by 'Spy', an honour which was also given another Trinity man, Oscar Wilde. But his biographer had not yet read the signs clearly understood in the Temple. 'He seems to like the disgrace of being stigmatised as Mr Balfour's Crown prosecutor: nor is he put out even when he is openly said to be as big a blackguard as ever was Peter the Packer; yet he is not without virtue. He has not much of a practice in England, but he has appeared in a case which arose out of a modern labour trouble, and it is possible he will get more clients. For he is a hard-working, painstaking, lynx-eyed practitioner who can speak strongly. He is a lean, pale-faced Irishman, who has as much wit and as much ability as Irishmen often have. He has not fattened even on robust Unionism.'

The appointment of the Attorney-General, Sir Charles Russell, to the position of Lord Chief Justice, removed from the Bar its real leader as well as its titular chief. His only contemporary rival was Sir Edward Clarke, who, wonderful orator that he was, was never quite able to take his place. He was too eloquent, and grew to rely too much on his wonderful gift. Carson was less afraid of him as an opponent than he was of far smaller men. He relied too much on his speech, and could never seem to pay enough attention to cross-examination. Now, it is the latter, far more than the former, which wins cases, and mere oratory is no shield or spear when the advocate is faced with the raking, penetrating questions of a Charles Russell or an Edward Carson. Sir Charles Russell's place was empty, and, as the newspapers had prophesied, it was another Irishman, hardly forty years old, and not the veteran Englishman, who climbed into it. It is also interesting to record that it was through Charles Russell's own son that Carson became the acknowledged leader of the Bar by one of the most famous and tragic cases that have ever been tried in the English Courts.

14. The Oscar Wilde Case

Young Charles Russell had decided not to follow in his father's footsteps: he preferred to seek a safer fortune in a solicitor's office; later, he founded the famous firm of Charles Russell & Co, which shares with that of George Lewis the greatest fame of all firms of English lawyers. Charles Russell had now a case of great difficulty to handle; he is said to have consulted his father, the Lord Chief Justice, as to the best counsel to be engaged for a most arduous task. His father is said to have recommended the name of Edward Carson. Charles Russell, who was to brief Carson in every big case for the next twenty-five years in which he could secure the services of the great counsel, went down to Dr Johnson's Buildings with a document in his hand which may be accounted historical in the story of English literature. It was the summons of the Court to the Marquess of Queensberry to answer to the charge of criminal libel concerning the celebrated Irish poet, novelist and playwright, Oscar Fingal O'Flahertie Wills Wilde. Wilde was now at the height of his fame; several of his plays were running to crowded houses in London; he was seen everywhere in Society. He was not merely successful, he was triumphant; and, as Frank Harris states, he had won what genius rarely wins in this grudging world – the applause of the many and the praise of the few; and success was hardening him: he could not endure criticism, and he arrogated to himself the rights to impunity of a god. Now Wilde was a great Hellenist, and a brilliant and learned scholar, but he had not learned the great theme of Aeschylus and Sophocles – that the *hubris* of mankind will surely incur the anger of the gods, who use, not thunderbolts, but the very *hubris* of their victims, as the main instrument of their own downfall. The legends of ancient Greece were full of warning to the man who sought to put himself above mortality. This was the story of Oedipus, of Creon, of Theseus, of Agamemnon, which Wilde had one time learnt by heart; yet, as he was later to propound to Carson, literature held no moral but only aesthetic lessons for him. All his learning had only taught him one side of the philosophy of Hellas.

There had been, it was true, ugly whispers concerning him for years. But so had there been, and so there will always be, of most men to whom the world gives fame and homage during their lives. Nor did the slanders come from very reputable people; good Society, as a whole, ignores what has not been blazoned in their powerful enemy, the popular Press. Was he not happily married to a charming and devoted wife, the daughter of a distinguished lawyer? Was she not constantly beside him at parties and at first nights, and entertaining his brilliant circle of friends in Tite Street? And, in any event, who could resist Oscar's infectious laugh, that gay, almost ethereal merriment, which redeemed and transformed the heavy, sensual lines of his great olive-coloured face? When he laughed the grossness of his features seemed to vanish away, and his companions felt that they were in the presence of a rare and gay spirit, obstinately young, and wonderfully brilliant. None of the photographs reveal even a hint of the strange charm which he was able to exercise, and they present to the modern eye an awkward, cumbrous body and the huge, self-indulgent face of a middle-aged man. Yet to his contemporaries the smile changed everything. Was not there some affinity between the magical, transfiguring smile and the tale of Dorian Gray?

Among those whose slanders of Oscar Wilde were well known and taken for granted was the Marquess of Queensberry. But his stories were hardly to be taken seriously; the bearer of a great name, he had little else to recommend him. Although he had been a fine boxer, and a fearless and successful horseman, he was separated from his wife, a cultured, sensitive and beautiful woman, whom he had treated abominably; he was a confessed atheist, and had lost his seat in the House of Lords, as a Scottish representative peer, for refusing to take the oath. He was a combative, obstinate fellow, who denied God and feared no man; yet he had none of the excusing nobility of Bradlaugh. Several of his children had not seen him for years. After a short period of service in the Navy, he had, despite fine natural ability, done little that was useful, and a great deal that was violent, cruel and eccentric.

Perhaps there was in him a streak of eccentricity which is near both to madness and genius; for he transmitted to his children undeniable talent. His eldest son, Lord Drumlanrig, who had died young, had been Lord Rosebery's private secretary, and was made a peer of the United Kingdom, as Lord Kelhead, in his own right by Mr Gladstone, before his promising career was cut short by an early death. The Marquess was furious, for now the son had a seat in the hereditary assembly from which the father was excluded.

More promising even than Lord Drumlanrig was his third son, Lord Alfred Douglas. He was as beautiful as a woman, but he did not show effeminacy: indeed, he had the making of a first-class athlete; he could easily have won his blue on the track. The writer remembers the late Lord Birkenhead, against whom Douglas was later to nurture implacable hatred, at an Oxford dinner describing the wonderful promise of this contemporary of his, and the brilliant impression which Alfred Douglas made upon him when they first met. He told me that they were once competitors in the same race; his intellectual promise was even higher: his first published poem in the *Oxford Magazine* was an earnest of the literary talent which was later to show itself in some of the finest sonnets of the English language. Lord Birkenhead, then at the height of his great prestige, mused sadly on the fate which distorted the career of this obvious favourite of fortune. 'It is said that the gods' favourites die young,' he said, 'but the real tragedy is sometimes that their life is long.' He told me that he was present in an Oxford room with both Oscar Wilde and Alfred Douglas: the reverent air with which his fellow-undergraduates treated the 'Master' sickened him. 'Tell us a parable, Master,' said one of them. A virile British expletive was heard, and the door slammed loudly, with a scholar of Wadham, and a future Lord Chancellor, on the right side of it.

It so happened that one day, in 1891, Lionel Johnson, an intimate friend of Douglas and a fine poet himself, took Douglas to Oscar Wilde's house in Tite Street. The exotic writer and the brilliant undergraduate were mutually captivated, and their friendship, begun then, precipitated the immediate downfall of the elder man at the height of his literary powers, and embittered, obsessed, and twisted the life of the other. It is not within the purpose of this book to measure the blame, but surely the view of the contemporary general public, so contemned by each of them, was right in assessing the blame, as it did, between the mature, distinguished man of letters, with all the glamour of his great reputation, and the spoilt child of fortune, twenty years old. The sustained and ingenious attempt, based largely on his own hearsay, of Mr Frank Harris to maintain the contrary hypothesis, does less than credit both to his great ability and to the credulity of his readers.

Although Lord Queensberry was the last man who had the right to play the part of a dutiful parent, his vain and combative nature took flame at the ugly rumours which coupled the names of Oscar and his son. Alfred Douglas left Oxford without a degree: his father discontinued his allowance until such time as his friendship with Wilde ceased; with the inevitable result, having regard to his son's proud and obstinate nature, that Wilde and Douglas were drawn more closely together. Queensberry was foiled, but he had drawn up the well-known 'Queensberry Rules of Boxing', and he did not recognise defeat in the first round. He went about swearing vengeance. 'I'll do it,' he was heard to boast, 'I'll teach the fellow to leave my son alone: I'll not have their names coupled together.' No doubt his pride had lashed him into a real sincerity. But his blows were not dexterous: he hit about wildly; he wrote a highly defamatory letter to his son concerning Wilde, relying on mere rumour for the grossest allegation, but making this reservation: 'If I thought the actual thing were true, and it became public property, I should be quite justified in shooting him at sight'. He then visited Wilde personally to protest in a most violent manner, but, on a suggestion by the writer of an action for libel, he said, 'No, the letter was privileged.' In a civil action for libel, a letter sent by father to son for the latter's protection would undoubtedly be, *prima facie*, a privileged communication, and it would have needed very heavy evidence of malice on the sender's part to convince a jury that the plea of privilege was in such a case displaced by malice. Finally, to a threat of personal violence, Wilde retorted with sublime insolence, 'I don't know what the Queensberry rules are, but the Wilde rule is to shoot at sight,' and turned him out of the house. Wilde was convinced that the Marquess knew nothing that could injure him, and at this stage this was almost certainly true. Queensberry's next move was farcical, and quite harmless. He had intended to raise a scandal at the first night of *The Importance of Being Earnest*, the comedy which was Wilde's dramatic masterpiece, at the St James's Theatre. He had purchased a stall, but Sir George

Alexander heard of his intention and returned him his money, refusing him admittance. Nevertheless, he presented himself at the stage door with a large bouquet of turnips and carrots, perhaps an allusion to the 'vegetable loves' of Bunthorne, Gilbert's extravagant caricature of Wilde. Opinion veered strongly round in favour of Wilde. Really, Queensberry was obviously mad. It was remembered that he had made a public disturbance 'as an agnostic' during the progress of a play, *The Promise of May*, by the late Poet Laureate, Lord Tennyson. He was rendering himself less and less dangerous: soon no one could bear to listen to this old bore, with his nasty obsessions and slanders on his son.

A letter from his son containing an open threat of a prosecution for criminal libel, and of 'seven years' penal servitude', however, determined him to face the issue: he consulted both the celebrated George Lewis, who refused his assistance because of his friendship for Wilde, and then Charles Russell. He was convinced now that Oscar Wilde would fight him in some way; indeed, he was alarmed, and he wished to choose his own ground. He was counselled to proceed with great care and moderation. Finally, he went down to one of Wilde's clubs, the Albemarle, and handed a card to the porter marked with the words, in a large scrawl, 'Oscar Wilde, posing as Sodomite'. There was cunning and finesse in these words. Even now he made no direct charge of any offence; but the whole world, whether sympathetically or not, considered Wilde the most shameless *poseur*, and this phrase both left a way of escape from a conviction, and also added strength to his case: the addition of this word served both as a shield and a spear. The discreet porter put the card in an envelope, and handed it, on 28 February 1895, to Wilde when he came in. No one else need ever have seen it.

As George Lewis said, when Wilde consulted him immediately after the trial, his proper course would have been to tear up the card with contempt. He could safely ignore the crude attacks of Queensberry, and no one would have blamed him. He was not in public life, and he had only to suspend his friendship with Alfred Douglas to be rid of Lord Queensberry. If everybody who received abusive postcards brought prosecutions for criminal libel, blameless reputations would be far more rare. Whatever Scotland Yard found out about him, the authorities would probably have given him the option of leaving the country, as they have in numerous other cases, no less heinous than that of Oscar Wilde. But pride and arrogance were drawing him on to destruction, and the pitiless chain of events which led to his disgrace and conviction, to the decay of his talent and miserable death, was set in motion by his own mad action.

Alfred Douglas and Wilde were both indignant that Queensberry, bad father and worse husband, should persecute them both in the role of a grieved and dutiful parent. The cautious words of the libel gave him further assurance. If it came to the point, which was the worst 'poser' of the two? A British jury should judge between them. There was logic and even justice in this point of view, and Wilde, like many a litigant before him, thought that he would find a Court of Law as easy to convince as his chosen friends and associates. His conversation had often won over to his side the most bitter enemies and critics. Besides, Wilde was supremely confident in his brilliant destiny. He would listen to no warning from his friends: he believed what he wished to believe. Queensberry had made his 'wonderful life' miserable long enough: it was time that the knot was cut.

On the advice of his friend, Robert Ross, he went post haste to a firm of solicitors, Messrs Humphreys & May, and instructed them to institute proceedings for criminal libel. Mr C O Humphreys, the senior partner in this first-class firm of solicitors, one of the most experienced criminal lawyers in London, listened with amazement to the story. He at once realised the gravity and importance of the case. Mr Humphreys asked him point blank on his solemn oath whether there was a word of truth in the libel. Wilde assured him on his oath that he was absolutely innocent. On the faith of this, Mr Humphreys consented to proceed. 'If you are innocent,' he said, 'you should succeed.' This was the sole basis of Wilde's oft-repeated assertion that his solicitors had advised him that he must succeed. On 1 March, Wilde went down personally to the Police Court to apply for a warrant for the arrest of Lord Queensberry, who was overjoyed at the turn of events. His enemy had walked into the trap. It is fair to state that, had he gone to George Lewis, that wise old man would not have placed the slightest reliance on Oscar Wilde's assertion of innocence. Perhaps that is why Wilde did not go to him. Mr Humphreys knew nothing of Oscar Wilde. Later he appeared in the Police Court to prefer his charge, wearing in his buttonhole a white flower, the sign of a blameless life.

When Charles Russell first undertook the defence of Queensberry, there was still strength in Wilde's position. Very little was known that was definite against him: it was nearly all hearsay, and based on his extraordinary clothes and affectations. Hence the cautiousness of Queensberry's accusation. It was essential for success to brief a man whose intellectual power could match itself against that of Wilde; much would turn on the view that the jury took of his works. Were there not implications of the alleged 'pose' to be found in the *Green Carnation*, the *Picture of Dorian Gray*, and the rest? It was a strange fate which led Russell to seek for the counsel who could stand against Wilde in Edward Carson.

It was the sound and plodding scholar of twenty years ago, with a love of a different kind for the same things which had laid the foundations of Wilde's work. He too had loved the legacies of Greece and Rome, and had preferred them to all other studies; but how different had been the lesson which they had taught him. In appearance and character he was the living embodiment of that *gravitas* which was said to be the root of the Roman character: the moral characteristic on which the Greeks laid most stress was *sophrosyne*, their beautiful word for self-control. Who ever showed self-control more clearly than Edward Carson? The study of the classics had perhaps contributed to his powerful character, but it had been their force and strength which had most influenced him. In the judgment of any work of art Carson would not pretend to be a connoisseur of aesthetic value, but he would always be quick to search and to find some moral meaning. Rarely has a classical education of the same kind produced two more contrasting types than Edward Carson and Oscar Wilde. The simplicity, the naked relevancy, the austerity behind all the best classical art and literature, had burnt itself into the deep and receptive soul of the toiling student, while the child of genius was seduced by the bypaths, sickly and corrupt, which steeply decline from the height and purity of the classical citadel. Pericles or Cicero or Horace would have recognised in Carson, the grave lawyer and courteous gentleman, a worthy student of their work, and a man in their own tradition, but Wilde would have appeared to them the most dreadful barbarian, whose spiritual home was properly in Babylon or Macedonia. And it was strange that fate should now place them face to face.

When Russell first brought the papers to Carson, the latter refused to take the case on the ground that it would be a hateful role to undertake against a fellow alumnus and classmate of Trinity College. Where, too, was the evidence upon which this prosecution – for in this case the defendant was really the prosecutor – of the man was to proceed? There was nothing to go upon but hearsay, which would be as likely to ruin the young son whom the Marquess was nominally protecting as to have any other effect, and the construction of certain books, 'which Carson had not read, and did not wish to read'. Carson has never quite held the orthodox view usually maintained by the great men of the law that a counsel is 'on the rank', and must take any case that comes his way in order that justice may be done and that the man even with the blackest appearance against him may find a bold defender. Carson could only fight if he could persuade himself of the moral justice of his cause, and he has frequently refused briefs which could not arouse this conviction in his heart. So Russell went away from Dr Johnson's Buildings disappointed, but he did not send the leading brief to any other man.

Meanwhile, private detectives had been busy searching London and Paris for definite evidence against Wilde, visiting restaurants and hotels. This evidence only confirmed what was already known – that Oscar Wilde and Alfred Douglas had stayed in the same hotel in many places and on many occasions; and Queensberry would still have to place himself in the most odious light in playing the part of his son's saviour and in ruining him at the same time. But, when the search seemed fruitless and the defence seemed to be in an almost hopeless case, proof suddenly became manifest. One of the detectives employed happened to visit a shop in the West End of London, which was being carefully watched, and for good reason, by the police. The detective engaged in conversation a girl employed there, whose real profession was 'the oldest in the world'; he asked her whether she was prosperous; she replied in the negative, and that she and her class were being subjected to low and abominable competition, which she attributed to the influence of Oscar Wilde. The detective now paid attention. 'Why do you say that?' he asked. The girl then said that he had only to visit an address in an unfrequented part of London, and break into the top flat, and he would find all the evidence that he required. He made off instantly, climbed up a dizzy flight of stairs, and knocked at the door. He was admitted by the caretaker, a miserable, frightened old woman, who tried vainly to prevent his entry: there he found a sort of post-box, which contained the names and addresses of many youths and young men of the humbler walks of life, and also documents which connected many of them with Oscar Wilde. These were put in the possession of the defendant's solicitors, who relentlessly pursued every avenue of information, and identified many of the poor creatures who were subsequently to appear as Wilde's accomplices. The meshes were gathering around Wilde, who was quite ignorant of this new turn of events. He still thought that all he had to meet was an attack on his books, which his genius could defend.

Charles Russell & Co now had much material to use which changed the whole aspect of the case: in criminal libel the defendant has a heavy task; a plea of 'privilege' has rarely succeeded; he may not plead 'fair comment on a matter of interest'. Moreover, he must not only prove 'justification', supplying meticulously and in detail particulars which justify his libel, but he must also prove that publication of his libel was in the public interest. Heretofore, Queensberry's draft particulars only contained references to passages in Oscar Wilde's books, some of which were of acknowledged literary excellence. In the light of the new evidence, however, not only was it possible to avoid all attack on Lord Alfred Douglas, but to go far beyond the words of the 'libel', which alleged 'posing'. The particulars of justification were now amended and supplemented by many folios.

With new instructions, Charles Russell came down to Mr Edward Carson's chambers. In view of the new situation, would he not now take the brief? It was monstrous that such a creature as Oscar Wilde should have the audacity to invoke the protection of the criminal law on his own behalf. If he succeeded, as he well might if he were not skilfully discredited, it would be making a mockery of English justice and the English Courts, and Wilde would probably boast to his friends that the man of genius was above morals and above the Courts, and write a play on the way a clever man can pervert the uses of justice. The only evidence against him was that of accomplices, and the Courts notoriously look with suspicion on such evidence, and juries most unwillingly believe it. Carson himself knew that the testimony of 'approvers' in Ireland often weakened rather than strengthened the case. Nor would any of these accomplices admit any offence on their own part, for obvious reasons. It was their account, rather, that Wilde had importuned them against their will. The advisers of Lord Queensberry were in no way acting for the Crown, but for a rather disreputable old man, and they had no authority to give immunity to those who came forward to turn 'King's evidence'. Carson was horrified at what was now alleged against Wilde. Russell assured him that in his view the evidence was absolutely true, and, indeed, told far less than the truth. Undoubtedly deep moral indignation boiled up inside him that this Irishman, this graduate of his own University, could come to London and corrupt and degrade these poor youths. To his simple and direct nature no kind of excuse presented itself which must present itself now to those who know Wilde's lamentable decline in later years, such as that Wilde's conduct was an affair for the physician rather than for the Courts. He knew Wilde well: in his view the man possessed a sensible and brilliant brain, with a keen eye for his own advancement. He was a public danger and pest, and a disgrace to his native land. It was not as if he was being asked to prosecute Wilde by the Public Prosecutor: why, the man was himself seeking to deprive another person of his liberty who had said of him far less than the truth, and this man had been a classmate of his own. He listened to all that Russell said, but still deferred his decision.

He was determined to take advice from the highest authority as to his duty in the matter: he went to Lord Halsbury, who had been Lord Chancellor during the Conservative administration. 'Should I do this? Is it right or not?'

'The great thing,' said the famous Lord Chancellor, 'is to arrive at justice, and it is you, I believe, who can best do it.'

This decided Carson, and he accepted the brief. It soon became known to Oscar Wilde that Carson was to be against him. This piece of news was immensely reassuring to the poet: it was not that he desired or expected mercy from him; he simply did not fear his antagonist. He did not regard him as a man who could be intellectually considered; he remembered his mediocrity in Trinity days, and his recent successes at the Bar and in Parliament made him think even less of these institutions than he had done before. He was immensely amused; he told his friends that 'he was to be cross-examined by old Ned Carson'. He had no doubt that, with him as his leading antagonist, the trial would merely enhance the reputation of Oscar Wilde: it was going to be too easy. What did Ned Carson know of literature – or of life, for that matter?

Almost on the eve of the trial, Wilde had dinner with Alfred Douglas, Frank Harris, and Bernard Shaw at the Café Royal. The two last-named urged Wilde to abandon the prosecution and go abroad, but Wilde and Douglas, taking great offence at this advice, rose abruptly and left the restaurant together. It is often said that Wilde could have escaped all his troubles by taking their advice. It is true that this dinner was after the Police Court proceedings, and that Wilde had seen all the particulars of justification, so that it may well seem that he was insane to proceed; but now it was difficult to turn back: at the very least it would have meant disgrace. For now, thanks to the detectives, Queensberry was in possession of information which would have justified a criminal prosecution against himself, and it is difficult to see how the Director of Public Prosecutions could have avoided bringing such a prosecution, had Queensberry sent his proofs. Unless he was willing to live abroad forever, his one chance was now to defeat and discredit Queensberry in this action, and, by a verdict won on the general issue, to burke every charge made against him. Moreover, his chances of success were far from hopeless. He had the leader of the Bar, Sir Edward Clarke, on his side, with Charles Mathews, the future Director and the most fierce and deadly prosecutor of his time. Lord Alfred, in the witness-box, could tell the jury a long and damaging story of his father's treatment of himself and his mother which might well alienate at once the jury's sympathy from him, make his role as a loving and dutiful father untenable and ridiculous, and hold him up to hated contempt and ridicule as a beast and hypocrite, upon whose accusations not the slightest reliance would be placed. Nor was Carson's real strength yet realised: many people accepted the underestimate that 'Jehu Junior' had expressed in *Vanity Fair*. The public – outside the Temple, at any rate – had no idea that he was a match for the great Sir Edward Clarke, and Oscar Wilde had no opinion of him at all. The evidence available goes to prove that Wilde was no longer in the mood of arrogant certainty in which he had launched the prosecution, for he had now read the Marquess's particulars:

he probably now bitterly regretted bringing the case; but he also saw, as a clever man, that a great deal was now at stake for him, and, if he wished to continue to live 'his wonderful life' in England, there was only one thing at this stage to do – to secure a conviction against Lord Queensberry. The only alternative now was disgrace and exile from everything that really made life worth the living for him. For, as yet, he had no place but in London. His writings, despite the fact that he had written *Salome* in French, were as yet unknown on the Continent, and ultimately it was his misfortunes which made his name second only to that of Byron's on the Continent among English writers of the nineteenth century.

The trial began on 3 April 1895. Before the case began, a circumstance arose which caused perhaps the greatest sensation abroad of the whole trial. According to English procedure, after a preliminary hearing in the Police Court before the magistrates, who may commit the prisoner to trial or not on the evidence, yet another preliminary enquiry must ensue: the facts must be laid before the grand jury. These are a panel of men with a property qualification, and they are usually well-to-do people. Before them the witnesses in the case appear, and, if the grand jury consider that there is sufficient evidence to justify putting the prisoner 'on his peril' they return a 'true bill'; if by a chance, which sometimes occurs, the jury think otherwise, they return 'no true bill', and the prosecution, except in very exceptional cases, is wiped out forever. Now it so happened that a very distinguished French journalist, who had lived for years in England and who spoke better English than the Englishmen, was mistakenly summoned to attend the grand jury at the Old Bailey. Out of courtesy, he went down to the Old Bailey to excuse himself as a French citizen, but, when he found the Wilde case was one of those which he was summoned to consider, he decided to remain. Indeed, so superior was his mien that he was asked to preside. The grand jury listened to the evidence and returned a 'true bill', but in the course of the testimony a far more illustrious name than Wilde's was mentioned. It was mentioned in its true context in the subsequent trials; the proceedings before the grand jury are private, and no British newspaper referred to it, but the Continental Press was made fully aware of the occurrence, and the news soon began to flow back to England. The mention of this name turned out to be another and critical misfortune to the unlucky Wilde. The Erinues were now in full cry. Had this name not been mentioned, as will later appear, Wilde might still have escaped a sentence of imprisonment altogether.

The case was heard on 2 April in the original Old Bailey, that terrible old Court of Tragedies. Judges and counsel had for generations denounced its sordid aspect inside and outside, together with its miserable proportions, and continued to do so until it was pulled down at the beginning of this century and succeeded by the present fine edifice. Everyone who entered the place was influenced by a sense of tragedy and gloom, and even by a feeling of imprisonment. For the Court was tiny; its air was foetid; the roomiest place was the dock itself, where thirty prisoners could be seated. And now it was crowded with fashionable people. There was not a seat or corner to be had. Somebody made a jest about 'The Importance of Being Early', and there was a laugh. When the Court was already packed, the tall figure of Oscar Wilde was seen squeezing his way through the crowd accompanied by Lord Alfred Douglas. He was elaborately dressed in a long Melton overcoat, and carried a strange, very tall, but conical-shaped silk hat. He was not wearing his white flower, but the entrance of this extraordinary person introduced an atmosphere of Gilbert and Sullivan. Somewhere in Court was the prisoner, who was on bail, but his squat little pugnacious figure could not yet be identified. Wilde seemed to be in high spirits; he chatted and laughed to his friends, and settled down into a seat at the solicitors' table.

Behind him sat the counsel; for Wilde, Sir Edward Clarke, Charles Mathews, and Mr Travers Humphreys, now a Judge; for the defendant, Carson, Charlie Gill, one of the greatest of criminal advocates, and his brother Arthur, later a police magistrate. Oscar turned round and smiled at Carson, who looked coldly past him.

There was a pause; the Judge was a little late; then were heard the usher's three knocks at the door. Everybody rose, and Mr Justice Collins entered in his scarlet and ermine robes, followed by the High Sheriff of London, carrying a sword and wearing court dress. The gentlemen of the Bar bow to the Judge, and the Judge to the gentlemen of the Bar. The Judge sits down, takes up the bouquet of beautiful flowers supplied for his use by old custom as a disinfectant against the plague; the Marquess of Queensberry steps into the dock; the charge is read to him; he turns an implacable look towards Oscar Wilde, and pleads in a clear voice that he is not guilty, that the words were true and published in the public interest.

Then Sir Edward, a short, stout man but of a great dignity, looking rather like an eighteenth-century parson, rises and opens the case for the prosecution. He soon shows that he is a master of words. The form is perfect. Carson afterwards said to a friend in the House of Commons, 'I never heard anything to equal it in all my life.' But which line was he choosing? Two courses lay open: one a course of extreme moderation; the other to anticipate attack by attack, and introduce the whole story of the Queensberry family, the Marquess's neglect and cruelty, and the bitter feud arising therefrom, in which his unfortunate client had been involved, and by reason of which Lord Queensberry was really pursuing him, as a friend of his divorced wife and estranged children. It would have been safe to prophesy that an advocate like Marshall Hall would have taken this course: he would have given battle over the whole front, and in every corner of the field. The Judge would have rebuked him and pulled him up again and again, but he would have succeeded in introducing such an atmosphere of prejudice against Lord Queensberry into the minds of the jury that some would have taken Lord Queensberry's side and some that of Lord Alfred and his mother, and Oscar Wilde's part in the story might have become quite a secondary issue. The terribly relevant and penetrating mind of Edward Carson might, perhaps would, have brought the jury back to the central issue of the trial, but it appears to the writer that a Marshall Hall at his best, flinging himself into the fray, with all his strength, might easily at least have secured a long consideration and a disagreement.

But Sir Edward Clarke had decided otherwise. Relying absolutely on Wilde's protestation of innocence, he was out for a conviction on the single issue, and was determined to avoid all irrelevancies. He considered that his client would suffer and not gain from a wide and bitter discussion of the Queensberry family history. The jury might then condemn Wilde for no sin of his own, but visit the sins of the Douglas children on Wilde's innocent head: such irrelevancies would widen and expose the front for attack by the angry Queensberry and his clever counsel. No doubt there were wrongs on both sides, and the more completely his client was kept clear of all this, the better for him. Besides, for such a plan of attack Lord Alfred Douglas was an indispensable witness; no jury would like to see a young son attacking his father in a criminal trial before his father had said a word in his defence. Lord Alfred was headstrong, eloquent, and full of bitterness against the Marquess; besides, the whole case arose out of the friendship between Wilde and Douglas, and it would be folly to subject a young nobleman to cross-examination as to this. Who knew what materials Queensberry had concocted or imagined and given to Carson? Sir Edward did not know that Carson was determined not, under any circumstances, to use such material in this trial.

It was a difficult decision, and it is easy to be wise after the event; it is always the golden rule for the prosecution to pursue a course of studied moderation; but this was no ordinary prosecution; here the real prosecutor stood in the dock, while the real defendant was to stand in the witness-box, exposed to the widest and bitterest attack on his life, on his works, on his very thoughts and ideas; but, had Clarke known all the information concerning Wilde on other charges which Carson had at his disposal, and the deadly use to which he would put it, and had he continued to hold his brief, without much doubt he should, for the sake of his client, have taken the other course.

From the moment that Clarke opened the case on these lines, perfect as his quiet argument was, Oscar's fate was really sealed. Though his counsel did not know it, he was really defending, not an innocent man who would be prejudiced by his friends' faults, but a guilty man, whose only chance of escape depended on the exposure of his enemy's malice and wickedness.

But, of course, Sir Edward held the close interest and sympathy of everyone: there was this great literary man, this acknowledged genius – and he was only forty years old – not indeed accused of any offence, but of whom a certain word with an obvious reservation had been used by an old nobleman so eccentric that he could hardly be held responsible for his actions. Nevertheless, Oscar Wilde could not let such an expression pass in connection with his name, although there had been no accusation of any offence. He had had trouble of this sort before. A man named Wood had found some letters in a pocket of a coat given him by Lord Alfred Douglas, and had come, when in great need, to Mr Wilde, asking for money. Mr Wilde had given him the money, but Wood had retained the most important letter for subsequent use. This letter had been used by two men named Allan and Clyborn to ask Wilde for more money; in the end they had given the letter to Mr Wilde. This was the first intimation the Court heard that Wilde had been the victim of low blackmailers. One reflects that, had Wilde prosecuted those men for blackmail instead of Queensberry for libel, they would have undoubtedly been convicted, and Wilde would have enjoyed the protection which the Court always gives to blackmailed persons with the courage to come forward. Thus all his troubles might have been averted.

As for this letter, of which the defence would make so much, there was really nothing in it: Sir Edward observed that it was a sort of 'prose sonnet' which had indeed been translated into a French sonnet. 'The words of this letter may appear extravagant to those who are in the habit of writing commercial correspondence' (the British jury laughed), 'or those ordinary things which the necessities of life force upon us every day, but the jury need place no hateful construction upon it.' Sir Edward then read the famous and amazing letter addressed to Lord Alfred Douglas by Wilde, 'My own boy, – Your sonnet is quite lovely, and it is a marvel that those red rose-leaf lips of yours should have been made no less for the music of song than for the madness of kisses. Your slim gilt soul walks between passion and poetry. I know Hyacinthus, whom Apollo loved so madly, was you in Greek days. Why are you alone in London, and when do you go to Salisbury? Do go there to cool your hands in the grey twilight of Gothic things, and come here whenever you like. It is a lovely place – it only lacks you; but go to Salisbury first. – Always with undying love, Yours Oscar.'

Mr Wilde, said Sir Edward, would satisfy the jury that there was nothing to be ashamed of in this letter. He looked up as if for reassurance at the jury, but they were far from satisfied. The foreman asked ominously, 'What is the date of that letter?' Sir Edward said the letter was undated, and passed on, having left, like the good advocate he was, the best to the last, to much surer ground. According to the plea in justification, Oscar Wilde was being attacked for something which he had never written; nay, more, the publication of which his influence had prevented. He had been invited to subscribe an article for an Oxford undergraduate paper called *The Chameleon*. He had obligingly sent them an article entitled 'Phrases and Philosophies for the Use of the Young'. They were brilliant and effective epigrams, and 'even wisdom in a witty form'. Perhaps some of the jury had thoroughly enjoyed such things in *The Woman of No Importance*, and Sir Edward smiled at the jury as one who shared with them the appreciation of good things. In the same magazine, however, there also appeared a disgraceful and indefensible short story, called 'The Priest and the Acolyte'. This was not written by Wilde, and, when he read a proof copy, he instantly wrote to the editor, who withdrew the magazine. How could this be urged in justification of this terrible charge? Nor was this the measure of unfairness: his client was to be assailed on moral grounds for his especial masterpieces, for his *Picture of Dorian Gray*. Could anything be more absurd? 'It can be bought on any bookstall in London. It has Mr Wilde's name on the title page. It has been published five years. The story is that of a young man of good birth, great wealth, and great personal beauty, whose friend paints a picture of him. Dorian Gray expresses the wish that he shall remain as in the picture, while the picture ages with the years. His wish is granted, and he soon knows that upon the picture, and not upon his own face, the scars of trouble and bad conduct are falling. In the end he stabs the picture and falls dead, and the picture is restored to its pristine beauty, while his friends find upon the floor the body of a hideous old man.' 'I shall be surprised,' concluded Sir Edward, with a side-glance at Carson, 'if my learned friend can pick upon one passage in that book which does more than describe, as novelists and dramatists may – nay, must – describe the passions and fashions of life.'

Sir Edward had finished his opening address. The conclusion had been made with consummate skill, which Wilde himself must have admired, in an absolutely just attack on the unfairness, ignorance, and confused logic of the plea in justification; nevertheless, the speech had failed of its full effect. There was no hint of apology or admission that Wilde had been indiscreet, weak, or foolish. He had not even excused Wilde's letter to Douglas. It left the defence to open its full assault without a foreboding. Throughout, Clarke, with studied moderation, was putting Wilde on a high pedestal, whereas he should have placed him in the arena, and stigmatised with ridicule and disdain the almost blasphemous assaults made on him, without in any way discrediting the assailants. He was putting his case altogether too high, and scorning in Olympian fashion to hit back. If Sir Edward Clarke had been defending William Shakespeare for stealing a deer, it would have been as well for him to have noticed the particulars of the charge, the poverty of his client, and the incidence of the game laws.

After the porter of the Albemarle Club, whom Carson did not cross-examine, had been called to prove the publication of the libel, Oscar Wilde went into the witness-box and kissed the book. Turning to Sir Edward Clarke, he adopted an attitude which seemed urbane and candid. He gave his age as thirty-nine, at which his old classmate, Carson, looked steadily at him and took a note. He went modestly through all the story of his good birth, academic distinction, and literary achievements. The first amusing incident in his evidence appeared when he described his interview with the blackmailer Allan on the subject of his letter to Lord Alfred Douglas. The man had said, 'A very curious construction could be put on that letter.' Whereon Oscar said that he replied, 'Art is rarely intelligible to the criminal classes.' The man persisted, 'A man has offered me £60 for it.' Oscar blandly retorted, 'If you take my advice you will go to that man and sell it to him for £60. I myself have never received so large a sum for any prose work of that length, but I am glad to find that there is someone in England who considers a letter of mine worth £60.' This was a touch the real Oscar Wilde, and the Court rose to it: he was a very engaging person. Nevertheless, Wilde admitted twice having paid blackmail on his letters. Even then, however, he had not been too proud to lavish his wit on the blackmailer. 'I am afraid you are leading a wonderfully wicked life.' The man replied, 'There is good and bad in every one of us.' 'You are a born philosopher,' Oscar flung at his retreating figure. Oscar was making a good impression. The man who could pay blackmail and laugh at the blackmailer at the same time was a very rare creature. His letter to Alfred Douglas was a work of art; the translation of it into French had been done by a French poet of great distinction, writing as 'Pierre Louys'. The 'Priest and the Acolyte' was bad and indecent: he had had nothing to do with the writing of it, and had stopped its publication. 'It was bad and indecent, and I thoroughly disapproved of it.' Then, as a final question from Sir Edward Clarke: 'Your attention has been called to the plea and to the names of persons with whom your conduct has been impugned. Is there any truth in these allegations?' – 'There is no truth in any of them.'

Now the real contest began: Carson rose to cross-examine. It was a painful and embarrassing moment as they faced each other. Many memories must have occurred to each of them, but Wilde smiled in a friendly way, as if inviting him to begin. Carson had now to ask his first question in cross-examination, which he always considered was the crucial moment in a case. He had puzzled long as to this first question. He knew how clever Wilde was, and how he could turn into ridicule the most serious and honourable matters. Up to the actual commencement of Wilde's evidence, he had not known how to begin. His plan was first to examine him on his literature and his views of morals as shown in his books, which was the weakest part of the plea, and then to pass to specific accusations which the information before him warranted. If he could obtain admissions from Wilde as to his writings, this would make the other dreadful evidence more credible to the jury. This, however, meant embarking on a literary enquiry on unequal terms with the cleverest writer in London, and on this ground it was an unequal contest. '*Impar congressus Achilli*'. Then Wilde quite unconsciously gave him his cue. He said he was thirty-nine: Carson knew that he and Wilde were almost exactly of an age, and he was forty-one. He had before him a copy of Wilde's birth certificate. Wilde, out of pure foolish vanity, had 'posed' as to his age. Wilde had put the first question into his adversary's hand.

'You stated that your age was thirty-nine. I think you are over forty. You were born on 16 October 1854? Did you wish to *pose* as being young?' – 'No.'

'That makes you more than forty?'

Wilde recovered himself; he made a gesture, and gave a long-drawn 'Ah,' as if he were congratulating Carson on his clever mathematics, and at the same time comically mourning his lost youth.

It was a small point, but nevertheless Wilde had told a vain and stupid lie in answer to the very first question put to him. But the age had a significance and a context. Carson passed on to ask Wilde the age of Alfred Douglas: he was now twenty-four, and Wilde had known him for three years. Wilde's answers showed that the two of them had stayed together in many places at home and abroad. Carson then passed on to cross-examine him on the literary side of the plea. He began with *The Chameleon*: it was true that Wilde had not written the 'Priest and the Acolyte', but the magazine began with Wilde's 'Phrases and Philosophies for the Use of the Young' and ended with 'The Priest and the Acolyte', written by a young man. It was an Oxford magazine; Wilde had been frequently at Oxford. Although Wilde had nothing to do with the writing of the tale, was not it attributable directly to his corrupting influence? Carson was tempted into this field; it was unfair to make the witness responsible for what he had not written, and Wilde scored again and again. Carson invited discussion of the whole inexhaustible subject of moral purpose in literature.

'You are of opinion there is no such thing as an immoral book?' – 'Yes.'

'May I take it that you think "The Priest and the Acolyte" was not immoral?' – 'It was worse; it was badly written.'

Everybody laughed; the jury were as delighted with their places as if they had been given free seats for *The Importance of Being Earnest*.

Carson put to Wilde the prurient details of the story: Wilde shrugged his shoulders, as if imputing prurience to the counsel who studied such things with care; really, he could not remember. 'I have only read it once, in last November, and nothing will induce me to read it again.'

Counsel pressed him as to whether the story was not blasphemous. Wilde answered that it violated every canon of artistic beauty: the story was 'disgusting', 'horrible', but not 'blasphemous'. Then he leant forward and said earnestly, 'I do not believe that any book or work of art ever had any effect on morality whatever.' This obviously seemed a surprising paradox to Carson: the man who said it could surely not be sincere.

Carson had again and again used the word 'pose' with ironic emphasis. He did so again. 'So far as your work is concerned, you *pose* as not being concerned about morality or immorality?' – 'I do not know whether you use the word "pose" in any particular sense.'

'It is a favourite word of your own?' – 'Is it? I have no pose in this matter,' answered Wilde, almost apologetically, dropping altogether his flippant air. 'In writing a play, or a book, or anything, I am certainly concerned with literature – that is, with art. I aim, not at doing good or evil, but in trying to make a thing that will have some quality of beauty.' This, though Carson had no sympathy with the point of view, was Wilde at his best and most sincere. Whether in the melodrama of *Dorian Gray* or *The Ideal Husband*, or the exquisite *Fairy Tales*, or in the sweet triolet, *Do you remember Sicily?* all that was sincere in Wilde was preoccupied with the search for beauty, and its expression in the English language. He did not seek to teach; he sought to reveal.

By a strange paradox, in denying the cause of morality in literature, Wilde had almost become morally earnest. But Carson's questions led him back again to flippancy. Wilde said there was no moral purpose in his work. Why then had he written his 'Phrases and Philosophies for the Use of the Young'? One by one they were put to Wilde. As spoken by Carson they sounded shallow and even pernicious, but

Wilde's retorts again and again blunted the edge of Carson's construction and irony, and showed the epigrams as something exquisite and delightful. Was not all this quite harmless, and, in Clarke's phrase, 'wisdom in a witty form'? Never was Wilde more entertaining in any of his comedies. Carson was like a knight in full armour attacking a dancer. He never faltered in his answers; nor were these always superficial. He passed easily from axiom to epigram.

'Listen, sir; here is one of the "Phrases and Philosophies for the Use of the Young": "Wickedness is a myth invented by good people to account for the curious attractiveness of others". You think that is true?' – 'I rarely think anything I write is true.'

'"Religions die when they are proved to be true." Is that true?' – 'Yes, I hold that. It is a suggestion towards a philosophy of the absorption of religions by science, but surely it is too big a question for you to go into now.'

'Do you think that was a safe axiom to put forward for the philosophy of the young?' – 'Most stimulating.'

'"If one tells the truth one is sure, sooner or later, to be found out"?' – 'This is a pleasing paradox, but I do not set very high store on it as an axiom.'

'Is it good for the young?' – 'Anything is good that stimulates thought, in whatever age.'

'"Pleasure is the only thing in life one should live for"?' This was surely only a restatement of what both Carson and Wilde had read in many philosophies down to the heyday of Herbert Spencer. The gloss was better than the epigram. 'I think that the realisation of oneself is the prime aim of life, and to realise oneself through pleasure is finer than to do so through pain. I am on that point entirely on the side of the Greeks.'

Carson next turned to *Dorian Gray*, and said that a decadent construction could be put on that work. 'Only by brutes and illiterates,' retorted Wilde.

'But an illiterate person reading *Dorian Gray* might consider it such a novel?' – 'The views of illiterates on art are unaccountable.'

Carson put further questions of the views of ordinary individuals on *Dorian Gray*. 'I have no knowledge of the views of ordinary individuals.'

'You did not prevent the ordinary individual from buying your book?' – 'I have never discouraged him.'

Carson then went on to put to Wilde views expressed by the characters in *Dorian Gray*, and referred to one character who had adored another man 'madly'. Had Wilde ever entertained such an adoration? 'I have never given adoration to anybody except myself.' There was loud laughter at this, but Carson treated it with cold scorn.

He put another passage: 'I have adored you extravagantly.'

'Do you mean financially?' Wilde asked.

Carson was angry now. 'Oh, yes,' he said, with deep irony. 'Financially. Do you think we are talking about finance?' – 'I don't know what you are talking about,' replied Wilde in mock despair.

'Don't you?' said Carson, reserved and cold again. 'Well, I hope I shall make myself very plain before I have done.'

Then came a cruel analysis of Wilde's strange letter to Alfred Douglas, which had already made such a bad impression on the jury. Wilde defended it on the highest grounds. 'I think it is a beautiful letter,' said Wilde. 'It is a poem. You might as well cross-examine me as to whether a sonnet of Shakespeare was proper.'

'Apart from art,' persisted Carson sternly.

'I cannot answer apart from art,' said Wilde.

'Suppose a man who was not an artist had written this

letter, would you say it was a proper letter?' asked Carson.

'A man who was not an artist could not have written that letter.' The laughter which greeted the sustained wit of this dialogue was now mixed with a low murmur of approval.

Carson's Dublin brogue had contrasted strongly, throughout the duel, with the classical accent of the most practised dialectician, and the best conversationalist, except perhaps Whistler, in London.

'Can I suggest, for the sake of your reputation, that there is nothing very wonderful in this "red rose lips" of yours?'

'A great deal depends,' retorted Wilde, with an air of politeness, and with obvious reference to Carson's Irish accent, 'on the way it is read.'

'"Your slim gilt soul walks between passion and poetry." Is that a beautiful phrase?'

'Not as *you* read it.' The taunt was now flung openly.

'I don't profess to be an artist,' replied Carson hotly, 'and when I hear you give evidence I am glad I am not.'

Carson took another of Wilde's extravagant letters to Douglas. 'Is *that* an ordinary letter?' he asked. 'Everything I write is extraordinary,' was the witness's disarming reply. 'I do not *pose* as being ordinary.'

So far the honours had all been with the prosecutor, except for the first few questions. It is true to say that Oscar Wilde had scored immensely. He had favourably impressed, not only the people in Court, but the contemporary Press. There had been something sincere in his talk about beauty and the Greek ideal. Very few people could have parried every powerful blow of Carson's by so skilful and light, and withal so good-humoured, a blade. The evening newspapers commented in a not unfriendly way on the strange attitude of this 'lover of the beautiful' who thought books could not be immoral, who was not concerned to do good or evil, but merely to create beauty: the 'wonderful intellectual force and flow of perfect language with which he had defended his positions' was praised, although some doubt was expressed as to what the very workaday British jury had thought of Wilde's views on the 'ordinary individual'. As in his plays, his wit had delighted the many; but to the few, to some who believed in Oscar's innocence and could not understand Carson's bitterness, the duel began to assume a symbolic form – the struggle of art against philistinism in its most intolerant and British form; to others who knew the truth, another antagonism presented itself: it seemed as if hypocrisy was about to baffle justice.

Carson had done his best. He had prepared his cross-examination with the same thoroughness and care as he had done in the case of Havelock Wilson, and he had failed. No tears this time; not once had he really pierced the joints of Wilde's armour. Well, for once he had failed; let him pass on. It was late in the afternoon, and the shadows of evening began to darken the old Court of Tragedies; and with the changing light Carson left the field of literature and began to question Wilde on a lower and more specific plane, where the Poet of the Beautiful joined company with valets and grooms and blackmailers in dim-lit, curtained, perfumed rooms. But even here Wilde was making a case for himself. He had a great contempt for social distinctions. Why should his characters all come from the drawing-room? He was a student and lover of life and youth. He dismissed the half-sovereign given to the blackmailer with a scornful gesture. 'I gave it out of contempt.'

'Then your way to show your contempt is by paying ten shillings?' – 'Yes, very often,' replied Wilde drily, and regained the sympathy of the Court.

Wilde had asked another young man, employed in a publisher's office, to an expensive dinner at an hotel.

'Was that for the purpose of having an intellectual treat?' asked the advocate.

'Well, for him, yes,' answered Wilde. Once more the jury laughed at the man's wit, but it was almost the last kindly laugh that the case aroused in any of the audience. The Court adjourned, and Oscar Wilde had undoubtedly scored a great intellectual triumph over the barrister; his evidence had been a sort of *tour de force*. But it was seen that Carson had many more pages to his brief, and his threat was remembered: 'I shall make myself very plain before I have done'.

Next day Wilde appeared at about ten minutes past ten. He began to talk and laugh with his second counsel, Charles Mathews, about the reports in the newspapers. Yet he did not look so well or so gay as on the day before. At half-past ten he was already in the box, again smilingly inviting Carson to begin. Today the questioning was far more serious: there was more about those darkened, perfumed rooms; of an old public school man named Taylor, who introduced Wilde to young men in humble situations of life; of specific dates and interviews; of champagne dinners attended by these two men, and young boys of no education or culture to whom Wilde gave presents of jewellery. Wilde must have been amazed at Carson's knowledge of his movements over a period of years.

'Did you know that one was a gentleman's valet, and the other a gentleman's groom?' – 'I did not know it, and, if I had, I should not have cared,' replied Wilde.

'What enjoyment was it to you to be entertaining grooms and coachmen?' – 'The pleasure of being with those who are young, bright, happy, careless and original.'

Carson: 'Had they plenty of champagne?'

Wilde: 'What *gentleman* would stint his guests?'

The Court laughed for the very last time – with Wilde.

Carson: 'What *gentleman* would stint the valet and the

groom!'

Name after name was mentioned; Sir Edward Clarke looked nervously at a letter of one of these people which Carson was handling. Surely it was hardly possible that Carson could be calling these young men to admit charges terrible against themselves. He said really, his lordship had better see a very ordinary respectful letter which Wilde had himself produced from one of the persons named.

'Never mind that,' said Carson grimly. 'Parker himself will be in the box, and the jury will see what he is like.'

A whisper of excitement went round the Court. So Carson had the evidence to prove his allegations after all.

Name after name was mentioned. Throughout this terrible ordeal Wilde had behaved with quiet dignity and restraint. No matter how wounding had been Carson's suggestions, this arrogant man had never faltered. His evidence yesterday had not been forgotten. The Press had been generous in praising his fine work. There was much that seemed fine about the man himself under this severe cross-examination by his own contemporary at college. If the case was not exactly the butterfly on the wheel, it seemed at any rate to be the man of genius on the rack; would the inexorable lawyer never leave the poet alone?

Wilde had never faltered up until now: Carson mentioned the name of a young servant at Oxford almost casually.

'Did you ever kiss him?' asked Carson with sudden emphasis.

Wilde made a gesture of disgust. 'He was a particularly plain boy. He was unfortunately very ugly. I pitied him for it.'

It was a deadly question and a fatal reply. That one question told the jury more than all the previous two days of questioning. Carson had almost finished his cross-examination, and this question had been a mere bow drawn at a venture. Both witness and counsel knew the truth was out. The former struggled to escape, but Carson would not let him pass from it. He fastened on to Wilde's answer like a hawk. Why had he given that reason? Why? Why? Wilde strove to explain. Several of his answers began inarticulately; some were broken off unfinished; all were excited and indignant. But Carson was relentless. Why had he mentioned the boy's ugliness? Wilde was almost in tears now, on the point of a breakdown like that of Havelock Wilson. Finally he pulled himself together, and gave the reason. 'You stung me by your insolence, sir. You are trying to unnerve me,' he cried out pitifully. This was a very different Oscar Wilde from the man who could not answer 'apart from art', and who had said, 'Not as *you* read it, Mr Carson'.

For he was broken: a further name, more suggestions. Wilde's recovered self-possession disappeared almost at once. Had he done this, and that? 'No, it has never occurred – never, *never*, *never*.' But Carson still pursued him with further questions. The witness, who had almost lolled in the witness-box, recoiled backwards, as if to shield himself: gestures of repudiation, disdain, disgust.

Finally came the words which must have been heard with relief by Oscar Wilde. Only one question more: would he know again a certain waiter at a Paris hotel? The witness winced. Yes, he thought that he would. It was the end of the most sensational cross-examination of those times, quiet but not without menace. Sir Edward Clarke rose to re-examine. Carson's attack had been so effective that he realised he must now reluctantly use the letters of Lord Queensberry to his son. These letters revealed the greatest malice towards his wife and children, especially to Alfred Douglas, whose legitimacy he questioned: no one, however august, who had been on close terms with his wife or children was spared from his attacks, not even the Prime Minister, Lord Rosebery, whose private secretary his eldest son had been, and Mr Gladstone, who had made him a peer. But these letters were of little avail now to obscure the prejudice which had gathered round Wilde; they might have been more useful at the beginning. Moreover, the introduction of entirely new documents gave Carson the right to cross-examine Wilde again, and so enjoy the last word.

Before this occurred, the Court adjourned until the afternoon. After the interval the Judge came back, and the whole Court waited for the prosecutor. The rumour started, and ran round the Court, that he had abandoned the case and left the country rather than face Carson again. The rumour soon proved a *canard*, for he appeared and apologised to the Judge on the grounds that the clock in his restaurant had been wrong. Carson then destroyed much of the effect of the Queensberry letters by reading a letter to Wilde written by Alfred Douglas to his father, which was full of hatred and bitterness. Then, at last, Wilde withdrew from the witness-box. Everybody expected Clarke to call Lord Alfred Douglas, whose friendship with Wilde was the prime cause of the whole case. Lord Alfred, who afterwards got the better of Marshall Hall, F E Smith and Douglas Hogg in the witness-box in various trials, fully expected it himself. He had been at Wilde's side all through the trial, and was more than anxious to give evidence. There was great surprise when Clarke closed his case 'reserving to himself the power to claim to call evidence to rebut anything that may be sprung upon him'. All who had followed the case were amazed at Clarke's decision. The last letters had been Alfred Douglas's correspondence, not Wilde's. The strikingly handsome youth had sat beside Wilde all through the trial, coming to the Court and leaving with him in his brougham. Why was Clarke not calling him? Was he afraid of the effect of his evidence or of Carson's terrible questions? It was most peculiar. Probably only lawyers realised that Clarke was pursuing the policy again of keeping Lord Alfred in reserve. While he still had not given evidence there remained something which might restrain Lord Queensberry and his advisers from making certain allegations against his son. But, after the letters had been read, a reply from Queensberry in any event was almost certain of rebuttal, and, on ordinary rules of advocacy, an obvious refusal to call a relevant witness, who was visible to all in Court, was calculated to do as much harm as any deadly cross-examination of that witness.

Carson now rose to open the case for the defence. Lord Queensberry, he said, withdrew nothing that he had said or written. He had done everything with premeditation and a determination at all risks and hazards to save his son. That was his client's one object. He was glad that the letter containing the Prime Minister's name had been mentioned, which showed that he was in no way connected with the facts of this case. Lord Queensberry's grievance there was purely political. Lord Drumlanrig had been given a seat in the House of Lords which was denied to his father, that was all. Carson then cleverly contrasted the artist and the man in Wilde, which the trial had shown. There was a great contrast between his books, which were for the select and not for the ordinary individual, and the way he chose his friends. Then his excuse was no longer that he was dwelling in regions of art, but that he had such a noble, such a democratic soul – Carson paused, while the Court laughed loudly against Wilde, who had confessed to 'no knowledge of the ordinary individual' – such a democratic soul, that he drew no social distinctions, and that it was 'quite as much pleasure to have the sweeping-boy from the streets to lunch or dine with him as the greatest litterateur or artist. 'I consider the position absolutely irreconcilable. On Mr Wilde's literature alone, Lord Queensberry's action was justified. A more thinly veiled attempt to cover the real nature of the letter to Lord Alfred, called a sonnet, has never been made in a Court of Justice. My learned friend has said that Wood had stolen the letters from Lord Alfred Douglas. But who was Wood? He too was Alfred, the friend of Wilde, the friend of Taylor. *One of the lot.* ... Taylor, the old public school boy, might have given a little useful information. He was Wilde's bosom friend. Wilde has said he was in close conversation with him only on Tuesday last. *Why has he not been called?*' Carson was now talking very slowly. 'Why did Wilde give Wood £16? The one thing that he was anxious for was that Wood should leave the country; so he paid his passage, and, after a farewell luncheon, he shipped him away to New York, and, I suppose, hoped that he would never see him again.' There was a pause. 'But,' said Carson dramatically, 'he is here, and will be examined.'

At this point there was a great sensation in Court. The Court had once more been growing darker all through this powerful and menacing speech. The atmosphere of comic opera and of high comedy which Wilde had introduced at the beginning of the trial had completely vanished. The evening shadows seemed only symbolic of the darkening shadows of the case itself. Everybody in Court seemed conscious that they were assisting at a great tragedy, the fame of which was indeed already ringing through the world. The climax of the drama had not been reached, but it now seemed to all certain and foredoomed. Even the cultured Judge, who had been obviously impressed, amused, and delighted with Oscar Wilde on the previous day, sat with his head buried in his hands. It was noticeable to everyone that throughout the speech no attack and little mention had been made of Lord

Alfred Douglas, except as the son of the defendant. The attack had been concentrated on Wilde. But at the very end Carson used his name. 'In view of these disgusting letters from Wilde to Lord Alfred Douglas, I wish to know, are you going to send Lord Queensberry to gaol? I ask you to bear in mind that Lord Queensberry's son is so dominated by Wilde that he threatened to shoot his own father. Lord Queensberry did what he has done most deliberately, and he is not afraid to abide by the issue in this Court.'

The Court adjourned at this point. Wilde's hopes had now fallen to the dust. His counsel was dumbfounded by Carson's advocacy, and what it had revealed. It had convinced Sir Edward Clarke that his confident assumption of Wilde's innocence, derived from the most solemn assurance from the man himself, was wrong. He was overcome by a sense of responsibility. If the case proceeded, and Carson, whom he was now sure was not bluffing, were allowed to call that terrible evidence, in the event of an adverse verdict Wilde must be arrested on leaving the Court. The Judge would impound the papers for the use of the Public Prosecutor. This was not the only evil. Lord Alfred Douglas was insistent on being called in rebuttal of evidence given, and, indeed, upon his evidence the only hope now rested. But how could he, a young man of impulsive mind, longing for vengeance on his own father, succeed where Wilde had been brought so low? Might not he too be involved in the tragedy? His duty as counsel, too, was far from clear. From a consultation with Wilde he was now convinced and certain of Wilde's guilt; how could he go on with the case? His junior, Charlie Mathews, was not in agreement with him. They had no right, as counsel, to assume anything against their client: their duty was to fight the case to a finish. With Carson's many witnesses, the case could be indefinitely prolonged.

The witnesses were themselves accomplices and criminals, and little reliance would be placed upon their testimony. The case was far from lost. In the meanwhile, Wilde would have plenty of time to escape if Hamilton Cuffe, the Public Prosecutor, was contemplating arrest. He could hardly prejudice the course of a criminal trial by taking steps against Wilde before the Queensberry case was over. If they withdrew the prosecution, the authorities would be free to act at once. Both men were actuated by high motives. In the mind of one, professional honour was perhaps foremost; in that of the other, the safety of his client. Oscar Wilde was like a man in a dream. He had lost all power of decision. He did not know what was best; a certain sense of pride and honour prevented him from leaving the country that night. On the other hand, he did not wish to involve Alfred Douglas in further trouble by allowing him to give evidence. He could not make up his mind either to withdraw the prosecution or to go on with it. The fact that Carson had Wood and the others in Court to give evidence against him had taken him completely by surprise. He could not make up his mind; he must try and get a little sleep.

Next morning the Old Bailey presented the same scene, but today there was a large crowd waiting outside the Court to see the main figures of the trial arrive. Public interest was intense and extremely hostile to Wilde. Inside the Court the same scene presented itself. There were still the fashionable crowds. There was the Judge and his bouquet; Carson, on his feet ready to begin; and Sir Edward Clarke, looking very white and miserable, sitting by his side. Everyone was present except the principal character, Oscar Wilde, although a pile of letters addressed to the Old Bailey awaited him. The last act was beginning without him. It was, however, noticed that Wilde was not in Court when Carson resumed his speech.

Counsel said that he had done with the literary aspect of the case, and with the relationship of Wilde and Alfred Douglas. 'I now, unfortunately, approach a more powerful part of the case. I have to bring before you these young men, one after the other, to tell their tales – for an advocate a most distasteful task. One word I will say. These young men are more sinned against than sinning. Let those who would blame them remember that.' Carson looked mournfully at the jury; with his sad dignity, he seemed to be like a recording angel. There was, he said, a startling similarity with all those other friendships of Wilde. They were neither his equals in age, in education, nor in social position. 'It may be a very noble and generous instinct in some people to wish to level down all social barriers. ... But if Wilde had wanted to assist them, was it a benefit for boys in their class of society for a great man of letters to take them to a magnificent dinner and prime them with the best champagne? ... After you hear the evidence you will wonder, not that the gossip reached Lord Queensberry's ears, but that the man Wilde has been tolerated for years in Society as he has.'

At the beginning of his speech Sir Edward Clarke had gone out, but he had now returned. He touched Carson's sleeve, and they began to consult together in whispers. Everyone guessed that something dramatic was about to happen. Had Wilde run away and left his counsel in the lurch?

Carson sat down, and Sir Edward Clarke rose. He began to speak with obvious embarrassment. He put the best face upon the matter that he could. But he relied with some ingenuity for his excuse on the part of the case on which the defence had manifestly failed. He said that it had become clear to Mr Wilde's advisers during the case that the jury might well excuse Lord Queensberry *as a father*, having regard to the passages relied on by the defence, for the expression which he had used. Mr Carson was about to make the most terrible allegations. Since, in his opinion, the jury might well return a verdict of 'not guilty' merely on the literary side, it would be manifestly dangerous and contrary to his duty to Mr Wilde to allow the prosecution to continue. For a verdict of 'not guilty' for Lord Queensberry, as a result of the literary evidence, would carry an implication of 'guilty' on his client on the whole of the allegations in the plea for justification, whatever view the jury might hold as to the terrible charges to be advanced by his learned friend. 'I am prepared to submit to a verdict of "not guilty", having reference to that part of the particulars which is connected with the publication of *Dorian Gray* and with the publication of *The Chameleon*. I trust, my lord, that that may make an end of the case.'

The device was transparent: Sir Edward Clarke was admitting a lesser charge, which had not been made out, in order to avoid far graver and more specific charges which he dared not face.

Mr Carson rose, and pointed out with terse and telling courtesy that a verdict of 'not guilty' would mean a verdict of justification on the whole plea. The Judge concurred.

'Then,' said Carson, 'the verdict will be that complete justification is proved, and that the publication was for the public benefit.'

Again the Judge assented, and so charged the jury. Once again, as in the Havelock Wilson case, Carson had succeeded without calling evidence for the defence. Once more he had broken down the witness. Once more the complaining party had proved the case for the defence.

There remained only the formalities. 'Do you find the complete justification proved or not?' asked the clerk of arraigns. – 'Yes,' replied the foreman of the jury.

'Do you find a verdict of "not guilty"?' – 'Yes,' replied the foreman.

'And that is the verdict of you all?' – 'Yes,' replied the foreman, 'and we also find that the publication was for the public benefit.'

There was loud applause heard in Court, which was taken up by a great crowd below. But the ribald demeanour and exultation of this crowd did little credit to British public opinion, or to the gravity of the occasion. As Carson and Sir Edward Clarke left the Old Bailey together, both exhausted and miserable, they passed through the cheering crowds, and saw loose women dancing wildly in the streets. 'What a filthy business!' said Clarke. 'I shall not feel clean for weeks.'

Oscar Wilde had come to the Old Bailey, but he had not come into Court. He had driven down rather late, and Clarke had gone into Court without further instructions. Clarke had been called into a small consultation-room, and, with his approval and advice, Wilde had decided to abandon the case. Charles Mathews's strong advice was to continue. He issued at once an explanation to the Press: 'It would have been impossible for me to have proved my case without putting Lord Alfred Douglas in the box against his father. Lord Alfred Douglas was extremely anxious to go into the box, but I would not let him do so. Rather than put him in so painful a position, I determined to retire from the case and to bear on my own shoulders whatever ignominy and shame might result from my prosecuting Lord Queensberry. – Oscar Wilde.'

After scribbling these words, and while Sir Edward Clarke was making his statement, he hurriedly left the Old Bailey with Lord Alfred Douglas in his brougham. He was observed to drive to the offices of Sir George Lewis in Ely Place.

As soon as Lord Queensberry had been discharged, another letter was written on behalf of the defence.

'37 Norfolk Street, Strand.

Hon Hamilton Cuffe
Director of Public Prosecutions
Whitehall
re Oscar Wilde
Dear Sir
In order that there may be no miscarriage of justice, I think
it my duty to send at once to you a copy of all our witnesses'
statements, together with a copy of the shorthand notes of
the trial.

Yours faithfully
Charles Russell'

Wilde's interview with Sir George Lewis was not
reassuring. 'What is the use of coming to me now?' he said.
'All this trouble was perfectly unnecessary.'

Wilde and Douglas then went to a private room at the
Holborn Viaduct Hotel. His carriage remained outside.
George Wyndham MP, Lord Alfred's cousin, came to see
them. He wished to warn Wilde to escape abroad, as a
warrant might be issued for his arrest at any moment. But
Wilde would not see him. After luncheon, he drove from the
Viaduct Hotel to the Cadogan Hotel, where Alfred Douglas
was staying. He passed through Fleet Street, where he had
worked and written, along the Embankment, past the Savoy
Hotel, where he had dined so often, through the Mall and
Birdcage Walk, past the early flowers and green lawns of St
James's and the Green Parks, until he reached his destination.
On his way he stopped at a bank, where he drew a considerable
sum of money by a cheque payable to self. It is impossible
to withhold pity from this man of genius, but yesterday so
arrogant and proud, now driving for the last time through the
scenes he knew and loved so well. What terrible reflections

and apprehensions must have been his as he drove along, past the familiar places, his 'wonderful life' wrecked forever. Did he know, as he sat huddled in a corner, that another carriage was following him?

He reached the Cadogan Hotel. He had decided to go abroad that night. A friend and neighbour of his was walking up Tite Street at about 6.45, and saw a cab piled high with luggage outside Wilde's house. He noticed that his mother, Lady Wilde, the distinguished Irish poetess, was superintending the loading of the cab. Alas, too late; a newspaper boy was coming up the street, shouting at the top of his voice: 'Arrest of Oscar Wilde.'

Shortly after six, Inspector Richards and Sergeant Allan of Scotland Yard found Wilde at the Cadogan Hotel. They had a warrant for his arrest. 'Really,' said Wilde, and he stumbled out of the hotel into a waiting cab. He was seen to be very drunk. He was taken to Scotland Yard and then to Bow Street, and charged. He spent the night in prison. He could not eat, and all night paced and paced his cell in deep and black despair. The Poet of the Beautiful. Poor Wilde, he was to see nothing of beauty again for more than two years, except what suffering could reveal from the depths.

Almost at the same time as that of Wilde's arrest, Edward Carson walked slowly into the precincts of the Palace of Westminster. A crowd of members and correspondents were waiting for him in the Lobby. Bitter political opponents like Tim Healy and Swift MacNeill, his countrymen and Wilde's, patted him on the back. 'Well done,' they said. Carson shrugged his shoulders. It had been a filthy business. He was tired and exhausted. Whatever else, it was certainly no cause for congratulation. 'Did you ever compete against Wilde at Trinity?' asked a Lobby correspondent. 'I was never an infant prodigy,' said Carson, and moodily walked off to the library to be alone. 'He does not seem to be in a hurry, even now,' said the correspondent.

Nevertheless, it was felt that justice had been done, according to Lord Halsbury's prophecy, and that Carson had rid England of a pest, at whatever cost to her fair name in the world; and the cost was great, perhaps not yet fully paid. Hundreds of congratulatory letters reached him, of which he kept only two.

'Central Criminal Court
City of London EC
5 April 1895

Dear Carson, – I never heard a more powerful speech, or a more searching cross-exam.

I congratulate you on having escaped most of the filth.

Yours ever
R Henn Collins'

Another tribute came from a distinguished firm of American lawyers, far away in New York State:

'First National Bank Building
Carlton, NY Ap 9 1895

Hale and Bowers
Counsellors at Law

Sir, – I judge from newspaper reports that your cross-examination of Oscar Wilde is one of the finest examples of the art of cross-examination in recent times. If you have a verbatim copy in pamphlet form I would esteem it a great favor to receive one. Or if you cannot supply it, will you kindly inform me where I can procure it.

Very respectfully yours
J P Hale'

But Carson's career was only beginning, and the future lay before him. For him was waiting a great cause, the love of a whole people, fame, and, despite bitter political disappointment and private griefs, as much personal happiness as falls to the lot of most mortals. While for Wilde, whose name, by an ignoble compromise, was then being removed from the St James's and Haymarket Theatres, where his plays, *The Importance of Being Earnest* and *An Ideal Husband*, were being performed, there remained overwhelming obloquy, imprisonment, poverty, a short-lived repentance, mental and physical decay, and an agonising death. The fact that his sufferings secured for his writings, which might otherwise have had a short-lived popularity limited to his own countrymen, after his death a worldwide and lasting fame, probably did not occur and certainly would have been no comfort to this child of his own time and of this world, who was, as Mr A C Benson has said, 'so gifted, so brittle, and withal so lovable'.

He was tried on a criminal charge, but Carson would have nothing to do with it: a prosecution was a different matter. The jury disagreed, and the Judge, Mr Justice Charles, it was said, would only have sentenced him to a six-months' term. Carson then went to his friend Sir Frank Lockwood, the Solicitor-General, who was to prosecute. 'Cannot you let up on the fellow now?' he said. 'He has suffered a great deal.'

'I would,' said Lockwood, 'but we cannot; we dare not; it would at once be said, both in England and abroad, that owing to the names mentioned in Queensberry's letters we were forced to abandon it.' So Wilde was tried again, this time immediately after the man Taylor, whose conviction was certain and guilt obvious. The immediately preceding conviction of a man known to be his associate was certain to prejudice him. This time a law officer, Sir Frank Lockwood himself, led for the prosecution: in the previous trial Mr

Charles Gill had led. It was thus that his conviction was secured. He was punished with two years' imprisonment, with hard labour – a savage sentence; and, had the Court of Criminal Appeal existed then, it is possible that either the conviction, owing to the circumstances of the trial and the uncorroborated evidence of the accomplices, or the sentence, which was a heavy one, would not have stood.

He was defended passionately on both occasions by Sir Edward Clarke, who charged no fee. In the interval between the two trials he was granted bail in thousands of pounds. One of the sureties was Lord Douglas of Hawick, Lord Alfred's eldest surviving brother. Such, however, was the obloquy into which the name of the once popular poet had fallen, that no other friend would stand bail for him. It was left to a stranger, a young English clergyman, to come forward to offer the risk of a heavy fine if Wilde escaped, to whom, as he said, Wilde 'had shown Beauty on a high hill'. During the interval Wilde was given the means of escape, and perhaps the authorities would have welcomed it. Wilde would not do it and leave his sureties in the lurch. Frank Harris, in his *Life of Wilde*, uses this as evidence of Wilde's weakness and lack of resolution. Should it not be credited to him for honour? That the verdict was just, there can be no doubt. Before the second trial he confessed to Harris, who was genuinely surprised. But, even so, to a lawyer at least, or to anyone interested in the administration of justice, it does not dispose of the question whether or no he was unfairly convicted.

There remains only to be recorded a circumstance as strange and terrible as the culminating scene in *Dorian Gray*. Some years afterwards, Edward Carson was walking by himself in Paris on a wet day in the early months of the year. He was about to cross the street when the driver of a *fiacre*, with Parisian recklessness, almost ran him down, and splashed his clothes with mud. He stepped back quickly onto the pavement, and knocked someone down. Turning round to apologise, he saw a man lying in the gutter, and recognised the haggard, painted features of Oscar Wilde. Like a flash, his mind went back to that occasion eight years before, in London, when Wilde's fine carriage had almost overrun him. The eyes of the two men met, and they recognised each other. Carson turned round and said, 'I beg your pardon.' Wilde, under the name of Sebastian Melmoth, was living in Paris, dying of a terrible disease, 'beyond his means', as he observed with the wit which never deserted him, preying on the generosity of his friends. In a week or two he was dead.

15. Leader of the Bar

In 1895, Mr Gladstone resigned after the House of Lords had rejected the second Home Rule Bill, and he retired to Hawarden to enjoy that interval between his life's work and the end, the desire for which he had often expressed, and which is vouchsafed to few leading statesmen. The Chief Whip, who had made the small Home Rule majority effective, succeeded to his father's peerage and went to the Lords, and the Liberal Government, elected on a Home Rule mandate, struggled on for a year, its reason for existence gone, bereft of its great chieftain, under the supercilious leadership of Lord Rosebery. But the voice of the prophet was silent, and, when the election came, once again the country voted decisively for the cause of the Union. Now, however, the Liberal Unionists, after many years in the wilderness, decided to take office with the Conservatives, and began to lose their separate identity as a party. So leading a position had Carson already attained, both in the Temple and in the House of Commons, during his short residence in England, that his appointment as Solicitor-General for England was widely canvassed. Even before the fall of Rosebery's administration, he had been considered in the Lobby 'as a good outsider for a law office in the next Tory administration', and, when that administration was actually being formed, his appointment was confidently expected, and its probability widely resented. The plodding Tory Queen's Counsel of many years' experience in the House, who may be designated as 'Messrs Paul, Byles and Benn', were angry that this Irish newcomer should climb so easily into a place for which their own labours had so well qualified them. Nevertheless, Carson was now openly acclaimed as the successor of Sir Charles Russell, and compared favourably in his performance with both Sir Edward Clarke and Sir Frank

Lockwood. 'Carson,' said one legal correspondent of this time, 'is as great a master of the sneer as Sir Frank is of the laugh.' Sir Frank had, like many others, been disposed to underrate Carson's ability at first. Charles Gill had warned him not to make this mistake, and Lockwood acknowledged to Gill that he had once lost a case of the first importance by trying to laugh the Irishman out of Court. The latter's appointment as Solicitor-General seemed all the more probable since Sir Edward Clarke now declined office when he was asked to comply with the new practice which required both law officers to surrender during their term of office their right to hold briefs for any client but the Crown. However, Carson was not appointed, and the new law officers were veterans of the English Courts, Sir Richard Webster, afterwards Lord Chief Justice Alverstone, and Sir Robert Finlay, afterwards Lord Chancellor. Carson would, of course, had he desired it, have been reappointed to one of the Irish law offices; but that would have meant retirement from his rapidly growing practice in London. As it was, he was merely rewarded for his vigilance in the Home Rule Parliament by being made a 'Right Honourable Gentleman' as a Member of Her Majesty's Privy Council in Ireland; moreover, his omission from the Government was of great advantage to him. For he was able for five years to consolidate himself in private practice, and to become the acknowledged leader of the Bar in cases of all kinds where matters of great or priceless value to private individuals, whether in money or good name, were at stake. Long years in which he was to be solely preoccupied with affairs of State awaited him, when he was to abandon all hope of future private fortune, and to sacrifice in a beloved cause much of that which he had already gained.

Any student of the eighteen-nineties, engaged in the search for some fact buried in the files of *The Times* newspaper, will hardly be able to avoid the name of Edward Carson as he turns the great pages. Almost every day it occurred while the Courts were sitting, and it is manifestly impossible to record more than a very few of the cases, every one of which was a romance or a comedy or a tragedy in itself, which were his daily routine in those years. Their titles could all be gathered from his fee-books; their reports can be found in *The Times*, or any other widely published newspaper of the period, and many of them could be enriched by the recollections of the advocate himself. A full collection of them would make a wonderful anthology of picturesque and striking advocacy, but by the present writer, in the nature of things, with so much of his task behind him and so much before him, only a few can be selected which are interesting for special reasons.

Briefs poured into Dr Johnson's Buildings in incredible numbers, but only a moiety at most were accepted. The clerk, who received of right a commission on all fees, told the disappointed clients that it was no use, as Mr Carson would do only one case at a time. It took Carson a little while to accustom himself to the idea that it was the clerk, not the principal, who fixed the fees; and the amount marked on the briefs seemed to be mounting day by day in the most alarming fashion.

One winter's afternoon, a visitor knocked at about four o'clock on the door of Dr Johnson's Buildings, and was admitted. He spoke with a broad Irish brogue. Mr Carson was out, and Hamilton, the clerk, eyed him suspiciously. They did say, although it was difficult to believe stories of the kind about such a quiet, courteous gentleman, that there were Irishmen who were after his master's blood. 'What name, sir?' asked the cockney clerk. 'O'Brien.' Hamilton almost slammed the door in the visitor's face. No, he was afraid that Mr Carson was still in Court. Mr Carson usually was in Court; he could not say when Mr Carson would return. The clerk's worst fears were confirmed. This must be the terrible criminal whom Carson had so often sent to gaol. Visions of the Phoenix Park murder rose before his eyes; he wanted no Fenian murder in the Temple. What had a respectable barrister's clerk done to deserve this? It was all Mr Darling's fault for bringing an Irishman into chambers. Scotland Yard must be informed at once. Then the stranger produced his card. The awestruck clerk read on the pasteboard, 'Lord O'Brien of Kilferona, Kildare Street Club, Dublin'. It was Peter himself. Hamilton was now all smiles. He showed the Lord Chief Justice of Ireland into Mr Carson's room, and drew up the armchair by the fire for his lordship. 'Mr Carson will be back very shortly, my lord,' he said. Peter looked at his old devil's desk, and round the room. Briefs, briefs everywhere, on the desk, on the ledges of the bookshelves, on the chairs: a sea of white paper and pink tape. He had heard so much of Ned Carson's phenomenal success in London, but he had not realised the half of its extent. 'I see,' Lord O'Brien observed, 'that Mr Carson has a great many briefs in the Queen's Bench.'

'Yes, my lord,' replied the impudent clerk, who had now completely recovered his self-possession, 'but I can assure your lordship that we are equally good in Chancery.' In due course Carson returned from the Law Courts over the way, and the two old colleagues embraced in an affectionate manner, as became two affectionate men who had faced danger together on many occasions; and O'Brien, who had saved Carson from the Irish County Court Bench, went away satisfied that he had set a great man on his way.

Carson was never greedy about his fees, and he often compelled his clerk to reduce them, but when his long rivalry began at about this time with another swiftly rising barrister, Rufus Isaacs, Hamilton thought it was time to make a stand.

'Mr Carson,' he said, 'Mr Rufus Isaacs's clerk is charging much higher fees than yourself. In future I propose to tell the solicitors that your fee is the same as Mr Isaacs.' Thereafter the clerk was adamant: if his master was asked to appear against Mr Isaacs, he would first confer with Mr Isaacs's clerk, and would always insist to the solicitor on 'the same fee as Mr Isaacs's clerk is charging on the other side.'

The fees went up and up, and finally Mr Isaacs's clerk had the audacity to demand five hundred guineas, an unheard-of fee in those days, when the pound was worth twenty pre-war shillings. Hamilton insisted on the same. The solicitor protested, and insisted on seeing Mr Carson personally. 'It's most unusual,' said the clerk; but eventually he had to show him in to the great man. It was dusk, and Carson's blinds had been drawn rather early.

'Mr Carson,' said the solicitor, 'I want to see you about that brief my firm sent down to you.'

'What have you to say about it?' said Carson, most courteously, with his charming smile.

The solicitor became more and more nervous: it was very difficult to talk to this great gentleman about money. 'The fee you ask is a very large sum.'

'I don't know whether he's right, I'm sure,' said Carson, 'but my clerk says I mustn't talk to you about it.'

'But it's a very big fee, Mr Carson.'

'You're quite right,' said Carson, 'I think it's a most exorbitant fee.'

'I'm glad you take my view,' said the solicitor with eager relief.

But Carson took his arm, led him gently to the window, and pulled up the blind. He then showed the attorney a sight which is familiar to every Templar as dusk falls on a winter's afternoon. All around were lighted windows; in some, men could be seen poring over papers or books; others holding conferences with clients; many waiting for work, talking to each other, pacing their rooms. They were all gentlemen of the Bar, who were seeking, or had sought, their fortunes in the profession. Who knows what stories of hopes and ambitions fulfilled, deferred, disappointed, what romances, comedies, tragedies, lie behind those lighted windows?

'Do you see all those rooms?' asked Carson. 'In every one of those rooms there's a light, isn't there? In all of them, you may assume, there's one man, probably two or three, who'll do the case as well as I'll do it myself, and most of them will charge a far more reasonable fee.'

'Oh, no,' said the solicitor, 'that's not my point. I wouldn't dream of letting anyone but you do it, with Mr Isaacs on the other side.'

'Well,' replied Carson, 'if you're such a fool as that, after all I've shown you, you'll just have to pay what my clerk asks you to pay.'

The fee was paid and the case was won.

It was a long rivalry between Carson and Rufus Isaacs: in almost any case of celebrity they were matched against each other. Their methods of advocacy were very different, but it was a rivalry of peers, both as regards intellect and fine, though contrasting, physical appearance. There is something heroic, as well as a rare nobility, about the outward mien of each of them. In the end, the intimacy of their continual contests in Parliament and in the Courts made them brothers in arms, as well as opponents, but at first there was a note of bitterness in their cases for which, it seemed to Carson, Rufus was to blame. The Irishman raised a laugh against the Jew once, after a bitter observation by the latter. When the Court adjourned, Carson took Isaacs by the arm. 'Look here, Rufus,' he said, 'we're going to be against each other a great deal for a great many years, I hope. If we are going to treat each other like gentlemen, let's understand it at once. If I don't laugh at you, will you promise not to bite my head off?'

Carson liked a fight to the finish; Isaacs was a superb settler of cases: he knew exactly when his case had reached the peak of its success, by a sudden skilful turn of the argument, or a fortunate change in the evidence induced by his masterly cross-examination; and he would often then arrange a profitable settlement for his client; he would leave nothing to chance, and was a master of detail. Perhaps – although here the writer, who never saw these battles of giants, speaks with the humblest respect – Lord Reading lacked Lord Carson's *flair*; or, at any rate, he was not prepared to back his own convictions about a case to the lengths to which Carson was prepared to go. Carson would leave the result of the case after four questions in cross-examination, and then sit down: or he would sometimes not bother to call evidence for his client if his cross-examination had been conclusive, as in the Havelock Wilson case. Against Rufus's wonderful knowledge of business routine and psychology, won from experience, Carson could set an imagination, a call to sentiment, even a sense of poetry, rarely heard in the English Courts.

These were the halcyon days of his life at the Bar. He was in the prime of life. His unexpected success was broadening and mellowing his nature, but neither hardened nor spoilt him. Mr A H Bremner, still practising in the middle 'eighties, the doyen of the Junior Bar and as great an expert on income tax law as any man in England, has given me an idea of the impression which Carson immediately made on his colleagues; they made friends at once, these two great gentlemen of the Bar. 'I go back,' said Mr Bremner, 'to Cockburn, Herschell, Day, Henry James, Lawson Walton, Edward Clarke; I have seen all the leaders who have taken their places till the present day, and I put Carson first. I was always deeply attached to him from being his junior. I, who was with him so much then, can say without hesitation that Carson was the most successful *nisi prius* advocate in my long career: if a point of law turned up suddenly, unlike many *nisi prius* advocates, he was always able to deal with it, and not only in matters of Common Law, but also on questions of Companies or Chancery. His manner was always quiet; many were the jury cases we won together; but he wanted no aid from me; he always knew every point; it was impossible to disturb him in Court. I don't think anything terrified Carson in Court or out of it; he was never hazy about either law or facts, as so many leaders are. His humour, too, was on a higher level than that of any leader I have known. Sir John Day was the only man who could come near him for this while he was at the Bar; but when he got on the Bench he thought he ought not to indulge in ridicule.

'Sometimes he would send me a note at about five o'clock, "Are you doing anything this evening? Will you come and have some dinner, and we'll talk over the case?" After dinner he would pick up half a sheet of notepaper; he would go through the whole case very carefully for two hours; when a good point arose for cross-examination, he would make some cabalistic little mark on the paper: that would be all the note he would take; but the next day he would remember it all, take his point, which would always be the right one, amplify it, and drive the witness into a corner. The witnesses could not get away; Carson mesmerised them; he was better than Russell, who put juries against him with his bullying. Then there were his long, dark eyelashes, his brogue, his captivating smile; he would lead the witness on into a number of answers which would destroy his case, and the witness's answer to his last question would be so ridiculous that the whole value of his testimony was gone; it was all so quietly done, and with such deadly effect, and his manners to his brothers at the Bar were always so delightful; he never missed the chance of paying a compliment to an opponent or a junior. Yet when he wished, he could assume so stern and majestic an air that not only his victim in the box, but every sensitive person in Court would feel awe, and even fear. He was the best speaker in the Courts of my time; I never heard him at a public platform, but they say he was wonderful there too. I did not see him as a politician at all, but as a colleague and a friend. He was a wonderful person, and a most lovable man; he secured the affection of everyone who knew him; it was impossible to know him and not like him.'

Like Carson, Bremner is a very modest man, and Carson considered him the most useful junior he ever had. Years afterwards he was sitting with Lord Finlay in a foreign hotel, and he caught sight of old Bremner in the lounge, and said to the distinguished ex-Lord Chancellor: 'There's Bremner, who has often kept me on the right side.'

Carson soon acquired a reputation as a deadly cross-examiner. There is a type of vain man who, when he goes to law, thinks he is a match in the witness-box for any advocate. Of this kind was a certain brewer, who brought an action to recover certain fees and commission from his company. Carson was leading for the company, and the brewer knew he was to be cross-examined by Carson, and made up his mind to be insolent to him in order to throw him off his guard, and make him lose his temper. 'These damned lawyers,' he said, 'one's only got to show them what one is prepared to stand from them and what one is not.' He began with a fearful insult to Irish Counsel, which would have made many Irishmen lose control of themselves, but he was only met with a kindly smile from this imperturbable antagonist. 'No, no,' said Carson, 'it is not a bit of use your being impertinent to me. I am too old a hand to be put off by that. You'll have to answer my questions, I'm afraid.' Thus he foiled a deliberate attempt to throw him off his guard. The witness had evidently based his plans on such an attack succeeding; when it failed, he absolutely collapsed. He was a perfectly honest man, and at heart a gentleman, and he seemed thoroughly ashamed of himself; he made admission after admission, and the company succeeded. This showed Carson's new colleagues how well prepared he was to deal with any tactics; yet, after all, compared to William O'Brien defended by Tim Healy, dealing with stout English brewers was easy money.

16. Ben Tillett and W S Gilbert

In March 1895, Carson appeared for the defence in a libel suit brought by another celebrated trade union leader, Alderman Ben Tillett, against the *Morning* newspaper. The trial was heard before Mr Justice Hawkins, and Mr Willis QC was for the plaintiff. It was another instance of the abnormal sensitiveness of the founders of the Labour Movement to criticism by their opponents, against whom they had themselves used the most violent expressions of public condemnation. The *Morning*, a Conservative newspaper, made fun of Ben Tillett for riding a bicycle, then an infallible token of affluence and respectability, and for receiving a salary derived from the small contributions of the Dockers' Union, of which he was the secretary and organiser. The newspaper went on to report a meeting of the union, from which, after certain criticism had been offered against him, the secretary prematurely departed, accompanied by some of his friends, who were likened by the *Morning* to a bodyguard. 'It must have been sad', ran the 'libel', 'to see the alderman saved by a bodyguard of his friends'. Mr Willis, in opening the case, described the great Ben Tillett as 'a mild and peaceful citizen' – a slander which Ben might greatly have resented outside a Court of Law – and almost as a person in whose mouth butter would not melt. Actually, however, Ben had frequently made the most militant speeches on behalf of his movement on Tower Hill, a great place at that time for Labour meetings. These speeches were so rich, even in the cold print of the newspaper reports, that they provided Carson with all the necessary evidence on behalf of the newspaper. In the course of the cross-examination Ben Tillett admitted to Carson that a man 'might' have shouted to him at the meeting of the union, 'My threepence a week is keeping you.'

'What did he mean by that?' asked Carson.

'Why should I answer you?' countered the trade union leader indignantly.

Mr Justice Hawkins reproved Ben for his insolence, and Carson pressed him. 'Come, sir,' he said. 'We are not on Tower Hill now.'

'No, nor in Ireland,' replied Ben Tillett aptly.

The Judge again sharply rebuked the witness, but Carson, who had himself thoroughly appreciated the answer, pleaded for indulgence to the witness. 'Does not your lordship think, in all the circumstances,' he said, 'that it was a fair retort?'

The plaintiff then asserted boldly that his attacks on his opponents had never exceeded fair criticism. Alas, his past speeches were about to be called up by Carson, like ghosts, to haunt him. He willingly admitted to Carson that he had described non-union workers as 'Judases, Careys, and Pigotts'. By that he meant that they were 'betrayers, informers, and perjurers'. Perhaps, after all, for a trade union leader this was excusable, and in the usual convention. He had described shipowners as 'dastards', but added naively that he would not object to such a term if applied to himself. It appeared that the witness had enjoyed a fling at every class in the community except his own: Carson worked up steadily from the police to the Bench of Bishops. Had not the witness said that the police at Hull were corrupted by the drink of the Masters' Federation? Had he not attacked the Judges, because they dispensed justice according to the excellence of the dinners provided for them by the merchants, and because, when they were shareholders with them, it was 'money first and law afterwards'. 'Men like Grantham,' he had said, 'are always ready to clap a man into gaol.' In general terms he had denounced those who disagreed with him as 'fat-gutted, full-pursed anarchists, from the Bishops upwards.'

'Whom do you put above the Bishops?' smiled Carson.

'Well, you, for one,' said Ben Tillett, with genuine admiration.

For no one was more amazed in Court at the record which Carson had been able to make against him than Ben Tillett himself. He had no idea that he had been such a rebel. 'Every wild statement', he writes in his book of memoirs, 'that had the slightest sting in it was cited against me in the mercilessly slow process of building up a case which Carson employed. To me was attributed, not merely attempts, but every determination of undermining the State. No man in that Court was more astounded than I was ... Nothing could be right for that wonderful lawyer.'

The comedy was picturesque and complete, with Ben Tillett there staring surprised into the cruel mirror which the advocate held up to him, and not recognising his own reflection; and once more Carson called no evidence for the defence. The jury saw the exquisite humour of the situation of the man who had exhausted the whole dictionary of vituperation at the expense of everybody not quite seeing things as he did, and yet who now brought a libel action against a newspaper for an innuendo. 'My learned friend Mr Willis,' said Carson, with a smile for the jury, 'is an eloquent, earnest, but somewhat imaginative advocate: it is the latter quality which accounts for his description of his client as "a mild and peaceful citizen". He has used the word "warfare" again and again. I make no objections, for it is "warfare" that the plaintiff has waged, whether on the police, the magistrates, the Judges of the High Court, secretaries of rival unions, and the whole Bench of Bishops. They are all lashed with the same whip, and are of the corrupt essence of humanity ... cut-throats, murderers, and anarchists. A man who has spent his whole life in slandering his opponents is surely not entitled to ask for damages in respect of a mild article like this. ... As to the charge raised against him of "remaining at his post" against the will of his union, if the plaintiff wins his verdict, we will probably have Ministers of the Crown suing in these Courts. No, it seems that Mr Tillett against the Press is all right, but the Press against Mr Tillett is all wrong.'

The speech was an admirable example of forensic satire, which was, however, so conclusive and good-humoured that even the plaintiff himself took it with excellent grace, although the verdict went against him, and the costs of the action ruined him. I called this case a comedy; but behind the comedy of the Law Court awaited the grim tragedy which so often attends the losing party when the sheriff calls with his officers.

Ben Tillett bore no malice, and, indeed, learnt to cherish a great admiration for his cross-examiner, which matured when Carson became a more important rebel than himself. Ben Tillett generously writes of him many years afterwards: 'I met him when he was a Cabinet Minister in the Coalition Government of Mr Lloyd George. I had demanded extra pay for soldiers' dependants, naval ratings, and for our own people, who were giving their lives and limbs in the surge and *débâcle* of war. I found a strong and enthusiastic supporter in Carson. As members of Parliament we met often afterwards in the smoke-room. I was glad to find him so human, in many ways so attractive. About his patriotism and stern rectitude I never had any doubts at all. But he knew how seared my soul had been. He realised that his caustic and remorseless power had blasted great endeavours on my part and had also sacrificed my home. The outcome of this case was almost total ruin for myself.' Poor Ben Tillett, he had been standing against very heavy metal. No wonder he was defeated. But the generous human sympathy which allowed him to admire the fine qualities of the advocate who had ruined him perhaps accounts for the great influence which his adventurous spirit has wielded in the Labour movement.

It was Carson's experience, however, that his own clients, whose good name or fortune he might have saved, were often very embarrassed at a personal meeting after the case, however profuse their expression of gratitude might have been at the time. The litigant's own advocate knows so much more concerning his client than even his opponent: 'I always made a practice of avoiding them; it was kinder,' said Carson of his successful clients.

Yet those who came up against Carson's advocacy were not always as generous as Ben Tillett. In vivid contrast to Alderman Ben Tillett, Sir W S Gilbert, who had ruthlessly caricatured Oscar Wilde as 'Bunthorne', nurtured against Carson an implacable dislike; the latter adopted in another libel action exactly the same tactics which he had used against Ben Tillett, with similar success. Like Napoleon Bonaparte, Carson was not ashamed to use the same plan on many occasions and diverse opponents, for both in the field of battle and in the Law Courts human nature reacts in the same way to similar treatment.

In this case Carson appeared for a theatrical journal called the *Era* against Lawson Walton QC and Marshall Hall. It was a veritable *Trial by Jury*, and the Court never lost the atmosphere of comic opera. Moreover, it was sensitiveness to criticism which made litigants out of both Ben Tillett and W S Gilbert. The last-named had recently written a play called *The Fortune Hunter*, which several London theatres had refused. It was then put on the boards, with moderate success, at Birmingham and Edinburgh. During the production the author gave an interview to a Scots newspaper, out of which all the trouble arose. When the interview appeared, Gilbert was reported to have called Mr Sidney Grundy, the well-known playwright, 'a mere adapter'; English poetic drama, he said, was doomed to failure, because no English actor, including Tree, Irving, Wyndham, Hare, and Alexander, could make a thirty-line speech at all interesting. Soon afterwards Sir Henry Irving made an angry speech about Gilbert, and the stage people generally were furious: an article appeared in the *Era* accusing him of unbearable conceit and ingratitude to the artists who had made his fortune. 'Mr Gilbert's self-esteem has with advancing years developed into a malady. In his own estimation he is a kind of Grand Llama or Sacred Elephant of dramatic literature. His good-nature has become obscured by the abnormal protuberance of self-esteem. That this – what's his name? – Grundy should have written successful original works, while he, the Great Gilbert, has met with failure after failure in modern drama, is preposterous and not to be borne.'

Gilbert, though a barrister himself, lost his temper and sued for libel. He recovered it sufficiently at the trial to make very good fun with Carson. It is easy to see how Carson proceeded, as he had done with Tillett, to show that Gilbert, though himself a savage critic of others, was very susceptible to criticism; however, he could hardly have hoped to make the old writer admit that *The Fortune Hunter* was a very bad play, but that he disliked the critics saying so. It appeared that the slightest breath of criticism was sufficient to break a friendship with Gilbert: he would not admit the notorious breach with Sullivan, but he admitted bitter feuds with D'Oyly Carte and John Hare, with whom he was not then on speaking terms. He confessed to cutting a lifelong friendship with Mr Clement Scott because of a severe criticism of one of his plays. 'I did say,' he replied, 'that it was no longer necessary for me to be a cockshy for a lot of low-class critics.' Moreover, it appeared that he was no better pleased by favourable criticism: really, W S Gilbert was a difficult fellow. 'I never read favourable criticisms,' he said; 'I prefer reading unfavourable ones. I know how good I am, but I do *not* know how bad I am.' At this moment it seemed as if Gilbert was about to break into rhyme; and, indeed, it only needed Sullivan's melody and the Savoy orchestra to turn the Court of Mr Justice Day (one of the best legal jesters who ever wore the scarlet and ermine) into an excellent scene of comic opera. Carson, now more experienced than he had been in Oscar Wilde's case in dealing with literary men, caught the spirit of burlesque, and put to the witness a passage out of his own *Rosencrantz and Guildenstern*:

> 'The acts were five – though by five acts too long,
> I wrote an act by way of epilogue,
> An act by which the penalty of death
> Was meted out to all who sneered at it.
> The play was not good, but the punishment
> Of those who laughed at it was capital.'

But Gilbert was not at a loss at the Irishman's quotation. 'Those were the words of Claudius of Denmark,' he retorted, 'not of myself. I wrote them, but I do not hold myself responsible for anything King Claudius says.'

'I leave it to the jury,' observed Carson, 'whether you did not repeat King Claudius's words in the box a moment ago'; and, indeed, had he not said that *The Fortune Hunter* was a very bad play, but that the critics should not have said so?

During Carson's speech, Gilbert lost his temper and walked indignantly out of Court. When the jury retired, the affections of the twelve good men and true were divided between the wonderful rhymester and the brilliant advocate, and they came back to state to the Judge that there was no prospect of their being able to decide between the two favourites – a truly Gilbertian end to this curious libel action.

The newspapers were full of this case, and, although the public soon forgot it, Gilbert never did. Years later, when the two of them met at Sir Squire Bancroft's for dinner, Gilbert turned his back on Carson and refused to speak to him; some months later, at another dinner, he repeated the same pantomime.

The interest of these two libel actions is the success which an identical method achieved both against the subtle mind of a writer and the native wit of a bluff dockers' leader. The principles, dear to the heart of a British jury, upon which Carson was working, and knew so well how to work, was that those who live in glass-houses should not throw stones, or, alternatively, that those who throw stones should not live in glass-houses and complain at the same time of damage done by neighbours. Perhaps the resentment felt and shown by the two plaintiffs, especially in the light of the material harm done respectively in each case by the powerful advocate, would also be a comparison not without interest to the psychologist.

17. The Jameson Raid Case

In July 1896, Carson was led by Sir Edward Clarke in a case which must rank as one of the great State trials of British history, which in its inception and conclusion is one of the most shining examples of British justice.[1] For the arch-criminal of all the five gallant men in the dock at a trial at Bar before a British jury and Lord Chief Justice Russell of Killowen, Mr Baron Pollock, and Mr Justice Hawkins, was himself a national hero, and a man in whose life all that was fine in the adventurous tradition of British enterprise and chivalry seemed to live again.

At the end of the nineteenth century there began to arise, for good or evil, a new spirit of imperialism: once more Englishmen began to feel in their hearts the world mission of their race. Mr Gladstone recognised the signs of the times and protested vigorously against the new imperialism. He wished that he had never lived to see it. But he was old – nearly twenty years beyond the allotted span – and Cecil Rhodes and his bosom friend, Dr Leander Starr Jameson – the redoubtable 'Dr Jim' – were in the prime of life, and, like two mediaeval knights, were winning a vast continent for their imperial country. Others, proud and jealous men too, were there beside them: they lacked the vision of the British, but they were determined to hold what they had won, especially from Britain, whose rule they had fled at the time of the Great Trek. They were resolved to reap where they had sown; to deny the rights of citizenship and naturalisation which all civilised States accord in some degree to newcomers; and to reserve political status for the original settlers alone. The land which they had found was rich; and in 1895 at Johannesburg,

[1] See, however, the editorial note at the end of this chapter.

the great city which was growing and thriving on the vast, new-found mineral wealth of South Africa, all the difficulties were already present which finally blazed forth in the Anglo-Boer War. The 'Dutchmen' maintained themselves as a small oligarchy in the Transvaal against the claims of a rapidly growing cosmopolitan population, and in defiance of the greatest Empire in the world, the old hereditary foe both here and in Europe, which was encroaching upon them on all sides. Never perhaps since the Spartans had lorded it in the plains of Peloponnesus over the unprivileged Lacedemonians and Helots, who greatly outnumbered them, had there been such a situation in a civilised State. Gold and diamonds were attracting adventurers of all kinds, good and bad, many of whom were British subjects. These *Uitlanders*, as they were called, were without political rights, although they contributed the great proportion of the revenue. 'Their rights?' said the grim old President in 1895. 'Their rights? They'll get them over my dead body.' It was, indeed, natural, under the rule of this jealous oligarchy, that the newcomers should feel insecure, quite apart from fiscal grievances and political inequality, and it was natural, too, that they should look north, south, and east to the representatives of the most liberal Empire in history. There was a widespread agitation in Johannesburg for a New Franchise Bill; the Reform Party was very strong, and it seemed as if in the end they must win; but their victory and admission to the franchise meant the defeat of the old President Kruger, whose party even then he had only maintained in power by the narrowest margin and the use of the most unscrupulous expedients; and the fear began to grow that he would not protect the malcontents from the worst kinds of pillage, disorder, and rapine which might break out in a cosmopolitan population, surrounded by, and in many ways dependent upon, native peoples. And so they turned their thoughts across the border to Matabeleland and Mashonaland, where Dr Jameson was acting as administrator over a vast territory protected by a British Chartered Company, the British South Africa Company, afterwards to be called Southern Rhodesia. They knew that he was full of resource, feared no man, and believed, as in a religion, in the genius of his race and the unity of South Africa. With a handful of British soldiers and police he had defeated again and again the hordes of warlike natives who had disputed his right to rule over the territory. They began to communicate with him, and all that year he was hither and thither between Johannesburg and his territory. It was arranged that he should raise, drill and equip a body of about eight hundred men on the borders of the Transvaal Republic, so that, if Johannesburg needed him, he could come to their aid. Meanwhile, Johannesburg itself began to arm: the foreigners themselves began to form associations for the protection of the *Uitlander* population. There were formed bodies known as the Cumberland, the Westmorland, the Scotch and American Associations, and a corps of unofficial police organised by the Mercantile Association. It is said that there were 20 000 armed men in Johannesburg, ready for a *lévee-en-masse*. It was arranged that, at the very beginning of the New Year, Jameson should march to their aid, and that there should be a simultaneous rising in Johannesburg to wrest political rights from Kruger, who would only listen to arguments of force. Undoubtedly the town was in a dangerous ferment of excitement and apprehension; rumour was everywhere, and fear was felt for the safety of the women and children. Public feeling was in a condition of smouldering discontent, and on 20 December 1895 a number of leading British *Uitlanders* communicated with Dr Jameson. 'At no distant period', they said, 'there will be a conflict between the Government and the *Uitlander*

population. The position of thousands of Englishmen is
rapidly becoming intolerable. Not satisfied with making the
Uitlander population pay virtually the whole of the revenue of
the country, while denying them representation, the policy of
the Government has been steadily to encroach upon the liberty
of the subject, and to undermine the security of property'.
Later the Boers withdrew the whole of the Government
police from the town – as they said afterwards, to avoid a
conflict with evilly disposed people. Perhaps this was prudent;
perhaps even it was with the approval of the *Uitlanders*; but it
was certainly an abdication of Government. Dr Jameson was
ready to strike. It was true that he had only 500 men armed
and mounted, but his action must not be judged as a mad
venture simply by reference to his subsequent failure. Before
the Raid, informed opinion both at Johannesburg and among
his own officers was that he could not fail to reach the city.
His force was in the nature of a *corps d'élite*, splendidly trained,
and it was thought that the Boers could not possibly mobilise
a force in time to stop him; and, once in Johannesburg,
anything might happen. He would have been welcomed like
a king, and a mighty army of determined men might have
marched on Pretoria, the State capital, to seize the arsenal and
demand by force the redress of grievances. It was only at the
end of December that his men learnt the purpose for which
they had been trained. 'I cannot tell you,' said Colonel Grey,
one of his lieutenants, in asking for volunteers, 'that you are
going by the Queen's orders, but you are going to fight for the
supremacy of the British flag in South Africa. We have had a
request from Johannesburg to assist the inhabitants to get a
better form of government. There will be no bloodshed.' The
utmost secrecy was observed in order to avoid a conflict. Not
until the last minute did the volunteers know that they were
to march on Johannesburg. As Dr Jameson said afterwards,

'When I started, it was with the feeling that if a single shot was fired, I should have failed.' The cavaliers set out during the last days of the Old Year from two points in the protected territory. The two columns, under the command of Dr Jameson and Colonel Grey, divided at first, united in Transvaal territory, and the whole body proceeded to advance towards Johannesburg.

Meanwhile, his confederates in the city were divided in a different sense. The magnitude of the adventure – for the issues were great – perhaps shocked the leaders of what was essentially a democratic venture. Two messengers were sent to Jameson, each by a different route, who, in effect, were ordered by the Reform Committee to retract the letter of a few days before. Further, the news reached the British High Commissioner far away in Cape Town, and he sent a galloper post-haste ordering the doctor to return. It is only fair to Dr Jameson to record that other messages from the city reached him, while on the march, counselling him to persist, despite the contrary advice given; and for him, indeed, the Rubicon was crossed. It was now or never: his *coup*, once initiated, could never be repeated. There could never be such a surprise from him again. To have retired would have meant a retirement forever from Transvaal politics, so far as he was concerned. He was aware of the doubts which must forever darken the counsels of a democratic committee embarked on a perilous adventure. He was convinced that only through him could a decisive course be taken. He had often before achieved the impossible; he decided to persist. To the High Commissioner's remonstrance, he replied: 'I am anxious to fulfil my promise on the petition of the principal residents of the Rand to come to the aid of my fellow-countrymen in their extremity. I shall molest no one. The above is my sole object, and then I shall desire to return to the Protectorate.' He marched on. At Johannesburg the *Uitlanders* waited on events.

The Transvaal Government now knew what the world knew: the *Uitlanders* were in a perilous and embarrassed position. They longed for the success of Jameson, and yet shrank from open complicity with his design. Then faith in his wonderfully lucky destiny, his brilliant personality, the training of his men, led them to believe that he must reach them. They heard that Kruger's old white horse was ready saddled in his honour's stables at Pretoria. But was the Government really taken by surprise? The President had recently taken a tour through his Republic 'for the benefit of his health'. It was afterwards ascertained that one of Jameson's men had communicated with his fiancé in Transvaal territory that he was expecting to be in the Transvaal for the New Year with many of his colleagues. Perhaps she had not kept silent. Kruger made an ominous statement, more than once, that if you wanted to kill a tortoise you must wait till he put his head out. At all events, the Boers mobilised quickly enough, and blocked Jameson's way to the city. They engaged him, and then he fell back, and, with the aid of a guide of doubtful loyalty, instead of taking the main road to Johannesburg, he attempted a disastrous detour and again found the Boers facing him in an impregnable position, with three times his numbers. He surrendered under a flag of truce. There was no timely assistance forthcoming from Johannesburg.

The people in the city could hardly believe the news: had they known of his danger, they would have marched out in their thousands, in their tens of thousands maybe, to assist him. But now all was lost, and he was, after most unpleasant and protracted negotiations, sent back to England with his principal officers. His attempt to solve the South African problem by a *coup d'état* had failed. Had it succeeded, Dr

Jameson would have been acclaimed as one of the bravest hearts in British history and the most astute politician in South African history. The Anglo-Boer War, with all its waste of life and loss of prestige to Great Britain, would never have been necessary, and many of the difficulties which still perplex South African statesmen might never have arisen. As it was, the Raid delayed progress and reform, and made conflict between Britain and the Boers almost inevitable. For the time all the advantage seemed to lie with Kruger and his oligarchy. He arrested, tried, and convicted the leaders of the Reform Party, first having induced them to disarm Johannesburg, while the lives of Jameson and his men, whom Kruger held as hostages, still lay in the balance. Their peril, disgrace and imprisonment could hardly have been greater had they risen in open rebellion. For the moment the cause of reform was lost, and the hands of the British Government were weakened immeasurably. There was, however, no enlightenment in Kruger's statesmanship capable of taking advantage of his new situation. For him the tortoise had put out its head, and been crushed forever. The policy of his party was vindicated. The sentence, trial, and punishment of the leaders of the *Uitlanders* is a disgraceful page in South African history, and, indeed, to civilised jurisprudence.

Meanwhile Dr Jameson was escorted back to England to face the justice of his embarrassed country, which had hitherto lavished honours and admiration upon him. But what offence had he committed? During the Franco-Prussian War, to stem the widespread enlistment of British subjects in the armies of the combatant nations, an Act known as the Foreign Enlistment Act was passed, 'to regulate the conduct of Her Majesty's subjects during the existence of hostilities between foreign States with which Her Majesty is at peace'. Heretofore there had been only one prosecution under the

Act, and the Crown lawyers prepared the indictment with the greatest care. Immediately on Dr Jameson's return to England, Sir Edward Clarke and Carson were retained for the defence, but, although it must always remain a matter of interest that the future 'King Carson', leader of the Ulster rebellion, defended the leader of the Jameson Raid, he had little voice in the conduct of the defence, and his advice, when proffered, was not taken. Against his view of what was wise and expedient, Sir Edward Clarke decided to take two preliminary and technical objections to the indictment. There was a doubt as to whether the territory from which the Raid had been fitted out was really 'British territory' within the meaning of the Act, or, even if it was so, whether the Foreign Enlistment Act had ever been made to apply to such territory with the necessary formality prescribed by its terms. If either objection could be made out, there was an escape for Dr Jameson on technical grounds. But Carson was strongly opposed to the taking of such objections. They were unlikely to succeed, and, if they did, such success would have a deplorable effect on public opinion throughout the world. The proud name of British law would suffer. He advised taking one of two bold courses: he would have fought vigorously on the merits, claiming that this was no military expedition as such against the Transvaal Government – what experienced soldier would embark on a conquest with 500 men? – but the execution of a public duty cast on Dr Jameson in a disordered country, whose Government had abdicated its proper functions, for the protection of his helpless fellow countrymen. The other course, which he was inclined to favour, was formally to plead guilty to the indictment, with a bold and proud statement that the prisoners gloried in their guilt, which had been committed in their country's cause and in order to save thousands of British people from danger and oppression. His advice was not taken, and the case dragged on wearily for over a week without Sir Edward Clarke seriously challenging the allegations of the prosecution on the interpretation put upon Dr Jameson's actions by Sir Richard Webster, the Attorney-General.

The Transvaal Republic supplied witnesses from whom the whole history of the intransigent, oppressive, and indeed cunning policy of the Boer Government to the *Uitlanders* might have been extracted. Again and again Carson pulled Clarke's gown and counselled him, 'You must pursue that, Edward,' but Clarke would not listen. 'I'll deal with that in my speech,' said the great orator. The case dragged on with hardly an adumbration of a valid defence, although it concluded with the adornment of one of Clarke's wonderful speeches. Even so, the jury were obviously reluctant to convict, in spite of a strong exhortation to do so from the Lord Chief Justice, whose summing up, according to *The Times*, 'recalled the judicial habits of an earlier age, and really constituted a more forcible statement of the case against the prisoners than the case of the Attorney-General for the Crown'. After a retirement of an hour and five minutes, the foreman said, 'The jury consider that the state of affairs in Johannesburg presented great provocation.' Further pressed by Lord Russell of Killowen, he said, 'We answered your questions categorically: we cannot agree upon a verdict.' Lord Russell then administered a sharp rebuke to the jury, and thus almost forced from them a verdict of 'Guilty'. Never was a verdict given more reluctantly.

Yet perhaps, after all, the great Irish Chief Justice was doing his duty. This was an exceptional trial, and no defence had been put forward by Sir Edward Clarke which justified any verdict but that of guilty. Lord Russell had commented on the antiquated state of the law which prevented the prisoners from giving evidence on their own behalf, a disability, if indeed it was one, which was soon to be altered by the Criminal Evidence Act. In any event, the verdict remains a shining example of the altruism of British justice. What other nation in the world, with a Conservative and imperialist Government in power, and a common jury, would have convicted of a criminal offence one of her national heroes, and four officers the pride and flower of her military caste? No challenges of jurymen, no Crimes Act, were needed here, and yet Dr Jameson probably held as high a position in the public esteem of Britain as William O'Brien had held in Ireland. The sympathy that was felt for the doctor in the highest quarters of the Government which prosecuted him, and which his failure had so grievously embarrassed, is illustrated by this anecdote. At an evening party, held shortly after the trial and sentences, Lord Salisbury, the Prime Minister, came up to Carson and said, 'I wish you'd brought "Dr Jim" with you.'

Jameson was sentenced to fifteen months' imprisonment without hard labour. His officers suffered lesser terms; but the public crowded round the dock before these exotic criminals, surely the strangest since Sir Walter Raleigh, were led away, in order to express their feelings of homage and admiration. 'They undoubtedly erred,' said *The Times* on the following morning, 'from excess of zeal for what they thought to be the interests of the Empire in South Africa, and of their fellow-subjects in Johannesburg. There is no doubt that these fellow-subjects were badly used, and that the interests of the Empire itself were assailed in more ways than one ...' Already the shadow of the Anglo-Boer War was casting itself forward, which Jameson's exploit, had it been successful, might have stayed forever.

Although 'Dr Jim' was treated as a first-class misdemeanant, he almost died during his imprisonment at Holloway, proudly refusing to make any representation to President Kruger, who, it was said, was willing to intervene on his behalf, for a mitigation of sentence. He came out of prison with his health broken, but with his spirit still the same, and lived – before he was laid to rest, after many years of separation, by the side of his beloved friend and hero, Cecil Rhodes, in the country which their comradeship had brought beneath the British flag – to become, ex-convict that he was and in spite of all, Baronet and Privy Councillor of Great Britain, Prime Minister of the Cape Colony, and the founder, with General Botha, of the South African Union. After all, he won by the arts of peace and by patience during nearly twenty years the self-same object at which he had snatched by a daredevil adventure of a few hours. The Great edifice of the South African Union, which the desperate Raid seemed to have made impossible forever, was raised by the very hand which seemed to have blasted it. As much to his influence as to that of any other man must be ascribed the fact that Boer and Briton have come together, it is to be hoped, forever. To the present writer these two men whom Fate brought together for a few days in the Queen's Bench, Carson and Jameson, seem to be spiritual and political brethren in arms. As a result of the work and the steadfastness of each of these two 'rebels', the one of whom was tried and sentenced, and the other of whom challenged, there stand today two great monuments, the Government of Northern Ireland within the Union, and the Union of South Africa.

The case of the Jameson Raid gave rise to a whole series of actions in which Carson was the victorious leading counsel. A number of Jameson's men, who had been wounded or imprisoned as a result of the Raid, brought civil actions against Jameson, and also Cecil Rhodes, as being ultimately responsible for their misfortunes, and having caused the whole trouble. Undoubtedly Cecil Rhodes was a close confidant and confederate of Jameson in all matters, but for the Raid he had no direct responsibility. The first of these cases came before Mr Justice Mathew, with whom Carson had quarrelled so dramatically on Morley's Commission in Dublin. He considered that Mathew, with his Irish sympathies, was the very worst Judge to whom he could present a case for Jameson and Rhodes. However, his fear proved to be completely unjustified. Mr Justice Mathew took a strong line against the plaintiff. 'It is quite a new thing,' he said in his charge to the jury, 'in English history to find a British soldier basing a claim for damages on the orders of his commander.' After Carson had won the first of a series of victories for him, Rhodes said to his counsel, 'This is my first happy day since the Raid.' Later Rhodes was able to make some recompense to his advocate for the successful issue of these cases, upon which far more depended than pecuniary loss, by giving Carson's son a farm in Rhodesia. The young man was there when the Anglo-Boer War broke out, whereupon he joined Rhodes's famous cavalry.

Editorial Note

Far from being 'a shining example of the altruism of British justice', the trial following the Jameson Raid was in fact a mockery of British justice. In his *Reminiscences* of 1922, Sir Graham Bower reveals that the top structure of the British government was involved in planning the Jameson Raid, and that a selection of dispensable scapegoats was used to carry the blame for the real culprits after the raiders were ignominiously captured by the Boers.

Bower, who died in 1933, was Secretary to the British High Commissioner at the Cape Colony from 1881 to 1897. He lied during the official London enquiry into the scandal in order to protect Chamberlain, Rhodes and other prominent people, in the process damaging his own career: he was dismissed from his position at the Cape, and appointed Colonial Secretary in Mauritius. He maintained silence throughout his life, from a sense of duty, but recorded the truth in his *Reminiscences*, which he directed not to be published until after his death. See *Sir Graham Bower's Secret History of the Jameson Raid and the South African Crisis, 1895-1902*, edited by Deryck Schreuder and Jeffrey Butler, Van Riebeeck Society (Second series Volume 33), Cape Town, 2002.

Moreover, and with respect to the learned author, Carson and Jameson were far from 'spiritual and political brethren in arms'. Carson fought within his own country to maintain the political *status quo*, whereas Jameson raided a sovereign state at the instance of his political bosses. They might both have believed in the Empire, but Carson was an Irishman fighting for what he considered to be the best interests of Ireland, whereas Jameson was a rogue adventurer making mischief in an independent country in a manner that helped precipitate a vast human tragedy in the form of the Anglo-Boer War.

18. Carson v Balfour

These were years of great prosperity for Carson at the Bar. In 1899 his fees gave him an income of twenty thousand pounds, an enormous income in those days of a far more valuable sterling and a negligible income tax; in the same year he refused briefs to the value of something like thirty thousand pounds. The bed-sitting-room in Bury Street, with all its anxieties, was now a thing of the remote past. He was now the owner of a mansion in Rutland Gate, and a charming country house at Rottingdean, where he rode on the Downs a fine old horse with a wonderful hunting record, which he had purchased from Peter the Packer. The horse's name was known as the 'Cob', and often used to take his master from Rutland Gate to the Law Courts in the morning. His wife had reluctantly left the Irish capital, which she knew and loved so well, and was never happy, despite the great material prosperity, in the new and wider environment of the great English city where her husband was becoming one of the leading citizens. His success puzzled and bewildered her, and it would be untruthful to say that either she or her husband were as happy together as they had been in the days of struggle and danger in Dublin. Indeed, material success was counterbalanced by deep personal anxiety. Anyone who has been admitted into Carson's intimacy will have remarked his great love of children. The present writer was invited to write one of a series of articles for the *Morning Post* to illustrate the beauty of the Bible, and went to Lord Carson for advice as to an appropriate passage. His advice, given with one of his transfiguring smiles, was 'Suffer little children to come unto Me, and forbid them not.' One of the families which lived close to his home at Rottingdean was that of Mr and Mrs Stanley Baldwin. The career of the former, which was still obscure when Carson's was at its zenith, was to be materially advanced by him many years later. Carson would delight in going down on his hands and knees to play games with the little Baldwin children, and he was known by them affectionately as 'The Black Man'. He had placed the highest hopes in his eldest son and namesake, but they never were fulfilled. Again and again the fatted calf was prepared for this prodigal son, but as often the father's heart was saddened, and finally hardened against him. There were moments of pride, as when his son wore the uniform of Queen Victoria and of King George in the Anglo-Boer War and in the World War; for his courage, which he had inherited from his father, was not to be questioned; but these episodes were but flashes of light in a sombre picture, which was one of the great and lifelong griefs which Edward Carson had to bear. Personal happiness came in the end to this strong and upright man in the evening of his life, and the calm waters were the more blessed by him after the stormy seas through which his spirit had passed.

But if in the Courts of Law Edward Carson had found a land flowing with milk and honey, in political life, by his own will during these years, he banished himself into the wilderness and became a rebel against his own party. Worse still, there came, with this rebellion, personal estrangement from the great man who had been his personal and political hero, and who was the patron of his success, both legal and political. Only those who have been personally attached to one of the great parties in English political life in the House of Commons can appreciate exactly how much it costs to take a line hostile to their own party. It means black looks from old friends, being cut and avoided in the Lobby, and the name 'traitor', 'rat' and the like from erstwhile colleagues. Politicians are sensitive folk and, without comradeship and good fellowship, life in the House of Commons is difficult to sustain. For Carson, being tied by bonds of gratitude and affection to the leader of the party in the House, Mr Arthur Balfour, to part from him on a matter of principle was all the more difficult. Yet it was a matter of principle, and Carson has shown again and again that, against that, personal and party considerations were of no importance. This is doubtless the reason why he never made a good Government man, and has never taken the first place in the State, for which his qualities seemed to have marked him down in a time and within a party when he had few competitors in prestige, political ability and personal character. He was never really able to play the party game, to exploit the adverse and unpopular elements in a particular policy for party advantage in opposition, and then to adopt that very policy for party advantage when on the Government side. This manoeuvre it is the constant fate of every politician to perform, in small matters or great, who aspires to serve the State through the party machine, and it is a blessed gift for a politician in power to be able to pass through the waters of Lethe when he takes office, and to forget the arguments which he has used in opposition. But Carson was cursed with the faculty of political memory, and he was never able to forget these things.

It is difficult not to read the debates on Mr Gerald Balfour's Irish Land Bill in 1896 without feeling that Carson was on the wrong side, but for the right reasons. The verdict must be that the Balfours were right as a matter of wisdom, but the verdict in their favour need not be unmixed with a certain measure of contempt, on account of the exactly opposite policy which they had exploited in the immediate past. It is hard now to realise the immense political importance at the time of a small number of evicted Irish tenants, and a few decisions of the Courts with regard to the Irish land statutes. In 1896, this was the burning question of political life; to such a narrow compass had the state of Ireland and the politicians reduced British political controversy. Nevertheless, the driving-force of Irish discontent and Irish Nationalism was undoubtedly the agrarian question – the ceaseless opposition of the Irish peasant, with his land hunger, and the hated but impoverished alien landlord with his mortgages and his diminishing proprietary rights. You cannot build up a beneficent capitalist system upon two classes, capitalist and worker, between whom there is a tradition of implacable hatred and, indeed, warfare. What landlord, especially if there is hardly any margin between his rent and his mortgage dues, will spend his small profits on tenants who hate him, and who are lying in wait to murder him? The case of Barlow Smythe is a clear illustration that good landlordism in Ireland was impossible. The only wise agrarian policy to be pursued in Ireland, if the Union was to be maintained, was to give the land to the Irish people, with fair compensation to the alien landlords. This process had been developing rapidly since the Land Court was opened in 1881. Judicial rents had been fixed over an acreage of 8 918 037 acres; £12 000 000 had been applied to land purchase under the two Conservative Acts; the miserable wages of the agricultural labourer had risen considerably, and at last he was sharing in the increasing prosperity of the country. But the full and intended scope of the Land Act of 1881 had been whittled down by judicial decisions; certain classes were thereby excluded, and the Courts had decided that, for the purpose of fixing a fair rent, the increased value of the land, due to tenants' improvements, could be taken into consideration for the landlord's favour. It had been the intention of the Land Act that the tenants should have the benefit of their own improvements. In the new Government Mr Gerald Balfour was appointed Irish Chief Secretary, and the Balfour brothers sat down to draft an Irish Land Bill to admit the classes excluded by judicial decision from the Land Act, 1881, to secure to the tenants their own improvements, and to expedite the purchase of land. To Lord Salisbury's negative policy of 'twenty years of resolute government', there was now added the positive policy of 'killing Home Rule by kindness'; and the foremost kindness that England could show, both to herself and to Ireland, was to remove forever the grievance of Irish peasant against English landlord, by giving the former the land with compensation to the latter. This would in the end take from the Nationalists their principal appeal to the masses. It was a sane policy; it was a wise policy; and it was the only policy which could maintain the Union.

It is fair to say that Carson did not take this view. He saw in the landlords a small and faithful garrison of Unionists, persistent in their loyalty to Great Britain, who had retained their love for England in the most difficult times, and who were now being despoiled by those upon whom they had relied as friends. He could see no hope in a policy which he regarded as a surrender to crime and lawlessness; and, after his upbringing and experience, who could blame him for this view? He complained that Englishmen regarded the Irish question in the abstract, instead of in the concrete. What was the reality of the situation? He knew only too well.

However, the Irish landlord had suffered greatly. He was now called upon, even with his compensation, to make further sacrifices, and the irony of the situation was that the Conservative Party, in opposition a year before, had exploited his grievances to the full. Carson had been appointed the leading spokesman of the Conservative and Unionist Parties on Morley's Committee on the Irish Land Act. He knew the distress of the Irish landlords from long experience, and all he said came from his heart and was spoken with the full assent of the Conservative leaders. Finally, seeing that his amendments were not being considered seriously, he withdrew, on his leaders' advice, with the whole Conservative representation. Morley was left alone with his friends to draw up his report; and it was this report which actually became the basis of Gerald Balfour's Land Act.

This was too much for Carson. No political or personal allegiance could make him blow hot and cold on the same question within the year. Had the Conservative Party not made use of him and his convictions for the purposes of obstruction against Gladstonian Government so shortly before, they might with greater justice have demanded submission from him, but for him to have to acquiesce now would have been a confession that the Conservative Party had used him as a tool. It is the accustomed fate of lawyers to be used and considered as tools by politicians, but Carson was not willing to join that goodly company of catspaws, and he at once entered the fray against his old chief. Indeed, it would have been more decent, in view of their adoption of his policy, if the Conservatives had given more co-operation and less hostility to Morley the year before.

He took a corner seat on the third bench below the gangway, from which Joseph Chamberlain, now Colonial Secretary, had waited on events for his seven years in the wilderness as leader of the Liberal Unionists. The observant eyes of the Press soon saw that Carson was marked out by nature as a leader of mutineers. When the Land Bill reached its committee stage, Carson was there with his sheaf of amendments. Always prone to express his opinions with complete outspokenness, he played the part of candid friend with such effect as almost to jeopardise the Government measure. The subject was, of course, his own, and from a varied armoury of wit, invective, and wary research into the speeches – still fresh from the printer – of his leaders, he drew weapons such as are rarely seen directed by a private member against the policy of his leaders. Close associations of the past did not influence him to give quarter. The Commons, used to the artificial and edifying courtesies and finesse of debate, saw something new and realistic in these methods. Again and again he would say, 'What is the reality of the situation?' and he would tear away every shred of consistency with which the Balfours tried to clothe their new policy. On 16 July 1896, speaking against a proposal to include properties of higher annual value in the benefits of the Land Acts, he said: 'Each successive Government thought it was necessary from time to time to bring in a Bill dealing with the Irish land policy, and, no matter how the law might have been settled, to take a small slice of what remained to the landlord. It is part of the everlasting attempt to make peace in Ireland by giving sops to one party at the expense of the other.' When the Government had accepted several amendments from Tim Healy, and had refused all of his own, Carson pointed an accusing finger at the Chief Secretary. 'It might have been thought,' he said, 'that since he has accepted six amendments coming from Louth, the turn of the Unionist Party might come. I really do hope that the Government has not come here simply for the purpose of pacifying opposition to the other side, and absolutely to refuse to consider any amendment coming from their supporters.' He was showing himself 'a master of gibes and jeers'; he justified his persistence by saying, with a look at Tim Healy: 'The discussion shows this – that if only one talks long enough on any amendment, and keeps the thing going for a sufficient time, everything will be given up by the Government.' He was beginning to win cheers now, and on every vote he led forty or fifty Unionists into the Lobby against the Government. But persistence has its reward, and, wary lawyer that he was, he at length led Mr Gerald Balfour into to a trap the depth of which the Irish Secretary did not at first appreciate. The amendment proposed by Carson was that in a demesne estate no application should be effective before a Court by a tenant if the freehold was owned only by a tenant for life, unless those interested in the reversion had been notified. Gerald Balfour thought this a very fair provision, and gave way. Tim Healy, however, saw that this might mean an exhaustive enquiry into title on every application, a process quite beyond the wit of the Irish peasant, who might not be able to read or write, or even speak English. Gerald Balfour now perceived the snare into which he had been enticed, and immediately began to make reservations. Carson rose, and addressed him in cold disdain. 'For the right honourable gentleman to say that he accepted the amendment, believing it to mean nothing, was really trifling with the House.'

The pain which Carson's attacks upon his brother had caused Mr Arthur Balfour, the Leader of the House, had been apparent throughout the debate. This last gibe was too much for him, and he rose, with a flush upon his face. 'I cannot help,' he said, 'regretting the line which my right honourable friend is taking. I cannot understand him taking the view he has taken, and expressing it with the trenchant hostility which has characterised his remarks.' This was a great deal from Arthur Balfour, but the rebuke had no effect upon the rebel. As soon as this discussion had been disposed of, he rose calmly to move another hostile amendment to the measure. 'I do not know,' he said, 'why the Chief Secretary has given the go-by to what he said a year ago, except perhaps that one's ideas of property alter according as one finds oneself on one side of the House or the other.'

The Leader of the House now hardened his heart against Carson. His amendments were treated impatiently and without courtesy. The chairman called upon him to move the next amendment which stood in his name, but Carson remembered Balfour's orders to retire from Morley's committee a few months before. He judged that to repeat the performance would remind and wound the leader now. Instead of moving his amendment, he said, 'I do not intend to move the next or any other amendment. It is quite apparent that no amendments of any importance will be accepted, and that, if they are accepted, the Government will go back on them.' He then walked slowly out of the House with some of his friends, amid the jeers of the Nationalists.

This Parliamentary gesture, taught him by Balfour himself, was not without its effect, but Carson was not done with the Bill. He was an Irishman: his pledge not to move amendments did not prevent him from intervening on amendments moved by others. The boldest speech of all was upon an amendment which sought to declare the law in favour of the landlords where improvements had arisen as a result of the 'inherent capabilities of the soil'. The Chief Secretary refused to deal with this vexed question at all, although it was declared in favour of the landlord in England. 'I do not rise to advise my friends to persist in this amendment,' said Carson with his greatest bitterness. 'I only rise to say that it occurs to me that it is an extraordinary thing that in one year all our views are changed because we are removed from one side of the House to the other. When a similar Bill was brought in last year, I opposed it, and I am glad to say that I had no greater supporter than the Leader of the House. But we move rapidly in these matters. In 1870, Mr Isaac Butt said that no one would think of alleging that the inherent capabilities of the soil were the property of the tenant. How are we to account for these transitions?'

Again Arthur Balfour was stung. 'What transitions?' he asked angrily.

'I call it a transition,' explained Carson coldly, 'when a right honourable member at one time professes certain principles as those which ought to be embodied in an Act of Parliament, and when he is on the other side of the House says that it is not necessary that they should be put into the Bill of his own Government.'

Loud cheers from Unionists greeted this statement, which the facts seemed to justify.

In answer to this speech, Mr Balfour made – a thing which for him was indeed rare – an emotional appeal to his late lieutenant. The latter's sincerity and bitterness had made a great impression upon him, and even Arthur Balfour could not take these taunts with his accustomed philosophy. John Morley spoke after Carson, and expressed the view that Balfour had betrayed his old principles by this Bill, and taken over the Liberal Bill of the year before. Mr Balfour replied in these terms, obviously deeply moved and made unhappy by what had passed: 'I do not think it worthwhile, and I am certainly not willing to reply at length to the right honourable gentleman opposite, but I confess that when I have to deal with a speech like that delivered by my right honourable and learned friend below the gangway, the case is different. My right honourable and learned friend and I have been political colleagues; we have fought side by side in times of stress; I have regarded him in times past with feelings of absolute confidence; I have felt that on his judgment I could rely; but when he turns round, and, on the subject of this Bill, makes an attack upon one who is certainly an old colleague, and who I hope he will consider an old friend, I admit I cannot allow his observations to pass without some remark. He accuses me and the Government of which I form a part of having changed our opinions in the last year, and of having, as he would generously imply, for the sweets of office, given up opinions which we once held and since defended from this side of the House. Then, indeed, I feel some explanation is due, if not to him, at all events to others who supported both him and me in those times, and in times still more difficult.'

Mr Balfour explained that he was simply refusing to decide the academic question of the right to the 'capabilities of the soil', either in favour of the landlord or of the tenant. A decision either way would rob the Bill of any useful or practical results.

'Is there any political dishonour, or anything that deserves the accusation of my right honourable and learned friend?' he continued. 'I ask the House to refuse an opinion one way or the other on a question which I say ought not to be dealt with in this Bill if it is to have any passing into law. That is the doctrine which I lay before the House. It is the doctrine I stand by. It is a straightforward doctrine. It is honourable. It is consistent with everything I have said or done, and I trust that every follower of the Government will support the Government in this clause in the course they are going to pursue.'

This speech was a gesture for reconciliation, generous and affectionate, such as the House of Commons loves, and the House immediately expected what it would have heard from ninety-nine men out of a hundred under such circumstances – some answering gesture of acknowledgment. When Balfour sat down after this speech, which was received with many cheers, honourable members shouted, 'Carson, Carson,' calling upon him to speak. But he was to be won into no public acknowledgment of reconciliation. As the *Westminster Gazette* records, the right honourable member for Dublin University sat 'grim, pale, silent', on his bench, his hat over his eyes. However, he could not let this personal appeal go by unanswered, and he wrote this letter to his old chief the next day:

'39 Rutland Gate SW
24 July

My dear Mr Balfour, – May I write you one line to say how deeply I felt your kind and generous allusion to myself last night, even tho' made in a speech censuring my conduct. One phrase alone pained me – the accusation that my criticism bore any suggestion of my leader's opinions being affected by 'the sweets of office'. Knowing well your views of office and at what a sacrifice you remain our only possible and most trusted leader, so mean a thought never crossed my mind.

When I was your Solicitor-General I gave a pledge in my election address to my constituents that I would resist to the best of my abilities any further interference with landlords' property in Ireland. If I have gone too far in carrying out this pledge it will no doubt justify a change in your opinion of my judgment and wisdom, but I hope it may not lead you to think I am the less grateful or devoted to the leader to whom I owe so much and whom alone I would ever consent to follow.

Sincerely yours
Edward Carson'

On the same day he received the following charming answer from the Leader of the House in his own hand.

'House of Commons
Friday, 24 July '96

My dear Carson, – Your note, just received, has given me great pleasure. I have ever felt confident that a friendship like ours, tried as it has been both by adversity and prosperity, was not destined to vanish and become as if it had never been. We have too often had to rely on each other in circumstances of difficulty and perplexity to permit our mutual confidence to be easily disturbed. I have watched your brilliant career at the

English Bar with the satisfaction of an old friend and the pride of an old colleague – but in my eyes it has been somewhat dearly purchased at the cost of the severance of our old official relations. However, I cannot expect you to take this view, and, though I do not get accustomed to seeing you off the front bench, I am delighted at the success to which that absence is due.

Yours ever

Arthur James Balfour'

But, despite this exchange of letters, Carson went to the Conservative Chief Whip, Akers-Douglas, and gave him notice that he no longer wished to receive the party Whip or daily notice to attend, which is the emblem and privilege of party membership. He repeated to Akers-Douglas Harcourt's warning to him a few years before: 'The Conservative Party never yet took up a cause that they did not betray'. 'Henceforward,' he said, 'I am resolved to take whatever course is best for Ireland.' The next day he consoled himself during a case in the Divorce Court by putting his feelings into satirical verse, as he often did. He wrote on his brief:

> The difference between Liberal and Tory,
> As each confiscates Irish land,
> Is that Liberals are more overbearing,
> While Tories are more underhand.

This was itself a parody of the famous rhyme of the days of the land war:

> The difference between Moonshine and Moonlight
> The people do now understand
> Is that Moonlight's the law of the League,
> And Moonshine's the law of the land.

The Bill was passed by both Houses, the House of Lords showing its accustomed pliability when a Conservative Government is in power; but, on its final stage in the Commons, Carson had a generous word to say to Gerald Balfour. 'I can only say,' he said, 'I am perfectly sure as I give him the credit, the right honourable gentleman will give me the credit for this – that all we have differed upon was as to the best method of promoting what we both have seriously at heart, the interests of Ireland, and the maintenance of the Union.'

19. Fighting for the Union

The maintenance of the Union: that was his cause throughout the whole of his political life. Moreover, he felt that the best interests of Ireland were bound up with that cause. How could Ireland, a small impoverished island, quite apart from the question of imperial safety and unity, stand by herself, deprived of the assistance of the immensely rich and powerful sister isle and her great market? The solution for him was a closer union of hearts which could only exist within a legislative Union. I suppose that the consensus of opinion must be that on the merits of this particular question the Balfours were right and Carson was wrong. The only hope of the maintenance of the Union was by the removal of the agrarian grievances, and it is impossible to make an omelette without breaking eggs. The eggs on this occasion were the unfortunate landlords. Yet, with it all, the cause of the Union was lost, as many concede, hopelessly, irretrievably, 'in the day of dishonour', as Gladstone had prophesied, by surrender after surrender to violence and lawlessness, with the loyalists shamefully abandoned; and Carson may be forgiven for tracing back the stages of surrender to its first precedents, when, in his view, measures, perhaps good in themselves, were brought forward, not on their own merits, but from fear of violence and crime. In any event, the interests of the loyalists had been sacrificed for nothing.

Yet even in those days he was no mere instrument of the landlords, as is often thought, though naturally they looked to him as a heaven-sent champion. He loved to advocate, with Irish members of all factions, the cause of the Irish peasant, of the Irish school-teacher, of the Catholic student. There was still much of the Liberal in him which in its purest inspiration calls out for justice to the poor and the oppressed.

It is true that he thought their cause was bound up with the Union with England, and, in words worthy of any patriot or humanitarian, he begged the Unionists in those sunlit days of Victorian prosperity to help Ireland to see this 'as a reality'. In 1898, despite a general improvement over the whole face of Ireland as a result of the quieter times, there was 'exceptional distress' in certain parts of the south and west of Ireland. He begged the Government to come to the assistance of the suffering peasants with relief. 'What do we mean by exceptional distress?' he said. 'Why, sir, at the very best of times these poor people for whom we are pleading live in a distressful condition; and when these people, and those interested in them, come forward to put before the House of Commons, to put before the British nation, what they call "exceptional distress", unhappy indeed must be their lot. At the best of times their living is of the lowest order, and it is a class of living which can only be called an existence; and, sir, what they are crying out for now is that they may be allowed to have that mere existence. In England, when distress of this kind arises, you are blessed with millionaires, with great wealth, with great factories, with rich employers who can well afford to be charitable. Unfortunately, sir, Ireland is a poor country, and we have no millionaires. We have no wealth and very little in the nature of trade. We have no factories and no employers who can cope with "exceptional distress". I am not going to say what is the occasion of that. It is not at all germane to the subject, and I think very little good is done in making attacks on the English Government of the past, when we want to deal at this very moment with the state of things which we now find in Ireland. ... If we do nothing, if the distress continues, I think it will create more ill-feeling towards England than any amount of "politics" can do. I appeal to His Majesty's Government to take this matter in hand. The people do not ask for much. They ask merely to be allowed to continue to exist. The congested district boards have done their duty well, but, sir, they have limited means; and when you have, year after year, these enormous surpluses on your budgets, which enable £1 000 000 to be taken off tobacco and matter of that kind, surely this rich country might join us in something nobler than this – in helping to relieve the sufferings of these poor Irish people.'

Carson, although a Protestant of Protestants, was one of the pioneers of, and most powerful advocates for, the foundation of a National Catholic University, which was finally given by the Liberal Government eight years later. The great argument against this proposal was that it would perpetuate the antagonism between Protestant and Catholic, and render their coming together impossible. Trinity College had thrown her doors wide to the Catholics. What more did they want? Carson's concrete mind again asked, 'What is the reality of the situation?' The Catholics would not go to Trinity College. Speaking in the Address in the House in February 1898, he said, 'As a member for the University of Dublin, and as one who has a belief in the advancement of our people by progress in education, I say our first object ought to be to see that education is brought home to them in a form which they can accept. Sir, I often think that members of this House, who meet habitually in England, do not thoroughly understand that the Irish Catholics are a people passionately devoted to their religion. They are a people who will not accept any institution in relation to the education of their children which is in conflict with their views; and, sir, this being the fact, and, all other expedients having been tried, what can be the use of believing that the aim of University education should be the idea of secularism, when the great bulk of the Catholic people in Ireland will not accept, and could not accept, that solution? I have often thought that English minds are very prone to deal with Irish questions in the abstract. I think we have to deal with Irish questions in the concrete. But the truth is that honourable members in their heart of hearts are afraid of something or other connected with the Catholic religion, which they will not suggest and which they will not explain. I ask, what is this fear of a Catholic University? That you lose the chance of a mixed education in the sense of the denominations coming together? But, sir, that system has already been tried, and it has failed. Do you think that the Catholics of Ireland will be worse off with the enlightenment of a University education than they are now when they are deprived of it? That is the reality of the situation. I can only say that, speaking for myself, I have no fears of a Catholic University.'

Is this the voice of a prejudiced diehard, of a bigoted Ascendancy man? Is it not rather the voice of a sagacious Unionist, who saw that the removal of all religious ascendancy was a necessity for the cause of the Union between the two nations? It is melancholy to record that many 'Unionists', who would not listen to his words then, were prepared long afterwards to abandon the cause of the Union, root and branch, as a lost cause.

One advantage which his independence brought him was that he was able on occasion to join a united front with his Nationalist colleagues in his country's cause. In the complicated arrangements which regulated Irish finance under the Union, from time to time blunders were made. Under the National Teachers Act, 1879, the British Treasury was found in 1896 to have paid £100 000 less than was due to the Irish teachers; at the same time the contributions of the Irish teachers for their Pension Fund were considerably short of the necessary amount. Carson advocated an adjustment in this direction by a simple application of the £100 000 to this end. But the matter was a complex one, and Mr Gerald Balfour preferred to meet the deficiency by an increase of contributions. Carson was the spokesman for all the Irish members on this matter. 'There is absolutely no difference of opinion among the members from Ireland on this question,' he said. 'In matters of this kind, which deal with the financial treatment of Ireland, the Government should act with scrupulous fairness to that country. ... It is this higgling which does so much harm. The Irish say, "If we are unable to get common justice from the Imperial House of Commons in such matters, how can we expect that in the broader political questions that come under discussion, and in which the happiness of our people is concerned, we shall be listened to?" I hope the Government will see its way to meet the unanimous voice of the representatives of Ireland, and if they do I shall not look upon it as a concession, but as an equitable and just carrying out of an Act of Parliament.'

Instead of welcoming and respecting the unanimous opinion of the Irish members, led for once by a Unionist, Gerald Balfour replied in a petulant manner, and concluded unfortunately with the words: 'The conclusion I am drawn to is that all the Irish members will invariably come down to the House and press for money, when they think it can be squeezed out of the Treasury.'

Carson again rose, and gravely rebuked the Chief Secretary in these terms: 'I think it is unworthy of the right honourable gentleman to suggest that Irish members are always prepared to come down to the House and make demands on the Imperial Exchequer, whether they are entitled to do so or not. This is not a demand on the British Treasury at all; it is simply a demand that Irish funds earned by Irish teachers shall be given to the men that earned them. No matter what may be the view, or the criticism, or the sneer of an Irish Chief Secretary, I will certainly, as an Irish member, have no hesitation in standing up for these men. I regret the tone of the right honourable gentleman, and I do not think that he improves the position of Unionism in Ireland or makes their task in this House easier.'

Was it wonderful that the Nationalists began to feel proud of him, or that one of them should state, in his cups, that he ought to be made 'leader of the Irish race at home and abroad'?

But Carson's father had been a Liberal Conservative, and so was his son. It was his view that liberty should go hand in hand with tradition. This, the true and straight tradition of Toryism, was apparent in a remarkable speech on the Evidence in Criminal Cases Bill. This was the Act which allowed prisoners to give evidence on their own behalf in criminal trials. It was brought forward in the cause of humanity, and was generally understood to be an Act in the interests of all prisoners, but Carson, with his vast knowledge as a criminal prosecutor, knew that it had always been a great advantage for the prisoner to be incompetent to give evidence on his own behalf. He said that the Act would, far from proving a boon, be oppressive to prisoners, and so exactly have his prophecies been fulfilled in the event that it is worthwhile to anyone interested in criminal jurisprudence to observe his remarks in a speech now forgotten, but highly praised at the time. 'The Attorney-General, with a persuasiveness against which it behoves us to be on our guard, has said that no prisoner need give evidence if he should not wish to do so. This, of course, may be the intention of the framers of the Bill, but, as a matter of fact, if the measure passes, every man tried for his life will be obliged to present himself for examination and cross-examination. In making this change, we will really be introducing the French system under which a prisoner is not only cross-examined by the prosecuting counsel, but also by the Judge. The man for whom I especially plead is the poor uneducated prisoner who is not protected by counsel or solicitor. I can conceive nothing that will lead to greater injustice than that an ignorant, undefended man shall at a moment's notice be requested to present himself in the witness-box and, having told his illiterate rigmarole, subject himself to cross-examination by the Crown. ... It is impossible for any ordinary man to have complete control of his senses or to do himself justice in these circumstances. We are putting an end to a great safeguard the citizens of this country have enjoyed for centuries, namely, that the Crown must independently prove its case.' As to putting a man in the box on a capital trial, he said, 'I think counsel will look upon such obligations as are thus thrown upon them with horror. There is also, to my mind, the great objection that a prisoner subjecting himself to cross-examination will leave himself also to be cross-examined by the Judge. If we are to subject a prisoner to this method of cross-examination and investigation of fact by the Judge, how far are we away from the French system? ... I can call to mind no case in all my long experience of any suggested miscarriage of justice by reason of a prisoner not being allowed to be called as a witness. It is a strange fact that it remains for a so-called Conservative Party to be the first to put forward these proposals in so extreme and stringent a manner, making revolutionary changes in the law.'

This speech had a deep effect upon the House, and was widely commended in the Press, but the Government view, strongly supported by Sir Edward Clarke, prevailed. Yet slowly and surely Carson's view proved true. An Act passed expressly in the interests of the prisoner has had, on the whole, a contrary effect. As Carson said, 'Judges are only human,' and a judicial cross-examination is now common form. At first, indeed, only very bold counsel would put their prisoners in the witness-box, and no comment was made by the Bench on either course being taken. But after Sir Edward Marshall Hall had put Wood in the box in the *Camden Town* trial, and had succeeded, the practice became general, and in a few years it was a bold counsel who refused to put his prisoner in the box. If he does not do so, it is almost certain to be the subject of judicial comment, and, in effect, contrary to the intention of Parliament, it is now a matter of obligation for a prisoner to go into the box. Prosecuting counsel often rely on cross-examination for a conviction, and as to the odious 'obligation' put upon counsel of which Carson spoke, it is interesting to record that Marshall Hall, the most celebrated and successful of all criminal defenders, refused to face such a responsibility in a capital case, and gave his prisoners an alternative form to sign: 'I intend to give evidence in this case / I do not intend to give evidence in this case'. Indeed, on more than one occasion he said that the affirmative choice had led the prisoner directly to the gallows. May not Carson have been right when he said that English liberty went hand in hand with tradition, and that, if it was not necessary to change, it was necessary not to change?

One instance of Carson's growing Conservatism was very curious. It was, indeed, his last speech before he became a Minister. A private donor had presented to Parliament a statue of Oliver Cromwell, and it was proposed to place the statue where it now in fact stands – in the precincts of the Palace of Westminster. Such an event was sure to raise an Irish debate. Mr John Dillon delivered a most waspish and ingenious oration. He said, if Englishmen had possessed the smallest national pride, a statue of Cromwell of the most magnificent kind would have been erected by public

subscription hundreds of years ago. What had poor Ireland
done for Daniel O'Connell? For Cromwell was almost the
greatest of Englishmen. This was too much for Carson. 'He
was a murderer,' he interjected. Dillon then said that as an
Irishman he could not possibly agree to the erection of the
statue in view of his tyranny in his country. Carson followed
him in the same sense. 'I think it is a slight to this House to
have a statue to Oliver Cromwell under any circumstances
within the precincts of this House,' said the lineal descendant
of General Lambert.

With this speech ended Carson's career as an Independent
member. By his independence he seemed to have lost much:
reputations are made and lost every day in the House, and
won and lost again as soon. But Carson did seem to have
thrown aside all chance of political advancement by fighting
his old patron in a hopeless cause. He suffered much personal
unpopularity at the time, but the House loves sincerity, and
in reality he had made himself known for the first time to
it. Gradually the House came to recognise that here was no
supple lawyer with a brief, but a fearless man of principle,
faithful, according to his lights, to a great cause.

20. Law Officer of the Crown

His active hostility to the Government bore fruits of advantage more swiftly than anyone had anticipated. Lawyers are very useful to their party in opposition, but, when their party is in office, unless they occupy the position of Attorney-General or Solicitor-General, their intervention is not encouraged by the party Whips and their Parliamentary talents usually lie fallow, or are forgotten. Carson had certainly saved his own from oblivion. Sir Richard Webster, who had been Attorney-General in three Administrations and, although not a brilliant advocate, had probably made more money at the Bar than any man up to that time, resigned from his position as Law Officer in May 1900 and became Master of the Rolls. Sir Robert Finlay, the Solicitor-General, succeeded him as 'Mr Attorney', and the Solicitor-Generalship had to be filled by a newcomer. The choice was known to lie between Mr Charles Alfred Cripps KC, now Lord Parmoor, and Carson. By the Whips the appointment of the former was favoured. For it is interesting, in view of the future, to record that never for one instant had his loyalty to the Conservative Whips failed. He had been a constant and dutiful henchman to the Party machine, whereas Carson had been a thorn in their flesh. Yet it was to Carson, the late Liberal Unionist and party rebel, that the appointment went. Perhaps the great Lord Salisbury is to be credited with a rare insight into the sort of Conservatism that really lasts. Before Webster resigned, and when Carson was still refusing the Conservative Whip, Arthur Balfour sent for the latter and asked him whether he would consider taking office again under the Crown. Carson said that there was no reason why the Conservative Party should offer him anything. Balfour looked gently into his eyes, and said,

'There are other questions besides Ireland, Edward.' Carson replied, 'I know that, but it's only for Ireland that I'm in politics.' Soon afterwards, Carson received a letter in Lord Salisbury's own handwriting, a courtesy not often exercised by modern Prime Ministers on such occasions.

> 'Hatfield House
> Hatfield, Herts.
> May 2, 1900
>
> Dear Mr Carson, – Arthur Balfour will have communicated to you our hope that you will be willing to accept the offer of the Solicitor-Generalship which is likely to be immediately vacant. Your acceptance would strengthen the Administration. I trust that you will see your way to do so.
>
> Yours very truly,
> Salisbury'

Perhaps the compliment of the personal letter from the great nobleman was decisive in winning back to the fold this powerful auxiliary. For, in spite of the sacrifice of many thousands a year and the loss of an independence which he greatly valued, Carson accepted the appointment. Immediately after he had written his letter of acceptance, Lord Justice Henn Collins, who had presided over the Wilde trial, sent for Carson and begged him not to give up the best years of his life in the service of the Government. 'Stay at the Bar,' he said, 'and be the greatest and richest advocate of our time. That is your real bent.'

On the same day on which he received and accepted Lord Salisbury's offer of office he wrote a letter of gratitude to Arthur Balfour:

'39 Rutland Gate SW
May 2, 1900

Dear Mr Balfour, – I felt so perturbed yesterday at our interview by all kinds of mixed feelings that I feel I really came away without conveying to you my very sincere appreciation of all that your generous friendship has done for me. I can assure you that my appointment as Solicitor-General for Ireland, and now as Solicitor-General, are trivial rewards to me as compared with the knowledge that in difficult times I had won your confidence. I know that in my new office, for a time at least, I will require some consideration from my colleagues, as many matters will be new to me, but I am certain you may rely upon my best efforts faithfully to serve the Government and the country.

With many thanks
I remain, sincerely yours,
Edward Carson'

Nevertheless, it seemed, at any rate to the friends of Mr Charles Alfred Cripps KC, as if promotion was regulated in a wicked world which preferred rather to muzzle vice than to reward virtue. The *Westminster Gazette* did not fail to improve on the occasion, and depicted Salisbury as a headmaster giving the term's prize to the Naughty Big Boy, to the evident chagrin of the Good Little Boy. There is no doubt but that the future Lord Parmoor – the creation was a Liberal one – was annoyed, but courteously went to Carson and told him that the appointment, had it been given to any other man but Carson, would have left him with a sense of grievance. Carson was, however, not deceived by this politeness. 'You know very well,' he said, 'that you've a sense of grievance now.'

The parable of the prodigal son was now enacted to the full. English and Irish Unionists competed with each other to do honour to the new Law Officer. He was twice banqueted by his colleagues at the Bar and in Parliament, and on one of these occasions the veteran Lord Chancellor, the Earl of Halsbury, took the chair and helped to slay the fatted calf for the senior member for Dublin University. For David Plunkett was now Lord Rathmore, and Carson was now the senior representative for Trinity, with the illustrious historian, Lecky, as his junior colleague. This was the first and only occasion on which an Irish Solicitor-General has become a Solicitor-General for England.

It may here be mentioned that the position of Solicitor-General carried with it a salary of £6 000 a year, with fees for Crown briefs perhaps equivalent annually to that amount, and yet the appointment was a financial sacrifice to Carson of at least £8 000 a year. Until 1895, Law Officers had been permitted to engage in private practice in addition to the Crown work, and in those days the Government lawyers used therefore to amass huge incomes.

With his appointment as Law Officer there went, as was customary, the honour of knighthood, and Carson was one of the first men to be knighted by the Prince of Wales, soon to be Edward VII. He had not known the old Queen personally, who had died on 22 January 1901. He had, of course, been presented to her and spoken with her; he had met her for the first time at a Windsor garden-party during the Jubilee Celebration of 1897. He was overcome by emotion when he saw the great old lady in her chair wheeled by her Indians, seeming to embody in her person and her attendants the breadth and majesty of the British Empire. He went behind one of the great trees and wept. 'This,' he thought 'was the girl to whom Melbourne and Wellington knelt, the woman of whom Palmerston was afraid, to whom Disraeli made love; and now she is going to speak with me.'

The future King, who rarely missed the chance of making a personal contact with a coming man, had already made friends with his Solicitor-General. He told Lady Savile that he wished to meet Carson at dinner. He had taken him aside at this dinner and said, imitating the Irish accent, not very successfully, 'How's dear old dirty Dublin getting along?' Carson replied, 'Just as when your royal highness left it.' But the Prince then showed the most shrewd and careful knowledge of Irish affairs, and was regaled with a sumptuous banquet of Carson's Irish experiences, such as the writer has tried to reproduce in this work.

With his appointment under the Crown there returned to him occasionally the duty of undertaking important criminal prosecutions, of which business he had made himself such a master in Ireland. He had not been long in office before he appeared in a case which, although the proceedings were scarcely more than a formality, by reason of the splendour of its pageantry and the rank of the prisoner may be accounted historical, and, it is hoped, the last of its kind.

Earl Russell, the grandson of the great Victorian Prime Minister, and himself a future Minister of the Crown, had been cursed with a miserable marriage. His life with the beautiful girl named Mabel Edith Scott, who had married him in 1890, had been a progress in bitter disagreement. The unhappy pair, despite numerous and varied applications to the Divorce Courts, were still legally tied to each other by the English law ten years later. Meanwhile the Countess, abetted by her mother, Lady Scott, had pursued her husband with the blackest calumnies until their mouths were stopped by a conviction for criminal libel and conspiracy against the latter at the Old Bailey. The earl, a young man of great personal magnetism and ability, still tied to the wife who loathed him, became attached to a lady named Mollie Somerville, and, since he could not obtain the evidence for a divorce under English law, determined to run away with her, and, after obtaining a divorce by the acquisition of a technical domicile in Nevada, to marry her. This was done against the strong advice of his friend and solicitor, Mr (now Sir) John Withers. On 14 April 1900, after a residence in Nevada which, as he was advised, qualified him for domicile under the laws of that State, he obtained a decree of divorce against his wife on the ground of desertion, and married Mollie Somerville the next day before a certain Judge Curler. But, whether or not his residence qualified him for a Nevada domicile under American law, this divorce could not have been valid in England, because English law requires, in order to found valid proceedings for the dissolution of an English marriage, that the husband must have changed his domicile according to the strict English requirements. To do this he must have formed the fixed intention to make his permanent home in another country. The ceremony before Judge Curler was therefore bigamous, and his countess forthwith petitioned for divorce on the grounds of bigamous adultery, and obtained a decree *nisi* on 24 March 1901.

In the meantime, Lord Russell had returned to England, and, after a long delay, the Crown decided to arrest him and indict him for bigamy. This was done on 17 June 1901, and by this act the Public Prosecutor invoked strange privileges and procedures of great antiquity, which are still the law of the land. Although the original distinction between felony and misdemeanour, as degrees of gravity in crime, has long since been blurred by the modern developments of our law, it still holds good that in cases of 'felony', but not for 'misdemeanour', a peer must be tried by his peers and not by a petty jury. Thus it came about that John Francis, the second Earl Russell, was tried by his peers in the Royal Gallery of the Palace of Westminster under the Presidency of the Earl of Halsbury, as 'Lord High Steward', on 18 July 1901. The last previous prosecution of this kind had been that of the fiery and eccentric Lord Cardigan in 1841 for his duel with Captain Tuckett.

Carson appeared for the prosecution with Sir Robert Finlay and others. England was facing the first dawn of the twentieth century, heavy with levelling fate and destructive change, yet this case seemed nearer to Runnymede and the race distinctions, caste privileges and penalties of the Middle Ages. Indeed, as was remarked by the smart young journalists of the time, there was a sense of something imagined rather than really experienced among the spectators. The magnificent gallery, adorned with Maclise's huge frescoes of Trafalgar and Waterloo, through which the King passes in all his regal glory with his retinue to open Parliament, had been converted into a hall of justice. Under the roof, with its glittering panels, moulding and chandeliers, at one end, was placed the throne, with its crimson canopy. On either side of the throne, the peeresses in their feminine finery and jewels, and the eldest sons of peers, were seated in opposite groups; at the other end, behind the Bar, there waited a large crowd of distinguished people, privileged to witness these strange proceedings.

It is a hot summer's day, and the great ladies of Edwardian society are fanning themselves with many-coloured fans until the Court is constituted and the trial begins. There is a loud buzz of conversation, which suddenly stops as the Crown lawyers, led by Finlay and Carson in Court dress and full-bottomed wigs, stalk past and take the seats prepared for them. They are followed by Mr Robson KC, Mr Horace Avory and the defending lawyers. Then a procession of elven Judges files in from behind the throne, all dressed in scarlet and ermine, except Sir Francis Jeune, the President of the Divorce Court, who wears his robe of black and gold. They take their seats along the Woolsack placed below the throne. They are followed by the barons, as peers of the lowest rank, who move in to the left of the throne, wearing their coronets, their scarlet robes and ermine capes. To the right enter the peers of higher rank, viscounts, earls, marquesses – among whom is the Prime Minister, Salisbury – and dukes. Altogether one hundred and sixty peers take their seats, prepared strictly according to their respective ranks. When they are all seated, they form two great banks of white and scarlet, which rise up, tier on tier, on each side of the throne against Maclise's paintings. Thereupon Sir Michael Biddulph, who holds the office of 'Black Rod', enters. Despite his title, he is wearing a gorgeous military uniform, and carries a white wand of great height. This is the emblem of the office of the Lord High Steward, who comes in last of all the members of the Court, a squat little figure of almost fantastic dignity, and climbs up into the gilded chair placed immediately below the throne.

The Court is now constituted. How different in its pageantry from the Courts which used to be 'constituted' by two resident magistrates in the days of the land war. Judge Curler of Nevada, who is in Court, must be amazed at the mediaeval splendour which his simple ceremony has called forth. The dead silence is now broken by a loud proclamation from the Sergeant-at-Arms, 'Oyez! Oyez! Oyez!' three times repeated. Silence is commanded in the King's name on pain of imprisonment, and the King's Commission is delivered on bended knee from the Clerk in Chancery to the Clerk in King's Bench, and read by the latter, also kneeling, while all other of King Edward's loyal subjects present rise and cry, 'God save the King.' It seems rather like some sort of religious service than a criminal trial. Yet criminal trial it is:

for now, escorted by the sable-clad yeoman usher, there soon enters a young man, clad simply in the fashionable clothes of an English gentleman. He is the prisoner at the Bar, and seems perfectly at his ease as he listens respectfully to the indictment. Yet he is the representative of one of the most historic families of Europe. If his claimed descent from the Saxon god, Thor, is not authentic, for the last four hundred years there has scarcely been a generation when a Russell has not taken an effective part in English history, more often than not on the progressive side. After the indictment has been read, Black Rod advances and leads the prisoner within the Bar. Before taking his place at a table near his counsel, he bows with meticulous care three times to the Lord High Steward.

'How say you, my lord, are you guilty or not guilty?'

Before an answer can be made, Mr Robson is on his feet strenuously making objection. Evidently he is taking exception to the indictment on a point of law, but nobody except the lawyers can understand, and they find it difficult to hear. He is arguing that no indictment can lie; that the statute under which the earl is prosecuted does not apply. There is a presumption that the King's law does not apply outside the King's dominions; this statute is not expressly stated to apply to offences committed outside the King's dominions, and it is to be feared that Nevada is no longer within the King's dominions, if it ever was. For hours the argument continues. The interest which had animated every face in the Royal Gallery is replaced by bewilderment, and then weariness. The interest of several lawyers, however, is seen to be aroused for the first time. They are more interested in Mr Robson's argument than all the pomp, and real business is being transacted. Nevertheless, full-bottomed wigs and ceremonial robes on a hot July afternoon are oppressive, and induce to somnolence. Even a scarlet-robed one on the

Woolsack is seen to nod. At last, to the relief of everyone, Mr Robson sits down, and Mr Avory 'follows' him. But Mr Avory's arguments have never been long, and, when he too has sat down, the Lord High Steward, whose vitality has never flagged, observes, almost with a snort, 'My lords, we have the advantage of having His Majesty's Judges here. I have been myself of opinion for some time that the matter which has been discussed at such inordinate length was really too plain for argument.' The preliminary point having been thus waved aside, it becomes the prisoner's duty to plead to the indictment. He stands up, and public interest is again awakened. 'My lords,' he says, 'under the advice of counsel, I plead guilty.' Soon, after a further plea from his counsel, the heir of Lord John Russell addresses his peers with deference, yet without humility, on the miseries which he endured from an early marriage and a merciless wife, before he has sought escape from his torture by a device which, as he thought, was within the law. His brother peers then pass out behind the throne into the House of Lords to consider the punishment. Presently they return, and Lord Halsbury pronounces sentence: 'Allowing for the provocation you have received, and the extreme torture which you have suffered during a long period of your life,' he gives a sentence of three months' imprisonment in the first division. Black Rod then hands the tall White Rod to the Lord High Steward. The latter, in obedience to immemorial custom, tries to snap it asunder with his hands: he cannot do it, and so forthwith breaks it across his knee. The prisoner leaves under escort, with a nod for Mollie Somerville, and the nobility of Great Britain, who have sentenced their brother peer, straightway cast off their robes – the July heat is great – and, carrying them on their arms, leave the Royal Gallery as ordinary gentlemen of the twentieth century.

In a few minutes the Royal Gallery is empty, and it remains only for the carpenters to remove the stage properties which have been constructed to carry out, according to custom, the last trial of an English nobleman for felony. It remains but to add that a few years later Lord Russell received a free pardon from the King for his offence, that he lived to become one of the ablest speakers in the House of Lords, and to hold high office, like Dr Jameson, under the Crown.

21. The Trial of 'Colonel' Lynch

If the case of the Jameson Raid had been the prelude to the Anglo-Boer War, the trial of 'Colonel' Lynch was the epilogue to that whole sad chapter.

In the so-called 'Khaki' election which followed the successful issue – after many vicissitudes and bitter humiliation – of the Anglo-Boer War, a remarkable candidate presented himself as an Independent Nationalist for election by the citizens of Galway. He was of Irish descent, had been born in Australia, and was at the time resident in Paris. His profession was that of a journalist. Unlike most candidates at that time, he made no reference in his election address, or in his reply to his committee's invitation, to the Anglo-Boer War. Nor did the Independent Nationalist candidate condescend to visit his electors. During the progress of the election, however, his opponents made it known that he was none other than the 'Colonel' Lynch who had commanded the 'Irish Brigade' in South Africa against Great Britain. Nevertheless, the men of Galway elected him as their member, and he wrote a letter to the Speaker of the House of Commons saying that his part in the Anglo-Boer War had not been actuated by feelings of hatred towards Great Britain; that he accepted the terms of peace in the same spirit as had his leader, General Louis Botha; and concluded by an appeal, in the words of Themistocles, that his fellow-members 'might not beat him, but hear him'.

His election as member for Galway, and his departure from France to take up his duties in the British House of Commons, was certainly an astonishing piece of audacity. He may have received some advice that he had a valid defence in law to any prosecution which was brought against him; but he was living safely in Paris, and his return to England was undoubtedly an act of courage. He arrived with his wife at Newhaven on 1 June 1902, and was forthwith arrested. Sir Edward Carson led for the prosecution in the very lengthy proceedings in the Police Court, and once more found himself against a prisoner who was also a Nationalist member of Parliament. There followed remand after remand, in order that witnesses and evidence might be brought from South Africa. It appeared that Arthur Lynch had gone to South Africa in the capacity of war correspondent to the *Journal*, which, like every other leading French newspaper, was taking a line adverse to Great Britain. It is possible that he did not contemplate any other action than the sending of anti-British despatches to the French Press, until he came under the sway of the magnetic personality of General Botha. Under the latter's influence it appears that in January 1900 he made application for naturalisation as a 'burgher' of the Transvaal, expressing at the same time his willingness to bear arms against Great Britain. For the Republic had, in order to enlist as many as possible in their army, relaxed the stringency of the conditions as to the admission of newcomers as 'burghers', which had been the root cause of the South African disturbance.[1] Under these new regulations Lynch became a naturalised Boer, and proceeded for some time to command a small force, composed of many nationalities, known as the 'Irish Brigade'. Men who had conscripted to serve in this brigade came to England and identified him, and one in particular gave evidence of Colonel Lynch commanding, and firing against British troops, at Sunday's River Bridge in Natal. Evidence was also available of a 'call to arms' which he had issued to Irishmen. There was, however, still more damaging evidence from an American citizen, a Mr G A Gregg, who had bicycled out as a sightseer

[1] With respect to the author, the pretext rather than the root cause – Ed.

to the Boer lines at Vereeniging. They were arrested as spies and interrogated before a Boer officer by Lynch. Gregg said to him, 'So you are Captain Lynch.'

'*Colonel* Lynch,' replied that officer, later observing to the Boer commandant, 'I want to show you these men are British spies, and ought to be shot.' Lynch strongly denied that he had acted in any capacity but that of an interpreter on this occasion, or had made either of these observations, but the witness was positive. 'He said we ought to be shot,' he said. 'These words made an impression on my mind at the time.' Another witness, a farmer named Handly, had remonstrated with Lynch, whose men were disturbing a neighbour's farm. 'I'm a British subject,' retorted the 'Colonel', 'and know the law as well as you do.'

'Then why are you fighting for the Boers?' asked the farmer.

'For fun,' said Lynch.

It is, however, fair to say that this was the account of witnesses for the prosecution as to what took place on these two occasions, and was denied by the prisoner.

At the last hearing before the magistrate the prisoner made a long statement in which he said what he could to excuse his actions, explained how his small troop had been dispersed, and how he had returned to Paris to continue his journalistic career before he returned to face his trial as member-elect for Galway.

The trial took place, not at the Old Bailey, but in the great Court of the Lord Chief Justice, before three Judges, Lord Chief Justice Alverstone, Mr Justice Wills, and Mr Justice Channell. For this was no ordinary felon: Colonel Lynch was the first man, since poor erratic Smith O'Brien had been tried for his pathetic attempt at rebellion in Ireland in 1848, to be tried for 'treason', and he was indicted under the old statutes which had been savagely used from the thirteenth until the seventeenth centuries. All the ceremony but none of the ancient barbarity of those times, such as the bitter invective of the prosecution and the vindictiveness of a Bench servile to the throne, against helpless and undefended prisoners, were observed in this State trial. Although the prisoner did not go into the box, this was at his express wish, and the Judges throughout the trial allowed the very able defending counsel, Mr Shee KC and Mr Horace Avory, to explore every legal avenue open to the defence. Nevertheless, the use in the indictment of the words of Edward III's old statute was a clear illustration of the antiquity and development of English jurisprudence, and during the trial there were continual references to the long pageant of English history which connected the England of Edward III with that of Edward VII.

For, in the reign of the third Edward, Parliament had made a definition of 'treason', and despite the arguments of Shee and Avory, the words still served. 'Whereas divers opinions have been before this time in what case treason shall be said and in what not, the King, at the request of the Lords and of the Commons hath made a declaration in the manner as hereinafter followeth ... that is to say ... if a man do levy war against our Lord the King in his realm, or be adherent to the King's enemies in his realm, giving to them aid and comfort in the realm or elsewhere and thereof be provenly attainted of open deed by the people ... then such person should be attainted and held guilty of high treason.' And so, in ancient style, was Arthur Alfred Lynch, international journalist, one of His Majesty's lieges, indicted as a 'false traitor' to her late Majesty, 'our Lady the Queen'.

The Attorney-General and the Solicitor-General appeared for the Crown, and the crowd was so great outside the Court that Carson, robed and wigged, was unable to make his way through. He appealed to a policeman for assistance. 'I'm the Solicitor-General,' he said. The officer shook his head wisely. 'That's what they're all saying,' he said.

The three days' trial was most remarkable for the persistence with which the defending counsel, especially Mr Avory, raised legal argument, some of it very plausible, for the defence, with regard to two statutes, one of the fourteenth and one of the nineteenth century. The prisoner was indicted for being 'adherent to the King's enemies in his realm, giving to them aid and comfort in the realm or elsewhere'. Mr Avory argued at the very outset that no indictment could lie, and that the prisoner should not be called upon to plead to it. But the Court held that the prisoner, in cases of treason, must first plead, and objections to the indictment must be heard later. So the prisoner pleaded 'Not guilty.' Later, Mr Avory ingeniously argued that the words of the statute could only apply either to a man who, while resident in the realm, had been adherent to the King's enemies wherever they were, or to a man who, wherever he was at the time, had aided those of the King's enemies who were within the realm. He argued that the word 'realm' meant only Great Britain itself, and that this statute did not cover the case of Colonel Lynch, who, outside Her Majesty's realm, had aided Her Majesty's enemies abroad. 'The Crown must absolutely omit,' he said, 'the words of the statute "in the realm" to make their indictment good.' Thus did a twentieth-century lawyer seek to escape from the words of an old statute, enacted for part of a small and sparsely populated island, and seven centuries later sought to be applied in a worldwide empire. But the Judges were not convinced by the argument, and held that the word 'elsewhere' made the statute applicable to the case. The other argument was based upon Colonel Lynch's naturalisation as a Transvaal 'burgher'. Here Mr Shee adduced a very eloquent argument based on the Naturalisation Act, 1870. Before this Act, since the old policy of the law was to retain rigidly the nationality of its citizens wherever they went, there were about twenty million citizens of the United States who could also claim British nationality. This was an Act to abolish the confusion of double nationality and to expedite naturalisation. It declared that where a British subject voluntarily became naturalised in another country, 'he shall be deemed to have ceased to be a British subject and be regarded as an alien'. Mr Shee argued that the Act was made for just such a case as the present. 'I submit,' he said, 'that the considerations which applied to Edward III's time are of little weight in the reign of Edward VII, and the whole aspect of the civilised world has been changed by facilities of transport and extensive emigration. The prisoner has transgressed no real law of allegiance, because he did not consider himself a British subject, and has resided for a long time outside British dominions. … There are traitors and traitors, the word in some instances imputing real treachery, but in others having no such connotation. For the first class no consideration can be shown. But the prisoner is not of that class. The "traitor" today is not the traitor of earlier times, the great territorial magnate with a large following.'

Mr Avory argued with even greater confidence that Lynch's naturalisation satisfied the Naturalisation Act, which in turn had removed him from the reach of the Statute of Treasons by exempting him forever from the obligations of Her Majesty's lieges. 'In order to support the indictment,' he said in his pithy way, 'you have to insert the words "this statute shall apply except in time of war".' By such technicalities, it seemed, was the prisoner at the Bar separated from a traitor's doom.

And here, as Carson showed, was precisely the answer to the argument. It is a commonplace of international law that, where two States go to war, all relations between their nationals, except those of a hostile character, cease. Therefore, just as a contract between two opposing nationals is at least in abeyance during the war, so an arrangement between a national of one country and the enemy Government must be void during a war. Otherwise whole regiments might, like Colonel Lynch, become naturalised for the purpose of joining the enemy, and legally desert in the hour of battle. As Mr Justice Wills said, 'This is such an extravagant conclusion that I think the foundation of an argument of which it is the logical result cannot possibly be sound.'

Thus both technical grounds of defence failed, and it only remained for Mr Shee to exercise his utmost eloquence on behalf of the accused. His concluding speech ranged over a wide sphere of human appeal and interest, and, in fact, amounted to a defence that the prisoner had acted throughout with the highest motives, and that Great Britain had no claim on the allegiance of this high-minded, cosmopolitan journalist. But Carson brought the jury back to the issues of the case. 'My learned friend has travelled widely from the issues,' he said, 'but, no matter how serious the case and grievous the consequences, you must come back to the main issue. For our part, counsel and jury, we have simply to see that the law is faithfully and justly observed. To do this we must first face the issue. Now what is the issue? My friend has made it appear to be whether a journalist can be convicted of high treason unless he himself believed he was guilty. That is not so. The law is that of adherence to the King's enemies. Thus the only real question is one of fact, not of belief. Did he adhere to the King's enemies? Why, there is no denial that the prisoner did take up arms against his country: there is nothing else to try.

… I will, however, deal with my learned friend's arguments, lest the jury think there is no answer. If you carry your minds back to 18 January 1900, you will remember the gloom that spread over the country because of our reverses. This was the moment when this gentleman applied to become a "burgher" and to take up arms against this country. Admitting in his application that he was a British subject, he voluntarily and without pressure elected to take up arms against his country, aye, this Empire, and his fellow-colonists. If there is no treason in that, treason is indeed a thing of the past. My friend has said that the prisoner was merely naturalised for Press purposes. Must a man throw off his citizenship to obtain honour in his profession? And here, gentlemen, we are dealing with an educated man. I do not believe that there is a man in the Empire, with the smallest common sense or patriotism, who believes that a man is entitled in the midst of a war to throw off his allegiance and fight against his country. My learned friend says that to hold otherwise would be to make the laws of England a trap and a snare for "Colonel" Lynch. It is difficult to treat such an argument with seriousness. I hope the day is far distant when a jury will find that a pretext so flimsy can cover a man's guilt. The facts are not in controversy. The prisoner became a member of the so-called "Irish Brigade". He admitted that by accepting his "colonelcy" he lost all his emoluments as a correspondent. So short a time does it take to turn an innocent journalist into an active soldier, and even a full colonel, three weeks later. Is that adherence to the Queen's enemies? That is what you have to find. How can it be otherwise when the prisoner became a colonel to fight against the Queen? Mr Shee has asked whether this was not a trifling act of treason in view of the general amnesty. But when the gentleman has gone to Sunday's River Bridge, showing men how to shoot, ordering them to shoot his fellow-subjects, how can one palliate or make light of such conduct? If this was not adherence to the Queen's enemies, what was? What is the use of talking of intent in the face of such undisputed fact? The case is crystal clear. You and I have nothing to do with the result. It is for you to find whether the acts proved to have been committed by the prisoner – a man of trained intellect – do or do not constitute the crime of high treason. That is the question before you. Your duty is as clear as clear. Whatever may be the consequences, with those you have nothing to do. Those consequences are entrusted to others.'

After a consideration of twenty-six minutes, the jury found the prisoner 'Guilty', and, in answer to the question put by the Clerk of the Crown, the prisoner said he had nothing to say. Thereupon three clerks arranged the squares of black cloth over the wigs of the three Judges, and everyone in Court rose. The solemnity of the occasion, always present when the death sentence is pronounced, was greater than ever, because of the high character and dignity of the prisoner and the historical nature of the trial. Mr Justice Wills, as humane a man as ever sat on the Bench, began to deliver the death sentence, the only sentence that could be delivered for the crime of high treason. Although he was in tears, he delivered a speech which might have been translated from Thucydides or Suetonius, and which stands as clear, contemporary evidence of the personal affection for Queen Victoria which was felt by the whole nation, and throws into high relief Victorian patriotism, loyalty and culture. It is very different from anything that is heard at the present time, and seems more out of date today than the Statute of Treasons itself.

'Arthur Alfred Lynch, the jury have found you guilty of the crime of high treason, a crime happily so rare that in the present age a trial for treason seems almost an anachronism. Civilised societies exist for the purpose of mutual succour and support, and they expect, in return, loyalty and allegiance; and if any man who disapproves of the foreign or domestic policy of his country were to be at liberty to take up arms against her, the very foundations of civilised society would be gone. The misdeeds which you have done in this case, and which have brought you to the lamentable pass in which you now stand, must surely convince even the most sceptical of the gravity and reality of this crime. What was your action in the darkest hour of your country's fortunes, when she was engaged in the struggle from which she has just emerged? You joined the ranks of your country's foes. ... You have sought, as far as you could, to dethrone Great Britain from her place among the nations. Nor can I forget that you have shed the blood of your countrymen who were fighting for their country. How many women have you made widows, how many children orphans, by what you and those under your command have done? You thought it safe in that dark hour of the Empire's fate, when Ladysmith, when Kimberley, when Mafeking were in the very jaws of deadly peril – you thought it safe, no doubt, to lift the parricidal hand against your country. ... You misjudged your country. She is seldom so dangerous to her enemies as when the hour of national calamity has raised the dormant energies of her people, knit together every nerve and fibre of the body politic, and made her sons determined to do all, to bear all, to sacrifice all, on behalf of the country that gave them birth. And against what a sovereign and what a country did you lift up your hand. Against a sovereign the best beloved and most deeply honoured of all the long line of English Kings and Queens, and whose lamented death was called back to my remembrance only yesterday as a fresh sorrow to many an English household; against a country which has been the home of progress and of freedom. ... Had you, and those with whom you associated yourself, succeeded, what fatal mischief might have been done to the great inheritance bequeathed to us by our forefathers ... that inheritance of power which it must be our work to use nobly and for good things – an inheritance of influence which will be of little effect for good unless supported by power, and of duty which cannot be effectively performed if our power be shattered and our influence impaired. You, who were prepared to do your country such irreparable wrong, must be prepared to submit to the sentence which it is now my duty to pronounce upon you. The sentence of the Court is that you be taken hence to the place from which you came, and from thence to a place of execution, there to be hanged from the neck until you are dead.'

The prisoner was taken away; and the Court emptied, shocked by the painful scene which had been enacted. The prisoner bore his sentence with outward composure; indeed, like a soldier. After his sentence, public opinion became more favourable to him, as his high motives were generally recognised, and the announcement that his sentence had been commuted to one of penal servitude for life met with general approval, as also did his release before he had served many months of his sentence.

The Crown was justified in its clemency. For, if the New York newspaper which prophesied that he would yet become a high official in the British Empire did not prove correct, it is interesting to add that he sat in Parliament as member for Clare from 1909 to 1918, and that he fought for the British Empire in France during the Great War. Moreover, by a strange chance, 'Colonel' Lynch of the 2nd Irish Brigade, who suffered sentence of death for high treason, became in those later days Colonel Lynch of the British Army. It was a pity that Mr Justice Wills did not live to learn of this permutation.

22. The Chapman Poisoning Case

Owing to the extraordinary success of Carson's advocacy, he had very seldom, since the trial of Oscar Wilde, visited the Old Bailey, where barristers sometimes find fame, but rarely fortune; now, however, his appointment as Law Officer occasionally took him to the grim old building. For instance, it is settled practice that, in poisoning cases, one of Law Officers should appear, and, on 16 March, Carson led for the Crown in the indictment of one of the most loathsome and successful murderers in criminal history. It may even be possible, as is suggested below, that he was in fact the best-known and most mysterious person in the annals of modern crime, and, despite all Carson's greater achievements, legal and political, the fact that he finally brought this miscreant to justice is an event which deserves to be recorded in its place.

The prisoner, who called himself 'George Chapman' but who was finally indicted under the name of Severin Klosowsky, a Pole thirty-six years old, was charged with the wilful murder of a young girl aged twenty, named Maud Eliza Marsh, who had been living with him as his wife. The trial was heard before Mr Justice Grantham, and Mr George Elliott KC was leading counsel for the defence. At the very outset it was apparent that this was no ordinary case, as Mr Elliott rose and argued that certain evidence as to the prisoner's previous life, which he knew the Crown intended to use, was inadmissible. Ordinarily English law will not listen to such evidence, and tries to isolate the facts of each particular offence, so that the prisoner is not condemned on his past record. Yet this rule has exceptions, and one of them is when evidence of similar acts by the prisoner is allowed to be given in order to rebut a defence of innocent intent or accident. After a short argument by Carson, the Judge held that the exception applied here, and that the evidence was admissible.

It was a strange and terrible story which Carson told to the Jury and to the crowded Court, in cold, unimpassioned tones. The contrast to the excited style of other prosecuting counsel of the time, such as Charles Matthews, was striking, and perhaps Carson set the example for the more deadly, objective review of evidence which is the pattern of all present-day prosecutors, far more effective than the older, more vindictive manner. 'I desire to state the facts absolutely without feeling and with moderation,' he said, 'because we are engaged in the trial of a man against whom the verdict may mean the loss of his own life. ... But if a distinction can be made in degrees of murder, I submit that no murder can be more determined and more malicious than by poison. Certainly no murder can be more demonstrative of the cruelty of the person perpetrating it than that of a man, standing by the bedside, day after day, of the person he professed to love, seeing her suffering torture and gradually sinking away from what he has by his own hand administered, upon the pretence of treating that person for maladies with which he professed to be acquainted.'

This is the cruel story upon which Carson based his opening speech, and all of which was proved in detail by scores of witnesses from many parts of England. On 22 October 1902, a comely young woman, known as Mrs Chapman, the wife of a well-to-do publican in Union Street, Borough, died shortly before her twentieth birthday. She had for some time been tortured by severe abdominal pains which had perplexed Dr James Stoker, her medical attendant. But her husband had nursed her with the greatest care, had given her the choicest liquor in his cellar, and she had had everything which sustained her, during her illness, from his own hands. His customers knew that he was 'something of a doctor', and he was often observed to read medical books behind the bar. So perhaps he was well qualified to tend his ailing young wife, and certainly his manner to her left nothing to be desired while she was alive. It was therefore all the more curious that he opened the house to the public on the day of her death. When she died, he broke down completely, and cried like a child. The girl's mother and father had been with her during her illness, but, apart from the fact that they had disapproved of her original employment with him as a barmaid and her subsequent hasty marriage, they had nothing to complain of in his treatment of their young daughter. Indeed, everyone spoke of his kindness to her and of their fondness for each other. He appeared to be a model husband. Mrs Marsh, the girl's mother, had, however, taken a taste of the brandy intended for her daughter, and had afterwards been ill. Old Mr Marsh then insisted on calling in his own family physician, Dr Grapel. Like Dr Stoker he was puzzled by the case, but, with less knowledge than Dr Stoker of the history of Mrs Chapman, he suspected foul play. It is probable that his suspicion was due to psychological conjecture rather than to medical skill, for he thought at first that the girl was dying of arsenical poisoning. He was too late to save the poor creature's life, but he insisted upon an inquest. On analysing the corpse, a deadly poison, known as antimony, almost tasteless to the palate and colourless to the eye, was found in every organ of her body. Chapman was arrested; but he was very confident, and, had not the circumstances of his past life been discovered, it is very possible that he might have escaped the gallows; but among his belongings were found papers which enabled the police to discover much of his strange history.

It now appeared that his real name was Severin Klosowski, and that he had been born in Poland in 1865. Moreover, as the proceedings at the inquest and the police court were made public, other persons who knew of his past life came forward to assist the police, and evidence was gathered against him from a variety of sources.

Perhaps the most important was that of a Brighton chemist, named William Henry, who had previously done business at Hastings, and who read a report of the inquest in the newspaper. He came up to London to speak to the police. He remembered having sold, in April 1897, one ounce of tartar emetic, of which the main ingredient is antimony, to a barber named 'Chapman', whom he knew well and whose customer he was. Chapman had been a clever barber, an 'exceptionally intellectual' man to talk to, who appeared to know a great deal about medicine. He had been at that time living with a buxom little fair-haired lady, who assisted him in his work. It was discovered that Chapman had left Hastings soon afterwards, and purchased the lease of a public house, the Prince of Wales tavern in Bartholemew Square off the City Road. Thenceforward, Chapman earned his living as a publican and practised no longer as a barber. There, after an agonising illness, 'Mrs Chapman' died, her body almost wasted away. Her real name was Mrs Shadrach Spink, and, like Maud Marsh, she had merely consented to Chapman's public statement that he had married her. Just before she died, the poor creature held up her emaciated arms towards him, and said, 'Do kiss me.' He was not able to do so before she died. He then leant over her and said, 'Polly, Polly, speak.' Thereafter he broke down and cried. Nevertheless, he opened his house to the public that day. Dr Rogers, however, made no trouble and granted a death certificate, ascribing the cause of the woman's death to phthisis.

Moreover, the widower soon consoled himself: he advertised for a barmaid, and employed a healthy farmer's daughter, Bessie Taylor, who was evidently very much to his liking. For he soon 'married' her by merely announcing the fact to his customers, and moved to licensed premises at Bishop's Stortford. There the health of this strong country girl began to fail, and on 13 February 1901 she died, after a prolonged agony. Four doctors were called in, all of whom differed as to the cause of her illness; nevertheless, one of them, Dr Stoker, the same as was later called in in the case of Maud Marsh, gave a death certificate. Everybody spoke of the kindness and affection which had existed between Chapman and his 'wife'. He had been at her bedside when she died, and had cried pitifully when he realised she was dead.

When these facts became known in the preliminary enquiries, the bodies of these two women were exhumed. Antimony was found in each of their bodies, and a gruesome sight met the eyes of the Crown physicians. For in each case the bodies of these young women, so long buried, were almost perfectly preserved. Their faces were easily identified, and even recognised, by their friends and relatives. 'The only difference,' said the woman who had nursed Mrs Spink, 'was that the hair had grown a little longer on the forehead; the face was perfect.' And Dr Stevenson said, 'The face and hands were those of a woman who might have been coffined the day before.' For antimony has this strange quality: while it destroys life, it preserves the body from putrefaction, and for years the bodies of these two women had lain preserved in common graves, to be conclusive evidence in the end against their murderer.

Many other witnesses came forward, and the Crown was able to supply Carson with much of the history of this triple murderer. Severin Klosowski had been a student of surgery in Poland, and in a Polish hospital had practised as such. Moreover, he kept, to the end, remarkable certificates as to his skill and application in that calling. After a necessary period of military service in the Russian Army, he came to England

and practised as a hairdresser's assistant in Whitechapel. The many customers whom he shaved there and at Hastings were charmed by the conversation of the clever barber, who knew so much of medical science and of the world, but they can hardly have realised their danger. In 1888 he married a Polish girl named Lucy Baderski, and two years afterwards emigrated to Jersey City in America. In 1892 he returned to England, and lived for a time in the same house with his own wife and a woman named Annie Chapman, whom he made his mistress, and from whom he took his English name. Fortunately for themselves, one after the other these women left him, and so survived, the latter after a severe illness. Doubtless he had tried to poison her. Both these women gave evidence against him. His next 'wife' was Mrs Spink, and so far as is definitely proved, his first victim.

Once the evidence as to the deaths of the other two women was admitted by the Judge, as in the case of George Smith, who killed the women by means of the bridal bath, the reader will appreciate that the defence was really hopeless. George Elliott did not put his client in the witness box: the prisoner pleaded 'Not guilty', and maintained his innocence until the last, but the writer has searched his defender's questions and speech in vain for any suggestion of a real defence. The case of Maud Marsh was the only one where an alternative theory in defence was put forward at all, that of suicide, for the reason that Chapman would not let her have children. The task was, indeed, a hopeless one, and Elliott was no Marshall Hall. He begged the jury not to be prejudiced against the prisoner as a hated alien, and that was really the only point made by him. He also maintained that there was an absence of motive. The first point was conceded by Carson, who, exercising the peculiar privilege of a Law Officer, had the last word with the jury. Carson began his final speech with dramatic emphasis on the exhumation of the dead women. 'We have wakened these poor women,' he said, 'from their long sleep, to give unassailable evidence against the prisoner. But I am sure, if they could have spoken, they would not have asked you to avenge them, but to do justice. Moreover, in this Court,' he said, 'we know no difference between the alien and the stranger and a citizen of this country. It is our proud boast that here, at all events, whatever it may be in other countries, it matters not to us who is the person on his trial, as all are entitled to the same law and the same justice.' As for the suggestion that there was no motive, he waved this aside. 'In this instance there is the most ample motive, for the prisoner's is a history of unbridled, heartless, and cruel lust.'

After an absence of only eleven minutes, the jury found the prisoner guilty, and Mr Justice Grantham, whose charge to the jury was hardly a model of judicial moderation, condemned the prisoner to death under his Polish name, without the customary adjuration: 'May the Lord have mercy on your soul'.

As Carson had conducted the case, his eyes had occasionally fallen on the man in the dock, whose eyes in turn were fixed upon his prosecutor with sullen malice. 'I have never seen such a villain,' said Carson of him. 'He looked like some evil wild beast; I almost expected him to leap over the dock and attack me.' After the trial it was discovered that, before he came to England, he had married a woman in Poland and had beheaded her. Yet he died protesting innocence. Who can say what thoughts were passing through that dreadful brain? When he was asked whether he would like to see his friends at the last, he said, 'I have none.' But there is very interesting evidence, ably epitomised by Mr H L Adam in his introduction to his edition of this trial, that justice had at last caught a greater criminal even than George Chapman, *alias* Severin Klosowski, appeared to be. When Detective-

Inspector Godley arrested him, he observed to his colleague, 'You've got Jack the Ripper at last.'

Jack the Ripper was the mysterious criminal who murdered women of the unfortunate class, at the end of the last century, by terrible mutilations. No man was ever brought to justice for these horrible crimes, but the following remarkable considerations may suggest that the man whom Carson prosecuted to conviction in his sole murder trial in the English Courts was Jack the Ripper. First, the Ripper's mutilations could hardly have been done save by a man with knowledge of surgery. Chapman was a surgeon. All the crimes of Jack the Ripper took place in the years 1888-1889. Chapman had recently come to England in 1888, and remained during the whole of that period. The venue of Jack the Ripper's murders was, in several instances, Whitechapel and its environs. Chapman was working at a barber's shop in Whitechapel during that period. In 1890, Chapman migrated to New Jersey, and, in the same year, a series of murders of the 'Ripper' type took place in the locality of Jersey City. In 1892 these Jersey murders ceased, when Chapman had returned to England. When it is added that the description of the man who was 'wanted' for the Whitechapel murders could also have been used with effect for the arrest of Chapman, had he been able to abscond, the identification becomes a little more than interesting conjecture. Can it have been that Chapman indeed led two lives, not a virtuous life and a perverted one, contrasting with each other like those of Jekyll and Hyde, but two abominable lives of crime, contrasting only in method? It may have been that, while he was living in comparative respectability with the first of the 'wives' whom he 'married' so easily, and before he met those whose lives he took with his corroding poisons, he was abroad in the streets at night, with his surgeon's knife concealed under his coat, taking unholy pleasure in hunting down the poor unfortunates for mutilation and murder, the most terrible 'physician' and 'surgeon' of all the annals of crime. At all events, unlike that of George Smith, his motive, as Carson said, was not gain, but lust; he soon tired of his victims, and, when this happened, neither medicine nor the law could help them. His success had made him arrogant; had it not been for this, the enemy of woman might have continued his career of crime indefinitely. No wonder he said of his last victim – in trying to persuade a new barmaid to be his mistress – with a snap of his fingers, 'If I give her that, there would be no more Mrs Chapman, and no one would know.'

For his confidence in his own success is less mysterious than the strange fascination which enabled him to capture, and apparently to retain, the affections of women who delivered themselves into this Bluebeard's hands. This remarkable power was also possessed by George Smith, and it may also be observed that each of them used with success exactly the same plan again and again until arrogance made them careless, and brought them to the gallows. The man who calls in the same doctor to provide the death certificate for two women, whom he has successively poisoned with the same drug, is confident indeed.

23. The Slater Agency Case

Although Chapman's was the only murder case in which he was involved, nearly all the Law Officer's criminal work for the Crown was done by Carson during these years, and he had not long been in office before the great strain of his combined duties in the House and in the Courts began to tell upon his health. In January 1901 he was laid up for a few days with neuralgia, and his very sensitive nature began to be affected by the idea that he was not doing his full duty. 'I do not think', he wrote to Mr Balfour, 'my absence for a short time will cause any serious inconvenience, as I know the A-G will willingly do all he can, which is a great deal. But, should there be any such inconvenience or should I be unable to return as soon as I expect, you will, of course, consider that you have in your hand my resignation. May I once more express my many obligations to you for your kindness and consideration, and I feel glad that, before I went to my incarceration, I had the pleasure of hearing your dignified and eloquent panegyric on our late beloved Queen. Please don't mind answering this. I know how busy you are, and I feel certain you will be sympathetic.'

Arthur Balfour knew Carson well by now, and of course paid no heed to the suggestion of resignation.

Another venue of the law in which the advocacy of the Law Officers is from time to time required, in cases of great importance, is the Divorce Court, on instructions from the King's Proctor. As is well known, it is the King's Proctor's duty to enquire, during the interval between the decree *nisi* and the decree absolute, whether the evidence on which the former conditional decree has been granted to the petitioner was true and candid. If such is suspected, on strong grounds, not to be the fact, the King's Proctor 'intervenes', and, if he proves his suspicions, the decree is rescinded. The case which is about to be recounted is one of great public importance in the history of the Divorce Court, and shed at the time a baleful light on the methods by which the advisers of parties who sought to escape from the bonds of matrimony, by pleading the only reasons valid under English law, were able in many cases to succeed. The facts revealed by the case of 'Slater's Agency' led to much stricter investigations into the circumstances of undefended divorces in the English courts. Perhaps, too, the fact that ill-used and innocent persons have been driven or led, by desperation, to such devices is not without its lessons to those who are concerned with the relation of law to humanity.

On 24 November 1902 an undefended petition, that of Kate Pollard against her husband Thomas Pollard, seemingly of a most ordinary kind, came on for hearing before one of the Judges of the Divorce Division; the facts seemed to disclose matters of the most common, if sordid, routine in that Court. The parties appeared to be of the middle class, and not at all well-to-do. The wife was a pretty businesswoman, who was the manageress of a café, and the husband, many years older than herself, was a not very successful businessman, who had been connected with the tea trade and with insurance work. He had married his wife in 1891; his health had failed, and he had been drinking heavily for years, according to his wife's evidence, and had treated her badly; the parties had separated, and the husband was now living with relatives at Plymouth. While he was residing there, it was alleged that there had been misconduct between him and a girl named Maud Goodman, who gave evidence as to this, and identified him by a photograph. The Judge, after a few minutes' hearing, granted the decree *nisi*. The case was not even reported in the newspapers, and it seemed that there was no reason why Mrs Pollard, who was of blameless reputation, should not look forward to her freedom in a few months' time.

The trial had been formal; the parties were humble, and only a few guineas had been marked on counsel's briefs, eminent though they were. The solicitor engaged always briefed eminent counsel. Miss Goodman had been paid little more than her expenses. But the truth, nevertheless, was that over five thousand pounds had been spent on obtaining that decree *nisi* for Mrs Pollard, of which six hundred pounds had gone to the solicitor who had prepared the case, and the rest elsewhere. Moreover, from this uneventful, if sordid, beginning, there evolved one of the most celebrated causes of the time, in which the principal leaders of the Bar were engaged, which occupied a month's enquiry in the Divorce Court, eliciting 8 738 questions and answers, and developed into a ten-day trial at the Old Bailey.

Soon after the decree *nisi* had been granted, Mr Thomas Pollard wrote to the King's Proctor saying that the evidence against him was fabricated, and that, if he had not been without means, he would have defended the suit. Such a communication obviously carried little weight, and it was not until he received far more significant information that the King's Proctor decided to intervene.

At this time there was a famous detective agency at work named 'Slater's'. It was widely advertised in many of the principal newspapers in London and Paris. These advertisements were most audacious. They stated that Slater's agency had not met with a single failure in the Divorce Court for seventeen years, and that the secret of this success was due to the fact that for seventeen years they had been able 'to secure reliable, independent, and corroborative evidence'. It was a matter of notoriety that a great number of wealthy people had obtained their freedom through the ministrations of Slater's, and the profits of that firm were enormous. They employed about forty detectives, and their office expenses alone ran from £8 000 to £10 000 a year. Most of the profits went to an individual known as 'Captain Slater', who was no longer seen in the office very often. He was now a rich man and left most of the work to his manager, who was known as 'Slater Junior', although it was understood that they were not related.

When the whole truth came out, the wonder is that the agency had been able to elude the law for so long; for their practices and their profits were such as to require the greatest 'loyalty amongst thieves'. The thing was so profitable and so easy. But at last two or three of their employees decided to leave the firm and start a rival agency of their own, which began to flourish as 'Simmonds' Detective Agency'. From this moment the clouds began to gather around Slater's. An employee named Cartwright was dismissed, was engaged by Simmonds, and took away with him the contents of his desk at Slater's. Among these contents were some papers relative to the Pollard divorce. These Cartwright took to the King's Proctor in January 1903. They were so conclusive and so incriminating that the King's Proctor forthwith determined to intervene. For years the authorities had had their eyes on Slater's, and here at last was their opportunity. The grounds of his intervention were stated to be that 'it was arranged by persons acting on behalf of the petitioner that the respondent should be induced to commit adultery in order that the petitioner might obtain a divorce from the respondent', and that 'a false case was presented to the Court on behalf of the petitioner', and that 'the respondent did not commit adultery as alleged in the petition'.

A powerful team of advocates was briefed for the King's Proctor, including Carson, the leader, and Charles Mathews, the future Public Prosecutor. They were faced by Sir Edward

Clarke, Mr Bargrave Deane KC, Mr Barnard, and Mr Valetta for Mrs Pollard.

The President's Court had not been so crowded since the famous *Hartopp* divorce case, and the presence of the Solicitor-General showed the case to be of the first importance. There was hardly a square inch of vacant space in the Court. The case opened on St Patrick's Day, and Sir Edward Carson was wearing a bunch of shamrock in his buttonhole, but, apart from this concession to the lighter side of things, he looked very grim indeed.

His opening was a sensational one, and lasted a whole day. It appeared that a gentleman named Mr Hugh Charles Knowles called at Slater's agency in September 1901: he had always heard that Slater's could work wonders. He saw a gentleman known as 'Slater Junior', whose real name was Mr George Philip Henry. He told them that a young friend of his, named Mrs Pollard, was leading a wretched life because of a worthless husband. Her one desire was to regain her freedom, and he, Mr Knowles, wished to see her through. The difficulty was that there was no evidence against the husband; but Mr Knowles was a millionaire, and money was no object to him. The husband's life in Plymouth must be closely watched, and the evidence obtained. Mr Knowles's part in the story was now a passive one; no doubt he was sincerely solicitous with regard to the misfortunes of the pretty manageress, in whose troubles he had taken a romantic and, it was clear, an innocent interest. Hereafter his only function was to pay, which he was willing to do to the tune of £5 000. Henceforth he left everything to Slater's. That enterprising organisation at once took the matter in hand, without so much as asking to see Mrs Pollard. They rang up a firm of solicitors with whom they happened to be connected at the time by a private telephone line; and from this time onwards a series of would-be benefactors – some of them desiring to make his acquaintance for the first time, and some claiming to help him for old friendship's sake, but all, strangely enough, in the employment of Slater's agency – descended upon the needy Thomas Pollard, who was eking out a precarious existence in the town of Plymouth, now and then entering a public house for a drink, but with very few other interests or pleasures in life.

The first reports of these agents were not encouraging: they reported that their quarry was morose and rather a recluse, and that it would be futile to try to pick up acquaintance with him in the street. 'What right,' asked Carson, 'has a detective to make acquaintance with a man to find information which would be detrimental to him?' It seemed that poor Mr Pollard really cared for his wife, and had no desire for the consolation of other women. It was therefore a waste of time to watch him. Slater's then devised another plan. If there was no evidence of misconduct as yet, could not Mr Pollard be induced into such misconduct by suitable encouragement? Thereafter, as time passed, reports became more favourable; acquaintance between Pollard and one of Slater's agents was consolidated into friendship at the Golden Fleece public-house; many drinks were consumed at the expense of Slater's agency, and finally their agent, Mr Cyril Smith, only lacked funds to 'complete the business'. 'I do not think,' he wrote, 'that the ordinary woman of Plymouth will serve the purpose. Having come across the two girls mentioned, who are smart and sufficiently dressy, I think that a look in at the theatre, followed by supper, would certainly lead up to "the finale". It must be made worth both these girls' while. I wish to point out that treating this man has cleared me out entirely. It is a very expensive matter. Given the necessary money, say £8 (in order to have a margin in case of necessity), in my opinion the matter should have an excellent chance of going through tomorrow night, when we are due to meet the two girls.'

However, nothing came of this suggestion. Slater's recalled Smith and sent down another man, John Davies, a young man who was to be introduced to Pollard and to represent himself as a commercial traveller, combining a little business with a great deal of pleasure. He looked like a typical 'toff' of the 'nineties, with enormous flaxen moustaches and whiskers. The landlord of the Golden Fleece said that he had overheard this conversation between the two in his bar: 'I'm sick of Plymouth; I'll go to Jersey,' said Davies. 'I have no money,' said Pollard. 'Never mind, I'll pay all expenses.' So, in March 1902, the two set off to Jersey: they appear to have consumed enormous quantities of liquor, and, in order to 'make evidence' for the wife's petition, Davies went to such scandalous extremes that the solicitor who had been preparing the legal side of it regarded the evidence thus obtained as too dangerous to use. The whole business had then to be repeated from the beginning. Meanwhile, thousands of pounds had been paid to Slater's by Mr Knowles, and nothing had been achieved. Charles Fielding, another ex-employee of Slater's, said that he had heard Mr Henry say to the solicitor, who had called: 'We are not getting on very well with the Pollard case at Plymouth.' The solicitor then slapped him on the back and said, 'Shall I go down and see what I can do for you?' 'I wish you would,' rejoined Henry.

The solicitor then went down to Plymouth with one of Slater's men, and there, as Carson observed, a series of events took place 'which was perhaps without precedent in the preparation of evidence.' He got into touch with a girl of the unfortunate class, named Maud Goodman, and tried to make her identify a photograph of Pollard as that of a man who knew her. On the same date, Pollard himself received a mysterious letter in these terms: 'Dear Tom, – Will you meet me at the Clock Tower at 11 o'clock, as I should very much like to see you. Just back from South Africa. Your old friend, Fred.' Pollard had not the slightest idea who his correspondent was – but went, out of curiosity. When he arrived, Maud Goodman was present, unknown to him, with the solicitor and his satellites for the purpose of identifying him as one of her friends. But she was not at all sure, and it was only after several interviews with the solicitor, and much argument, that she finally signed a statement identifying Pollard. The solicitor paid her a few pounds for her signature, and returned to London in triumph, having achieved far more by his single visit to Plymouth than all the hirelings of Slater's agency. But these worthies had at least made an attempt to create evidence and then to record it. The statement which Maud Goodman signed turned out to be a simple fabrication. Moreover, it was very difficult to keep her up to the mark when the time for the trial arrived. She did not want to come to London, and it took the solicitor and two detectives to persuade her, and then she said she would only come if a Mrs Longden also came; and Mrs Longden said she would only come if a Nelly Bell came too. 'And so,' said Carson, with his bitterest smile, 'this interesting party left Plymouth for the precincts of the Divorce Court, composed of these women and two detectives as a bodyguard, and, in order that there might be no illegality, there too, in full force, was the solicitor himself, all coming up to London to prove one single act of misconduct on the part of the husband. ... A more scandalous and heinous arrangement could hardly be conceived,' said Carson, commenting on the whole case. 'Apart from whether this evidence was true or false, the Divorce Court does not exist in this country for the granting of divorces when one person has caused the downfall of the other: it would be an extraordinary state of things if the party who had brought the other into such a condition had the right, because of that condition, to claim a divorce.'

During the many days which this case occupied in the Divorce Court, a mass of evidence was called on both sides, and provides a vivid contrast between the styles of advocacy of Sir Edward Carson and Sir Edward Clarke. The latter was unable seriously to shake the evidence of Cartwright, whose evidence was so damaging to Slater's agency and to the solicitor, imputing to them a criminal conspiracy, or that of Mr Pollard, who denied even acquaintance with Maud Goodman, who said in turn that she was sure that she did not know Mr Pollard, and had been frightened into giving evidence at the previous trial by the solicitor. When Mrs Pollard entered the witness-box, she surprised everyone by her charm and sincerity. 'I wanted to be free,' she said again and again, 'and to end this miserable life.'

Clarke also put the proprietor of Slater's agency into the box. He was a tall, handsome, grizzled man, with the hard looks of the soldier who has seen service abroad. He called himself 'Captain Scott'. In truth, he had no right, except through his personal appearance, to his military title, as was shown when Carson cross-examined him. He looked so obviously 'the Captain' that everyone had called him so for years. He had passed, it appeared, under many names: he had been a pawnbroker's assistant, a jeweller's assistant, a solicitor's clerk, and a clerk to a mortgage broker who was also a detective, named Henry Salter. But he looked every inch a soldier, and a fine one.

'Why did you take the name of Slater – was it to confuse clients and to do harm to Salter?' asked Carson.

'No.'

'I was only anxious to see how you got your name,' said Carson grimly.

An article had been published against him, calling him

Tinsley, his true name, and describing him as an 'exposed creature, still practising as Slater's bogus agency', and Carson was putting this document to him.

Mr Bargrave Deane objected. 'I am rather surprised that a public officer ...' he began.

'A public officer,' retorted Carson slowly, putting the whole force of his personality into the words, 'will do his duty regardless of your sneers.' At this, Bargrave Deane felt the full weight of Carson's powerful personality, and made no further protests.

A significant incident occurred when 'the Captain' failed to produce his bank-book, and Carson, on being told that it contained thousands of names, including many important ones, did not insist on its production, on the grounds of public policy. Many other advocates would have insisted on the production of the book, but Carson saw the red light at once; it was no part of his duty to spread the scandal of this business far and wide. It is said, indeed, that one of the highest judicial functionaries in England had paid Slater's £1 000 for obtaining a statement from a certain individual. Scott was certainly a detective of great accomplishments, and the mismanagement of the Pollard case was probably due to the fact that he did not any longer supervise the activities of his subordinates. He made a loud protest that Cartwright had stolen the Pollard papers from his office.

'Oh, but Captain Scott,' commented Carson, in a soothing voice, 'those papers were quite *harmless*: there are nothing but *harmless* papers in your office.'

He asked Scott why he had not dismissed the man Davies after his scandalous expedition to Jersey with Pollard. Scott replied, 'Because Davies was the only support of his parents.'

'Was it not really because he might have been a dangerous witness against you and your institution?' asked Carson.

'Need Christian charity enter into this?'

'Yes, and I have for years contributed to charitable institutions,' said Scott. The extent of Slater's practice can be judged by the fact that Davies, one of forty detectives, had been engaged in a hundred cases since the Jersey episode a few months before.

Another interesting witness was the rich young man whose money had made all this possible. He had spent £5 000 on the case; yet he said he was not *particularly* in love with Mrs Pollard, and he would spend an equal sum on anyone who had been treated as she had. 'You will probably have a large clientele,' observed Carson.

During its progress the case had been assuming at every stage a graver aspect, and at last the President, Sir Francis Jeune, said: 'It is no use mincing matters. The case has come to this: did Maud Goodman speak substantially the truth, or did the solicitor in the case induce her to state what was entirely false?'

It was this serious situation with which Sir Edward Clarke had to deal in his final speech, but, instead of concentrating on it, he launched into an eloquent defence of Slater's agency, an attack on Simmonds' agency, on the King's Proctor, and on the severity of the divorce laws. His case was that the evidence of the King's Proctor was based on a conspiracy at Simmonds' agency to ruin their older rivals; he condescended to a strong vindication of the solicitor in the case and of Slater's agency; but the best parts of his speech were an appeal on behalf of the petitioner. 'Mrs Pollard,' he said, 'came here hoping that this investigation would release her from a marriage which could never be more than a formal one. Now, owing to a combination of the respectability of the King's Proctor, and the cunning of Simmonds' agency, she is in peril of losing the relief she has obtained by her decree and severing an association with a man who has become odious to her; again and again, her cry has been: "I wanted to be free".'

Never had Carson enjoyed an opportunity of testing his own theory of advocacy, and the consummate skill of his terribly relevant mind, than he had on this occasion. The contrast between the two methods was never more apparent. Clarke had made an appeal to the simpler emotions; Carson brought the jury back to their duty, and in his way appealed to a more refined emotion and a far broader issue than did his veteran opponent. His speech lasted into two days, and its interest never flagged. He began by an ironic reference to Sir Edward Clarke's gratuitous defence of Slater's agency. 'I am glad,' he said, 'that Slater's agency has had the benefit of Sir Edward Clarke's advocacy, but *I* appear solely in the interests of the public. I sympathise with my learned friend's peroration with regard to Mrs Pollard, but, assuming that all this is true, it is not the case with which you and I, gentlemen, have to deal. This is a case which raises questions far and away beyond our sympathies and feelings. This is a case which goes to the root of the administration of justice in this country. If it is true that Slater's exists as the agency for procuring the registration of dishonest evidence as a decree of a court of justice, if it is true that the solicitor in the case – an officer of the Court – has presented a false case to this Court in consideration of a large sum of money, we are confronted with a grave danger to the administration of justice in this country, and we must put aside all feelings against Mr Pollard and in favour of Mrs Pollard. Sir Edward has said that documents have been stolen, but the question is not whether they were stolen but whether they are genuine. The question is not how they were obtained, but whether they are true, and whether Slater's is an illegitimate business to procure evidence, rightly or wrongly, to earn these enormous sums.

... As for Mr Knowles, the millionaire, I accept that he is not in love with Mrs Pollard, but the remarkable thing is that, not being in love, he has spent close on £5 000 on this case. Sums of £100 were paid by him with that cheerful simplicity and chivalry which must commend itself to all honourable men; and, having paid them, he would repair to the shop where Mrs Pollard was being employed and tell her of the wonderful results which Slater's was bringing about. ... Whatever the result of this trial may be, it is high time that Slater's should be exposed. What are they? I find it difficult to restrain my indignation when I speak of that association. For, if their own statements are to be believed, for seventeen long years they have had no failure in this Court. It is indeed high time that they were exposed. I charge them, gentlemen, before you, with being from beginning to end the manufacturers of illegal evidence. I say that so far as any legitimate business is concerned, Slater's does not exist. Consider, too, the solicitor, who affords counsel the opportunity for saying, "Will you believe these women before me, a gentleman who pays £600 a year rent, and keeps thirteen clerks". It is necessary for you, sirs, to brace yourselves to this task. At the best, this detective business is a dirty business, conducted even with the greatest honesty. But Slater, with 2 000 names on his books, employing between forty and fifty detectives, he did not care, as he has admitted, how his business is carried on. All he wants is the filthy profits of his dirty business. After Davies's return from Jersey, Knowles paid £250 in golden sovereigns to Slater's. But, when looked at in cold blood, this Jersey evidence was considered too dangerous to use by the solicitor. Then that solicitor tries his own hand at it; and, gentlemen, it does seem a serious matter for him to go round the brothels of Plymouth and interview these wretched women, who were only there to sell their souls and their bodies for five shillings or ten shillings, these outcasts from society, who did not care whether their shame was known or not; for, after all, their shame was their daily employment. His conduct was but a trick to get one prostitute to obtain a statement from another, and this becomes evidence in a court of law! And yet, gentlemen, you are discharging a great and valuable public service in hearing this case. ... For, above all, in the interests of justice itself, you should take care that no one shall be allowed to tamper with the truth: we must see that the justice which is administered in these Courts is pure and undefiled.'

The President, in his final charge to the jury, commented on the splendid advocacy which had been shown in this long trial. When he had finished, the jury, after five minutes' consideration, found that the man Davies, 'acting under the instructions of Henry with the knowledge of the solicitor and Slater's, had induced Pollard to commit adultery'. They further found that, 'to the knowledge of, and by the procurement of the solicitor and Slater's, a false case had been presented to the Court'.

Even so, the case was not concluded. Sir Edward Carson slowly rose and said, 'I ask that all the documents in this case be impounded for the use of the Director of Public Prosecutions.'

'Yes,' said the President. Everyone knew what was to happen now.

As a result, on 25 October 1903, Henry Scott (*alias* Henry Slater), George Philip Henry, his managing director, John Pracey (*alias* John Bray), Cyril Smith, and John Davies, their employees, and the solicitor in the *Pollard* case were all indicted for conspiring together to 'pervert and defeat the due course of law and justice'.

A criminal prosecution was a far more difficult matter

to deal with, and Rufus Isaacs was briefed to defend Henry Scott, and Charles Gill to defend the solicitor. Other counsel were briefed to defend the other prisoners. Carson took two days to open the case, in which he 'challenged an institution, carried on in this way, as not being a genuine business, and as one which cannot bear the light of day, and whose transactions cannot be tested in a court of justice.'

The case was tried before Carson's old companion, Darling, now a Judge, and was a contest of legal giants, with the three great jury advocates of their time, all at the height of their powers, representing the parties. Gill never missed an opportunity to make a good Old Bailey point. He attacked poor Mr Pollard for the financial support which had been given him to keep him in London as King's evidence.

'You had a grey suit at Bow Street, and now you have this blue one,' he rasped.

'Really, Mr Gill,' interrupted Carson, 'we could not bring him up naked.'

'If they had not dressed him,' observed the Judge, referring to an actual incident in Pollard's married life, 'he might have pawned the sheets.'

'The real terror, my lord,' said Carson with a smile, 'was that he might have pawned the new suit.'

Rufus Isaacs brought very heavy metal against the prosecution's witnesses. He made use of the theory that the case was a conspiracy of the rival Simmonds' agency, and attacked the witness Cartwright on those grounds.

'Don't you think,' he asked the witness, 'that if they could ruin Slater's it would be a fine thing for Simmonds'?' Cartwright could not give a reply, being now an employee of the latter agency and the main witness against Slater's.

'Come,' said Mr Justice Darling, 'don't you think that, if anyone turned the Solicitor-General out of office, it would be a very fine thing for the person who turned him out?'

'I am not quite sure about that,' observed Carson, reflecting upon Rufus's enormous private practice. 'I should be very glad to exchange with Mr Isaacs.'

Darling's wit was prophetic: after the defeat of the Conservatives in 1905, Rufus Isaacs eventually succeeded Edward Carson as Solicitor-General, and their positions were reversed.

At the end of the case for the prosecution, Rufus Isaacs had established that Henry Scott, the proprietor of Slater's, was actually away from England in Australia at the material dates in the Pollard case, and therefore, although, in Carson's words, 'his were the methods, the business, the system', the Judge had no alternative but to discharge him, which he did with obvious reluctance, 'acquitting him of nothing but this particular indictment'. Carson had built up a very powerful case against him and his agency, but his absence from England absolved him from responsibility in this specific case, and the agency was not on its trial on a general charge. Rufus Isaacs carried tremendous weight with the Bench at this time. He was once stating what was the law, to old Lord Justice Vaughan Williams, when the latter said, 'Wait a little, Mr Isaacs, until you come up here on the Bench, as you assuredly will.' That was the way the Judges treated him. Rufus's argument paid tribute to the powerful case that Carson had built up, but claimed that it was against the principles of English law to visit criminal responsibility on a man's head for previous actions when he had personally had nothing to do with the charge alleged in the indictment, a charge of a conspiracy with regard to a specific matter. So 'the Captain' walked out of the dock, looking every inch a soldier. Well might he say, as he looked at Rufus, '*Sic me servavit Apollo*'. None of the prisoners elected to give evidence on their own behalf at the Old Bailey, having endured the terrible ordeal of having been cross-examined by Carson in the Divorce Court. They preferred, wisely enough, the security of the dock.

With regard to the solicitor, but really speaking for all the prisoners, Gill made one of the finest speeches of his career; he always had a sense of inferiority when opposed to Carson, and liked nothing better than to be led by him. But on this occasion he laid about him properly, and, even as it stands now in the cold lines of rotting newsprint, it is impossible not to be carried away by the virility and force of this speech. Knowing he had a difficult case, he seized on two matters which he knew would have an effect upon the Old Bailey jury. In all criminal cases a Law Officer has a right to the last speech, and Carson intended to use this right. There was also no Court of Criminal Appeal at this date, and Gill made tremendous play with these two facts, which could have been used in any criminal prosecution. 'The Solicitor-General can speak last as Law Officer and speak at any length, and I cannot answer him. … One of the relics of the barbarous times of our criminal law is the privilege of reply accorded to the Law Officers of the Crown. In criminal cases, too, this monstrous state of things exists: that a man whose liberty and character are at stake has no opportunity of reviving the trial, because the law says the verdict of the jury is final.' It was amusing to see how lightly the old warhorse took his fences. The terribly damaging evidence as to the collection of evidence from prostitutes for money was swept aside. 'In the Divorce Court, where adultery is alleged, a very ordinary way of proving it is by calling the woman. Such a woman would not be willing to come forward; she would have to be persuaded. It is idle for my learned friend to hold up his head and cry, "What a terrible thing it is to pay a witness!" Witnesses are paid every day. If my client went too far at

Plymouth, that is a matter for professional investigation by the Law Society, not by a criminal jury. ... If I could change places with the Solicitor-General, it would be the most interesting thing in all your lives to hear him comment on his own speech. ... With such a miscarriage of justice as in the *Adolph Beck* case before their eyes, people woke up to the fact that there was no Court of Criminal Appeal and wondered why there had never been one. The same arguments apply to the barbarous custom which gives the Solicitor-General the right of reply.' At the conclusion of this speech there was loud applause in Court. This was all the more remarkable because, at the beginning of the trial, the prisoners had been entirely out of the public sympathy.

Carson realised that Gill's speech might secure the acquittal of all the prisoners in the dock, such was its effect. He bent himself to his task, and answered Gill, as he had answered Clarke, by a speech full of irony and dignity. It is almost a model as a reply for the prosecution to a passionate appeal by a brilliant defending advocate. It infuriated Gill, who was his kinsman and his oldest friend at the English Bar. 'I will,' Carson said, 'pass over the personal remarks of my learned friend about myself, because it is the privilege of counsel for the prisoner to abuse anybody and everybody. You must analyse his speech, because the best of it consisted of eloquent and passionate abuse of the various subject-matters with which he had to deal, and which have nothing to do with the case. My learned friend is angry with the existing law – that there is no Court of Criminal Appeal. I may or may not agree with him, but how can it possibly affect your deliberations? Erring mortals that we are, we must do our best until that great Court is established; and when it is, infallibility will pass from this Court to that Court, and one hopes that my learned friend's new Court will be absolutely infallible. Mr Gill was very angry with the Law Officer's privilege, but the law has placed the duty on us to exercise the best discretion we can in the public interest. Really, all that eloquent passage showed was that Mr Gill resented the fact that I, and not Mr Gill, should speak last. I am not sure that Mr Gill does not only resent my speaking, but my presence here at all. ... But what I have done has been according to my conscience; it has been my best in the interests of the public.' Then he spoke very slowly as he came to his most impressive passage. 'I do not care one farthing for the result of this case. It is nothing to me. I want nothing of what my learned friend calls "the triumph of the prosecution". I want no triumph. My learned friend has criticised the divorce law, and I do not know whether there was anything more eloquent in his speech than when he told the jury that the divorce law was unjust because it does not allow Mrs Pollard to have her marriage dissolved. It may be a very unjust law that a woman, because she has a bad husband – it may be a very hard thing that, when she meets a wealthy man – cannot discard her husband. It may be a very bad state of the law. But we are not accountable for the law. That is the law. The issues here are far higher than the matrimonial disputes of Mr and Mrs Pollard, or anybody else. You are trying here a great and important question. Gentlemen, there can be no more important question in the interests of social order and the government of this country ... namely, whether the sources of justice can be tampered with for the most sordid motives, the acquisition of wealth in the transaction of this nefarious business which the prosecution alleges was being carried on by these people.'

Here Gill rose and protested violently: 'I must protest against these outbursts of eloquence against the men in the dock.'

'The main part of the objection,' said Darling, 'seems to be that the Solicitor-General was eloquent. I cannot interfere in the exercise, by the Solicitor-General, of a natural gift.'

'The matter on which we most pride ourselves,' resumed Carson, 'in this country is the administration of justice. There are highly paid officials, great Judges, solemn trials. There are men paid to preside over these Courts who are absolutely above suspicion, and juries perform their duties with no less care and devotion in the administration of the law. But what is the use of all this, if we are to allow for a moment any interference with the evidence that is brought before the Court? For this must taint the very fountain of justice itself.'

After a consideration of an hour and a half by the jury, they found all the prisoners guilty except the solicitor, as to whose guilt they could not find any prospect of agreement. His case was sent over for re-trial until the next sessions, and ultimately the Attorney-General decided not to prosecute again. The other men, the 'Captain's' manager and agents, were punished with terms of imprisonment. The purpose of the prosecution had been served, and a great public service performed by their conviction. Henceforward it became far more difficult to manufacture or fake evidence for the Divorce Court. The 'golden age' of the detective agencies as *agents provocateurs* was over and done with. Henceforward they knew that the eye of the law was upon them, and was ready to punish them, and came to perform their proper function, that of the detection, rather than the manufacture or fabrication, of evidence, and are now carried on in a respectable manner by responsible people. A mere study of the number of cases dealt with by Slater's, as shown by this case, shows how far the net was spread, and the 'Captain' stated in the Divorce Court that there was nothing very exceptional in the treatment of the Pollard case. This result was largely achieved by Carson's advocacy in the Divorce Court. He won the sympathies of the jury away from Mrs Pollard to a much higher plane, and public gratitude is due to Carson for scotching a real and growing scandal in the administration of justice.

24. The Alaska Boundary Case

His conduct of this case brought Sir Edward an offer of high judicial office. At the end of the term of office of Sir Francis Jeune as President of the Probate, Divorce and Admiralty Division, the Chancellor, Lord Halsbury, thought that Carson, with his strong character and penetrating mind, was the ideal man to sift the evidence and do justice as President of that Court. He accordingly offered him the Presidency. Mr Justice Darling was in his old chambers when the Chancellor's letter came, and must have had a peculiar pleasure in seeing this tribute to his old protégé. Carson said at once, 'I don't want the appointment, Darling; I love my work at the Bar.' Darling was shocked at this perfunctory refusal of one of the highest judicial positions. 'No, really, Edward,' he said, 'you can't treat such an offer like that. Give the matter a little thought before you refuse it.' So Carson gave it deeper thought, and considered it so seriously that the leaders of the Conservative Party, to whom he had now become invaluable, began to be alarmed, and begged him not to leave the House of Commons just when the Tories were on the eve of a dangerous General Election. How near he came to accepting this offer is revealed by the following correspondence.

'5 Eaton Place, SW
23.1.'05

Confidential
Dear Prime Minister, – I have had a letter from the Lord Chancellor offering me the office of President of the Admiralty and Divorce Div. He has asked me to give him an answer at once, and before doing so I must write you a line to ask if my acceptance of it wd meet with your approval.

You have been so much to me and so good a friend during my career that I shd feel sorry indeed if you thought I placed my personal feelings or advancement before what you wd consider right and best under all the circumstances.

I am quite willing to go into Opposition if I am of any real use to you and the party, and my only anxiety is that in any course I take I shd meet with yr approval.

I feel bitter pangs at the idea of severing my connection with politics and, above all, at leaving yr service.

Will you please send me a wire to 4 Temple, London.

Yrs sincerely,

E Carson'

Next day, Mr Balfour telegraphed to Carson: 'Lord Chancellor informed me of proposed offer, which I entirely approved. Your loss will be deeply felt, but I think you should do what suits your own view. Whatever course you take I shall approve. Arthur Balfour.'

He also telegraphed to his private secretary, Mr J S Sanders, at 10 Downing Street: 'Have received letter from Carson. I am confident he means to accept the offer.'

However, after a long conversation with Sanders at Downing Street, Carson wrote the following letter to the last named.

'5 Eaton Place, SW

Jan 25, '05

My dear Sanders, – You were very kind and showed me great friendship yesterday, and I feel grateful. After a good deal of hesitation I have declined the offer of the LC. Whether I have been wise or unwise matters little, as I have acted upon my own instincts and my own wishes in the matter.

Yrs v s,

Edward Carson'

So, at length, the man who had applied for an Irish County Court Judgeship at the age of thirty refused one of the highest judicial posts in Great Britain at the age of fifty. Mr Balfour was relieved, and his secretary, Sanders, wrote from Downing Street on 20 January 1905: 'Just before leaving for Manchester to join the Chief, let me tell you that I had a word of thanksgiving from him on hearing from me that you had declined judicial office, and that you had accordingly elected to stay by his side in our future strenuous fight in Opposition. So don't think him ungrateful, for grateful he is.'

One of the interesting aspects of this correspondence is that the Conservative leaders themselves anticipated certain defeat at the next election.

Yet the idea of the Bench had always been at the back of Carson's mind, and the more he had reflected on Lord Halsbury's offer, the more it had attracted him. The position of Law Officer, which combines the duties of advocate and Minister, is the most strenuous, if also the best paid, in the Government. The work and private cares were telling upon his never very robust constitution, and in the end he refused the position against his own inclination. Had he been raised to the Bench and a judicial peerage, he would never have taken a further part in politics. Perhaps Fate was at work, and reserving a place in history for him, and as leader for Northern Ireland.

However, the fact is that, had he accepted the Chancellor's offer, his appointment would have been void under an Act of Parliament for which the Chancellor himself was responsible. His appointment would have required a special amending Act to be passed by Parliament. The Chancellor had forgotten this fact, and neither Mr Justice Darling nor the Solicitor-General knew it until after the offer had been refused; and so Lord Halsbury was not only breaking the law of England in making this offer, but breaking one of his own laws. For, by section 2 of the Supreme Court of Judicature Act, 1891, which had been introduced by Lord Halsbury himself, the office of President of the Probate, Divorce and Admiralty Division can only be filled by an English barrister of not less than fifteen years' standing. Carson had only been called as an English barrister in 1894, and so had not nearly fulfilled the necessary apprenticeship for that high position.

Yet another duty which from time to time falls on the Law Officers is to appear for Great Britain in international disputes; and therefore his part in the Alaska Boundary dispute – one of the greatest lawsuits in which two civilised States have ever engaged, and by which the possession of many thousands of square miles, as valuable minerally as any in the world, was settled between the British Empire and the United States – must be included in any summary of his legal career.

The dispute arose in this manner. In 1867 the United States, through the advocacy of Senator Sumner and by the sagacious act of Mr Seward, the Secretary of State, purchased Alaska from the Russian Government for a few million dollars. This year was also historical in North American history for a different reason. For this was the year of the British North America Act by which the Canadian provinces federated themselves into the Dominion of Canada, and received a Constitution from the Imperial Parliament at Westminster. As soon therefore as she became a nation, the new Dominion found herself cut off from development in the north-west by the purchase of a tract of land as large as France by the United States for a very small sum. For many years, however, it seemed as if Canada had lost little in substance, and the United States for years did not set very high store on its new possession. It was known by the critics of the Government as 'Seward's Ice Chest', and the administration of this vast, icebound, apparently barren territory was generally considered more trouble and expense that it was worth. The boundary between Alaska and British North America was understood to have been settled by a treaty signed between the Russian and British Governments in 1825, all the rights and obligations of which the United States had taken over by its act of purchase. The country was, however, considered so valueless that no general survey was taken and no boundary drawn.

Little was known of this distant corner of the earth. Alaska was associated with grinding ice floes, burning mountains, and everything weird and fantastic. In the eighteenth century the redoubtable Captain Cook had made a survey, and Vancouver had made a claim to sovereignty of Alaska for his own country; but the achievements of early navigators had long been forgotten when the Russian Government made in 1821, by a ukase, an extravagant claim to exclusive rights of navigation within 100 miles of the whole Pacific Coast of North America. This was naturally challenged by Great Britain, and, by a treaty of 1825, Russia's title to the territory of Alaska was recognised, the boundary between Alaska and British territory 'described', but hardly defined, and the rights of Great Britain to trade and sail freely along the coast conceded.

It was not until the year 1897 that Alaska really challenged the attention of the world; and then it suddenly became one of the best-known and coveted parts of the earth. Gold was discovered in the Klondike, part of the Yukon, in the mid-summer of 1896; the discovery became universally known in the following winter, and there followed one of the great 'gold rushes' of history, in 1897 and 1898, to this hitherto despised and neglected territory. Myriads of prospectors and adventurers flocked to the new goldfields from all parts of the world, with journalists and artists from countless newspapers.

The Yukon produced £100 000 000 worth of gold in less than four years, and the country was also found to be rich in copper, coal, and other minerals. The promised land of the prospectors could best be reached by the mountain passes at Skagway and Dyea, and the natural harbours provided by the many deep inlets on the coast became of the first importance, especially that which was known as the Lynn Canal. These were quickly appropriated by the United States; Skagway and Dyea were seized and organised as American towns, and, by the winter of 1897, the Americans had planted settlements as far inland as Lake Bennet in British Columbia. At last, as was inevitable, the Governments of Canada and Great Britain made protest, which was to lead to bitter disputes until the matter was finally settled in 1903. The British and American lawyers and geographers pored over eighteenth-century maps, and deduced respectively, from the treaty of 1825, meanings which conclusively gave all that was valuable in the disputed territory to their own country; and, indeed, as will be seen, the treaty was susceptible of two entirely different interpretations. Nor was the situation without the gravest dangers for peace. Public feeling both in Canada and the United States was raised to a very high pitch, as the years passed and no solution was found. The situation was comparable to that on the Rand at the time of the Jameson Raid, except that here the two richest countries in the world disputed the title to the soil that suddenly gave forth its new and unexpected burden of treasure. At any moment new gold might have been discovered in any part of the territory claimed by both powers; this would have meant a rush of miners to the place; and, with a shot fired by a Canadian or American adventurer at another of the opposite nationality, any disaster might have been possible. While there was a general desire that this perilous situation should be settled once and for all by some form of arbitration, neither side seemed willing to concede one iota of their national claim. The atmosphere in Great Britain was hardly favourable to arbitration owing to the intervention of American diplomacy in the dispute between Great Britain and Venezuela, and the unfavourable result of that dispute to Great Britain. Yet it was the American Government which refused the offer of an independent arbitrator; however, after long pourparlers, in January 1903 a treaty was signed between the two powers by the Governments at Westminster and Washington, which decided that the whole matter should be referred to a Commission of six 'impartial jurists' of repute, three to be appointed by each of the two Governments. Thus the only chance of a decision was that one Commissioner, on either side, might decide against the claims of his own country. Canadian opinion was hardly reassured when it was announced that America's three 'impartial jurists' were Mr Elihu Root, Secretary of War in President Roosevelt's Cabinet, Senator Lodge, and Senator Turner. Mr Root had been the first American Minister to send troops into the disputed territory; Senator Lodge and Senator Turner had each, according to newspaper reports, committed themselves to the strict American view. Shortly before his appointment, Senator Lodge had said: 'No nation with an ounce of self-respect could but admit the justice of America's case'. A Government official was reported to have said, 'Any American who granted Canada's claims, or any part of them, could not continue to live in this country. We put our trust in the likelihood that there will be at least one fair-minded man on the other side.' For the British Empire were appointed Sir Louis Jetté, ex-Lieutenant-Governor of Quebec, Mr A B Aylesworth KC and Richard Webster, who had become Lord Alverstone and was now Lord Chief Justice of England.

The venue of the proceedings was the great hall of the

Foreign Office in London, and the tribunal sat under the presidency of the Lord Chief Justice. The United States, Great Britain and the Dominion had all briefed the flower of their respective Bars. For the United States there appeared the Honourable Jacob M Dickinson, Mr T D Watson, the Honourable H Taylor, and Mr C D Anderson; for the Dominion, Mr Christopher Robeson KC, Mr F C Wade KC, Mr Geoffrian, and Mr Duff; for Great Britain, the Attorney-General (Sir R Finlay), the Solicitor-General, Mr Rowlatt (now a Judge), and a Mr J A Simon, then in his first youth as a barrister, now perhaps the greatest English lawyer in modern legal history.

In the last name there lies one of the romances of the Bar. This was the first really great case in which Sir John Simon was engaged, and the repute which he gained by his services did much for his future success. Sir Edward Carson, as every busy lawyer must, occasionally sent out work – opinions and the like – to be devilled by other men. He did not always know the names of the men who devilled for him, but he began to notice that some of his work, written with striking and recognisable calligraphy, was always done with exceptional originality, learning and accuracy. He enquired from his clerk as to who this talented and careful 'devil' might be. 'He must be a man of great experience,' he said. But he was told that the handwriting was that of a certain Mr John Simon, a young Oxonian of exceptional brilliance. At this time there occurred the great tragedy of Simon's life. At the outset of their joint adventure upon a career of which the promise of brilliant success seemed almost certain, his young wife died, and left her husband overwhelmed with grief and uncertain how to direct the course of his life. Sir Edward Carson, who had been recalled from his summer holiday to prepare the presentation of the British case in the Alaska dispute, heard of his young 'devil's' sorrow. Carson wrote to him at once, advising him truly that the only possible assistance for a heart full of grief was the preoccupation of unceasing work, and asked him to spend the rest of the summer staying at Cowes in a country house which he had rented, preparing the Alaska boundary case.

It was, indeed, a weary pilgrimage upon which these two great lawyers embarked. When Carson first saw the high piles of documents in the case, which nearly filled the library in his new house in Eaton Place, he almost burst into tears; it is impossible in a short space to give an impression of the complexity of this dispute, but the main contentions on each side can perhaps be briefly stated.

The controversy between the two Powers concerned a narrow strip of land, mountainous, irregular in outline, indented and cut by deep tidal inlets, and running from Mount St Elias in the north to the Portland Channel in the south, over four degrees of latitude on the North Pacific coast contiguous to Canadian territory. Opposite this line of coast is an archipelago of islands; and narrow waters, of a width varying from a few hundred yards to thirteen miles, separate the islands from the mainland and from each other. There were two main matters in dispute: the width of the strip of land along the coast which the Americans had a right to take from their Russian title, and the ownership of the Portland Channel and certain neighbouring islands at the extreme south of the disputed territory. The first question was by far the most important. The country had not been accurately surveyed at the time of the Anglo-Russian treaty of 1825, which was signed far away by diplomats in St Petersburg. The Russians' main purpose was to secure for themselves the archipelago of islands, and they seem to have desired, for the better protection of their traders or those islands, a narrow strip of coast on the mainland from Mount St Elias to the Portland Channel. The British negotiations first suggested that the base of the mountains should be taken as the frontier, but the two Powers ultimately agreed that the frontier between Russian and British North America should be 'the crest of the mountains running parallel to the coast, subject to the condition that, if the line should anywhere exceed the distance of ten marine leagues (34½ miles) from the ocean, then the boundary between the British and Russian territory should be formed by a line parallel to the sinuosities of the coast and distant therefrom not more than ten marine leagues'. Now upon this one sentence were based both of the two interpretations, the one of which gave the heads of all the inlets, of vital importance to navigation, as well as the mountain passes into the gold country, to Great Britain, and the other to the United States. Shortly, the Canadian contention as to the frontier line was this: that, although there was no one continuous 'chain' of mountains 'parallel to the coast', there were mountains within the meaning of the treaty near the coast, and that a line drawn along the tops of the mountains nearest the coast should be taken. Great Britain further contended that the word 'coast' meant the general trend of the mainland coast, and not the edges of the tidal inlets, which ran far inland. The United States, on the other hand, contended that, as there was no continuous mountain range running parallel to the coast as described in the treaty, and the negotiators must therefore have been deceived as to the geography of the place, it was necessary to fall back upon an artificial frontier, not defined by nature, ten marine leagues inland, running parallel to the 'sinuosities of the coast'. The 'coast', by their interpretation, meant literally the rugged edges of the mainland, including those of the deep channels and inlets. The result of this definition of 'coast' was to throw back the frontier much farther inland, and to give the United States all the heads of the inlets and the mountain passes. In a sentence, the British interpretation gave to America a strip of 12 000 square miles, and to Great Britain the heads of the inlets and the mountain passes vital to Canadian commerce and communications. The American interpretation gave the United States a strip of 32 000 square miles, together with the heads of all the inlets and the mountain passes.

For several weeks, Carson worked day and night on the documents in this case, and insisted that John Simon should be present at all the consultations with the High Commissioner for Canada. He took great pains to consult him at every opportunity, in order that the High Commissioner might grasp, what Carson already knew, that there was no one engaged in the case who understood the dispute better than this young junior. At length the Commissioner said, 'Who's that young man, Sir Edward? He seems to know more about it than any of us.' 'That's young Simon,' said Carson. And so Simon was briefed, as fourth counsel, in his first big case, and indeed, in all his distinguished career, he never was concerned in a greater litigation.

The proceedings were conducted by alternate speeches by the leading advocates, lasting singly two, three, and even four days. The delivery of these speeches made the greatest demand upon the energies and abilities of the great advocates present. Old books of explorers and geographers; ancient maps and charts and travellers' tales, particularly those of Vancouver; the correspondence and conversations of statesmen, both historic and forgotten; the obscure adventures and claims of merchants, sailors, and trappers over a hundred years; the contrary claims and acquiescence to such claims of several Governments; together with the most modern surveys and photographs of a wild, mountainous, and often trackless country, and a maze of ocean channels through an archipelago of islands – all had to be sifted and examined and brought together in relation to each other in order to support one of the two opposing theories in this great international lawsuit.

The Attorney-General opened the case for Great Britain, and it was closed by Sir Edward Carson. It may truly be said that there was not a single speech which was not a fine intellectual effort; and the present writer may perhaps be forgiven for considering that the British lawyers had the best of the argument. Carson made a contribution most typical of his mind; all his speeches, legal or political, in small things or great, bear the marks of his gift of analytical deduction, that power of his of reducing the most complicated subject-matter to the narrowest compass and the clearest issue. The American case depended largely on being able to introduce maps, correspondence, claims to sovereignty and other events previous to the 1825 treaty, together with principles of general international law. It is a well-known principle of English law that, when a contract has been reduced to writing, if the terms of the written contract have a clear and unambiguous meaning, previous correspondence cannot be introduced to vary or supplement it. No one was more skilful than Carson in showing that everything was clearly expressed in the document itself, and that recourse to extraneous matters was unnecessary; and in this, as regards the Alaska boundary dispute, was the strength of the case for Great Britain. The hopes of the United States lay in showing the inadequacy and obscurity of the document, and then in introducing previous negotiations and subsequent events to justify their own interpretation. Many a time had Carson made this point in a case of contract in the Waterford County Court, and here he was making the same argument as regards a treaty in the great hall of the Foreign Office in this mighty international dispute.

His aim was to bring the tribunal back to the simple words of the treaty, now almost forgotten in the mass of historical and geographical arguments which had been brought forward by the United States. 'I ask the tribunal,' he said, 'to keep to the treaty itself, until we arrive at some difficulty which requires external assistance. ... If Mr Middleton's account of his conversation with Stratford Canning is to be accepted as interpreting the treaty, we might as well have no treaty at all. I ask the tribunal to answer broadly whether the treaty can mean that Russia should have a strip of 34½ miles round the heads of all the inlets, without any distinction between one inlet and another, even if the result is, as in the case of the Lynn Canal, to give Russia a strip over 100 miles wide, and even if it is utterly impossible to draw such a line 34½ miles back parallel with those inlets.' If, however, previous negotiations and events were to be referred to, he showed that the United States Government itself had again and again denied Russia's right of sovereignty to this strip of land at dates before their own purchase of Alaska. In truth, 'Russia did not desire any part of the mainland as a substantive territory, but only as a means of support to her settlements of the islands.'

With regard to the vexed question of the 'mountains', he said, 'The British case is that the line of mountains was "defined", but not "identified", and nothing further could be done in an unsurveyed country. The British view is that the mountains might be nearer than ten marine leagues from the sea, but the strip of coast was not to exceed ten leagues in breadth. It was not the mountains which were to be the boundary, but the line along the summits, so long as their distance from the coast should not exceed ten marine leagues. My learned friends object to the line of mountains suggested, but offer no alternative. They actually suggest that there are no mountains to satisfy the treaty; and this is in a country where it is impossible to go far in any direction without coming across a mountain or a mountain pass.' So far, he argued, from being a dearth of mountains, there was an embarrassing richness of them. As to the artificial construction put by the American counsel on the word 'coast', to mean the literal edge of all the inlets, however deep or narrow, he said: 'The language of the treaty must be construed according to the ordinary rules of language. The treaty speaks for itself, and it is clear that "coast" means the edge of the ocean. The "ten marine leagues" was to be from the ocean. ... The usual sense of "ocean" is the vast body of water separating continents, and is entirely out of place in connection with an inlet, a river or an estuary. A look at the map shows the utter impracticability of drawing a line parallel to the sinuosities as interpreted by my learned friends.' 'Why,' said Carson, pointing towards the direction of the River Thames, 'if the ocean is to be taken as wherever one can find salt water, this enquiry is perhaps being conducted on the edge of the ocean.' Even from this weary pilgrimage of historical and geographical survey he could not exclude a gesture of picturesque advocacy. He concluded by a compliment to the American lawyers, and a reference to the fact that this was the way – by an argument in which no bitterness or heat had been engendered – that, in the future, great and friendly nations, like individuals, would solve their disputes, and so serve the peace of the world.

Mr Dickinson, who ended with the last and finest speech for the United States, no doubt felt the force of Carson's concentration on the treaty, and at once sought to escape from the narrow issues to which Carson had brought the controversy. He appealed to the tribunal not to take a narrow view and decide the matter on a narrow construction of the meaning of words. He made a strong plea for the consideration of all relevant events, documents and surveys, before and after the treaty. He conceded that it would be impossible to draw a line parallel to the 'sinuosities of the coast', inlets and all, according to the United States's interpretation. But he argued that the expression 'sinuosities' excluded the British interpretation of coast as meaning the 'general trend' of the mainland. 'Great Britain's interpretation,' he said, 'would give her every safe harbour and anchorage, and every point useful for the defence or protection of trade.' He said that the maps of 1823 showed that it was not to the mountains bordering on the sea, but to the mountains passing round the heads of the inlets, that the negotiators referred, and there was no such continuous range of mountains. 'It becomes necessary for Great Britain to select a set of peaks. There is nothing in the treaty to justify the selection of peaks nearest to the sea. The Solicitor-General skips from peak to peak, like Ariel.'

After a four days' speech from Mr Dickinson, and after the necessary compliments had been exchanged between the two Governments and the President, the advocates' task was over, and it remained only for the Commissioners to confer, and, if possible, to reach a conclusion. All six Commissioners were banqueted in the Guildhall by the Lord Mayor and by the Pilgrims' Society, and a general atmosphere of peace and goodwill prevailed. Soon, however, rumours began to grow which caused consternation in Canada, that Lord Alverstone had made a statement committing himself in the main to the American contention; and, although he denied having made this statement, this is substantially what he decided. When, about a fortnight later, he published his judgment, the Canadian Commissioners refused to sign the award. Lord Alverstone's decision is certainly neither a satisfactory nor a convincing document. The main purport in the award, which is not without paradox, is that in principle, with regard to the mountain frontier as opposed to the artificial ten-league frontier, his judgment decided in favour of the main British contention; but, by his construction of the word 'coast' in accordance with the American view, he deduced a mountain frontier which robbed Canada of all for which she had been striving. He rejected the main American argument that there were no mountains within the meaning of the treaty, and therefore he refused to draw the purely artificial frontier so long claimed by the United States at ten marine leagues from the heads of the inlets; he accepted the British contention that there were mountains within the meaning of the treaty, along the peaks of which the frontier could be drawn; but, by in effect deciding that, in drawing a line along 'the crest of mountains parallel to the coast', the word 'coast' meant, not the general trend of the coast, but the tortuous edges of the inlets, he chose as a frontier, not the mountains nearest to the coast, but a series of peaks further back, along a line behind, and roughly parallel to, the deep inlets. The result of taking such a line rather than one parallel to the mainland coast, which would have cut across the inlets, was to give the Americans half only of the actual area which they claimed, but along with it all the valuable inlets and mountain passes, and so to cut off Canada from access to the sea over more than four degrees of latitude, and in particular to deprive her of free passage up the Lynn Canal to the Yukon territory, the most convenient, and at some seasons the only, mode of access. It is also fair to state that the territory granted to the United States was far less valuable to the United States than it would have been to the Dominion, to whom the communications were of vital importance. It is true that the other question, of the Portland Channel, which depended on the identification of a certain route taken by the explorer Vancouver, was substantially decided in favour of Great Britain, and Canada received two of the Islands, Wales and

Pearce Islands, whose possession followed from that decision; but, for no very clear reason, two other islands, the possession of which had been assumed throughout the proceedings also to depend on the Portland Channel decision, were given to the United States. Altogether, the Canadian Commissioners considered that the decision was not a judicial one, and was a 'compromise between opposing and entirely irreconcilable views of the true meaning of the original treaty'. Although Lord Alverstone was at once hailed by the American Press as taking his place 'among the great Lord Chief Justices of England' for his decision, it is to be feared that their view of his judicial talents was exaggerated, and the Canadian view of his judgment is unhappily corroborated by reference to most of his judgments in the King's Bench. His method of arriving at a decision was often a not very happy compromise between, and even a confusion of, opposing arguments. In the *Dictionary of National Biography*, Mr Justice McKinnon, a high authority, writes of him: 'Perhaps the truest and most modest remark in Lord Alverstone's *Recollections* is that, throughout his life, he had been favoured by good fortune; he was not a very clever man, nor a learned lawyer, nor a good speaker in the Courts or in Parliament. As a judge he was dignified, though not distinguished. But the reports will be searched in vain for judgments of his that are valuable as expositions of the law.' It is to be feared that Canadians will not be consoled for their loss of a large part of the Pacific coast by reading this biographical essay, which concludes with a reference to Lord Alverstone's amiable but somewhat boisterous disposition, and to the fact that 'during forty years, he sang in the choir at Kensington parish church'.

Even if the Alaska award was correct, it might perhaps have been more convincing and more consoling to Canadian opinion if we could have looked back with pride to a great impartial judgment of unquestioned authority, which had been the work and the thought of one of the several great English jurists alive and available for service at that time.

It will, however, have been observed that the whole decision, with all its results and implications, was finally reduced to the comparatively small compass of the meaning of the word 'coast' in the treaty; and to that question, it is submitted, those who are interested in the merits of the controversy should apply themselves, and, in so doing, carefully consider the clear, common-sense arguments of Sir Edward Carson, which are quoted above, on that very matter.

However, American public opinion was naturally overjoyed, and regarded the award as a great triumph for American diplomacy, as indeed it was. Even English opinion found consolation in the fact that the permanent solution of a question which offered wide opportunities for discord between the two great kindred nations was an advantage that far outweighed any disappointment. At all events, Great Britain had suffered, after the adverse settlements of the Alabama and the Venezuelan disputes, another heavy loss in the cause of international arbitration. As an international litigant it will be admitted that Great Britain has proved very patient and singularly unsuccessful.

However, Canada mistook such resignation for complacency. The feeling grew that official Britain cared more for the friendship of the United States than for the whole Dominion; that Dominion interests had been sacrificed to make an Anglo-American holiday. Even Sir Wilfrid Laurier, the Prime Minister, demanded that, for the future, Canada must have an independent treaty-making power, and other politicians openly advocated secession. Those who had worked for years in the cause of closer Imperial co-operation were confounded. The name of Lord Alverstone was held in hatred and contempt by Canadians, and even the name of Great Britain became unpopular for some time; and it is to be feared that the movement for the legal dismemberment of the British Empire – which, it is to be hoped, has finally been crowned by the Statute of Westminster in 1931 – received a great momentum from this award. But it is best to draw the curtain on this unhappy incident with the dignified speech of the Canadian, Mr Aylesworth, when he returned home, and to accept his conclusions. 'Canada,' he said, 'must bear with the award graciously and with submission. The ties that bind Canada to the Motherland will stand the strain of many Alaska awards.' There, and in the permanent removal of a cause of discord between the British Empire and the United States, we leave this vexed and difficult question.

25. George Wyndham and Lloyd George

During these five years, it can readily be seen, Carson's time was very fully occupied in the Courts. Meanwhile the Government was engaged in the last great attempt at the conciliation of Ireland under the Union. By George Wyndham's celebrated Land Act of 1903, the purchase of land by the tenants was greatly facilitated, the Government speeding the parting landlord with equitable compensation. Trinity College was itself one of the landlords, and Carson only intervened in the debates on this Bill, not as Solicitor-General, but as the member for Trinity College determined to see justice done to his constituency. Such independence in a Minister, whose voice, as a rule, is raised solely on behalf of the Government, is rare, if not unprecedented. At times his championship of the rights of the university caused the Government considerable anxiety, especially on one occasion when he went in and took his seat, not on the Government bench, but in his old seat below the gangway. During the progress of the measure the Chancellor of the Exchequer, Sir Michael Hicks-Beach, sent for him, and said, 'Carson, you haven't the elements of statesmanship in you.' 'I know I haven't,' retorted Carson to the formidable 'Black Michael', 'and when I come to understand those who have, I'm rather glad.' In the end he won the concession for Trinity College for which he had striven so uncompromisingly. On yet another occasion, he spoke, when Solicitor-General, in almost direct opposition to the Government. The vexed question of a Catholic university for Ireland was raised once again in April 1901. The Conservative Government had made no advance towards the foundation of such an institution. 'I desire to intervene,' said Carson, 'not as a member of the Government, but as representing Trinity College in this

House. I have taken up this attitude for many years, and I have upon every occasion, I think, on which this question has come before the House, expressed my views fearlessly and I hope clearly. ... For my part, I value so highly a university training that I would make almost any sacrifice which would enable Roman Catholic young men to receive the benefits of such a treasury ... I prefer Roman Catholicism highly educated to Roman Catholicism in ignorance, and the only way in which that result can be brought about is by the establishment of a generous system of higher education. ... I will always give any assistance in my power to put within the reach of the great mass of the people of Ireland the benefits of university education.'

The Government was proud – indeed, justly proud – of the immense improvement in the state of Ireland which had followed upon its policy. George Wyndham's Land Act met with Carson's approval because, unlike Gerald Balfour's Bill, which he opposed so violently, it did not seek to solve the Irish question at the expense of the landlord. In this Act adequate provision was made by the immensely rich British Treasury for the landlord. The Conservatives were firmly convinced that they had killed Home Rule by kindness, and that they had found a permanent solution to the Irish problem by removing the causes of agrarian discontent; so, perhaps, they might have done, had it not been for the British party system, and the swing of the political pendulum under the weight of quite different problems than the Irish question. Meanwhile, Conservative statesmen spoke proudly of a permanent solution and of the 'last Irish Land Bill'. But Carson was not so sanguine: he had a deep foreboding that this was not the end of the Irish question. The Conservative Party was already losing its whole strength and inspiration, from divided counsels – for reasons that will appear later.

He knew that political agitation must come again, as soon as the Unionists lost their majority. 'They call this the last Irish Land Bill; they talk of a permanent solution,' said Carson in a speech at Oxford. 'I have been hearing of a last Irish Land Bill, and of a permanent solution, all my life, and I have no doubt that I shall hear of them again.' The Government resented this criticism of their achievement, and there was a difficult interview between Carson and Arthur Balfour. When, afterwards, Carson walked through the Lobby, the journalists crowded round him, hoping to get the first news of his resignation. But Carson did not resign, and he was kept busier than ever in the Courts. The explanation of his attitude on this matter, and of his Oxford speech, is to be found in a letter sent to Arthur Balfour on the same night as that in which their interview took place.

'House of Commons
4 May '03

Dear Mr Balfour, – I am very anxious to make it clear that, in what I said at Oxford with reference to the Irish Land Bill, I never intended in the least to be disloyal to you or the Govt. It is quite true that, when I stated I would give the Bill the "minimum of support which my official position required", I had in mind the dislike of my constituency to the policy of land purchase (and which I share) and its probably effect in the university, but I thought that, in adding that I gave it this support "because I had no alternative", it would be clear my view was that, however disagreeable this policy was, it was my view that it was the only one. I see it has been represented that I said I had no alternative but to support it, which was not in the least what was intended and which would be ridiculous.

It is, of course, very difficult to understand the exact circumstances under which I was speaking, but I should like to add that I was replying to a speech plainly prepared for Wyndham and not for me, and which described the Bill with an enthusiasm which I could not, as representing Dublin University, adopt. I hope you will understand this explanation. I need hardly add that, so long as I have the honour of serving under you, I never could intentionally do a disloyal act.

Yours sincerely
Edward Carson'

Having regard, however, to the high hopes that had been raised by the new Land Act, it was particularly unfortunate that George Wyndham, its author and the Chief Secretary for Ireland, should become embroiled, just at the moment of triumph, in an unfortunate affair which led to his own resignation and to a growing lack of confidence in both Arthur Balfour, who had succeeded his uncle as Prime Minister in 1902, and the Conservative Administration. Against Arthur Balfour's judgment, George Wyndham had appointed as his Permanent Under-Secretary at Dublin Castle an Indian Civil Servant of great distinction, Sir Anthony MacDonnell. Balfour's objection to the appointment was that, by repute, MacDonnell was a Home Ruler. However, George Wyndham, most charming and self-willed of men, had his way. MacDonnell from the first seems to have understood that he had been charged with greater powers and responsibilities than are usually given to a Permanent Under-Secretary belonging to the Civil Service, and Arthur Balfour would have known himself to have been more than justified in his original antagonism had he known how Sir Anthony was employing his time. Lord Dunraven, as Chairman of the Irish Reform Association, was interested in a scheme of devolution for Irish government, in which Irish finance and other matters were to be transferred from Westminster to a responsible council, drawn from all Ireland, composed partly of elected and partly of nominated members. Sir Anthony became interested in this scheme, and gave counsel and assistance in the draft, which was written on official Dublin Castle notepaper. But, when Dunraven's scheme was published in September 1905, and a storm of criticism rose against it, especially from the Irish Unionists, George Wyndham repudiated it and denied all knowledge of it. It soon became known, however, that Sir Anthony MacDonnell, supposed, as a Civil Servant, to have no politics, and employed under the Crown at Dublin Castle, had taken a leading part in the draft, and it was impossible to quell the indignation of the Irish Unionists, who regarded this as a disguised form of Home Rule and as surely leading to a Nationalist and Catholic ascendancy in finance. This ill-timed raising of the constitutional question was particularly unwelcome and inopportune to the Government, which had placed such high hopes in their 'final' solution of the agrarian problem; indeed, they were robbed of much of the credit and popularity of their Irish policy by this unfortunate incident.

Carson himself was among the most indignant: he regarded it as a monstrous thing that a Civil Servant in such an important position should have been responsible for a scheme so much at variance with Unionist opinion. How far George Wyndham himself was involved was unknown, and has only recently been made public by an article in the *Quarterly Review* by Mrs Edgar Dugdale. In a strong speech at Manchester on 7 February 1905, Carson committed himself to an unequivocal condemnation of the policy of devolution. He denounced it as a 'fatuous, ridiculous, unworkable, impracticable scheme, lately set going in Ireland by certain gentlemen whose names had been attached to it.' The Ulster

Unionists had intimated to the Whips that they no longer had confidence in the Administration, and Carson, although a member of the Government, defended them. 'The grievance of Ulster Unionists,' he said, 'is, rightly or wrongly, that the scheme originated with a permanent official retained under a Unionist Government in Dublin Castle.'

This time the threat of resignation came from Carson. He at once informed the Prime Minister that he could no longer serve in a Government whose Chief Secretary was in any way committed to a scheme of devolution which might put Ulster under the Catholic majority, and offered his resignation. 'You know, A J B,' Carson said, 'it's only for the sake of the Union that I'm in politics at all, and this idea is a particularly insidious attack upon the Union.'

'I know it is, and I think George has been very indiscreet,' said Balfour, but he added, putting his arm affectionately round Carson's shoulders, 'now, do help me; I'm in a great difficulty. Besides, I can make a very good logical defence of George.'

The advocate and the philosopher faced each other. 'A J B,' said Carson, 'what would be the use of my saying to one of my juries, "My client comes before you, gentlemen, with a very good *logical* defence"? What I must know is whether you have a *real* defence for him. What are the *realities* of the matter?'

The realities, not known for certain at the time by either Carson or Balfour, were that, while Wyndham was abroad on a rest cure, Sir Anthony MacDonnell had made mention, in two long and closely written letters, of the part he was playing in the Dunraven proposals, but that George Wyndham had either not read the relevant passages or had failed to appreciate their meaning. Indeed, the passages were so casual that even the mind of a man who was not an invalid might easily have missed them.

Carson wrote to J S Saunders: 'The present situation is

an intolerable one, and I sincerely hope the PM is going immediately to end it. For myself, I feel acutely the position in which the PM is placed after all his splendid work, but it seems hopeless for even the most devoted followers to do anything.'

The end, however, was that Carson did not resign, but that Wyndham, his health growing worse, bowed to the Parliamentary storm which was growing daily in intensity, and surrendered his office. In any event, his failing health would have made his continuing tenure of that difficult post almost impossible.

Balfour immediately sent for Carson and offered him the position of Chief Secretary. After some discussion, and with some reluctance, he accepted it; and, although his appointment was never published, it can be said that he was Chief Secretary for a day. He informed Arthur Balfour that, if Sir Anthony MacDonnell were not immediately sent back to the India Office, he would insist that all official communications must come to him direct without passing through the hands of the Under-Secretary. However, after his formal acceptance of the offer, other difficulties arose. John Atkinson was considerably senior to Carson at the Irish Bar, and had been his Attorney-General in 1893. Atkinson was still Irish Attorney-General in 1905, and would now have to serve under Carson if the latter became Chief Secretary. Carson was unwilling to embarrass or wound the feelings of so old a friend, and on this ground begged to be excused from his appointment, which finally went to Mr Walter Long.

Carson had only one considerable opportunity of showing his Parliamentary abilities while he was Solicitor-General. He was put in charge of the Licensing Bill of 1904. The excessive number of public houses was an acknowledged social evil. The justices of the peace, in whom the power resided to refuse the renewal of publicans' licences, did not, as a rule, choose to exercise this power, because it would mean turning men into the street and depriving them of their livelihood without compensation. Suddenly an enterprising member of the Chamberlain family began refusing to renew licences in Birmingham, and brought the trouble to a head. Insurance companies then began to refuse to insure publicans' licences. The Conservatives devised a Bill giving power to the magistrates to distribute compensation to publicans whose licences they refused to renew. It may seem that this Bill gave small scope; but it aroused widespread public interest, and gave rise to a battle between the sacred rights of property and the cause of temperance. The protagonist on the one side was Carson, and on the other was Mr David Lloyd George. From May to July 1904, when the Bill passed its final stage in the Commons, Carson made over ninety speeches on the measure, and Mr Lloyd George must have done nearly as well. They were a good match for each other. When, night after night, two men are engaged in Parliamentary warfare, it is impossible that a kind of intimacy should not spring up between them; and, in this way, Carson grew to understand and appreciate the brilliant Welshman, and got to know him, with all his wonderful Parliamentary resource, extremely well. Mr Balfour, however, had not yet learned to like him, and, one day, when Lloyd George was speaking, said to Carson, 'What a pity; there's a first-rate man – so very clever – but there's always something in every speech that spoils it. I suppose it was ingrained in him as a country solicitor.' 'Then I'm a good match for him,' said Carson, 'for I was only a country lawyer when you first knew me.'

Once more, Carson reduced a complicated matter to a simple issue. 'We are agreed,' he said, 'that the number of licensed houses in almost every district in the country is excessive, and yet neither party has been able to make any progress for the last thirty years. ... The whole question in this case is: ought there to be compensation or ought there not? The moment you agree there ought to be compensation, I say that our Bill will hold the field until you give us a better alternative.' Mr Lloyd George argued that a publican's licence was not, and never had been, in the nature of property, and showed that, from the time of Henry VII, the legislature had taken power to suppress common ale-houses, a cause of much mischief in the realm. He went behind the rights of the publican to the rights of the public, from the rights of property to the well-being and efficiency of the whole people.

This was the one measure of first-class importance which Carson ever piloted through the House of Commons; all the rest of his notable achievements had been, and were to be, in attack. But here he performed his task splendidly; always courteous, even in the small hours, and even to the most rabid apostle of temperance; never at a loss, even on the most intricate point; never obstinate in the face of an obvious improvement to his measure; he won golden opinions, such as are rarely won, from his opponents; many remarked that, if only he could give up the Courts, he would make a splendid Leader of the House of Commons. When Mr Asquith moved the rejection of the Bill on third reading, he said, 'I do not complain in the least of the manner in which the Bill has been conducted. The Solicitor-General has shown, in the conduct of it, uniform courtesy, unfailing lucidity, and, I must add, inexhaustible resource.' Otherwise, the main burden of Mr Asquith's speech was the classic and accustomed protest against the use of the guillotine closure. In Carson's reply there was a recollection of old conflicts, and a presentiment of mighty battles still to come with this generous opponent. 'I myself,' said Carson, 'have a very vivid recollection, when

I was not a very old member of this House, when I sat on the Opposition side, of the hardships of the guillotine, not upon a question whether publicans should have compensation, but as to whether my country should be separated from that of the right honourable gentleman.'

After Carson had made his last speech on the Bill, Mr Channing, the member for Northampton, a bitter opponent of the Bill, voiced the general feelings of the House when he said, 'We all acknowledge the uniform courtesy and consideration which the Solicitor-General has given, during the discussion of this Bill, to those who have differed from him.'

26. Home Rule and Protection

Meanwhile, while the House of Commons discussed Irish land and the grievances of publicans, the Cabinet was divided on greater issues, and opinion in the country was veering round towards the greatest reversal since the Reform Bill. The Conservatives had been in office for nearly ten years. Not only were they rapidly losing the confidence of the country, but they could not agree among themselves on the main question of policy. Mr Joseph Chamberlain, who, by joining the Conservatives on the question of the Union with Ireland, had inaugurated and then consolidated the long period of Conservative supremacy, now, by his campaign for Imperial preference, created a new line of division in the parties which he had united; indeed, the wound made by that division, which made defeat at the next election certain, has never entirely healed. Not for nothing had this fearless man, with his penetrating and audacious mind, presided over the Colonial Office for so many years. He resigned office in 1903 to study the great question of Imperial economic unity, and to gather strength for his great campaign. His plan was none other than the reversal of the policy of Free Trade upon which England had seemed to thrive so wonderfully throughout a half century. But Joseph Chamberlain saw even then that the tide had turned, that foreign nations behind tariffs of their own were able to keep out British products, which had enjoyed a monopoly so long; and he saw that by a strange irony those foreign industries had themselves been developed by British capital, while the great expanses of British territory remained undeveloped. He saw the richest heritage of any country in history divided, neglected, ignored. No wonder he said almost at the outset that he was not afraid of food taxes. Yet he raised a spectre of which politicians are afraid to this day. Even Conservatives in the citadel were afraid. Had not Disraeli agreed at last that Protection was not only dead, but damned? There were many in the Conservative Party who refused to support the Chamberlain proposals; there were more who gave them but cold support; there were some who embraced them with fanatical zeal and expressed them with the crude faith of religious converts; and the Prime Minister, where was he? Nobody knew. He showed himself a master of evasion; it was said that there were no clearer and analytical arguments for Free Trade than the declarations of the Prime Minister in favour of tariffs. Even when the election came, no one knew where he stood; and before his constituents at Manchester, his phrases were Delphic and ambiguous. 'If you return us to power, we shall consider fiscal reform in the very forefront of our political constructive programme'. Yet the Government clung to office, long after their divisions had become notorious, and thus made their condition hopeless. The country, asked to decide on a momentous change in policy, could hardly be expected to do so at the instance of a party itself by no means convinced of the necessity or wisdom of the step, and whose leader spoke in riddles. It is tragic to the student of the politics of these times to see how, by a mere inability to decide boldly, the Conservatives missed the chance, which has never come again, to make one united Empire without bar or barrier. During the twenty-six years that were to follow before the issue was to be raised in a practical form again, the great British Dominions were, deprived of a guiding hand, to diverge from Britain and themselves so widely that any scheme of customs union or federation presented a far more intricate and difficult problem than in Joseph Chamberlain's day. Meanwhile, Chamberlain, having failed to win the united enthusiasm of the faction, could hardly expect to gain the verdict of the nation. Further, the very names of the leading politicians had begun to weary the nation, drawn, as they seemed to be, mainly from a few families and an exclusive caste. All the signs in the firmament were against the Conservatives. The great fiscal change which determined leadership might then have achieved, under a safe roof, was postponed for twenty-six years until grim necessity and dire poverty enjoined it; and the Conservative leaders seemed almost to be inviting the British people to throw away one of the greatest chances they ever had. Finally, in December 1905, Mr Balfour at last resigned, and Sir Henry Campbell-Bannerman formed an administration, preparatory to an appeal to the electorate.

Yet, as a result of Unionist policy, the name of Great Britain stood high in the world. The problems of South Africa, which might be called a direct legacy from Mr Gladstone, had been solved. Ireland, as a Liberal Chief Secretary was to acknowledge, was in a more contented and prosperous condition than she had been for centuries. England had ensured her position in the world by friendship with France and alliance with Japan. On the latter the Conservatives placed especial value. Indeed, it was said that the Japanese alliance, initiated in 1902, falling to be renewed in 1905, was the real reason of Mr Balfour's retention of office. As Carson said at Maidstone on the day after Mr Balfour's resignation, 'I do not recollect in my lifetime when the name of England stood as high abroad. The Unionist Government have laid down their office when they may well be proud of their achievement. Never has England been counted as a friend and an ally as she is at the present time. Yet, when the Unionist Government came into power, England was scoffed at for her betrayal of Gordon, and despised for the surrender of Majuba Hill.'

During all the discords over the fiscal controversy, Carson had been unhesitatingly in favour of Mr Joseph Chamberlain, so long as his support did not involve a personal choice between him and Balfour. Chamberlain's son, Austen, came once to canvass him. 'Are you for my father?' he asked. 'Yes,' replied Carson, 'and if I wasn't, I should long to be.' For Joseph Chamberlain had become a great hero to Edward Carson: in his considered judgment Chamberlain was the finest man he ever met in political life. 'I loved and revered Arthur Balfour,' he said to me, 'and owed him so much; but Joe was different; he had qualities which Arthur Balfour lacked. He was a great man.'

Yet Carson was torn between divided loyalties. The Press and the public were counting heads in the Conservative Party, defining the leading men as friends of Balfour or of Chamberlain, and, when it came to an issue between the two men, his loyalty to Balfour was predominant. Carson's well-known views on Tariff Reform caused his name to be mentioned by the *Morning Post* as a partisan of Chamberlain. But, although he was with Chamberlain on policy, he could never contemplate disloyalty to Balfour in a personal way. This was a question which, unfortunately, he never really made his own, and did not involve the question of the Union, which was deep in his heart and the only question which could and did estrange him from Arthur Balfour. It is this very personal loyalty to political leaders which often delays a vital change in policy until it is too late. The strength of Balfour's position lay in the support of men like Carson, who refused to consider any other man as leader so long as he was willing to remain. Decided leadership of some kind would have been a blessing beyond price for the Conservative cause at this time, and the Muse of English political history may regret that Carson, who on any question of the Union of England with Ireland was willing to fling all personal considerations to the winds, could not take the same bold and objective course when the Union of the whole Empire was hanging in the balance. The pity of this is the greater because the participation of Ireland in the advantages of an economic Empire, with the full right to Imperial preference for her goods, would have provided a great argument for the continuation of the Union, and a decisive one against rebellion and separation. The bitterness of the constitutional question might have diluted and disappeared in the wider economic solution he conceived in the interests of the whole Empire. Here, however, is his letter written at this critical time, which speaks for itself.

'5 Eaton Place, SW
30.1.'06

Dear Mr Balfour, – You may have observed statements in the Press, eg *Morning Post* of today, classifying the party into your followers and those of Mr Chamberlain. As I am classed amongst the latter, Sir E Clarke suggested to me I should write to the Press contradicting the statement. That course does not commend itself to me, on many grounds; and I do not see that a newspaper should be in a position to require notice being taken of what they are pleased to insert for their own purposes. However, as Clarke thought the matter of some importance, in order that the City might know the classification was incorrect, I thought I might mention the matter to you. ... I need hardly say I am only loyal to you.

If you agree with me, please do not mind answering this. I am very distressed over the whole situation, and it will be a great help to me when you come back.

Sincerely yours
Edward Carson'

Carson had become one of the most powerful platform speakers of the Conservative Party, and he is to be found, in the very early days of Tariff Reform, lending the full strength of his advocacy to the Chamberlain proposals. For instance, in 1904, we find him speaking at Kidderminster for a certain Mr Stanley Baldwin, who was to be the Conservative candidate at the next election, but not a member of Parliament until four years later. He appealed for the 'glorious edifice of a world-wide united economic Empire'. He appealed for tariffs as a guarantee of the standard of life of the wage-earners. 'How can we compete in the manufacture of goods with countries where the factory laws are different, where wages are different, and whose exports are subsidised by grants from the State?' he asked, afterwards adding: 'It cannot be beyond the wit of man to find a method whereby the mother country can treat the colonies, and the colonies treat her, in a manner which will give them both some advantage over those who are strangers in blood and strangers in language.'

For him a General Election carried with it no electoral anxieties. He had merely to present himself before a crowd of friends and admirers at Trinity College who greeted him at each election with greater admiration and affection. For there, too, in his own country, he was not without honour. They had long respected their senior member, and now they were beginning to love him, as is clearly shown by his correspondence with his constituents. Freed from a campaign of his own, he threw himself with all his energies into the national campaign, and spoke all over the country on behalf of Tariff Reform. Yet, from a sense of loyalty to Arthur Balfour, he referred to neither Joseph Chamberlain nor Chamberlain's specific proposals, and his election speeches were more guarded than his earlier ones. This serves as striking proof of the extent to which personal loyalties were confounding the great issue at stake, which it was the duty of the Conservative Party to place before the country. For he was not without misgiving. He clearly saw that this issue was dividing the Conservative Party, whose defeat seemed almost certain. Through all his speeches on the campaign there ran a note of warning on that other issue, which was his own, and the whole reason for his entry into politics – the cause of the Union. Almost as soon as he became Prime Minister, Sir Henry Campbell-Bannerman made a declaration in favour of Home Rule. He could not count on an overwhelming victory, and the Irish vote was important. Yet, strong Home Ruler that he was, there were those who enjoined moderation upon him. Irish Home Rule had wrecked the Liberal Party twice, and driven it out of office for a generation. It was important that it should not once again ruin everything at a time when all else seemed to be favouring them. Sir Henry Campbell-Bannerman made a speech at Stirling in which he advised the Irish Nationalist Party to accept their full policy by progressive stages.

Carson was determined that the country should understand that the Liberal Party had not turned their backs on Home Rule, and that the maintenance of the legislative Union was still an issue between the parties, and he wrote the following letter to *The Times*.

'Rottingdean
December 31, 1905

Dear Sir, – The ingenious attempt of the Prime Minister and Mr Asquith to delude the electors of the United Kingdom into the belief that Home Rule is not an issue in the coming election, by use of the words "independent Parliament" and "supremacy of the Imperial Parliament", ought not to be allowed to deceive anyone. Will the Prime Minister or any of his colleagues answer this single question? Have they abandoned the policy of setting up a separate Parliament in Ireland, with a separate Executive accountable to such Parliament? If they have, will some member of the Government explain what the Prime Minister meant at Stirling when he advised the Nationalists trustfully to accept "an instalment of representative control, provided it were consistent with and led up to the larger policy"?

What is the larger policy?

These are simple and definite questions, and the answers to them will decide whether Home Rule is or is not an issue in the coming election.

> Yours faithfully
> Edward Carson'

Of course his questions were not answered by his opponents, whose one object was to avoid the Irish question as a major issue; and indeed, for once, Ireland was forgotten. The last three elections of the nineteenth century had been fought on the Irish issue, and the first of the twentieth had been the 'khaki' election. The growing electorate in 1906 were interested in many things: in the Taff Vale judgment; Oriental labour in the Transvaal; above all, the fiscal question dominated the election. They were not particularly interested in Ireland. Yet, in every speech, Sir Edward reminded his audiences that a Liberal Government would mean trouble in Ireland, and that the days of political agitation would be renewed. 'Sir Henry Campbell-Bannerman,' he said at Putney, 'has once more raised the Home Rule flag, and I as an Irishman regret it. I regret it because I hoped that the recent legislation passed by the Unionist Government, under which extended local government was given to Ireland, and under which 120 millions of the taxpayers' money was either invested in or promised to that country, would have been allowed to work itself out and bring about, as we desire, beneficent results, without raising once again the question of the dismemberment of the Empire.' In another speech he said, 'It should never be forgotten that we are a Unionist Party, and it is our first duty to maintain the Union. There are forces gathering which may necessitate our girding ourselves once more to go forth to do battle for the good cause.'

In his advocacy of Protection he was anxious to show to the electorate that there need be no sudden change from the greatest measure of Free Trade to High Protection. He pleaded this issue with studied moderation. 'Why should this matter make everybody call each other names?' he asked. He placed the question as a matter of business before the people. He considered that the Protectionist zealots had played into the hands of the Free Traders by the extreme contrast which they drew between the two policies. 'Are you satisfied,' he had said in Manchester in February 1905, 'with fiscal conditions as they now stand, where English goods alone are taxed in the markets of the world? It is a gigantic business question for the nation. Are we going to refuse the hand which the Colonies hold out to us? There is no need of a great reversal of policy. We must act tentatively and scientifically. We must try and evolve by scientific arrangements some system which will put us on an equal footing with foreign countries in the great industrial competition in which we are now involved.'

Thus, with foreboding in his heart, Carson went up and down the country pleading that the cause for which he stood, the Union of England and Ireland, should not be forgotten in the wider discussion of proposals for fiscal reform, which would make possible a worldwide Union of the British Empire.

27. Opposition and Private Practice Again

The defeat was unexpected only in its overwhelming nature. The Conservatives and Liberal Unionists returned to Westminster with a total strength of 157. The Nationalists came back with 83 members. But the outstanding feature of the election was the Liberal majority of 84 over all parties, including the Labour Party, which emerged for the first time as a potent factor in British politics, with a roll of 53. This great Liberal victory had been obtained despite a division in their ranks hardly less serious than that among the Conservatives. Lord Rosebery, from the outset, had refused to serve under Sir Henry Campbell-Bannerman, who had fearlessly opposed the Anglo-Boer War in its inception and prosecution. The man upon whose shoulders the mantle of Gladstone had fallen was no political Elisha: yet, mediocre in his abilities as he was, he had sterling moral quality, and was not untypical of the genuine reaction in favour of reform which had swept over the country. Moreover, the Cabinet which he was able to gather together was indeed one of all the talents. With Asquith, Haldane, Morley, Bryce, Grey and Lloyd George in the Cabinet, and with Winston Churchill in a minor office, it was at once apparent that it was not only in numbers that the Liberals were superior to the forces of Toryism. For Balfour, although he was soon to find a seat in the City of London, had been defeated at Manchester, and Joseph Chamberlain was soon to become but a shadow of himself. Of the rest, the majority of that small band of men, from whom was to develop perhaps the most efficient and persistent Opposition of recent political history, the greater part were old men grown so grey and so well-beloved in the service of their constituencies that even so mighty a landslide did not affect their security. There was, indeed, one young barrister of outstanding brilliance, Mr F E Smith, whose political destiny was to be closely bound up with that of Carson. He was soon to challenge the Liberal Government at the outset in a maiden speech audacious in its insolence; but as yet no one knew his quality. Apart from Arthur Balfour, there was no parliamentarian of outstanding capacity in the Conservative Opposition except Sir Edward Carson. Upon him, therefore, there devolved a great duty. Despite his commanding position at the Bar, and the really cruel demands which this made upon his brain and body, Carson bent himself to the task of maintaining the traditions of His Majesty's Opposition, not only in the House of Commons, but on the public platform. Never since the days of Mr Gladstone's second Home Rule Bill had he worked with such devotion and abandon in the House of Commons. Nor was the task ever a light one. Of the Conservatives, for the most part veterans, who survived the landslide, only forty at most could be found to be active in the cut and thrust of debate. Arthur Balfour himself was never more brilliant; he soon impressed an unsympathetic assembly, which had been inclined to regard him at first with hostility and disdain, and Carson again sat beside him as his principal lieutenant, all the joy of battle once more lit in his heart. He did not underestimate the strength of the Liberal leaders, but this added all the more zest to the struggle. Almost at once F E Smith was attracted to this great advocate, and learnt to love and venerate him as he did few people in the world. The former's instant success at the London Bar, whither he had migrated from Liverpool on his election, soon won him the silk gown of a King's Counsel and a Rolls-Royce motor car. The latter won the envy of Carson's chauffeur, who had faithfully served him from the earliest days of motoring. At this time he drove his master about in an old-fashioned

Daimler, and tactfully but in vain suggested that Sir Edward should not be outdone by that swaggering young fellow F E Smith and his Rolls-Royce.

The Liberals at last enjoyed a majority which was independent of the Irish members. Their pronouncements upon Home Rule had been so ambiguous at the General Election that they could hardly have revived Mr Gladstone's proposals at once. For whatever reasons they had won their verdict, and it had not been on the question of the Union. It became understood that there would be no proposals for a separate Irish legislature during the life of the present Parliament, which might last for seven years, that the Government would proceed on the basis of Home Rule by instalments, and that the first of these instalments would be a Bill on the lines of the Dunraven-MacDonnell draft which had brought such a storm about the head of George Wyndham.

Meanwhile, it was clearly their duty to turn their hands to measures for the social reform of Great Britain herself, for which they had a clear mandate from the electorate; in the field of education, licensing and trade union law, there was a great weight of public opinion for a generous policy of Liberal reform. Not the smallest influence which had restored the Liberal Party and created the Parliamentary Labour Party was that of the judgment of the House of Lords in the Taff Vale case. This judgment decided that a trade union could be sued for the acts of its agents, and its funds annexed by successful plaintiffs in civil claims against it for damages. 'Conspiracy' is a wrong at common law, and conspirators are liable for any damage done in the pursuance of their conspiracy; the ordinary strike was clearly a conspiracy at common law; and, although the organisers of an industrial strike were expressly exempted by previous statutes from criminal liability, trade union funds, the very sinews of the movement, became liable to seizure.

Almost as soon as Parliament met after the election, the Government was called upon to deal with this question. The Labour Party at once introduced a measure of their own completely exempting trade unions from any form of civil liability, although a Royal Commission had sat and reported strongly against any such general immunity. The Government also, through the Attorney-General, Sir John Lawson Walton, introduced a Bill dealing with the same subject-matter. Under the Bill, however, trade unions and their executive committees were made responsible for certain breaches in the law committed by their members. Sir John, adopting the conclusions of the Royal Commission, insisted on the necessity of this provision: the other course, he said, would create a 'privileged proletariat'.

However, this safeguard so strongly antagonised the Labour Party, and even many Liberals, that the Government gave way, and it was the humiliating task of the Attorney-General to come down to the House of Commons and announce that the Government had surrendered to the trade unionists. And so the measure was passed, which seemed at the time to give complete and absolute immunity to trade unions to conspire, not only against their employers, but against the State, which undoubtedly led, twenty years later, to the General Strike.

This was the first blow to the prestige of the Government, as serious as it was unexpected. Upon Carson fell the duty of leading the attack. His speech on 3 August was merciless against Lawson Walton, who was a personal friend of his. But the Attorney-General had allowed himself to be used as a catspaw, and had done something of which Carson's nature was simply incapable. By his action Carson considered that Walton had degraded his profession and justified all the cheap sneers which are often made at the expense of lawyers. Carson's speech was a real philippic against his unfortunate colleague. 'There is no precedent for this,' he said, 'in all the laws of this country. What the Attorney-General ought to have said so as to make the thing quite complete was, "as regards wrongful acts committed by trade unions, all the laws of this realm, whether statute or common, are hereby repealed". ... Or he might have put it in another interesting form. He might have said, "The King can do no wrong; neither can a trade union".' Then, pointing a finger of scorn and accusation at the Attorney-General, he said, 'I want nothing more to condemn this proposal than the words of the Attorney himself, which he has now ignominiously eaten. The honourable and learned gentleman apparently thinks it consistent with the great office he holds, and with his high position in the profession and in this House, to come down now and say: "I told you on a previous occasion that black was black, and now I tell you that black is white". Is it any wonder that our profession is almost universally held in contempt by successive Houses? Anything more preposterous than the line that has been taken by His Majesty's Government with reference to the amendment I can hardly conceive, and it is all the more preposterous because we know what is the claim of honourable members below the gangway, a claim for immunity. The Government had that claim before them, and they came down to this House, and through the mouth of the Attorney-General denounced, in language which I will not myself dare to use, the proposal for the abolition of the rule of law that the wrongdoer should be made to redress his wrong. ... Such a policy the Royal Commission declared would be opposed to the very idea of law, order and justice. And what does the honourable and learned gentleman, the Attorney-General, do, who is accountable to the House for law, order and justice? I do not envy the position of the honourable and learned gentleman. Even with the emoluments of office, I should be sorry to be in the position of the Attorney-General who now proposes that which he has before denounced, and which a Royal Commission has declared to be opposed to the very idea of law, order and justice.' As if spurning the whole Liberal Front Bench, he turned to the Labour members. 'I do not pick any quarrel with the honourable members below the gangway. They know what they want. Indeed, I respect them; but, for my part, I believe that no one should be beyond the scope of the law. ... To me personally, and to my constituency, it matters nothing. If I have any interest in it at all, it is in the litigation which I foresee will necessarily arise on this Bill.'

When the Bill was completed in committee, and was reported to the House, Carson took occasion, to the surprise of his friends, to congratulate the House on having reached another stage in this Bill. But his congratulations were deeply ironical. There had been much discussion as to so-called 'peaceful picketing' and as to safeguards in the Bill to prevent 'besetting' and 'intimidation', and now the congratulations were given because, 'I had not the least doubt after what had already taken place in connection with this Bill since it was introduced, that if the same crop of concessions had gone on at the same rate, by the time we had reached the next stage not only would the word "peacefully" have disappeared, but we would have been asked to insert the words "with turmoil and violence". I cannot understand why this discussion is allowed to go on. Why does not the Attorney-General get up and say, "Just as I had to give way on a previous occasion with reference to the opinions I so strongly felt, and continue to feel, so here, now, I am prepared to throw over my principles"?'

In the course of the discussion, the unfortunate Lawson Walton had allowed himself to state that there might be some prejudice against trade unionists in the tribunals before which they appeared. Carson again fell upon him for this indiscretion. 'The Attorney-General is not yet satisfied, and so he must go on and attack the tribunals before which he has practised. He, the Attorney-General of this country, who ought to be the upholder of the administration of the law, has not hesitated on this occasion to bring forward the argument that they could not trust the tribunals before which he has practised.' Carson's concluding observations on this Bill were in the same vein of bitter irony. 'I regret,' he said, 'the ignominious surrender which the Government has made. ... It is most unfortunate that the Government has not shown itself able to resist the "peaceful persuasion" which has been addressed to it, and the "intimidation" which has resulted in an utter change of front.'

There has seldom been as bitter an attack by one member of the Bar against another in the House of Commons. The comradeship of the Bar usually makes them tender to one another. But Carson could show no tenderness where a man appeared to him to have been false to his political convictions, and he showed no tenderness here. Yet no more generous tribute to Lawson Walton came from anyone than from Carson in the following year, when the former was removed forever from the bitterness of Parliamentary strife. Presiding over the Primrose League, in the heart of the Tory citadel, Carson went out of his way to refer to the dead Attorney-General. 'It is to me a real personal loss. He was an enemy, and at the same time a great and dear friend. We have been opposed to each other very many times in the Law Courts, and we had bitter hostilities in the House of Commons, but during all the long years we were never

anything but the greatest real friends. I mourn his loss, and
I think the public does too.'

*   *   *

There are, perhaps, two main tenets, the protection of
property and the maintenance of the British Empire under
the Crown, for which modern English Conservatism stands.
These ideas were also the mainsprings of Carson's mature
political faith, and they are to be found clearly expressed in
all his political speeches. His best years and abilities were
given to the latter cause in special relation to the Union
between Britain and Ireland; but the new contentment in
Ireland arising from the Conservative land reforms, and
the decision of the Liberal Government not to introduce
as yet a third Home Rule Bill, enabled him for a time to go
outside the main stream of his political life, and to give his
advocacy to the former theme. For the Conservative the safe
possession of property is, after the protection of life itself,
the distinguishing mark of civilised society; and one of the
first duties of the State is to ensure it. The root objection
to Mr Lloyd George's legislation with regard to licensing
and the taxation of land in his 'people's budget' was that it
was of a confiscatory nature. The possession of property in
some form is widely distributed over the citizens of Great
Britain, and the suspicion that the State, instead of protecting
property, was actually confiscating it, undoubtedly led to the
reaction among the myriads interested in property in one
form or another, which again gave the balance of power to
the Irish Party and brought back the Irish question as the one
dominant issue. Moreover, had not the veto of the House of
Lords complicated the issue and estranged a large mass of
the electorate, the reaction of democracy would have gone

back, in full circle, to Conservatism. After their attacks on the Conservative Licensing Act, it was certain that the Liberal Party would redeem its pledges to its temperance reformers. The Conservative Act had, however, worked efficiently, having reduced the number of licensed houses at the rate of about 1 200 in one year. In their celebrated Licensing Bill of 1908, the Liberals proposed to effect a drastic reduction of public houses, at an accelerated pace, by allotting licences according to the density of the population. They also proposed to limit compensation to dispossessed licensees to a period of fourteen years. The controversy on the latter proposal raged around the academic question of whether the licence was or was not a form of property, or only an 'expectation'. It was conceded by both Liberals and Conservatives that, if a licence was in the nature of property, it was entitled to respect, even as against the cause of temperance. The whole of England became interested in this almost metaphysical discussion, and owners of all forms of property, quite apart from the half-million shareholders in brewery companies, began to feel insecure. The Bill was introduced in February 1908 by Mr Asquith, as Chancellor of the Exchequer, but by 4 May, when the Bill came up for second reading, he had succeeded Sir Henry Campbell-Bannerman. Mr Lloyd George, the new Chancellor, therefore moved the second reading. The contrast between the classical, sedate oratory of Asquith and the whirling rhetoric of his lieutenant was never more clearly discernible than in their two speeches introducing the Licensing Bill. On each occasion Sir Edward Carson led the Opposition, and his speech in opposition to Mr Lloyd George had a great effect in the country, and immensely strengthened the agitation against the Bill. The people's Chancellor had concluded a very emotional speech with a moving peroration. 'Whenever,' he said, 'you find these poor creatures gathered together whose brain is shattered; whenever you find human beings huddled together in loathsome squalor and wretchedness; whenever you find men living in a condition of vice and crime; they all bear testimony that drink is the prime agency in the creation of all this unsightly mass of pain and degradation; and I say that the Government would fail abjectly in its duty if, through any base fear of any force or combination of forces, they were to shrink from doing all in their power to cut out from the social organism this most malignant growth that drains the vitality of the nation.'

Carson then rose to reply for the Opposition. All the afternoon and evening he had sat on the front bench without eating, but before making his speech he had fortified himself with a half-bottle of the best Burgundy to strengthen him for the fight against the temperance men. Yet he began with extreme diffidence, and with an apology for assuming the place of his leader, Arthur Balfour, whose health kept him away. 'I have not the least ambition,' he said, 'I never have, to trespass on the patience of the House. I have no ambition to make speeches. On this occasion, however, it has fallen to my lot to wind up for the Opposition. I shall do my best, and that is the most that I can do. I listened to that very able speech of the Chancellor. It was a brilliant speech, and may I say that its peroration, although I think it was more suited to the platform than the House of Commons, very much affected me. The right honourable gentleman, although he differs from me in politics, I hope does not imagine for a moment that he abhors the evils of intemperance any more than I do. ... On the question of intemperance, I can assure him that I agree with every word he said. ... But he forgot to show us, and he could not explain to us, what was the connection between the number of licences and the amount of intemperance which he was so vividly depicting to the House. The truth is, there is no joy in any Bill proposed by the right honourable gentlemen opposite unless it does an injury to someone.' Then Carson began to deal with a deeper aspect of politics – the limitation to party legislation which every party must have in mind if its work is to be permanent. Under the party system, every Government must remember that it will be succeeded by another, probably by its bitterest opponents, and that if its work arouses too wide and deep an opposition, that work will surely be swept aside like chaff before the wind. 'You have never been able to settle much,' he said, 'since you came into power, and that is because you have refused to settle anything by taking away the sting as regards those to whom you are opposed.' He reminded the Government that not the brewers alone, but half a million people, were directly interested in the brewery trade, but that this was only the beginning of the discontent which the Bill was arousing. 'Members should be careful in establishing precedents of this kind, for a time-limit as to compensation for recognised interests may be applied to every species of property which derives its sanction from the House of Commons. Take the case of railways. I think I could make a very pathetic speech as to the community's relation to railways by asking where do they get their monopoly, and contending that, since the House of Commons has conferred this monopoly, it has the right to rescind it. Then there are tramway companies, gas companies, electric lighting companies, all of whom have received monopolies from this House, which, according to the argument that has been used, can rescind them by giving fourteen years' notice. That is the precedent you are laying down by this Bill. That is why great forces are being arrayed against you. ... The Chancellor asked me a question, and I will answer him. "Has the State," he asked, "the right to get back the monopoly which it gave?" I do not deny it. They have the right. The reason they have the right is because they have the power. Yes, sir, that is the real reason. ... I believe that, altogether above and beyond the opposition to this Bill, the fear of the country is that you are by this measure creating a precedent as regards other property, and, so far as I am concerned, I will with all my heart oppose it.'

This was an immensely effective speech, and, on sitting down, Sir Edward received a great ovation. His old friend and Viceroy, Lord Londonderry, sitting up in the Peers' Gallery, could hardly restrain himself from applauding. He went at once and wrote a note of congratulation: 'My dear Edward, I must write you one line on your speech. It was *magnificent*: you simply pulverised the other side. It took all my time to prevent myself applauding you from the Peers' Gallery. *Well done*, you.'

Carson's haunting diffidence has been clearly shown in the opening of this speech. He was generally growing to be considered the future leader of the party. He knew this, and the prospect held no allurement for him. He could not think of himself as the supplanter of his beloved Arthur Balfour, and he had no confidence in his abilities beyond the Irish issue, to which he regarded himself as wedded. 'If you go on like this, Ned,' said Sir Thomas Comyn Platt, one of his intimate friends and admirers, as the two walked down the steps of the Carlton Club, 'you'll be Prime Minister.' 'How would I be Prime Minister?' said this incurably modest man. 'What would I ever know of foreign affairs?'

Yet, during any of these years, the leadership of the Tories would have been his for the asking; indeed, had it not been for a combination of causes, personal to himself, it must have fallen into his lap. Balfour's indecision on the Tariff issue; his aloofness from the rank and file of the party, despite his brilliant fencing in debate, was making his retirement from the leadership only a question of time; and no one stood as high in the party's esteem and regard as Sir Edward Carson. There was not a man, save Balfour, of his intellectual quality among the Tories. No one could attack in the House of Commons as he could. In directness of character, singleness of purpose, in contempt for the things of this world, he stood alone; he charmed all who knew him; and the future was to show that above all things he was a leader of men. In October 1908 he was chosen by the Unionist Committee at Aberdeen University to stand against the new Prime Minister, Mr Asquith, for the Lord Rectorship. The women students, suffragettes all, supported him against Mr Asquith, 'who imprisons British women rather than grant them the measure of justice to which they are entitled'. The Unionist literature urged his election because 'Carson is a brilliant orator, and Asquith is a dull dog'. Although he was defeated by 434 votes to 370, the fact that he was selected to oppose the Prime Minister in this classic annual contest shows the reputation he was gaining, especially among the youth of the country. It seemed as if, almost against his will, he would be forced into the first place. Indeed, had not been for his preoccupation with Ireland, his heavy practice in the Courts, his almost morbid distrust of his health, and his incurable modesty, the place must surely have been his.

28. Redmond, Birrell and 'Limehouse'

However, just when Carson was beginning to take the lead in the field of British politics, Ireland called out to him once more, and, while political controversy raged round the Licensing Bill, which the Lords threw out without alienating the sympathies of the nation as a whole, there were graver matters which called for the attention of thoughtful people. In Europe the German Emperor was challenging the supremacy of the British Admiralty by a most ambitious naval programme, and in Ireland disorder had broken out once more. On 9 November 1908, Carson made a speech at Oxford to the Stafford Club which ridiculed the indifference of the Government. 'When Europe,' he said, 'is seething with unrest, when Ireland is in chaos, when the unemployed are knocking at our gates, not one word are we allowed to speak on matters of imperial or national interest, but we spend our time solemnly discussing whether a policeman who is to enter a club is to be in or out of his uniform.'

Ireland, indeed, was in chaos once more. The benevolent Conservative land reforms had indeed removed the agrarian grievance so far as the tenants were concerned. By March 1909, 228 958 tenants had signed agreements in the previous five years for the purchase of their farms. But a new and more dangerous agitation had grown up, in the interests of not the tenants, but the landless. In 1897, William O'Brien had founded the United Irish League, for the purpose of assisting the landless to acquire an interest in their native soil. The large grazing farms became the object of attack by this organisation, and it spread far and wide with its many branches all over the country. Nevertheless, under the Conservative Government, the lawless methods of the agitators made little progress against the Crimes Act, and when Mr Birrell took office in 1906 he was able to give testimony as to the peace and contentment which prevailed over the land. It was impossible for a Government which had so long denounced the Crimes Act to retain its procedure, and once more Ireland was restored to the rule of its ordinary juries and magistrates. Moreover, the Liberal Government likewise decided not to renew the Peace Preservation Act, under which the importation of arms into Ireland was forbidden.

The failure to enforce the first and to renew the second Act had grave results in the history of Ireland; the lapse of the latter Act, strongly criticised by Sir Edward Carson at the time, was to be relied on by him in one of the most audacious actions ever perpetrated by a subject under the British Crown. In contrast to the melancholy progress of events which constitute the history of Ireland during the five years preceding the introduction of the third Home Rule Bill, one happy event for which Carson had worked for many years against the wishes of his political friends stands out clearly. For to the Ulstermen he was still only a brilliant Dublin man, who happened to agree with them on most subjects. His opinion did not yet run as the law of the land. In 1909, the British Parliament founded a real National and Catholic University for Ireland. In the debate, his junior colleague for Trinity College, Mr James Campbell, afterwards Lord Glenavy, who had succeeded Lecky, strongly criticised the measure, and the Irish Unionists voted almost in a body against the Bill for the sake of the Protestant religion. Carson, however, ignored their representations and those of many of his constituents, and made his last appeal for the Catholic University. 'I think,' he said, 'that the debate should not close without some speech being made different in tone from that of my right honourable colleague representing Dublin University. I may hold views that do not entirely commend themselves even to many of those who think with me in Ireland. I believe it is the duty of every Irishman, of whatever creed or politics, to wish godspeed to these Universities, and do his best, in a spirit of noble generosity, to make them a great success; and I hope that the bringing of them into existence may be a step forward in the union of all classes and religions in Ireland for the progress of our country and its education.'

This speech, delivered at a time when the disturbed state of Ireland was making the Government of that country a subject of bitter disputation between Carson and Birrell and the Southern Irish members, and in vivid contrast to his usual fighting speech, was recognised as the sincere expression by an implacable opponent of his generous nature. The heart of the House of Commons was touched, and Mr Birrell, so often the target for Carson's attacks, announced that 'the remarkable and striking speech to which we have just listened has made me, I am willing to confess, a happy man.'

He received many letters of congratulation from distinguished men and old friends on this speech. The Provost of Trinity, Anthony Traill, wrote: 'My dear Carson, – I write a line to congratulate you on your splendid speech last night, which made Birrell a "happy man". You spoke my mind exactly. I have lost no opportunity here, public or private, in putting forth the same views. I am disappointed with Campbell's speech, but perhaps he thinks his seat not quite as sure as yours, and has therefore to "speak for a certain gallery". Yours sincerely, Anthony Traill.'

His friend and colleague of old days, Sir Dunbar Plunket Barton, at that time a judge in Ireland, also wrote him a charming and affectionate letter. 'My dear Ned,' he wrote, 'I waited to read your speech in *The Times* and now write to congratulate you on its success. It was a most timely and effective speech. It makes your friends, like myself, proud of you. It would have seemed ungracious and unfitting, if no such speech had been made from your bench. The true Unionist statesman ought, while maintaining law and order and all essential institutions and rights, to seize any reasonable opportunity of wishing godspeed, as you have done, to every legitimate effort to raise Ireland to something better and higher in culture and education. Believe me that you raise yourself by doing so more than you realise. Yours ever, D P Barton.' Another letter from an Irishman said of this speech: 'To have heard it was an event in my life.' Testimony as to Orange opinion came in a letter from the Ulster Club, Belfast: 'Dear Sir Edward Carson, – I cannot refrain from expressing the deep satisfaction with which I read your speech on the Universities Bill. I think the course taken by Ulster Unionist members shows a complete want of appreciation of the real merits of the situation and a really purblind political judgment. ... We should have gained much by adopting a more sympathetic attitude even on the part of those who are only reconciled to accepting the inevitable. Yours faithfully, Adam Duffin.'

*   *   *

With the relaxation of the criminal law and a return to unpaid magistrates and common juries, the agitators of the landless came into their own. Their victims were now not only the Saxon landlord, but every farmer who owned too much of the sacred Irish soil. Such was the state of public opinion in Ireland, fanned by men like Lawrence Ginnell, that it was well-nigh impossible to obtain convictions before common juries; moreover, even magistrates refused to do their duty. With the object of breaking up the large grazing grounds, the stock belonging to prosperous graziers was seized by night and day, and driven and scattered miles away over the countryside. If their owners ever recovered them, the poor creatures were found starved or mutilated, and all the barbarities of the 'boycott' were again revived against the enemies of the new 'Plan of Campaign'. The political agitators, literary and rhetorical, were of course spared the martyrdom of prosecution, and juries and magistrates had perhaps some reason in refusing convictions against the humble and ignorant peasants, whom speeches and leading articles had persuaded and encouraged to break the law.

By the autumn of 1907, the same year in which Mr Birrell had paid his famous tribute to the peace and contentment of the island, conditions were once more so serious in Ireland that the Government became alarmed. By the Irish Council Bill of that year they had attempted to carry out the MacDonnell-Dunraven proposals, and to redeem their pledge of 'Home Rule by instalments'. Mr John Redmond, leader of the Irish Party, sympathetic in London, when he crossed to Ireland, found the force of Irish opinion too strongly opposed to the proposal, and it was condemned at a great meeting at the Mansion House in Dublin. The Bill was withdrawn, and the Liberal Government was left without a policy; for they were determined not to allow Home Rule to be the dominant issue at a General Election. It will be seen later how this issue was never again allowed to become the dominant issue at an election, although it was to dominate Parliament itself for many years and to be the cause, more than once, of rebellion and civil war. There were only two courses now to be pursued by the Liberals: devolution, the way of compromise, was dead. They had to choose, as Mr Gladstone had done, between the Crimes Act, which meant enforcement of the law, and a bold policy of Home Rule, mandate or no mandate. They chose neither: as Mr Tim Healy observes in his book, Liberal principle died with Mr Gladstone. The Liberals had so often denounced the Crimes Act as tyranny that they dared not use it now. 'What,' said Mr Birrell, 'was the position of the Liberal Party? They opposed the permanent Coercion Act with all their vehemence. We have year after year voted for the repeal of it, and to ask us to put it into force, except upon a case of overwhelming magnitude, is simply ridiculous.' There comes a time when statesmen should be bold and confess their faults. This the Liberals refused to do, and so cut themselves off from the only way in which they could undertake the obligations of government in Ireland. And so for four long years they allowed the administration of the law to fall into even greater contempt, and the condition of the country to degenerate once more into lawlessness and anarchy. As early as November 1907, Carson was able to quote in a letter to *The Times* a charge of Judge Curran to an Irish grand jury, which graphically describes the condition of the country: 'Bodies of men, secretly at night, and in many cases armed with sticks and staves, breaking locks and gates, have driven out and scattered over the country the cattle of their neighbours, with the intention of terrorising them into complying with their demands. One can scarcely credit we are living in a civilised country. No mercy has been shown to these parties by their opponents, who are merciless in their persecution.' Mr Birrell admitted that magistrates were refusing to convict in perfectly plain cases, but maintained that the Government 'had done all that a Government can do within the powers of the law to put these things down.' The Attorney-General for Ireland acknowledged that in certain parts of Ireland conditions were worse than those existing among savages on the West Coast of Africa. Quiet, law-abiding citizens did not know when their cattle would be seized and mutilated, or when a bullet would come through their windows, yet for two years there was hardly a conviction. Carson concluded his letter to *The Times* with these words: 'Sir, but for the seriousness of the subject-matter, one might feel amused at this farcical comedy. But some of us wonder how long these things will continue under British rule.'

For the next four years all Carson's political efforts were directed towards compelling the Government either to enforce the law or to declare openly for a specific Home Rule Bill so that the electors could decide. It was his fear that after elections fought on other issues, the Government would introduce a Home Rule Bill and claim a mandate, after affairs in Ireland had been allowed to reach a condition of hopelessness owing to the weakness of justice and government. In the event, precisely what he feared came to pass, in spite of his strenuous and vigilant attempts to prevent just this thing from happening.

In November 1907, to increase this bitterness against the Government, two of his own kinsfolk, a landowner and his mother, as they were leaving their church on a Sunday, had been murdered. On 8 December, at Macclesfield, he made a memorable speech which attracted general notice. 'My own kinsmen,' he said, in tones of great emotion, 'only three or four weeks ago, were shot as they were leaving their worship on Sunday in the presence of a jeering and cheering crowd. This is a disgrace to civilisation under the British flag. I warn the Government and Mr Birrell that no man ever made a greater mistake than to play with crime in Ireland. I speak vehemently as an Irishman to the English people, and say that if you are not prepared to govern Ireland according to the ordinary elementary conditions of civilisation that prevail in every country, then get out of Ireland and leave us to govern ourselves. ... I was born and bred loyal to your sovereign, who is my sovereign. I was taught at my mother's knee that no nation, either in history or at the present day, was so keen and anxious for justice and liberty as the English nation. I believed it. I am beginning to doubt it when I see people in this country standing up and giving consideration and welcome to those who they know have only one object, and that to sever your country from mine. I do not like to make changes, but it almost seems to me that when the Radical Government deliberately refuses to put the law in motion against ringleaders who are carrying out a nefarious system of crushing down liberty – because they happen to be members of Parliament who support them in the House of Commons, and yet go through the pretence of prosecuting the dupes and corner boys who carry out the behests of the ringleaders – I say that the time has come when loyal Englishmen should pull themselves together, make their voices heard, and let the Government know that these are things they will not tolerate. We are in despair in Ireland. There is no use mincing matters: we are in despair, because we have asked the Government to enforce the law indiscriminately against all law-breakers, and we have failed to get any favourable response.' The reader is asked to remember Carson's exhortation to 'govern Ireland or get out'. This was 'the reality of the situation' in 1907, and it was not recognised until, after fifteen years of civil war, strife, vacillation and compromise, the Coalition Government adopted the latter course.

In every public speech he made, Carson tried to bring home to the comfortable people of England who came to political meetings the true state of affairs in Ireland, where 'Captain Boycott' was allowed to stalk through the land. In February 1909, he said to a meeting at Brierly Hill: 'Do you know what a boycott in Ireland means? Do you know that a mother cannot get milk for her dying babe; and that it will be allowed to die, simply, forsooth, because the father or mother is under the boycott? A farmer cannot go to bed without knowing there is a chance that next morning he may find his cattle with their tails cut off or their eyes gouged out. It is a state of savagery, and a blot on the English name.' There was a great increase in the number of attacks with firearms, and the responsibility for these murders and other crimes Carson fastened on the Liberal Government, which had allowed the Peace Preservation Act to lapse and so 'put the arms into the hands of these men'.

In the House of Commons he threw himself once again into the field of Irish politics, and, by his constant and devastating attacks on the inactivity of the Irish office, he disturbed into anger even the kindly equanimity of Augustine Birrell, who complained that Carson was 'offensive and disagreeable'. Mr Asquith, too, usually imperturbable, was stirred into an irritable restlessness before the Irishman's accusations, as he reclined on the Treasury Bench.

He had an opportunity, on 4 February 1908, to raise the whole question on the Conservative amendment to the address which regretted 'that the speech of His Gracious Majesty has failed to refer to the increase of agrarian crime and disorder in Ireland', or to give any assurance as to the adoption of measures for the better protection of the lives or properties of His Majesty's subjects. He had been taunted by one of the Irish members as a tyrant and as 'Coercion Carson' in the old days of the land war. 'If this was meant as a reproach,' retorted Carson, 'I will only say that there is a great difference between the view of the honourable member and myself. He advocates the coercion of the mob. I advocate, if necessary, the coercion of the law, and if I, in my earlier legal days, were engaged in pulling down tyranny and intimidation in Ireland, I tell him at once that, even after this longish period, when I can perhaps take a better perspective view of the situation, I can say that I have done nothing which I in the least regret, or of which I am in the least ashamed.' Birrell had referred to most of the cases of 'boycotting', which had increased from the previous year to 116, as being of a 'minor character'. 'There are only nine cases where a man has carried a life in his hands,' answered his merciless antagonist. 'So, these others are *minor* cases. What are these *minor* cases? ... One of them was that of a lady who left Sligo to seek employment in Longford. Because her father was boycotted in Sligo, when she obtained employment at Longford, she was turned out of it by the ban of the League. What is the next? A man refused to leave the employment that he had been in for twenty years, and when he died his own brother was refused timber to make a coffin that he could be buried in. And what was the third one? It was that of an old woman who for over twenty years had received at the hands of the parish priest a few pounds for cleaning out the chapel, and, because her husband remained in an employment that was not popular, this poor woman was compelled by the priest, at the dictation of the League, to give up that employment. These are cases of *minor* boycotting, and they have increased from 24 to 116 under the kindly and beneficent rule of the right honourable gentleman during the last twelve months. ... I was glad to hear him last night describe boycotting as the negation and repudiation of Christianity. ... But how many men has the right honourable gentleman brought to justice during the last twelve months for the negation and repudiation of Christianity? Not one. Ponder this fact for a moment. ... In addition, we have 381 cases of cattle-driving in five or six months, and not a dozen convicted. ... I think a more disastrous speech than the one delivered by the right honourable gentleman last night has seldom been delivered in this House by a responsible statesman. ... With these statistics of crime before him as to the paralysis of the law, all he says is, "I shall do nothing". He has given us a reason for allowing this state of things to go on. He has told us that after all you must look at the origin of the crime, and the hopes held out to these people. Ah, I wish I had plenty of time to argue that question with him. All I can say is, no more dangerous proposition can be laid down by this House than that pending the redress of grievances you are to allow people any latitude in the commission of crime. I do not know how far this is to be allowed to go on, but, if you are going to say, because there is not enough land to go round in Ireland, therefore you are to excuse and palliate deeds of this kind, I say you are preaching Socialism pure and simple, and Socialism of a more advanced type, I venture to think, than anything that has been put forward by honourable members inside or outside the House, who are said to have raised the Red Flag.'

If Mr Birrell's philosophical composure had occasionally been disturbed by this bitter attack, it was soon restored; he had also been deeply impressed by the speech, and wrote a letter to Carson on the following day from the Irish Office, which is a striking example of the personal friendliness which men, bitterly opposed on questions of policy, can show to each other. But the great gulf that was fixed between the two men on policy is also clearly apparent behind the friendliness.

'Irish Office
Wed, 5 Feb, 1908

My dear Carson, – Now that we have got cattle-driving out of the way (possibly, I agree, only for a time), I should like very much to have a confidential chat over the University question. Any time you like to name, and any day, in my room here, will suit me.

I thought, if I may say so, you spoke with great force last

night, and you will, I am sure, heartily believe that I am not blind to the dangers of the situation. But your argument really amounted almost to this, that, when there are half a dozen really bad cases of tyranny and oppression which the ordinary law is powerless to protect, the ordinary law should be superseded and justice done, at any cost and at whatever risks. I can't go as far as that.

I may have been wrong in not putting Ginnell on his trial. He would, of course, have got off. Edward the Third[1] of blessed memory doesn't apply to such cases as his: but I don't believe one bit in G's influence or that the cattle-drivers were his "dupes", although I do recognise that a Dublin or Cork or Limerick jury, anxious to justify their perjury, clutched at the argument presented for the defence, that it was a great shame to prosecute these cattle-drivers and let off the orator! I had not thought of this. But I have no right to bore you with my meditations after the battle.

A B'

If his efforts had deeply impressed his opponents, his friends were transported with delight: several among them could not rest that night until they had written to him. Sir Ian Malcolm wrote from the Carlton Club, 'My dear Carson, – I can't go to bed without telling you how greatly impressed I was by your speech – far the finest thing in the debate; for it soared to a level that nobody else could touch. I never saw a Government so punctured, nor a Minister so miserable, nor a party so hushed, as the feeble horde that had to face your terrible denunciation. It made me proud to be connected even in the humblest way with the work you are doing. – Yours, Ian Malcolm.'

[1] An old statute of Edward III was used in certain cases for prosecutions in Ireland.

Walter Long, the leader of the Irish Unionists, wrote in the same vein: 'My dear Carson, – I can't go to bed without thanking you for your magnificent wind up. I know how great a strain it entailed upon an overworked man, but it meant a very great deal to this country and the party, and makes me wish with all my heart you could give more time to politics. Once more a thousand thanks. – Yours ever, Walter H Long.'

A telegram of congratulation came from Dublin, sent by the Lord Chief Justice – Peter the Packer of old days – the next morning, and Carson was overwhelmed with other congratulations.

This was only the first of a series of memorable speeches with which he raked the Government Front Bench on their Irish policy. He derived a melancholy satisfaction, in a debate on the Irish Estimates, from showing that the fees of the Law Officers for Ireland in respect of prosecutions, when there were scarcely any convictions and disorder was rampant, had nearly trebled 'in this year of grace and conciliation that of the average year of the "wicked coercionists". The Attorney-General,' he said, 'thinks that cattle-driving has largely been put down by abortive prosecutions. Therefore, in future, the law will be administered in this way. Juries will be advised not to convict, as it is more successful to acquit than to convict. ... But for my part, I know nothing that could have a worse effect than day after day exhibiting to the public who were inclined to break the law, the paralysis of the law itself.'

A year later matters had become even worse in Ireland, and in the debate on the address on 24 February 1909, Carson gave an even greater warning to the Government, and challenged them to face the electorate boldly with their constructive policy: in the course of this speech he turned away from Mr Birrell for a moment, and challenged Mr John Redmond to cross over at once and denounce the crime in Ireland, which he professed to disapprove.

'Is it denied,' he said, 'by anyone that the position of Ireland is deplorable? It is deplorable: it is growing worse. ... The honourable and learned member for Waterford [Mr John Redmond] gave the House a great deal of information last night about crime in England. Nobody doubts it. But what is the whole difference between crime in England and crime in Ireland? It is that in Ireland crime is organised for the purpose of stamping out liberty, whereas in England it is sporadic, the work of individuals, sometimes from malice, sometimes due to poverty and various other causes. ... Every day I read of people being summoned before the Land League Courts, and fined by decrees of the Land League. ... I read of persons who have attended before the League, and at its dictation, and through terror, have surrendered their farms. The right honourable gentleman has been again and again attacked for not putting the Crimes Act into operation. I quite understand that he never can, and never will, use the Crimes Act: I think it quite vain to keep rubbing the Crimes Act into the right honourable gentleman. He dare not use it. How could he? He has said over and over again that he would never use it. ... The country, according to the right honourable gentleman's own view, was, when the present Government came into office, quieter that it had been for six hundred years. Yet in two years a situation has been produced the gravity of which can hardly be exaggerated. ... I should like to say a few words about the non-renewal of the Peace Preservation Act, because to my mind it is one of the most serious acts done by the Government. I ask the Chief Secretary this question. Does he say there is no connection between the refusal to renew the Act and the increase of outrages by firearms? It is a very simple question.'

Finally Carson put plainly to them the only honourable

alternative to the Crimes Act. 'As the honourable and learned member for Waterford said last night, the alternative of the Liberal Government is at once to bring in a Home Rule Bill, and to put the whole responsibility on to the Irish people. That is not your policy. You have undertaken not to bring in a Home Rule Bill, at all events during the present Parliament, and as far as I am concerned it is an issue likely to be removed as far as possible from the next General Election. Is it devolution? You told us you had a mandate to bring in a Devolution Bill. It was rejected, not by the House of Lords, but by the Irish Convention. ... The situation under the present Government is an impossible one. You are not prepared to follow out to its logical conclusion your Home Rule theory; you are not prepared to take your courage in your hands and ask the electors what they think of your Home Rule theory. I say that any Government that wavers between Home Rule and Unionism is doomed to failure.'

Only one major Bill of a constructive nature in relation to Ireland was brought forward by the Government during these years – the Irish Land Bill of 1909. Owing to the fall in value of Government securities, which was the basis of Wyndham's Act, the financing of the Act had broken down, and expenses of the purchases fell heavily on the Treasury and the Irish ratepayers. Birrell introduced a measure in effect decreasing the bonus payable to the landlords, and raising the annuity payable by the purchasing tenant; but these very proposals were calculated, by making land purchase less attractive to both landlord and tenant, to discourage and obstruct the peaceful revolution which was going on. Whereas the purchases of land under Wyndham's Act had been on the basis of voluntary agreement between landlord and tenant, Birrell also proposed to give powers for the compulsory acquisition of land by the State for distribution among the landless. These proposals Carson regarded as the triumph of the League, and as a surrender to the crime and lawlessness of the past three years. Carson remembered bitterly the talk of a 'final Irish Land Bill' in 1903, and dealt with the whole question in his speech on the second reading of the Bill on 31 March 1909. 'Agreement,' he said, 'which was the basis of the Bill, is being torn up. Compulsion is being introduced. Now is it not a pity – is it not more than that; is it not almost a crime – not to make some real effort to promote the carrying on of the work which has been done? ... There is not one line which will accelerate land purchase. Agreements are waiting completion to the extent of £56 000 000, but the financial provisions have broken down. After coming here and saying you are not able to carry out in any reasonable time the commitments which have been entered into voluntarily, you proceed to ask for powers for compulsion. Just consider the situation: £56 000 000 worth of agreements to be carried out! Tenants and landlords rushing over each other into the office to try and get their agreements, and the right honourable gentleman is so enamoured that he means to bring in these compulsory powers. ... This ought to have been an agreed Bill, because all of us now admit that the question of transfer from landlords to tenants must be carried out: the only point remaining is how best to finance the matter. I certainly would not lay down that every man in Ireland who sufficiently agitates is to get land, and that is what the Bill lays down: so it is. Do you contemplate where you are going? Do you contemplate what you are doing when you lay down that principle? Do you contemplate what the extension of it will be?'

At the end of 1908 and 1909, Ireland, which Carson bitterly described as 'the football of political parties', was again at the forefront of political controversy. Ireland was the 'running sore' of Liberal administration, and its administration was becoming well known as a public scandal. It looked as though the Liberal Government would be forced to give in to Carson's importunities and to fight the next election on the issue of Home Rule. In that event there was little doubt in the minds of political managers that the Tories would once more have swept the country. Mr Lloyd George is reported to have said at the end of 1908 that the Liberals would not come back more than one hundred and fifty strong. After the death of Campbell-Bannerman, the whole inspiration for reform, which had brought them to power, seemed to have ceased. As Carson said in a public speech, 'There never was a Government which came into power with greater opportunities than the present. It had the largest majority on record, but at the end of two years it has lost the confidence of the country. Once the waves begin to flow in against the Government, they soon increase in force until it is swamped.'

Had it not been for one thing, the Government would have been compelled to take their courage in both hands and face defeat on the Irish issue when their popularity was at a low ebb. The country was thoroughly tired of the indeterminate Tory aristocrats in 1906, but now it was equally weary of the indecisive Liberal lawyers. Each Government had failed to make a decision on the main issue, in one case on Tariff Reform, in the other on Home Rule, and it seemed as if the people, once sickened by privilege, were now disillusioned by reform, and that this Government would share the fate of its predecessor. Was there no way of stemming the tide of the popular reaction? There was, indeed, one issue on which the general will might be aroused – the question of the House of Lords. By absolute power of veto, the Peers had jettisoned a series of Bills, introduced by the Liberals, which included the Licensing Bill. The English people, willing enough to assent to general principles of reform, but always opposed to prohibitions and concrete restrictions, had hardly stirred. Men were inclined to say: 'Thank God we have a House of Lords'. There was, however, one limit, though only at the highest a constitutional convention, to the powers of the House of Lords. It was a cherished tradition that the Commons alone had power to decide the raising of finance in the annual Budget. There had been disputes between the two Houses, but on the whole the claim of the Commons had prevailed. On the other hand, the Lords had from time immemorial given their 'assent' to the Finance Bill each year, and could claim to reject it as a strict matter of right. At about Christmas 1908, Mr Winston Churchill and Mr Lloyd George began to attack the House of Lords with especial vehemence, but the country was inclined to agree with Carson when he attacked them bitterly as a pair of buffoons, and said: 'All this palaver of theirs about the House of Lords is a kind of Christmas pantomime.' But it was not pantomime, as the early months of 1909 clearly revealed.

Whether the events which followed mark the results of deliberate policy to frustrate the 'knavish tricks' of the Tories, and win back the popular favour, is a secret locked within the hearts of the surviving Liberal leaders of that day, and may never be a matter of official political history; but the facts speak for themselves. Mr Lloyd George in 1909 introduced into his Budget proposals, embodying the ideas of Henry George, for the taxation of land values. Eventually the taxes were to become part of the law of the land; they were to be in force for a decade, and the expense of organising them was to exceed the revenue they raised. But, spectacular failure that they proved to be in practice, these proposals left their mark in history: from the introduction of these taxes there came, as a direct result, the Parliament Act and the third Home Rule Bill. These specious land proposals, glorified by

Lloyd George's imaginative rhetoric, had all the elements of popularity. Never had such matters, which really amounted to new legislation of a most drastic, complex and far-reaching character, been included in the annual Finance Bill. If the Commons denied the right of the Lords to reject the Budget, the Lords could logically reply that this Budget was not a measure to raise revenue for the year, but a Land Bill to place burdens upon one form of property forever. How cleverly was the net spread in sight of the bird. All summer the battle raged in the House of Commons, and Carson was once more in the thick of the fray, sitting up night after night into the small hours arguing intricate amendments, designed to stultify the new taxes, and denouncing the whole plan in general terms. 'Many of us believe,' he said, 'that this is an unjust and impossible tax, but we all look upon the machinery under this Bill as vague, arbitrary, tyrannous and fraudulent.' So successful, however, was the opposition in the Commons, that the Bill, when presented to the Lords, was shorn of many of its principal objections, and the Lords could have consented, had they willed, to a very costly measure for the taxation of land, which, however, left the rights of property quite secure, and could have been repealed in the first week of a Conservative administration. So heavy were the disadvantages of rejection of the Budget by the Peers that many were in favour of acquiescence. The view began to prevail that the Lords should let the emasculated Bill go by, and it was said that the Liberal managers were mightily afraid that the counsels of moderation would prevail. Then Mr Lloyd George, who had argued his Bill in the Commons, 'like any political Dr Jekyll', with great tact and patience, added fuel to the flames by his Limehouse speech in July, in which he appeared as a veritable Mr Hyde and put the Lords in the dock as a class, and with all the vocabulary of ridicule and invective, and amid every demonstration of extraordinary popular support, appealed to the people. 'Without you we can do nothing; with you, we can brush the Lords aside like chaff before the wind.'

If his intention was to harden the opposition in the House of Lords, he was completely successful. Those wise people in the Tory citadel who counselled moderation saw that their cause was lost, and many of them were converted to the other view. Carson, whose speeches as regards the course pursued by the Lords had been cautious, now came out openly for rejection by the Lords and immediate dissolution. For him the gloves were off. He regarded Lloyd George's speech as pandering to class hatred of the worst kind. He described him as a 'demagogue and a *farceur* who had graduated in abuse.'

'May I suggest,' he wrote to *The Times*, 'that the speech yesterday made by the Chancellor of the Exchequer opens a new page in political controversy? In the House of Commons the Chancellor has been posing as a Minister anxious to meet objections to the Finance Bill, and as a responsible trustee for the public welfare and peace. In his speech at Limehouse, Mr Lloyd George has taken off the mask and has preached openly a war of the classes, the satiation of greed, and the excitement of all the passions which make possible the momentary triumph of the unscrupulous demagogue. ... The shallow pretence of discussing finance is given up. The result appears inevitable that, before such a policy can prevail, it must be endorsed by the people, and the sooner that opportunity is given, the better for the nation. All necessity for discussing constitutional precedents is now at an end, when a Minister of the Crown responsible for the finance of the country proclaims that he is about to legislate, not for a Budget, but for a revolution.'

The Lords rejected the Budget in *toto*; nor did they temper the edge of their veto. Lord Milner's 'Let us reject the Budget and damn the consequences' roused a howl of democratic indignation. And so His Majesty was left with no supply for the year. An immediate dissolution followed, which could not in any event be delayed for long, and might have been fought with very different results to the nation and to the parties. The Liberals, by accident or design, had been given exactly the battleground that they would have chosen for themselves. Ireland was forgotten; the unpopularity and shortcomings of four years were forgiven. The Liberals could no longer appeal to the people on the grounds of lofty ideals and constructive reform, but they could say: 'The Lords have thrown out the people's Budget because their interests as landowners were assailed'. Lloyd George's words rang round the country. 'Without you we can do nothing; with you, we can brush the Lords aside like chaff before the wind.' Thus, in a wonderful election campaign, he was able to reap the benefits of the storm which he had himself aroused by his Limehouse speech. Without that the Lords might well have accepted the Budget, and staked their hopes on a reversal of its land provisions after the General Election resulting in a Conservative victory.

So, beyond their hopes, were the Liberals saved from the consequences which usually befall an Administration of whom the country has grown tired.

29. Cadbury v Standard Newspapers

On the very day on which the Lords threw out the contentious Budget, after a debate of high distinction, on the democratic ground that they were not justified in giving their assent to the Bill until it had been submitted to the judgment of the people, and during the week in which Mr Asquith introduced into the Commons a motion censuring the Lords for unconstitutional action and calling for a dissolution and an election on the broad issue of 'Peers against People', Sir Edward Carson was engaged for seven days on the Midland Circuit in a case in which the interests of politics, the Press, morality and big business were curiously intermingled. The case was tried at Birmingham by Mr Justice Pickford, afterwards Lord Sterndale. The weather was bitterly cold, and, although Carson's fee was in the nature of a king's ransom, he determined that no financial consideration would ever induce him to face the discomforts of a provincial hotel for a week. Indeed, it was the last case he ever fought on circuit. Carson appeared in an action for libel for the defendants, the Standard Newspapers, a Conservative newspaper association which controlled the *Standard*, the *Evening Standard* and the *St James's Gazette*. He led a distinguished team of colleagues – Mr Eldon Bankes KC, afterwards a Lord Justice, Mr H A McCardie, afterwards the bachelor Judge, Mr Profume and Mr St John Field. He was opposed, as he usually had been in all the great *causes célèbres* of the last four years, by Mr Rufus Isaacs KC, who was supported by Mr John Simon KC, Mr Norman Craig and Mr H H Joy. Rufus Isaacs's clients were Cadbury Bros, the famous Birmingham manufacturers of 'Bournville' cocoa and chocolate. The Cadbury family came of fine Quaker and Radical stock, and, indeed, were one of the main pillars of the Liberal Party and Free Trade. However, they controlled the *Daily News*, the principal Radical newspaper of national importance, which had at the previous General Election most violently denounced the Conservative Government for allowing Chinese indentured labour in the Transvaal, and condemned it as slavery; and now they were taking action among their own people of Birmingham, near which their world-famous Bournville factories were situated, to defend their honour against a charge of conniving at slave conditions in the production of their own raw material.

For Messrs Cadbury were famous, not only for their wonderful chocolate, but for philanthropy, both to their employees and in a more general way. Their great family concern was a private company with a capital of £2 000 000. Like the firm of Messrs Lever, whose celebrated case against the *Daily Mail* will be recounted next, the story of their vast undertaking is a romance; as in the action of Messrs Lever, their case was tried among their own people; and, like Messrs Lever, they were model employers. But chocolate cannot be made alone by the efforts of the happy men and women fortunate enough to be employed at Bournville by the benevolent Cadbury brothers. The raw material gathered from the cocoa-bean has to be gathered from far, scorched corners of the earth. The delicious bars of nutritive chocolate consumed by millions of English children contained the products gathered by the negro working under the tropical sun far away. Messrs Cadbury themselves owned a small estate in Trinidad, where they showed the same care for their workers which distinguished their factory at Bournville, but from 1900 to 1908 a great part of their raw material was shipped from the islands San Thomé and Principe, which were possessions of the King of Portugal on the West Coast of Africa. In 1901, an old gentleman informed Mr W A Cadbury that slave conditions of a terrible kind prevailed in these islands in the cocoa fields. Thereupon he spared no pains to discover for himself the truth, and to force reforms from the Portuguese Government. He went himself, at great risk to his health, to the tropical islands; he paid personal visits to Lisbon to intercede with the Portuguese Government. His visits to Africa were satirically referred to by the *Evening Standard* as those of a 'Quaker filibuster'. Finally, at the cost of thousands of pounds, he equipped a commission to report impartially on the whole situation in the islands. All that the old gentleman had told him was found to be true. Conditions of slavery of the very worst kind were found to prevail; nor was the Government of Portugal disposed to pay a great deal of attention to the representations of Messrs Cadbury. New reforms were promised; certain regulations were in fact enacted, but they were not enforced, and during all these years the unhappy lot of the indentured negro labourer did not improve. Then Mr Burtt, the Cadbury commissioner, sailed home with his report: it was a terrible document, and Mr Cadbury went with it to the Foreign Office to see Sir Edward Grey. All these years Messrs Cadbury had still been buying cocoa from these dreadful islands. Their view was that, if they ceased to buy, they would lose all influence by which they could improve the lot of the unfortunates, the product of whose labour would merely be transferred to another buyer. Sir Edward Grey was against the immediate publication of the report, and he had the diplomatic aspect of the matter to consider. Although Mr Cadbury expressed absolute willingness to discontinue his purchases from these islands, the view of the Foreign Office seems to have been that Mr Cadbury should take no steps either to publish Mr Burtt's report or to discontinue his purchases until diplomatic pressure had been exercised by Great Britain on Portugal, with whom His Majesty's Government was on terms of cordial friendship. The commercial interest of Messrs Cadbury in the islands would immensely strengthen any diplomatic action which the Foreign Office might see fit to take. However, other investigations were being pursued, and a gruesome book appeared from the pen of Mr Nevinson, who had paid a visit to these unhappy islands on a commission from *Harper's Magazine*. A General Election was imminent, and the Standard Newspapers, which had previously sneered at the Cadburys' efforts to improve the lot of the unhappy negroes, could not now resist the opportunity offered to attack the family which controlled the *Daily News* on the very ground on which that journal had with such deadly effect attacked the last Conservative administration. Surely, also, this was an illustration of the logical conclusion of the doctrine of Free Trade, which must have led Mr Cobden, if his letters on the subject are to be believed, to have mitigated something of his dogma.

On 26 September 1908, when it had been announced that Mr W A Cadbury was himself to visit the islands, they published an article full of gibes and sneers and innuendoes, but containing no open charges. 'It was left to others', the article ran, 'to throw light on those favoured portions of the earth's surface which enjoy the rule of Portugal in Africa. Other observers have anticipated Mr Cadbury, and have described the state of affairs in certain of these districts. ... It is not called "slavery": "contract labour" they call it now, but in most of its essentials it is that monstrous trade in human flesh and blood against which the Quaker and Radical ancestors of Mr Cadbury thundered in the better days of England. ... There is only one more amazing thing than Mr Nevinson's statements, and that is the strange tranquillity with which they are received by those virtuous people in England whom they intimately concern.' The *Standard* commented: 'In the plenitude of his solicitude for his fellow-creatures, Mr Cadbury might have been expected to take some interest in the owners of those same grimed African hands whose toil also is so essential to the beneficent and lucrative operations at Bournville'.

In January 1909, Messrs Cadbury, the Anti-Slavery Society, and the Foreign Office, having all failed to ameliorate the conditions on the two islands, the Cadbury firm brought an end to their relations with the Portuguese colonies, and bought no more cocoa from them.

Meanwhile a writ was issued for libel against the *Standard*. It was one of the cases in which the defendants not only stood by their 'libel', but aggravated it by their defence. They pleaded justification in so far as their article consisted of statements of fact, and fair comment upon the rest. Their defence, and the 'particulars' thereto, consisted of sixty closely printed pages, which included many of the articles in the *Daily News* which had condemned Chinese indentured labour in the Transvaal before or during the 1906 election. The defence, in effect, admitted the steps which had been taken by Messrs Cadbury to induce reform in the colonies, but alleged that this was merely an attempt to anticipate attack. Thus undoubtedly, as Rufus Isaacs said in opening the case, they aggravated the libel and rendered the task of the defending advocate far more difficult. The defence, as finally delivered, had developed into a charge of hypocrisy against one of the proudest and most honourable names in British commerce.

The great public interest in the case was increased by the political crisis and the imminent General Election, and also by the fact that the greatest Conservative leader of the day was engaged for a Conservative organ against the most brilliant advocate in the Liberal Party, who was in turn attacking on behalf of the honour of a great Liberal family, not unconnected with the most powerful Liberal organ. The case recalled one of the bitterest specific issues of the previous election, which had undoubtedly lost many seats for the Conservative cause, and beneath the surface the whole ethical foundation of the doctrine of Free Trade was in question. To the single combat that was to ensue between the two great advocates, while the issues were being formally declared at Westminster, the eyes of England were turned; indeed, it seemed almost as if the General Election was being fought at Birmingham in miniature. The interest of the case was heightened by the announcement that Sir Edward Grey himself, the Foreign Secretary, had undertaken to give evidence on behalf of the plaintiffs. Rufus Isaacs and Edward Carson seemed almost like knights chosen to fight at a tournament by their respective factions, as in mediaeval days.

Rufus Isaacs opened the case for the plaintiffs in a masterly speech: he laid great stress on the wonderful way in which the Cadbury brothers had carried on their business in the interests of their workpeople, and skilfully marshalled all the facts which showed that the condition of the poor slaves in the islands had been their first care for a number of years. Against all this he contrasted, with rhetorical exaggeration, the attack which had been made upon them by the *Standard*. 'The issue in this case,' he said, 'is whether it is true to say that, when once the knowledge was brought home to my clients, they did nothing. ... The defence is, in essence, that the plaintiffs are a lot of canting hypocrites.' He urged that the defendants had first alleged that Messrs Cadbury had done nothing, then that they had done a great deal, but that all that they had done had been a mere pretence.

When Rufus Isaacs finished his opening speech, there was cheering in Court, and the hopes of the defendants seemed to have become forlorn, especially as the *Standard* had undoubtedly sneered a short while before at Mr W A Cadbury for making any effort at all to interfere in the affairs of the islands. Mr Cadbury was clearly an upright and honourable man who had made this matter his first care, and he had been hypocritically attacked by a newspaper of opposed political views. Mr Cadbury's evidence lasted three days, and he was subjected to one of the most rigorous cross-examinations of Carson's career. But immense prestige had gathered round Carson since the trial of Oscar Wilde. He was recognised as one of the leaders of the country, and his personality itself carried a sometimes decisive weight in a Court of Law. When a decision had been taken by his client, or his client's adversary, which of two views might legitimately be taken, he had a marvellous power of enlisting the opinion and the prejudices of the jury heavily on the side of his own client. The old Irish wig and gown were very torn and ragged now, but somehow, when Carson stalked in, he seemed to fill the Court and dwarf every other personality in it. He could not make a gesture without dignity, or utter a word without weight. Devices which in others would have seemed trite or pretentious were endowed with originality and grace when he applied them. Even the handsome Judge in his scarlet and ermine, sitting above him on the Bench, seemed to lose in importance and stature. And his questions were indeed sometimes so terrifying that not only the witness, but disinterested spectators in Court, felt a feeling of awe; and always he could bring back the mind of the jury from a variety of general and complex considerations to some very simple issue. Rufus Isaacs had said that Chinese slavery was not an issue in the case. What was the reality of the situation? It was that Messrs Cadbury, who had a controlling interest in the *Daily News*, had for years bought raw material from planters who to their knowledge had used slave labour.

His first questions were directed to this issue, and admitted of answers only in the affirmative. They were all derived from information contained in Messrs Cadbury's own report. The questions, simple in themselves, but backed by Carson's masterful personality and melancholy dignity, grew in gravity, starting from an admission of mere slavery, and passing from cruelty to atrocity, and from atrocity to licensed murder on a large scale, until the plaintiff seemed to stand there as defendant in all but name, and sharing responsibility for the sorrows of the backward world.

'Is it a fact that San Thomé cocoa has been slave grown to your own knowledge for eight years?' – 'Yes.'

'Was it slavery of a very atrocious character?' – 'Yes.'

'The cocoa you were buying was procured by atrocious methods of slavery?' – 'Yes.'

'Men, women and children taken forcibly from their homes against their will?' – 'Yes.'

'Were they marched like cattle?' – 'I cannot answer that quite. They were marched in forced marches down to the coast.'

'Were they labelled when they went on board the ship?' – 'Yes.'

'How far had they to march?' – 'Various distances. Some came from more than a thousand miles, some from quite near the coast.'

'Never to return again?' – 'Never to return.'

'From the information which you procured, did they go down in shackles?' – 'It is the usual custom, I believe, to shackle them at night on the march.'

'Those who could not keep up with the march were murdered?' – 'I have seen statements to that effect.'

'You do not doubt it?' – 'I do not doubt that it has been so in some cases.'

'The men, women and children are freely bought and sold?' – 'I do not believe, so far as I know, that there has been anything that corresponded to the open slave-market of fifty years ago. It is done now more by subtle trickery and arrangements of that kind.'

'You do not suggest that it is better because done by subtle trickery?' – 'No.'

'The children born to the women who are taken out as slaves become the property of the owners of the slaves?' – 'I believe that the children born on the estate do.'

'Was it not the most cruel and atrocious form of slavery that ever existed?' – 'I cannot distinguish between slavery and slavery. All slavery is atrocious.'

'Knowing it was atrocious, you took the main portion of your supply of cocoa for the profit of your business from the islands conducted under this system?' – 'Yes, for a period of some years.'

'You do not look upon that as anything unusual?' – 'Not under the circumstances.'

All through, Mr Cadbury had answered these questions with perfect frankness, and on the next day it was the same. The questions were so put that it amounted to a long catechism, every answer to which was in the affirmative.

He put to the witness a quotation of a report of the Board of Messrs Cadbury which read: 'There seems little doubt that public opinion would condemn the existing conditions of labour if the facts could be made known'.

'Did that represent your view?' – 'Yes.'

'There would be no difficulty about making the facts known?' – 'There would be no difficulty.'

'If you had made public the facts, public opinion would have condemned the conditions of labour, and you would not have gone on?' – 'I think so.'

At the end of the long cross-examination, however, Carson asked one question which elicited a sincere and embarrassed negative, repeated several times.

'Have you formed any estimation of the number of slaves who lost their lives in preparing your cocoa, during those eight years?' asked Carson.

'No, no, no,' answered the witness, with unhappy agitation.

On the following day Mr George Cadbury was called, the principal director of the *Daily News*. He made a splendid witness when Rufus Isaacs questioned him concerning the suggestions of the *Standard* as regards his sincerity in the matter. 'I can say that there is no truth whatever in it, and I can look any man in the face,' said the great manufacturer, with a fierce look towards Carson. He said that he looked on slavery with eyes of abhorrence. But Carson was not thus lightly to be defeated by a bold gesture.

'And on anyone trying to make money out of slavery?' he asked. 'What do you think of that?'

'Sentiment told me that the slavery ought to be stopped, but common sense told me I should do no good by stopping buying at that time,' replied Mr George Cadbury.

'And common sense was against your sentiment?' rejoined the advocate.

Questions were then put to Mr George Cadbury as to his connection with the *Daily News*, and as to the policy of that newspaper with regard to the indentured Chinese labour in the Transvaal. Nothing, however, had been said as to the conditions at San Thomé. There was, however, an explanation for this. 'We found it injudicious,' said Mr George Cadbury, 'at that time that anything should appear that might jeopardise the efforts that were being made to improve the conditions of affairs in San Thomé.'

Although the great Foreign Secretary himself was called,

who corroborated the account given by the Cadburys as to their relations with the Foreign Office, and bore witness to their perfect good faith, Carson's cross-examination had made an effect which charged the whole atmosphere of the Court. He realised this himself, and felt himself strong enough to adopt the same strong line which he had taken in the Tillet case. Despite the grave allegations against the plaintiffs, which called aloud for explanation, contained in the particulars of defence, he elected to call no evidence for the defence and to rely on his speech alone. It is safe to say that no other advocate, living then or now, could have afforded to take course this course. But Carson, the most modest of men outside the arena, was fully conscious of his strength within it, and applied himself to his difficult task, knowing that Rufus Isaacs was to enjoy the last word. He began with a bold vindication of the original article, which he described as remarkable for its modesty.

'If the *Evening Standard*,' he said, 'believed they were wrong, they would not have been unwilling to say so. On the other hand, if they have published an article on a great public question, an article vital to civilisation itself, no matter at what expense, they must be challenged; they are bound in the interests of civilisation not to save themselves either trouble or expense in vindicating the position they have taken up. ... Let there be no mistake. There is no crawling down in this matter. We stand by our colours. ... The plaintiffs put themselves forward as the champions of proper conditions of labour, whether at home or among the coloured races abroad, and they have put themselves upon a plane of very high public morality. They were, most of them, subscribers to associations for putting down slavery. ... This slavery was of the vilest type. You have heard that children are born on these islands as calves or lambs are born. Mr Isaacs says that slavery is not an issue, but I say that slavery is *the one vital issue*; and I say that for eight long years this condition of affairs was supported by the money that went from this country through the Cadburys to the plantations of Portugal – Messrs Cadbury have paid £1 200 000 on slave-grown cocoa. ... Upon the plain facts of this case, and upon the knowledge that they had of the existence of this slavery, it was the plaintiffs' duty, the moment they knew of the conditions under which this raw material was produced, to wipe their hands of the whole thing. What is the plaintiffs' explanation? They say shortly, "Oh, we continued this for eight years for humanitarian purposes: we did it, very much against our sentiments, in the interests of the people of St Thomé and Principe". The plaintiffs say, "What is the use of our giving up 'the accursed thing' when someone else will take it up?" If this were generally followed, it would relieve anybody from doing anything that is right. It would be a splendid defence to the receiver of stolen goods. It is a strange phase of morality to say, "I know it is through our money that the whole business was carried on, but if I didn't supply the money, someone else would". Gentlemen, if the thing was wrong, the duty of the plaintiffs was to get rid of it at once. That was exactly what they did not do. I submit that, if they had had the real interests of the people at heart, they would never have allowed all the long years to go by in which the bartering of men, women, and children was the foundation of the products which were being sent for the making up at Birmingham. ... I ask the jury to look upon this as being a matter of public interest on which the defendants have a right to comment, as raising a public question which is of importance as regards the whole character of our dealings with foreign commerce.'

No report or comment can recapture the moral effect of the speech. The advocate's triumph is at the moment, and at the moment alone. When Rufus Isaacs rose to reply, his complaint was that not a single witness had been called, but that the defence 'had relied on a speech of singular power and scorn and invective by Sir Edward Carson.'

'The defendants,' he observed, 'are wise in their judgment.' Rufus Isaacs's speech was a powerful argument also, not unworthy of the occasion, and was received by the tribute of loud applause in Court. It was then the Judge's turn to charge the jury. Rarely has there been a charge more favourable to one party. From beginning to end it was a direction to find in favour of the plaintiffs, and to question and undermine the foundation of Carson's argument. 'Gentlemen,' said his lordship, 'unless you find that the plaintiffs have acted dishonestly, the plaintiffs are entitled to succeed. It is not a question of fair comment; above all, it is not a question of the difference of politics between the *Standard* and the *Daily News*. ... The gist of the matter is whether, for the purpose of preventing an attack upon their character, Messrs Cadbury took steps which were not real steps.' But the Judge had managed his jury badly. They obviously considered his summing-up too one-sided, and several of them turned their backs on him in Court.

In this case each side had put its case exceedingly high. There was no climbing down in either quarter. At the time, when the people's Budget had been rejected by the Peers in the name of the people themselves, political feeling ran as high as it had ever run in Great Britain, and, great as were the issues involved in the action itself, the whole case involved the deeper, nationwide antagonism of the two great factions in the State. Birmingham, the home of the beneficent Cadbury firm, whose name was a source of national pride to the whole of Great Britain, was also the home of Joseph Chamberlain, the founder of Liberal Unionism and the arch-foe of free imports.

It was almost impossible that among twelve reasonable men these considerations should not, to some extent, affect and divide their minds. How would they decide?

When they filed in, in answer to the Clerk of Assize, the foreman announced that they found for the plaintiffs. There were loud murmurs of approval. And the damages? 'One farthing.' There followed varied murmurs in which derision and approval were predominant. Carson immediately rose and asked that the Judge should allow no costs to the successful party. But his lordship ruled sternly that the costs must follow the event.

All the heavy costs of this expensive action therefore fell upon the *Standard*, but they could at least claim a moral victory. This moral victory was ascribed by everyone to the advocacy of Sir Edward Carson. Without his scathing tongue and towering personality, the newspaper could hardly have escaped a verdict of many thousands. As it was, the damages were contemptuous; the jury, in obedience to the Judge's direction, acquitted the plaintiffs of bad faith, but they deferred to Carson's view of 'the reality of the situation'. The plaintiffs, in the hope of ameliorating the conditions of the negro in San Thomé and Principe, had continued to keep their hold on the situation, with the best intentions in the world, by continuing to purchase. But all their representations, and those of a Free Trade Government, had failed, and they were forced in the end to reverse their policy and to boycott the islands. Would it not have been better if they had done it sooner? Would not an immediate boycott have been more consistent with the traditions of England and of William Wilberforce, who had persuaded hundreds of thousands of his countrymen over a period of years not to touch sugar, because it was produced by West Indian slave labour? Carson did not fail to remind the jury of William Wilberforce. In criminal cases a British jury must decide 'Aye' or 'No', but in civil cases the smallest coin of the realm provides sensible British opinion, on many occasions when its mind is perplexed, with a convenient compromise. But it is fair to say that only one advocate, having regard to the bitter and aggravated nature of the defence, could have obtained so favourable a result for the newspaper. This was really one of his greatest forensic victories. Eldon Bankes, his second counsel, had been quite in despair about the case, both in and out of Court.

30. Lever and the Daily Mail

Carson and Rufus Isaacs had taken precisely opposite roles in another great libel action two years previously. Two of the mightiest business enterprises in Great Britain – at the head of which were two of the greatest business personalities of our time, both men of genius – opposed each other before Mr Justice A T Lawrence in Liverpool. This was the celebrated action of Lever Brothers against the Associated Press. In this case Carson appeared for the plaintiffs, and was supported by Mr Horridge KC, now a Judge, Mr F E Smith, and Mr Hemmerde. This was, incidentally, the occasion when Carson first really made the acquaintance of the brilliant F E, and it made their friendship. Rufus Isaacs, who led, Mr Duke KC, now Lord Merrivale, Mr Norman Craig and Mr Branson, now a Judge, appeared for the defendants.

Mr W H Lever MP, afterwards Lord Leverhulme, was at the head of the plaintiff company, and the defendant association, whose principal newspapers, the *Daily Mail* and the *Evening News*, already enjoying a vast national circulation, was controlled by the great Lord Northcliffe, then better known as Sir Alfred Harmsworth. The histories of the gigantic businesses which each had built up were in themselves wonderful romances of commerce. In the early 'eighties, before the days of *Answers*, Mr Lever was working humbly in a grocer's shop, and had learnt that all soap in general use was greatly adulterated by unsavoury substances. He conceived the idea that the manufacture of pure soap might be made into a great commercial success. He set up a small factory at Warrington, turned out 20 tons a week in his first year; and 450 tons in his second. In 1887 he moved to Port Sunlight, where, in 1906, 3 000 tons were turned out weekly, and 3 500 hands were employed. The beneficence of Lever

Brothers to their employees had already become proverbial, and a proffered reward of £1 000 to anyone who could prove the adulteration of their soap had never been claimed. Their capital amounted to many millions of pounds. Their goodwill had been built up by an expenditure of £2 500 000 in advertising in England alone, half a million having been spent on advertising in the Press. Messrs Lever Brothers had therefore acquired a commanding position in this branch of commerce. In 1906, the price of the raw material for soap rose owing to its new-found use in the manufacture of margarine and other foodstuffs, and a general price increase was agreed to by all the soap-makers. Messrs Lever Brothers had to make up their minds whether they would raise the price of their one-pound tablets of soap or slightly reduce their weight. The company dealt only with retailers, and not directly with the public, and their agents strongly recommended against an increase in price. Mr Lever decided on the other course, and gave notice to all his retailers of a reduction of weight by a paper attached to each carton of soap. At the same time the famine in raw materials continued, and Mr Lever considered that in bad times the expensive competition, which had been carried on at fever heat by the soap manufacturers, with lavish advertising, might be allayed by an amalgamation; and a large scheme of amalgamation was actually set on foot. The formation of such a trust would certainly have resulted in a great reduction in advertising revenue to the newspapers, and it also became a matter of common rumour that the trust was being formed, not to reduce costs, but to exploit the public by 'cornering' the raw material and raising the price of soap all round to the consumer. It is the legitimate duty of a great newspaper from time to time to take considerable risks in order to warn or protect the public against schemes which are inimical to its interests, and the *Daily Mail* had often fearlessly played this role to the benefit of the public. But there is usually, in the life of every great newspaper, at least one occasion when it overreaches itself on an adventure of this kind, with disastrous and sometimes fatal results. It took *The Times* years to recover from the effects of the publication of the Piggott forgeries and the Parnell Commission, and on this occasion Lord Northcliffe made the one great mistake of his life. He considered that the proposed soap trust was a conspiracy against the public interest, and believed that he could prove it. In short, he felt himself justified by the information before him in fighting and attempting to smash the amalgamation with all the strength of his mighty association of newspapers.

But, as *The Times* pointed out in a leading article after the trial, he himself had an obvious interest in the matter, as the amalgamation of the soap companies would eliminate a great deal of competitive advertising. In October 1906 he sent a letter to Mr Lever assuring him of personal friendliness, but soon afterwards opened fire in his newspapers with a deliberate and prolonged attack upon Mr Lever and his proposed soap trust, which continued through October, November and December of that year. First and foremost, the *Daily Mail* seized on the fact that the threepenny tablet of Messrs Lever Brothers' soap, which had weighed one pound before, now weighed only 15 ounces, as evidence of a general conspiracy to exploit the public. The *Daily Mail* argued that, although the retailers might have had notice of the change, the information had never reached the consuming public. But this was only one phase in an attack which covered a very wide field. The attacks had a disastrous result, both on the sale of the Lever soap and on the value of their shares, and Mr Lever was compelled to protect his goodwill, which had cost him millions to build up. The proposed amalgamation had to be abandoned, and Messrs Lever Brothers were compelled to go back to the one-pound tablet of soap for threepence. Meanwhile, the *Daily Mail* vaunted and gloried in the havoc which their campaign had inflicted in the soap world.

As in the Cadbury case, the suit was tried in the plaintiffs' own citadel at Liverpool, but with very different results. Rufus Isaacs had done his best to remove the trial to another venue, but had failed. Perhaps he was afraid of 3 500 of the best-treated employees in the world, who lived in the vicinity of the Liverpool Assize Court at Port Sunlight. Indeed, when the jury were empanelled, there were numerous excuses made by jurors who were interested in one way or another in the plaintiffs' concern.

It was anticipated that the action would last a fortnight, but Carson made up his mind to finish the case in a day or two, on his opening. He felt confident that on the facts before him he could blow the defendants' case sky high, and induce them to settle outright for an enormous sum. He was convinced that Lord Northcliffe did not know the strength of the case against him. His plan was to make the most formidable opening of his career, put Mr Lever in the box, and challenge Rufus Isaacs to do the like with Lord Northcliffe. Whereas he was sure that Mr Lever had the means of answering every question which Rufus could put against him, he determined to reveal to Lord Northcliffe at the outset that his campaign had been based on inaccurate information and was utterly unjustified. He knew that by a powerful treatment of his subject-matter, he could make the great journalist realise how far he had overreached himself.

Mr Lever entertained his counsel in great style: he lent them his house in Birkenhead, and saw that they lived off the fat of the land during the progress of the case. In these luxurious surroundings Carson, assisted by his team of lawyers, put the finishing touches to the speech that was to win the greatest sum for libel damages which had ever been awarded to a plaintiff.

His opening speech was a two-day effort, and it certainly was a devastating performance. 'This libel, gentlemen,' he began, 'is of a very exceptional and serious character, deliberately carried on for several weeks, and was made with the object of smashing up Lever Brothers. It is a libel which has been persisted in up to the present moment. ... The plaintiffs' complaint is that the defendants, having made up their minds to smash the combine, instead of attacking it in a fair way, have stooped to methods of libel, which have rendered Mr Lever and his company liable to be branded as men with whom no honest man could have any dealings in this country. The first and most serious charge is that the plaintiffs sold their soap in such a fraudulent manner as to deceive the public as to the weight of the soap. The next charge is that the plaintiffs, in consequence of the combine, have dismissed large quantities of employees. Another charge is that they have cornered all the raw material in the market. Messrs Lever Brothers are also accused of having, along with others, attempted to bribe and buy the Press, and it is suggested that the attempt had to be abandoned because high-class and patriotic papers like the *Daily Mail* refuse to be bribed. A number of the libels also contained hostile criticism of certain brands of the plaintiffs' soap, and allege that unsavoury fish oil has been used in their manufacture which they have fraudulently concealed by scenting it. After suggesting that the conduct of the plaintiffs in the matter of the combine tends to the oppression of the poor, the libels finally shake the foundations of the plaintiff company by alleging that the Lever preference shareholders, by a certain manipulation, are to be got rid of for the benefit of Mr Lever himself.'

Against this dark background of the libels, Carson drew a glowing picture of Mr Lever, the pioneer of pure soap, the quality of whose merchandise had never been challenged, the model employer, the generous philanthropist, who from small beginnings had built up one of the greatest businesses of the world. He skilfully explained that the alteration in weight – weight never having been guaranteed – and the scheme for a combine, had a fair and logical explanation in the increased cost of raw materials. Then he passed to one of the most sensational claims for damages which have ever been made. 'If you find,' he said, 'that Messrs Lever Brothers are not robbers and swindlers, fraudulent traders and all the rest of it, and if you find that all the other charges are untrue, what are the damages to be given to them? The damage is incalculable. ... No money can wipe out the sufferings of weeks and months during which the charges were hurled against the business of Lever Brothers. You must, without shirking, try to assess something that will be compensation for what has been done. For the rest, up to the time of the issue of the writ, the plaintiffs' trading losses have been £40 000. Those losses have continued. The *Daily Mail* has not only admitted, but gloated over, these losses that have been caused by them. But that is a small part of the total loss. The whole company has been shaken from top to bottom. Two million preference shares have been reduced in value £1 apiece, with a loss, to those who held the shares, of £200 000. On the ordinary shares it is impossible to say what the loss has been. The whole concern has been shaken up as if by an earthquake. Then you have to ask yourselves how the goodwill of the company is to be restored, and at what price. It has to be rebuilt to some extent, and that can only be done by a verdict of the jury.' Carson's final gesture was one of consummate skill: with a wave of his hand he directed Mr

Lever to go into the witness-box. 'And now, gentlemen,' he concluded, 'I have put my first witness – my client, Mr Lever – into the box. Let my learned friend, Mr Rufus Isaacs, cross-examine him to his heart's content, and, when his time comes, I hope he will be able to follow my example and do the same, and call as his first witness his own client, Lord Northcliffe. I hope he'll be able to play cricket with us.'

Mr Lever made a most competent witness, and all Mr Rufus Isaacs's subtlety could not make him damage his case. Indeed, he made a score or two against the great advocate. Rufus asked him why he had not placed the notices of alteration of weight on the soap in a more prominent place. 'I am perfectly sure,' rejoined Mr Lever, 'that, wherever we had placed them, it would never have pleased you, Mr Isaacs.'

Rufus Isaacs's last question was, 'Do you know that, before the first article appeared in the *Daily Mail*, there was a meeting in Birmingham at which a resolution was passed about what was called "the trick of the fifteen ounces"?' – 'I do not,' replied Mr Lever, 'and, if there was, it was most unjust.'

'That is for the jury to determine,' observed Isaacs, but the jury looked so unsympathetic at this that perhaps he regretted making the comment.

The plaintiffs' counsel went off in high spirits to the luxury of Mr Lever's house. Carson knew Rufus well, and was convinced that there would be a settlement. As he and F E Smith motored down to the Court after an excellent night's rest, free from all anxiety, he said with a smile, 'Well, poor Rufus will have had a very bad night of it. He didn't like that challenge of mine to call Harmsworth. He doesn't know what to do. I'll wager he's been on the telephone with Harmsworth all night, and he'll be on the steps of the Court waiting to make me an offer.'

When the car reached the Court, there was Rufus alone

on the steps, as Carson had prophesied, looking tired and worried. He was not accompanied by his client, as Carson was. 'Well, Rufus,' said Carson, with a broad smile, 'you look very tired. You look as if you'd been up all night. Where's Harmsworth? Are you going to make me an offer?'

'We'll give you £10 000,' said Rufus.

Carson and Lever treated the figure with contempt, and walked into Court. When the trial seemed about to be resumed, Rufus was observed whispering to Carson. This is what he was saying: 'You can't stop me withdrawing my defence and going to the jury on an assessment of damages alone.'

'No,' said Carson.

Rufus Isaacs then rose, and with a great show of generosity, announced that after Mr Lever's evidence the defence could not persist, and would ask the jury to assess only the damages. This was a clever device to soften the jury by a demonstration of magnanimity. But Carson was not to be thus deprived of the full spoils of victory. 'Mr Lever can accept no compromise. For months and months an attempt has been made to blacken Mr Lever's character, and the company's. ... On behalf of Mr Lever I cannot accept as mitigation any tardy retraction by the *Daily Mail*. Mr Lever must be allowed to go to the jury and obtain such damages as will vindicate his reputation.'

Carson, who had expected this to happen all along, added with his most innocent air, 'The course adopted by my learned friend has taken me completely by surprise. I ask for time to bring witnesses, on the question of damages, to the Court.'

But at this point there took place the most humorous scene that Carson ever observed in a Court of Law. There, in open Court and in audible tones, Rufus Isaacs began raising his offer for a settlement like a buyer at an auction, while Carson passed on the offer to Mr Lever, only to have it refused at once by that redoubtable plaintiff. 'I never saw a more determined man,' said Carson.

'Look here, Ned,' said Rufus, 'you can have £15 000.'

Carson leant over to his client, sitting below him.

'Look here, Mr Lever, here's Harmsworth offering you £15 000.'

'I won't have his £15 000.'

Rufus's offer jumped up to £20 000, to £30 000, to £40 000. Finally came the offer of £50 000.

'What do you say to that, Mr Lever?' asked Carson.

'That's a substantial offer,' said Lever. 'I'll take it.'

Mr Lever was loudly cheered by the crowd as he left the Court, and was almost mobbed by the enthusiasm of his employees at Port Sunlight when he visited them to announce a holiday for them all as a celebration of the greatest sum of damages which had ever been obtained in a libel suit. Yet this was but the beginning of the losses which fell upon the Associated Press as a result of their campaign against the soap trust. There were a number of other claims for damages against their various newspapers, and Mr Lever's first £50 000 set a standard which involved the association in a total loss, it is said, of a quarter of a million pounds.

Despite this staggering blow, Lord Northcliffe bore no malice against the great lawyer, whose flawless advocacy had won these enormous damages from him, and their destinies were often in the future to touch and join each other. Both during the Ulster crisis and in the Great War, Lord Northcliffe gave great assistance to Sir Edward Carson, and had a profound respect for him. Northcliffe said to him some time afterwards: 'Carson, you're the biggest enemy I ever had.'

Carson replied: 'Why didn't you employ me, then? I daresay you'd have won.'

Perhaps, in all the circumstances, it was not surprising that in the course of time Sir Edward became the standing leading counsel for the *Daily Mail*, and won many a verdict for them. Years later, in 1915, at one of the most critical moments in English history, when Carson was playing a dominant role in the councils of the nation in the hour of her peril, the great journalist wrote: 'Your noble action of yesterday adds to the admiration I have always felt for you, despite your criticisms and soap brigandage. I believe you will save the situation. Your sincere Northcilffe.'

31. J B Joel v Robert Sievier

The *Cadbury* and the *Lever* cases are signal examples of the triumph of Carson's advocacy over that of Rufus Isaacs. Figurative similes are inadequate, but so contrasted were their methods that these victories may be compared to the triumph of the eagle over the serpent. But it was not always thus. Sometimes the serpent won. A notable instance of this was the prosecution for blackmail brought by Mr J B Joel against Robert Sievier, the editor of the *Winning Post*. This book has recorded many actions, civil and criminal, to which supreme and permanent interest, both of individuals and even of the nation, attached. But no capital trial, no great dispute between citizens or nations, aroused more public excitement than the Sievier prosecution. Mr Robert Sievier, that astonishing adventurer of the Turf and of Fleet Street, was in June 1908 very short of cash. He was a man of which at least this could be said: he was singularly punctilious about payment of his 'debts of honour', and at this time these obligations were pressing hard upon him. He had a slight, a very slight, acquaintance of a personal nature with Mr J B Joel, the South African millionaire. J B Joel had on one occasion run up the bidding for a mare on which Sievier had set his heart, and Sievier had made it his particular business to find out ever so much about Mr J B Joel. He had paid a visit to that mausoleum of information, the British Museum, and in a newspaper had stumbled across evidence of a youthful indiscretion by Mr Joel in his early business career. In his newspaper he ran a series of satirical articles on eminent individuals, entitled 'Celebrities in Glass Houses'. Mr J B Joel was the victim-subject of one of these articles, and every week his life was made miserable by attacks, both veiled and open, on his commercial past and his sporting present.

Finally Mr Joel heard that an early portrait of himself was to be printed in the *Winning Post* depicting him 'standing between two murderers'. Events then moved rapidly to their conclusion. Mr Joel, through two intermediaries, one the especial and trusted confidant of Mr Robert Sievier, lent the latter £5 000, with which he immediately discharged his debts of honour, and the attacks on Mr Joel abruptly ceased. But the police had been warned about the transaction, and a material part of the business had been observed by a Scotland Yard inspector concealed behind a curtain. Mr Joel applied for a warrant for Mr Sievier's arrest for proposing to Jack Barnato Joel to abstain from publishing certain matter with intent to extort money.

Carson was briefed for the prosecution, and Rufus Isaacs for the defence. The cross-examination of the Jewish millionaire by the great Jewish advocate was a dramatic, a merciless, and a masterly performance. The latter especially attacked the witness for using one of Sievier's closest friends to arrange this transaction. 'It was an unfortunate thing,' said the witness. 'It was a dishonourable thing,' retorted Mr Isaacs, with heat. The plight of the witness was made no better when he said that Sievier would have trusted nobody else but this particular man. The defence was that Sievier had made no proposals to abstain from publishing offensive matter about a man whom he hated, but that the rich man had taken advantage of his sworn enemy at a moment of great financial embarrassment, and had set a trap for him to silence him forever. Sievier in his way was a very popular figure, and a man of the greatest audacity. He was on bail during the trial, and drove down to the Old Bailey in a spanking carriage and pair. One day he forced his way into the Court by the Judges' entry. He was late and a great crowd of his partisans outside the Court further delayed his progress. 'You can't come in here,' said the police officer. 'Who are you, anyway?' 'Well, you can't damn well get on without me,' said Sievier. 'I'm the prisoner.' All through the trial he was nodding and smiling from the dock to his friends. He seemed to be enjoying himself immensely. Certainly the prisoner at the bar was the hero of the hour. The whole of Rufus Isaacs's cross-examination of the witnesses for the prosecution had been based on the hypothesis that the two intermediaries had been used as dupes, and had had no intention to harm Sievier. He had dealt very mercifully with the two men on this basis. Then Rufus put his client into the box without making a preliminary address. The mercurial and engaging witness was bored by this defence, and started a new hare. Carson, attempting to discredit him, suggested that Sievier's view was that his two friends were low and mercenary conspirators. Blandly, Sievier agreed. 'Of course,' he said, 'they were manufacturers of evidence against me.' 'Your friend is an awful liar, then?' pressed Carson. 'Either he is, or I am,' answered the witness naively. Farce was never far away with such a personality as the prisoner. The witness had an explanation for everything. He was asked for an explanation of the proposed picture of Mr Joel, 'standing between two murderers'. He gave one: the two supporters of Mr Joel were not murderers; they were clever caricatures of Labour leaders by Mr Starr Wood. Why had he ceased publication of the attacks on J B Joel? Mr Leopold de Rothschild, whose word was law on the Turf, had told him to stop them.

Carson did not shake the prisoner. Charlie Gill, who was his second counsel, kept on telling him he was not being sufficiently severe. Rufus Isaacs called no witnesses but his client, and in the ordinary course this gives the right to the prisoner's counsel to address the jury after the prosecutor, and so have the last word. But Rufus had put in a number of documents, which strictly entitled Carson to this last word.

When he had concluded Sievier's re-examination, Rufus sat down. Carson did not rise, and the Lord Chief Justice looked from one to the other of them, quite perplexed. An argument followed in which each of the great counsel squabbled for the last word with the jury. At last Carson gave way with a gesture of impatience. 'If there is the smallest doubt about it,' he said, 'I think the prisoner ought to have the benefit, and I waive my right.'

The prisoner, back again in the dock, bowed politely. 'Thank you very much, Sir Edward,' he chirped.

'I don't want any thanks from you,' replied Carson. His objective prejudice in favour of fairness to 'the prisoner' had no basis in any subjective sympathy for Robert Sievier.

If his cross-examination had lacked severity, he made up for it by his speech, which was in his most sardonic vein. 'If anybody has been looking with satisfaction on the proceedings for the last few days, it is the blackmailers,' he said, 'and are you going to lay it down that the prosecution must fail because the evidence was obtained in an unfortunate way? If you do, this will be a day of Magna Carta for blackmailers. ... I appeal to you not to let any popularity of the prisoner, and the cheers of any people outside or inside the Court, prevent you from doing your duty.'

Carson gained a great deal of ground by his powerful speech, but Rufus Isaacs won it all back by his last word. 'If they had not known,' he submitted, 'that Mr Sievier had had a bad week in June, the money would never have been dangled before him. ... They knew Sievier was broke, and I put it to you that his thought was: "Here is my opportunity for getting rid of the man for heaven knows how long. He is broke, and here is an opportunity for my money. I must get someone to help me ...". I imagine them getting hold of the man's best friend and confidant.'

Loud applause broke out at the conclusion of counsel's speech, during which Mr J B Joel sat with his bowed head in his hands.

After a colourless charge by Lord Alverstone and an absence of the jury for over an hour, the latter filed in. It had been a nice question of fact for them to try. But it was eminently one for a jury. A phrase or a word, some little difference in the facts or the setting, might convert an innocent application for a loan or for assistance into a threat with a view to extortion. Their minds had been swayed by the two greatest advocates of the age at the height of their powers. Though undoubtedly they had been swayed by Rufus Isaacs's vivid picture of the rich man making overtures to the poor man, Carson had made the most of the accomplished fact of the loan, after which the scurrilous attacks had ceased, and had painted in terrible colours the public dangers of blackmail. How had they decided? In answer to the Clerk of Arraigns, the foreman said, 'Not guilty.' Immediately the packed Court burst into loud cheering, which was taken up again and again, and which the ushers found it impossible to repress. Outside, there was being enacted an amazing scene. From Newgate Street across the wide front of the Old Bailey to a point beyond Sea Coal Lane, a crowd some four or five thousand strong had gathered, and, as soon as the verdict reached them, the people gave a great shout and at once made a rush for the main door to greet Mr Sievier as he came out. The police were quite unable to deal with the situation. Even Mr Sievier was afraid of so intense and violent a popularity, and he escaped in his fine carriage by a side door in Newgate Street. But he was at once recognised, and the crowd ran after his carriage and surrounded it, cheering madly. When Rufus Isaacs emerged, the anti-Semite mob gave him a tremendous reception, shouting 'For he's a jolly good fellow'. Moreover, for a full twenty minutes they refused to move away, and continued their jubilations. For Carson the scene must have evoked many memories and reflections. He remembered the murderous crowd at Mitchelstown, the loud rejoicings after the *Wilde* trial; and here were four or five thousand Anglo-Saxons going mad with joy because of the acquittal of a journalist of the Turf. Moreover, the almost unprecedented scene outside the Old Bailey called forth reflections and misgivings of a general nature: this was more like the exuberance of a Roman mob in the time of the decadence than the traditional behaviour of the English public. The best forensic and the highest judicial talent had been expended for days in determining a private dispute of a not very elevated character which was of little or no consequence to the community, apart from the aspect of blackmail; and here were the people cheering as if a Waterloo had been won. 'We are rapidly becoming,' said *The Times* in a leading article, 'the most emotional of people; and one of the most mischievous forms of uncontrollable feeling is an outburst of enthusiasm, or, it may be, the opposite, as to someone on his trial. Today it may be for the innocent, tomorrow for the guilty.'

32. The Archer-Shee Case

Despite the furious campaign against the Peers and the 'dear loaf' carried on by the Liberal leaders, the disillusionment of the people in their party was apparent in the result of the first General Election of 1910. The powerful popular cry against the arrogance of the hereditary legislators did not prevent them from losing a hundred seats to the Unionists. The Liberals themselves had but a majority of two over the Unionists; once more they had lost their independence, and required the support of the Irish and Labour Parties. Mr Redmond was overjoyed, and said that the Nationalist Party could not be in a more favourable position; the Liberal Government could not remain in power for a single day without him. The Irish, at heart a conservative and even primitive people, had no sympathy with Henry George's ideas of taxation of land values, which might be valuable in a new and rapidly developing country full of mineral wealth, such as California, but had no relation to a nation of peasant proprietors, which was the ideal of all good Irish patriots. They had no grudge against the Lords for what they had done: an independent Irish legislature would no doubt sweep aside the taxation of land values. Their enmity to the Lords arose out of the certainty that they would reject any Home Rule Bill, and the probability that this rejection would be endorsed by the people. They now had the power to make Mr Asquith 'toe the line', but first the Lords had to be swept aside. The marvel is that, with the cries of 'Peers and People' and that of the 'dear loaf' against them, the Unionists did so well. For the first time since Mr Gladstone's last Administration, neither party could govern by itself, in the absence of agreement between themselves, without the Irish vote. The Liberal

Party decided to carry on by themselves on a Home Rule policy. Only by Conservatives had the Home Rule issue been raised as a dominant one, and it was on the speeches of their opponents that the Liberals, who had been almost universally silent and evasive on the question, were rather curiously to rely for a mandate. Although no mention had been made of Home Rule in the Prime Minister's election address, a perfunctory and ambiguous statement concerning Irish self-government, under the supreme authority of the Imperial Parliament, was found to have been made in a long speech which dealt otherwise with Free Trade and the House of Lords. The Prime Minister claimed that the election had been won on Free Trade, and other Liberal leaders claimed a mandate for the abolition of the House of Lords. No serious person suggested that Home Rule had been the issue. But the bargaining started at once. For neither in the South nor the North of Ireland was there any doubt as to the real situation. Ireland had come into her own again. The leaders of the Nationalist Party met frequently to consider the exact methods of coercion which they had best adopt against Mr Asquith. But neither were the Ulstermen idle. Ever since Lord Randolph Churchill had said, 'Ulster will fight', preparation had been a tradition in the North. Their organisation was as strong and as perfect as a political organisation can well be; by means of the Orange Lodges it had its roots in the people. The Ulster Unionist Council, composed of several hundred delegates, had been constituted in 1905. The Council contained an inner Cabinet, known as the 'Standing Committee'. They had a score or so of representatives at Westminster. They were sworn to the maintenance of the Union as to a religion: there was something mediaeval in the singleness of purpose of this Protestant community. They lacked but one thing for effective action, and it was a necessity. Among themselves they had no leader. There was no single man in all that massed and formidable confederacy, from aristocrat to artisan, who had the authority and mental power to lead, to restrain, to protect, and at the same time to state the case for a movement which needed all the advocacy it could obtain in the immediate future, and all its own strength for the last resort. It was decided by these clannish people that there was only one man, and he was a stranger and a Southerner. In January 1910, Mr James Craig MP, afterwards Lord Craigavon, was deputed to ask Sir Edward Carson to accept the leadership of the Irish Unionist Party in the House of Commons.

It is with a sense of the beginning of a totally new and great departure that the writer deals with this offer and its acceptance. It is the conventional view that Carson was from his earliest youth devoted, like Hannibal, to his cause: it was not so. Nor did any gift of moral fealty or even of affectionate sympathy from the Ulster folk go with this offer of Parliamentary leadership. Like the practical folk they were, they looked about for the most efficient instrument at hand, and they saw that Carson was the only man. Indeed, had they appreciated how much of the South was in him, they might have paused. Yet, although it was formally only the question of the leadership of a small Parliamentary group, it was realised, both by those who offered and by the man who was to give his assent, that this was no ordinary political chairmanship. It meant, sooner or later, the surrender of all private interests; it meant the surrender of all wider political hopes and ambitions. For the leadership of Ulster, with an obligation in the last resort to lead resistance by force, was not consistent with the leadership of the Conservative Party. The most that the leader of the Conservative Party could demand was that the people of Great Britain should decide the question at a General Election.

It was an exacting demand upon a man of fifty-six, whose health had always been delicate and troublesome, who had bitter private cares and worries, who loved the law rather than politics, and whose ambition, several times frustrated, had been the peace and quiet of the judicial bench. It was a bold request from men of very different lineage and traditions from his own. He had never sympathised with the narrow dogma of the Ulster Scot, and was as different a man as can be from those who needed his service. It was a great sacrifice to ask from a man who had only to go into Court to earn a thousand guineas, who had had the leadership of the Conservative Party for four years within his grasp, and at any moment might be importuned or compelled to take it. They were asking that a certain Lord High Chancellor, a probable Prime Minister of England, and a man who had always loved peace and quiet, should forsake all and become at best the leader of a score of followers on a single issue, at worst a rebel chief and a man convicted of high treason. For Edward Carson, the greatest advocate of the time, with the highest destiny of all in front of him, there was no glamour or glory in what was offered; only duty, danger, and self-sacrifice.

It is safe to say that almost any other man in Carson's position would have refused. He thought it over for several days. He made it clear to Mr Ronald McNeill that an affirmative decision would cut him off from all promotion, legal or political, and the latter agreed with him. Nevertheless, this was the cause for which he had entered politics – the cause of the Union. Through Ulster the cause of the Union could best be served: only through Ulster could the cause of the Union be saved. Was he to prove false to a lifelong cause because it was dangerous, and he was getting old and idle and ambitious? His inherent sense of justice, which had often urged him on to fight many a battle in the Courts, urged him to accept. He saw Ulster almost as a client upon whom a great injustice was about to be inflicted by a corrupt conspiracy between forces far stronger than herself, without her own consent, without the consent even of the only lawful authority with the right to inflict the injury. In the end he wrote a letter of acceptance. It was a great brief for which he had been retained, a brief the only reward of which was the honour and gratitude of a whole community. And this was the man whom Joseph Devlin, the leader of the Nationalists in Belfast, was to describe in the House of Commons, after four years of perilous devotion to the Ulster cause, as a 'politician on the make'. But it was much more than a brief. For his acceptance was unqualified. He would be their leading advocate, their Prime Minister, and, if necessary, and only in the last resort, he was willing to march into battle at their head as their general. It was a great undertaking, and the like of it has rarely, if ever, come the way of a tired barrister fifty-six years old. The destiny of a great man is indeed a narrow and a fateful path. Upon the man of words, who might, but for Peter O'Brien, have been a County Court Judge in Ireland twenty-five years before, and who might, but for an interview with J S Sanders, have been President of the Divorce Court, there devolved, by the choice of others and his own consent, a great political task fraught with danger, and calling for swift and determined action. This decision, coming as it did so late in his life, meant the parting of the ways. Had he said 'No', a far greater destiny might have had to be recorded by his biographer, or his career might have gone forward on the conventional lines of steady promotion for the party lawyer. But in either event the name of Carson would have conveyed nothing of the special prestige and meaning now associated with it.

*　　　　　*　　　　　*

And yet, before he was wholly absorbed in the cause to which he had dedicated himself, there was one parting obligation of a legal nature which he was bound to fulfil. It is a case which reveals more than any other his advocacy in its most perfect and powerful form, showing him as a true and faithful friend, a defender of the weak against the strong, and as an indomitable fighter against tremendous odds. For years, as advocate and counsellor, he waged this legal battle against a great department, with the whole weight of the Liberal Government of the day against him. In October 1908, Mr Martin Archer-Shee, a Roman Catholic gentleman who had recently retired from the agency of the Bank of England at Bristol, received a most distressing letter from Admiralty House concerning his boy, George, a lad of thirteen who was at that time a cadet at the Naval College at Osborne. Although George was not particularly studious, and the authorities at Osborne had made this known to his father, he had won, in his short life, golden opinions as a boy of a conspicuously straightforward character, both at home and at Stonyhurst, where he had recently been at school before entering Osborne. There was nothing, therefore, to prepare his father for the grievous blow which he was to sustain when he read these words: '*Confidential.* I am commanded by My Lords Commissioners of the Admiralty to inform you that they have received a letter from the Commanding Officer of the Royal Naval College at Osborne, reporting the theft of a postal order at the college on the 7th instant, which was afterwards cashed at the post office. Investigation of the circumstances of the case leaves no other conclusion possible than that the postal order was taken by your son, Cadet George Archer-Shee. My lords deeply regret that they must therefore request you to withdraw your son from the college.'

The old gentleman wrote to the Admiralty saying that he would never believe his boy was guilty, and went down at once to Osborne with a much older son, Major Martin Archer-Shee MP. He found there was no alternative for him but to take his poor little son away. From the enquiries which they had made, the authorities were already convinced of his guilt. The following are, shortly, the events which led up to this young boy being branded as a thief and a forger.

Two cadets, George Archer-Shee and Terence Back, had arrived at Osborne in the same term; they were in the same class; they occupied adjoining beds in the same dormitory, and were thoroughly well known to each other. At breakfast on October the 7th, Terence Back received, in a welcome letter from home, a postal order for five shillings. He told his friends at breakfast of his modest windfall; ultimately he put the order into his writing-case, which in turn he secured in his locker. He spent the afternoon taking part in a rowing-race, and, on his return at about 3.45, he went straight to his locker to get his postal order and cash it at the canteen. The postal order was missing. He reported his loss to the chief petty officer. That individual remembered that he had given leave to Cadet Archer-Shee to go to the post office, which was at a few minutes' distance from the college, sometime that afternoon. He became excited, and mentioned Archer-Shee's name to Back, and went down himself to the post office to interview the postmistress. Now, it so happened that only two cadets had obtained leave to visit the post office that afternoon, and they had both admittedly gone about postal orders. Next morning the postmistress was sent for by Commander Cotton of Osborne College, and she gave the following account. She said that, shortly after two o'clock on the day before, a cadet named Arbuthnot had come to buy a postal order, and, about an hour afterwards, a cadet had come and asked her to cash a postal order for five shillings endorsed 'Terence H Back'. She added that after he had done so, the same cadet asked for a postal order for fifteen and sixpence, and had received it. Now Archer-Shee had undoubtedly gone to the post office on 7 October to obtain a postal order for fifteen and sixpence. All his friends knew that he had set his heart on a model steam-engine, which he had seen priced in a London catalogue at fifteen and sixpence. He had told his best friend, Cadet Patrick Scholes, immediately before he went down to the post office, that he was going to buy a postal order for the engine. Seven cadets were paraded before her, and she was unable to identify either Arbuthnot or Archer-Shee; but, if she was right in her recollection that it had been the same cadet who had both cashed the postal order for five shillings and bought the fifteen-and-sixpenny postal order, there was hardly any need for identification. For someone had stolen Back's postal order, made a clumsy imitation of his signature, and cashed it at the post office. It was proof manifest against Archer-Shee. This seems to have been the view taken by Commander Cotton. He sent for the boy and questioned him, and told him to write Cadet Back's name. He wrote at once 'Terence H Back'. The commander thought it curious that Archer-Shee should at once write down the exact form of signature which appeared on the endorsement of the postal order. Archer-Shee's writing of 'Terence H Back', together with the postal order, was sent to Mr Gurrin, the greatest expert on handwriting in England, who pronounced them both to be the work of the same hand. Upon this evidence the authorities wrote to Mr Archer-Shee asking him to remove his boy. It can well be understood the disgrace and shame which fell upon him and his parents. Yet the boy himself had shown the greatest composure and self-restraint throughout the proceedings. He said to Commander Cotton, 'I swear by Almighty God that I am innocent,' and he never faltered in this declaration of his innocence throughout his ordeal. The poor child was naturally unable to refute the chain of circumstantial evidence which had fastened suspicion upon him. 'All I can say is that I never did it,' he said again and again. Nor in this hour of cruel tragedy for this little boy and his family was there lacking some consolation. At the Catholic school of Stonyhurst, such was the recollection of his character that, when the charge was made public, his old schoolmates met together and declared that Archer-Shee was incapable of such an action; even the rector of the college, Father Bodkin, at once wrote to his father that he would be glad to receive the boy back. This noble and Christian offer, which was gratefully accepted, redounds to the lasting glory of this fine school.

Meanwhile, the Admiralty would give the family none of the information on documents which had decided their course of action, and the family had therefore only the word of the boy himself. This was good enough for them, and, in an hour of inspiration, Major Archer-Shee took his brother to see Edward Carson at Dr Johnson's Buildings on the very day on which he left Osborne. The major, as a young MP, had learnt something of both the tenderness of Carson's heart and the strength of his advocacy. 'There is only one man who can help us,' he said, 'and that's Edward Carson.' Sir Edward knew more than a little about Osborne, as his own sailor second son, Walter Carson, had gone through the college; and strangely enough it was Carson who as First

Lord was to close the place down altogether He was deeply moved by the sight of the boy, still dressed in the smart cadet's uniform to which he was no longer entitled, with his sad, strained little face. At the same time he understood well that unblemished honour is an essential condition for all officers in His Majesty's Navy, and he was determined not to interfere with the discretion of the Admiralty unless he first convinced himself that an injustice had been done. With kindliness, but with absolute thoroughness, Carson cross-examined the lad on every aspect of the story, and the reader will now understand that this was no small test of his veracity. But the boy completely satisfied him, and, at the end of it all, Carson was quite convinced of his innocence – and there was no better or more experienced judge of the demeanour of a witness than Edward Carson. One curious independent fact at once impressed Carson: Archer-Shee's own locker had been broken into on 7 October.

Now that Carson had made up his mind to help, he threw himself heart and soul into the case. There was great difficulty about the manner of procedure. It was at the time quite unknown upon what documents or statements the Admiralty had acted. Numerous applications were made to the Admiralty for disclosure of these facts, but Messrs Lewis & Lewis were able to get very little satisfaction from the Admiralty, except an offer to show the postal order itself, and a statement that 'the Admiralty had not acted on documentary evidence alone'. It soon became apparent that the Admiralty were not very anxious to be helpful, and the Archer-Shee family proceeded to make enquiries of their own which were not unfruitful. It was discovered that the boy had, on 7 October, £2 3s 0d in the school bank, and £4 3s 11d in the Post Office Savings Bank, so that there was no need for him to pilfer five shillings. Moreover, on the very day, 7 October, he had obtained a chit from an officer for the withdrawal of sixteen shillings from the school bank for the purpose of buying an engine. He had actually withdrawn that sum, and there seemed to be a strong presumption that he had bought the postal order for fifteen and sixpence with it. Also his friend Patrick Scholes came forward with helpful evidence which impeached the correctness of the recollection of the postmistress. She had put the time of Archer-Shee's call as being after three o'clock. Scholes could swear positively that he parted from Archer-Shee shortly after two, and saw the latter go off to the post office.

The family now felt the case was strong enough to justify a judicial enquiry under the auspices of the Admiralty; to this request the Admiralty refused to accede. It is true that Mr George Elliott KC was sent down to hold a departmental investigation, and that Mr R D Acland KC, the Judge Advocate of the Fleet, conducted an enquiry into the matter, but on each occasion the department refused to allow Archer-Shee to be represented by solicitor or counsel. There was therefore no sifting of the evidence by cross-examination, and it is not surprising that the original decision was not disturbed.

The attitude of the department seemed to Carson indefensible, yet it was difficult to see how, without their help, the boy's reputation could ever be vindicated. Endeavours were made to induce the Director of Public Prosecutions to bring a prosecution; then a plan was entertained of persuading some friend to bring a collusive prosecution. For over a year, Carson worked indefatigably, like Zola and Maître Labori in the case of Dreyfus, to obtain an impartial reopening of the case. All his efforts were in vain, until finally he conceived the idea of proceeding by 'petition of right'. The maxim 'The

King can do no wrong' is one which applies literally in the Courts. But redress is given to his subjects, not as of right, but as a matter of grace, when damage accrues as a result of a breach of a contract by the Crown. By ancient custom, when a subject humbly 'petitions' the Crown in respect of such a breach of contract, the Attorney-General on behalf of the Crown endorses the claim 'Let right be done', and the Crown thus waives its immunity. A contract between the Crown and the subject is the foundation of procedure by petition of right. Could a contract be established between a parent, whose son is sent to be educated as a naval officer at an official naval college, and the Crown? At any rate, the experiment was worth the trial. As a matter of business, some sort of agreement seems to be implied in such an arrangement in a country whose officers are trained and recruited from an early age on a voluntary system, largely through the express consent and will of parents. In return for a parent devoting his child, still of tender age, to the prescribed career of naval service, the King may be said to guarantee to train the child for that service. If the parent withdrew the child from Osborne, he could be sued by the Crown. Why should not the reverse apply by petition of right?

At all events, it was on this basis that 'the tragedy of Archer-Shee' was brought before the Courts, and thereby before the public. In strict law, Carson had a difficult case to argue, for the absolute prerogative of the Crown is an obstacle difficult to surmount for any litigant, if the Crown elects to rely on it. But, in morality and abstract justice, Carson had an overwhelming claim to be heard. Had George Archer-Shee been a few years older, and a full midshipman, he could have claimed the right of every one of the King's sailors or soldiers, a trial by Court Martial. Since he was only a cadet, was he, innocent or guilty, to be deprived of all right to a hearing, either in the criminal, civil, or naval Courts? It was a case, like that of Dreyfus, in which justice itself cried aloud for at least an impartial hearing. It seemed impossible that the Crown could object in any formal way to the trying of the facts of the case before a jury. The Crown surely would not dare to condemn a helpless and perhaps innocent child to lifelong ignominy by sheltering behind the prerogative claim of the Crown to immunity.

Yet this is precisely the plea which Sir Rufus Isaacs, who had become Solicitor-General, was instructed to raise against George Archer-Shee's father when his claim by petition of right was at length heard for the first time before Mr Justice Ridley on 12 July 1910. Sir Edward Carson, with Mr Leslie Scott KC, afterwards Solicitor-General, and Mr Eric Hoffgaard, appeared for the petitioner, and Sir Rufus Isaacs, leading Mr Horace Avory KC and Mr B A Cohen, for the Crown.

Sir Rufus relied strictly upon the immunity and the absolute right of dismissal by the Crown of one who, it was claimed, had entered the service of the Crown. This was to Edward Carson the most shameless injustice. The Crown had allowed the Archer-Shee family to incur all the heavy costs of a lawsuit without this objection, and at the eleventh hour claimed this technical immunity and refused to allow the facts to be used. It seemed to him tyranny in its worst form. When Mr Justice Ridley began to show that he felt himself compelled to take the view of the Crown, on the ground that it was impossible to distinguish the service of a cadet from that of an officer, Carson rose in his wrath and uttered no mincing words.

'The Crown,' he said, 'is shirking the issue of fact. It is a public scandal. The Crown can, I suppose, be high-handed out of Court, but in open Court it is not to be tolerated.'

The Judge suggested to Sir Rufus that, whatever the exact

legal position, it might be better for the Court to listen to the facts.

'My lord, I am entitled to your judgment,' insisted the Solicitor-General.

'My lord,' pleaded Sir Edward, 'I hope you will hear the facts. We have been persisting for two long years under the most aggravating circumstances that ever occurred.'

But, when the Judge felt constrained to cut short the proceedings on the point of law, Carson became stern once again, and, like a figure of justice itself, he rose to his great height in righteous indignation.

'This,' he said slowly, with a gesture of unutterable disdain in the direction of the Crown lawyers, 'is a case of the grossest oppression without remedy that I have known since I have been at the Bar.'

'All I can say is that there have been various enquiries,' said Sir Rufus lamely.

'Only hole and corner enquiries, in which the boy was not represented,' answered Carson.

'That is not so,' protested Sir Rufus, 'Mr George Elliott KC went down.'

'Yes,' observed Carson, with his bitterest emphasis, '*that* was our enquiry.'

'Assisted by the Admiralty,' added Sir Rufus.

Carson turned to Rufus, almost with personal antagonism. 'It is a gross outrage by the Admiralty, Mr Solicitor,' he said, and stalked out of Court.

From that time on, Carson devoted himself to the expedition of an appeal to a higher court and a second hearing. He made all the necessary applications, usually delegated to a junior counsel, himself, and, owing to his untiring efforts, the appeal was heard in the Court of Appeal six days afterwards, on 18 July, before Lords Justice Vaughan-Williams,

Fletcher-Moulton, and Buckley. He put his whole soul into his argument, skilfully introducing the untried question of fact at every turn of the argument. 'Your lordships,' he said, 'may be interested to know that the charge against the boy is that he stole a postal order and forged the payee's name. This charge is totally devoid of any foundation.'

The intense feeling behind his argument did not fail of its effect before these three great lawyers. 'I shall never forget,' said Carson to me in describing this appeal, 'how old Vaughan-Williams, who was a great lover of justice, responded to my argument. "Yes, yes," he said, "where are the facts. We want the facts".'

Yet still Sir Rufus, on behalf of the Crown, persisted in relying on the strict immunity of the Crown, until, after a long argument, the united weight and hostility of the Bench were too strong for him, and compelled him to abandon a position which would have been disgraceful, even if it had been tenable, in any free and democractic country. By the sense of justice, and the independence, of the three Lords Justice who heard the appeal, the whole aspect of the case was altered, and, when the case of George Archer-Shee came before a jury the second time, he came as a citizen whose right to be heard had been decreed by one of the highest Courts in the land.

Thus, not for the first or the last time, did the Judicial Bench of England strike a blow for the liberty of the subject against the tyranny of a modern Government department which had attempted to revive and to use the worst weapons of the Middle Ages. The Lords Justice sent the case back for rehearing, with instructions that the facts should be tried by a Judge and jury before the legal objections were argued at all.

After a powerful application by Carson personally before the Lord Chief Justice for a speedy trial, the case again came before the Courts only nine days later. It was tried by Mr

Justice Phillimore and a special jury. After two years of the law's delays, Carson took the case from one Judge to the Court of Appeal and back again to another Judge with a speed which is unhappily rare indeed.

But, in this last phase of the long legal struggle, new and unexpected difficulties arose. The learned Judge, from the very start, leaned strongly to the support of the Crown. This, however, seemed only to add zest to the task which the great advocate had taken upon himself. All through the trial, Carson is to be seen at his very best, the champion of the oppressed, sparing himself nothing in a cause which he knew to be just and right. He was ill; his mind was full of private cares and the tremendous responsibilities which he had taken upon himself by accepting the leadership of the Irish Unionists. Yet for four days, in the stifling July heat of that crowded Court, he threw himself into the cause of this young boy as if he had been his own son. It was the culminating round in a long fight conducted by an individual champion against the Government of a great country; again and again the latter had placed obstacles in his way; as often he had brushed them aside. It is not too much to say that the great heart of England, with its deep love of liberty, went out to him, and began to know and understand the inner character of this man, tender and indomitable, which had up to this time only been known to an affectionate inner circle of friends. This heroic and masterful effort not only dominated that Court, but attracted to him the admiration, interest and attention of every man and woman in England who loved to see justice done and a great champion fighting for the right with all his soul and strength. Among the thousands of admirers who felt drawn towards him, as to a hero of romance, was a certain young Irishwoman in her early

---

[1] Later Carson's second wife, after the death of his first wife. – Ed.

twenties, named Ruby Frewen.[1]

The whole basis of his argument can be summarised in the words, 'Let right be done', the traditional words, as we have seen, in which the King waives his royal immunity in every petition of right. It was for the jury to see that this endorsement was no mere empty form in this case. He made an appeal which would have been hard for any jury to resist. 'This case,' he said, 'is one of an unusual nature, because the King cannot be sued in the ordinary way in his own Courts. But, where there has been an alleged breach of contract by the Crown, the King endorses the writ with the words, "Let right be done", as has been done in this case, and then the action proceeds in the ordinary way.' After outlining the contract which he claimed existed between the 'suppliant' and the Crown, he passed on to the facts of the case.

'It is important to remember, gentlemen,' he said, 'that the boys enter this college as mere children. ... This little boy – from his birth, in 1895, until 1905 – was brought up at home, where he did not give his parents one moment's anxiety. In 1905 he went to a preparatory school and then to Stonyhurst. There he obtained the very highest character and the confidence and the affection of all those who came into contact with him. In 1908, by examination, he entered the Royal Naval College. ...' Referring to the letter which the father had received from the Admiralty, Carson said: 'By this letter this little boy of thirteen was branded as a thief and a forger, labelled and ticketed as such for the rest of his life. In the investigation which has led to this disastrous result, neither the father nor any friend of the boy was allowed to be there to hear what was said. I protest against the boy being branded in this way as a thief and a forger. But the little fellow from that day up to the present moment, whether when called before his commander or under the softer ordeal of the enquiry before his own parents, has never faltered in the declaration that he was innocent. Two years have elapsed since then. We have pressed again and again for a judicial enquiry into the matter – not a departmental enquiry, but a judicial enquiry – but we have pressed in vain until this petition of right was brought, and even this was opposed until we constrained them by an order of the Courts. If the boy's character is to be cleared, it will not therefore be by any action of the State, but by a verdict of twelve of his fellow-citizens, and that will be the only satisfactory ending to this case. The suppliant only asks for his son that which every street arab obtains. Indeed, he does not ask for so much. The latter has the protection of a trained magistrate, of a grand jury presided over by a Judge, of a petty jury presided over by a Judge, and finally the Court of Criminal Appeal. But naturally the department, having taken up a certain attitude, will never go back. They have fought and are fighting to the bitter end. ... I suppose, gentlemen, that a department has no heart, and does not understand a father's broken heart. ... So, two years ago, the father took his little boy away. I will not trouble you with the technical defences, but I will put the boy before you on the plain issue. Is he a thief and a forger, or is he not?'

He then dealt with the scanty information which the Admiralty had consented to give to the suppliant, which included the report of the great expert on handwriting, Mr Gurrin. 'Perhaps, gentlemen,' observed Sir Edward, 'I will have an opportunity of asking Mr Gurrin questions as to evidence given by him on other occasions.' This remark caused the first of his many clashes with the Bench.

'That observation is unworthy of you, Sir Edward,' said the learned Judge. 'Everybody knows Mr Gurrin.'

'I resent that observation, my lord,' replied Sir Edward; 'I hope you will at once withdraw it.'

The Judge looked pained and surprised. 'I cannot do that, Sir Edward,' he said.

Carson then turned away from the Judge and addressed himself to the jury alone. 'Well, then,' he resumed, 'I don't mind it, gentlemen; I shall try not to become upset in this case, and will try to do my duty.' He then told the story of the postal order, and criticised the commander's suspicions arising out of the incident when George Archer-Shee had written the signature of Cadet Back as 'Terence H Back'. 'The commander made an extraordinary remark: "It is funny you know Back's Christian name." Why? They slept next to each other. They entered the college together, and they were class-fellows from morning till night. Why was it extraordinary? When once a suspicion gets into the mind, gentlemen, it is extraordinary what small things seem to confirm that suspicion.' He then dealt with the two so-called enquiries. 'We asked to be represented, but the Admiralty replied that the enquiry was not one in which "representation on your side, in the sense in which you use the term, is appropriate". Why in all the world, gentlemen, would it not be appropriate?'

Here, again, the Judge was disposed to soften the bitter edge of counsel's speech. 'You are censuring me, my lord,' Carson complained, 'on what you supposed I was saying.'

'And *you* are censuring everyone, and I suppose it is my turn now,' said the Judge.

Carson shrugged his shoulders. 'Now, I suppose, your lordship is censuring me again,' he observed, but he had nearly finished.

'The day has now come, gentlemen, at last, when the matter can be sifted and tried in open Court, and I need not remind you of the vital issue which depends on your verdict, whether or not the boy is to be cleared, now in his childhood, of the charge hanging round his neck. I will first call the father to speak to some necessary matters, and will then take the earliest opportunity of letting you see the boy, and of hearing him cross-examined by the Solicitor-General. Whatever the result may be, we will rest satisfied that we have had an investigation, for which we have waited for two years, by an absolutely independent tribunal.'

The old father was then called. He was a living type of the old-fashioned English banker, dignified, reserved, and palpably honourable. 'I have never at any time,' he said, 'had reason to suspect my son's honesty. His character is conspicuously open and straightforward. There is nothing secret about him.' Sir Rufus Isaacs cross-examined him as to the signature on the postal order. While he was chief agent of the Bank of England at Bristol, the witness had had occasion to study signatures. 'I know nothing about the signature,' he said, 'but whoever forged this signature on the postal order used a feigned hand, and that person was not my son.'

George Archer-Shee, a handsome boy of fifteen, was then called, whose frank face and manner seemed to bear out the high character which his counsel and his father had given him. Carson took him through the sad story briefly, and asked him finally, 'Is there any truth in the charge made against you?'

'No, certainly not,' he replied.

He then for two days faced the cross-examination of one of the ablest counsel who have ever practised at the Bar, but he was quite equal to the ordeal. His evidence was not merely unshaken at the end of his cross-examination, but was even strengthened. Nor did he lose, throughout, his composure or his courtesy towards his powerful antagonist. His manners did the very greatest credit to his home and to his Catholic school. There was only one circumstance which could be said to tell against him. When he was first questioned he had said that he had visited the post office between three and four o'clock, which would have corroborated the account of the postmistress. The boy admitted this frankly. 'But I corrected myself at once,' he added. 'I suggest,' said Sir Rufus sternly, 'that it was not until Messrs Lewis & Lewis came upon the scene that you alleged the time to be 2.30.'

'No,' replied the boy stoutly.

After his re-examination, the Judge asked him several searching questions, but the witness's testimony survived this test, and, indeed, caused some amusement in the packed Court.

'If there is any more laughter in Court,' said the Judge, 'I shall clear the Court. I will be glad of any excuse to do so, as it is inconveniently crowded.'

The next witness was Archer-Shee's bosom friend, Cadet Patrick Scholes, who was now a cadet at Dartmouth, the senior naval college. He said that he distinctly remembered Archer-Shee asking him to accompany him to the post office on 7 October, as he was going to get a postal order. The time was about a quarter past two; he had to refuse because he was expecting a visit from friends. But he knew that Archer-Shee wanted to get a postal order to buy a toy engine.

'How do you fix the time as "quarter past two"?' asked the Solicitor-General in cross-examination.

'I remember the time well,' replied the witness, 'as I kept looking at the clock to see what time my friends were arriving.'

'Did you say at one time that Archer-Shee said that he was going to *cash* an order?' – 'I have never said that Archer-Shee was going to cash an order.'

When Sir Edward re-examined him in relation to this suggestion, an incident occurred which very much impressed the jury.

'Was any suggestion ever made to you until yesterday that you had said "cash" and not "get"?' – 'No.'

'Was it made to you yesterday by the Treasury solicitor?' – 'Yes.'

It was apparent that the jury did not like the fact that the Treasury solicitor had made this last-minute enquiry for the first time of this young witness before he gave his evidence.

Arbuthnot, the other cadet who had obtained leave on 7 October 1908 to go to the post office to cash an order, was then called. He had gone immediately after dinner at about two o'clock. 'As I came out of the post office,' he said, 'I met one of the cadet's servants, but I did not know him by name or by sight.'

A telegraph boy, named Frederick Charles Langley, gave evidence which was very helpful to the suppliant's case. He said that one cadet came in about 2.10, and another cadet came in a few minutes afterwards and left at 2.30. He had been asked about it soon afterwards, and had always given the same account.

Then followed a number of witnesses as to character, from the family, from Stonyhurst, and from Osborne. His brother said, 'I have always found him singularly honourable and truthful.' Father Davis of Stonyhurst said, 'I was in close touch with Archer-Shee in 1907. He was always straightforward, honourable, and truthful in every dealing.' Mr Gordon Gorman, master of the Navy class at Stonyhurst said, 'I found Archer-Shee one of my most interesting pupils, candid and honest in the highest degree.' Another witness said, 'I think he is the most open, frank, and straightforward boy I have ever known.' Mr Lievesay, Archer-Shee's tutor at Osborne, said very much the same thing. Father Bodkin, the principal at Stonyhurst, said, 'He is a conspicuously straightforward boy. I received him back willingly when he left Osborne.'

That closed the case for the suppliant, and the Solicitor-General opened the case for the Crown. He reduced the case to the single issue: 'Was the boy who bought the fifteen-and-sixpenny order the same boy who cashed the stolen order? If you believe that, the suppliant's son is necessarily guilty. I will call the postmistress, and she is positive on this point. ... When questioned in the first place, Archer-Shee said that he had been at the post office between three and four. This is important in ascertaining where the truth lies. Sir Edward Carson has made a severe attack on the Admiralty. I am here to justify their action. For questions of great importance are involved. They honestly believed in the boy's guilt, and honestly thought that he should not be allowed to associate with the other cadets. It is not suggested that the Admiralty have acted from malice or spite, or from any ulterior motive. I am most anxious that that should be made clear. The question is: have they reasonable grounds for their belief? ... They submitted the postal order to an expert – at any rate, the most accredited among them. Mr Gurrin reported that it was Archer-Shee's hand on the postal order. ... The family asked for an independent enquiry. This surprises me. It would be hard to find a more experienced, high-minded, and capable person than Mr Acland, the Judge Advocate of the Fleet. He will be called before you. ... What you have to determine is whether the boy or the postmistress is telling the truth. Gentlemen, I will have the opportunity at a later stage of dealing with the case more fully.'

The postmistress was examined by Mr Horace Avory. 'Are you sure that it was the same cadet who cashed the five-shilling order as bought the one for fifteen-and-six?' he asked her. – 'Perfectly.' She admitted that she could not identify any of the seven cadets who were paraded before her, but she did not remember that any of the cadet's servants had visited the post office that afternoon.

The postmistress was clearly an honest woman, who was

giving her evidence to the very best of her recollection, and Carson dealt gently with her. No counsel knew better than Carson when to use the soft pedal and to exert all his charm. He, who had been so stern and unbending, even to the Judge, almost coaxed her into candour, and out of her positive frame of mind into one of dubiety.

'Is there anything in your books to show the order in which the postal orders are dealt with, or the time?' – 'No.'

'So that, on the point whether the same person cashed the five-shilling postal order as bought the one for fifteen-and-six, we must rely upon your memory?' – 'Yes.'

'Are not all these cadets very much alike?' – 'Yes.'

'All smart, good-looking boys about the same age?' – 'Yes.'

'When did you first know anything was wrong?' – 'The petty officer came up that night, and asked me if a cadet had cashed a postal order, who had no right to it.'

'It was he who first suggested to you it was a cadet?' – 'Yes.'

'Did he say he had given leave only to two cadets?' – 'I am not sure.'

'Did he say that such people were not wanted in the Navy?' – 'Yes.'

'Was he in a very excited condition?' – 'I thought so. I have said that he was almost raving.'

'Did you say a word to anyone that evening about it being the same boy who bought the fifteen-and-sixpenny order who had cashed the five-shilling order?' – 'I did not say it to the petty officer.'

'Did you even say it was a cadet who cashed the order, before you saw Commander Cotton the next day?' – 'If I said "I did not" to Mr Elliott KC, it must be correct.'

'Can you remember anyone else at all having a transaction or conversation with you at all that day?' – 'No.'

'Do you remember the appearance of anyone at all who

called that day?' – 'No.'

'Do you remember if any of the cadets' servants called?' – 'No.'

'So you paid no attention to anybody else that day?' – 'No.'

'And no one has ever attempted to test your memory on that point until now?' – 'No.'

When this witness left the box, Carson had almost completely demolished the damaging effect of her evidence-in-chief, without in the least discrediting her character. The general effect of her testimony was that of a very honest woman, whose recollection had been twisted by suggestion and blurred by lapse of time. Yet upon her account, on which as it now stood no just man would hang a cat, the authorities had taken their action. It was a great cross-examination of the gentler kind, and did no harm to the postmistress or anyone else. Yet had another counsel, perhaps Marshall Hall, dealt with this witness in a harsher manner, the effect of her testimony might have been disastrous to the suppliant's case.

But the case was telling painfully on Carson. His brother, Colonel Walter Carson, came in to see him at Eaton Place immediately after the hearing, and found him dripping with perspiration, and very unhappy and anxious. When he returned home, he found he had some very difficult political work to do in the Ulster cause. When the Court assembled for the third day of the trial, he told the Judge that he was determined to finish the case himself, but that he might have to ask for an adjournment, as he was very unwell, and had had to sit up late with some other work of great public importance. 'Perhaps, however,' he said, 'I may get better as the case proceeds.'

The next witness was Cadet Back, whose postal order had been stolen. He admitted to Carson that about sixty cadets were at his table when the postal order arrived, that they, together with the cadets' servants, might have seen his postal order, which he had shown to others. But Archer-Shee was not at his table, and had not, to his knowledge, seen the postal order at all.

'Was it the chief petty officer who brought in Archer-Shee's name?' – 'I think it was.'

'You knew Archer-Shee's name was George, and he knew yours was Terence?' – 'Yes.'

'Had you seen Archer-Shee sign his name, and had he seen you sign yours?' – 'Yes.'

The chief petty officer, who had reported the matter, was the next witness. His testimony was inconsistent in several vital matters with that of the postmistress and Cadet Back. He said that she had mentioned a cadet to him as being the culprit before ever she had seen Commander Cotton. She had told him by telephone the night before.

'Then, when you went to see her, did you ask whether it was a cadet?' – 'No, I did not need to. I knew it already.'

'Would you say, then, that the postmistress was telling an untruth?'

Here the Judge intervened, and protested that this was an unfair question to put to the witness. Carson looked steadily at the Judge. 'Does your lordship *seriously* rule that I cannot do so?' he asked.

'No, I do not do so,' replied the Judge testily.

Carson then questioned him as to the breaking open of Archer-Shee's own locker.

'Do you suggest that he had broken open his own chest?' – 'No.'

Carson then read a passage from the witness's evidence before Mr Elliott in which he had made that very suggestion: 'I can only think that he broke into the chest himself.'

'Have you not formed a very strong opinion about Archer-Shee?' – 'No.'

The witness added that Cadet Back had been wrong in saying that he had mentioned Archer-Shee's evidence, but admitted that there had been a number of other thefts both before and after Archer-Shee's departure, and that the culprits had not been found.

When the Judge Advocate of the Fleet was called, Carson objected to the admissibility of any evidence as to the enquiry, as it had not been held in the boy's presence. He made his objections very strenuously. 'All this was done behind our backs,' he said.

'Once and for all,' said the Judge, 'I say that I do not take the view that this was done any more behind your back than behind the back of the Crown.'

'That is nothing to me,' replied Sir Edward. 'The Crown was not being tried. But I will put my point in any way your lordship likes. I shall say "in our absence".'

Mr Justice Phillimore overruled the objection, but Carson made a demonstration of asking only one question of Mr Acland, who had sat as a Recorder.

'When you try a prisoner as Recorder, you'll hear both sides, I suppose?' – 'Yes.'

After a number of cadets' servants had given evidence, Commander Cotton was called, but his cross-examination was postponed. Before the Court rose, Carson and Isaacs again wrangled for the last word with the jury.

'I do not suppose,' said Sir Edward, 'that the Solicitor-General will claim the Law Officer's privilege to have the last word with the jury. I have never known it claimed in a civil case, and I was a Law Officer for six years.'

'I am sorry to say,' interrupted the Judge, 'that my experience goes back longer than that; I have known it to be so claimed, and I can give instances.'

'They are getting out of date,' observed Carson drily.

But the Crown showed no sign of relenting from contesting every inch of the ground, and would not waive even this advantage, and Carson prepared that night with meticulous and laborious care the cross-examination of the commandant and the captain at Osborne. He made every preparation for the remaining stages of the hard-fought battle, knowing well what the great effect of Rufus Isaacs's last word might be.

Next morning Carson was surprised to hear Rufus Isaacs ask that the cross-examination of Commander Cotton be postponed. Captain Christian went into the box instead. He gave an account which seemed more appropriate to a man excusing his own action than blaming another's. 'I formed my opinion,' he said, 'entirely apart from the question of handwriting.' The whole atmosphere of the trial seemed to have changed from one of attack to one of defence.

Then suddenly a most dramatic thing happened. The Solicitor-General, after a hurried consultation with Sir Edward Carson, rose and made a statement. 'As to the issues of fact, the Court and the jury will not be further troubled. ... I say now, on behalf of the Admiralty, as a result of the investigation which has taken place, that I accept the declaration of George Archer-Shee that he did not write the name on the postal order; that he did not take it; and that he did not cash it; and that consequently he was innocent of the charge which has been brought against him. I make that statement without any reservation of any description, intending it to be a complete acceptance of the boy's statements. ... On the other hand, my learned friend, Sir Edward Carson, accepts the statements of the Admiralty as to their action, and agrees that those responsible for all that has happened were acting under a reasonable and *bona fide* belief in the truth of the statements which had been made to them. ... In justice to the postmistress, upon whose evidence so much reliance has been placed, it is right to say that it has never been suggested that there was any want of *bona fides* on her part, and, indeed, the cross-examination of Sir Edward Carson was only directed to show that she was mistaken.'

Sir Edward Carson, who had been completely surprised by the sudden collapse of the case for the Crown, rose and began to speak. It was the proudest and happiest moment in his whole career at the Bar, because the case for this child was in his heart as no other lawsuit ever had been in the past, or was to be again. There were tears in his eyes. 'The complete vindication of his son, George Archer-Shee, was the object of the suppliant in bringing this action. That object has been entirely achieved. This is the first issue of fact. With regard to the two other issues, I agree that those responsible acted *bona fide* under a reasonable belief in the statements put before them. The whole action has now been disposed of, but I suppose the points of law will now stand over.'

That Rufus Isaacs had only anticipated the verdict of the jury was apparent by the scene which followed. The jurymen clambered out of the jury-box to congratulate Mr Martin Archer-Shee and Sir Edward Carson. Members of the Bar and the public did the same thing. The surprise of the sudden end prevented a much greater demonstration. But there was one person whose absence was realised at once – the central figure of the drama. For some reason George Archer-Shee was not in Court. Carson soon left the Court, and made his way downstairs to his room in the Law Courts. After a short while he heard a knock at the door; it was George Archer-Shee, who had come to thank him for all he had done.

'Why was it you were not in Court, George?' asked Carson.

'Well, sir,' said the boy, 'the truth is that I was taken to a theatre last night, and I overslept.'

'What a strange boy you are,' said Carson, who had been able to think of nothing but this case for weeks. 'Didn't you feel too nervous to go out to the theatre?'

'Nervous, sir?' replied George. 'I never had the slightest nervousness: when I got into a Court of Law, I knew I'd be all right. Why, I never did the thing.'

'After all, that's a very good way of looking at it,' said Carson, looking at his young client admiringly.

This was the end of the litigation, but the family had still to wait for a year before they were able to wring any redress from the Crown. It will have been remarked that by a singular oversight, although Rufus Isaacs's retraction was without reserve, his speech contained no word of regret on behalf of the Admiralty for the dreadful pain and suffering they had inflicted on the Archer-Shee family. Moreover, no offer came from the Treasury to settle the enormous bill of law costs which they had been forced to incur through the cruel obstinacy of the department in opposing a judicial enquiry, and the proposals for £10 000 damages put forward by Messrs Lewis & Lewis were treated with scorn. Indeed, to add an element of farce to this strange story, the Admiralty callously claimed that the boy might have suffered no great damage after all, since they conveniently remembered that they had sent, before the theft of the postal order, a warning letter to his parents on the subject of their son's lack of industry in his studies. As Mr George Cave MP, afterwards Lord Chancellor, said in the House of Commons, 'The suggestion seems to be that, because you have not been very diligent in your studies, you ought not to mind being charged with theft.' The matter was raised in the House of Commons on the Navy Vote, when George Cave moved to reduce Mr McKenna's salary by one hundred pounds in order to call attention to the matter. Mr Ramsay MacDonald distinguished himself on this occasion by asking the chairman 'whether the whole of the day was to be devoted to the discussion of what was an attempt to blackmail the Treasury. This observation was received with great indignation, and very properly withdrawn under pressure from George Cave, and a debate of great distinction followed in which F E Smith, Lord Charles Beresford, Alfred Lyttelton, Rufus Isaacs, and Mr McKenna all took part. Mr McKenna, the Liberal First Lord, was not very conciliatory, and still tried to pour scorn on the claim for damages. But F E Smith at once settled him with a picturesque argument, which really touched the heart of the House of Commons. 'Is £10 000 too much?' he asked. 'Let any honourable member apply the circumstances to his own boy. If the boy had been a relatively poor boy he might not have had the services of the right honourable and learned member for Dublin University, and would probably have been branded as a thief and a forger. The Government ought not to measure with too nice a scale the amount of compensation.' Mr Alfred Lyttelton expressed himself deeply shocked that 'these children of tender age are not represented by a next friend or counsel' and at the fact that no expression of regret had come from the Admiralty. 'What objection could there be,' he asked, 'for the representatives of the Navy, the custodians of one of the most generous and honourable services in the world, to give to the father of the boy an expression of regret?' But only after an outburst from a Liberal MP, Mr Roch, did Mr McKenna finally yield. 'No father in the House,' exclaimed the honourable member, 'would say £10 000 or £20 000 would compensate it. It is in the discretion of the First Lord of the Admiralty. Let him get up and do it like a man.'

It was then that Mr McKenna rose and offered to leave the question of compensation to a tribunal composed of Lord Mersey, Sir Rufus Isaacs, and Sir Edward Carson. Ultimately, £7 120 was paid by the Treasury to Mr Archer-Shee in respect of costs and by way of compensation. Thus the happy end of the famous case of *Archer-Shee v The King*. Nevertheless, even this conclusion can hardly be called 'happy'. Poor Martin Archer-Shee's heart had been broken by his son's disgrace, and he died a few months afterwards, and his death was undoubtedly accelerated by all that he had suffered. Nor could the Admiralty have known how precious were those two years, in which they had allowed George Archer-Shee to remain under a cloud, to the boy himself. For all they could see, this candid and promising boy had a long life before him.

Four years or so after the trial, Carson went down to the War Office to obtain news of his nephew and godson, Teddy Robinson, who had been on the casualty lists reported as killed. As he went in he met Mrs Archer-Shee, the widow of the 'suppliant'. She told him that poor George was dead. He was one of the first British officers to be killed in the Great War, and he had, at the age of nineteen, given his life to the country whose 'official mind', by its obstinacy and callousness, had darkened two years of his short life.

By the conduct of this case Carson added cubits to his stature in the nation's estimation. Mr J L Garvin, who did not know Carson personally, voiced the feeling of intelligent contemporary observers of this trial when he wrote this rare tribute to his fellow-countryman: 'Full recognition has not yet been given to one aspect of the Osborne cadet case which seems to us to eliminate all the rest in real drama. ... There is not a parent in the land who has not been amazed by the cruelty of the procedure adopted at this business at Osborne, and who does not feel that such measures must be taken by the Admiralty as shall make a peril of this intolerable kind impossible for the future. But the acquittal of the cadet, and his reinstatement in the service, have not been so much the triumph of law as the triumph of a great lawyer, and Sir Edward Carson's whole conduct of the case has been one of the finest things in the annals of the English Bar. Even law may be dead and impotent without personality. A good cause has been lost again and again by weak handling. The abstract justice of a cause is not necessarily anyone's security. In this instance a powerful advocate, who is also a strong man, took up the cause in a spirit of generous championship and indignant conviction as to its merits, and by sheer personal force beat down against all odds a terrible wrong, and established the innocence of a lad unjustly accused of theft and falsehood, and sentenced almost to moral death. If his health had been always as robust as his mind and character, Sir Edward Carson, as every Unionist knows, might have held a far greater position in political life than he has ever cared to assert. But he has won this time something above party distinction. His splendid courage and will have assured his permanent place in the public regard, and make him a national figure. We are all proud of him.'

Ulster, too, was watching, and with no disinterested mind had observed how great a fighter she had chosen as her Parliamentary leader. She must have appreciated that this was no ordinary lawyer. It was clear that he had faith, the root of the matter in him; and many an Ulsterman must have read with special satisfaction the accounts of Carson's persistence and ultimate triumph in this case. Ulster is well versed in Scripture, and knows that 'He who is faithful in small things, is faithful also in great'.

Mr Garvin's words were almost prophetic. Carson was on the threshold of great events in the history of his country, in which he was to take a never-to-be-forgotten part. At last political greatness was to be thrust upon him, not by ambition, but by his own sense of duty and the choice of a whole community, who, like poor George Archer-Shee, were in desperate case, and needed just such a champion as he had proved himself to be.

Index to Main Cases

Alaska Boundary case   368
Archer-Shee case   471
Cadbury v Standard Newspapers   440
Chapman poisoning case (Jack the Ripper?)   338
Clanricarde, Marquess of,   160
Croagh Orphanage   76
Dorset Street Tragedy   51
'French Paste'   195
Gilbert, W S, v the Era   276
Hayes and Moriarty   136
Jameson Raid case   280
Joel, J B, v Sievier, Robert,   465
Lever v the Daily Mail   455
Lynch, 'Colonel'   327
O'Brien, William, MP (Mitchelstown Massacre)   118
Russell, Earl,   320
Slater Agency case   347
Smythe, Mrs Henry,   54
Tillet, Ben, v the Morning   272
Wilde, Oscar, v Queensbury, Marquess of   215
Wilson, Havelock, v the Evening News   200